# THE HANDBOOK OF

# Clans & Tartans

# OF

# Scotland

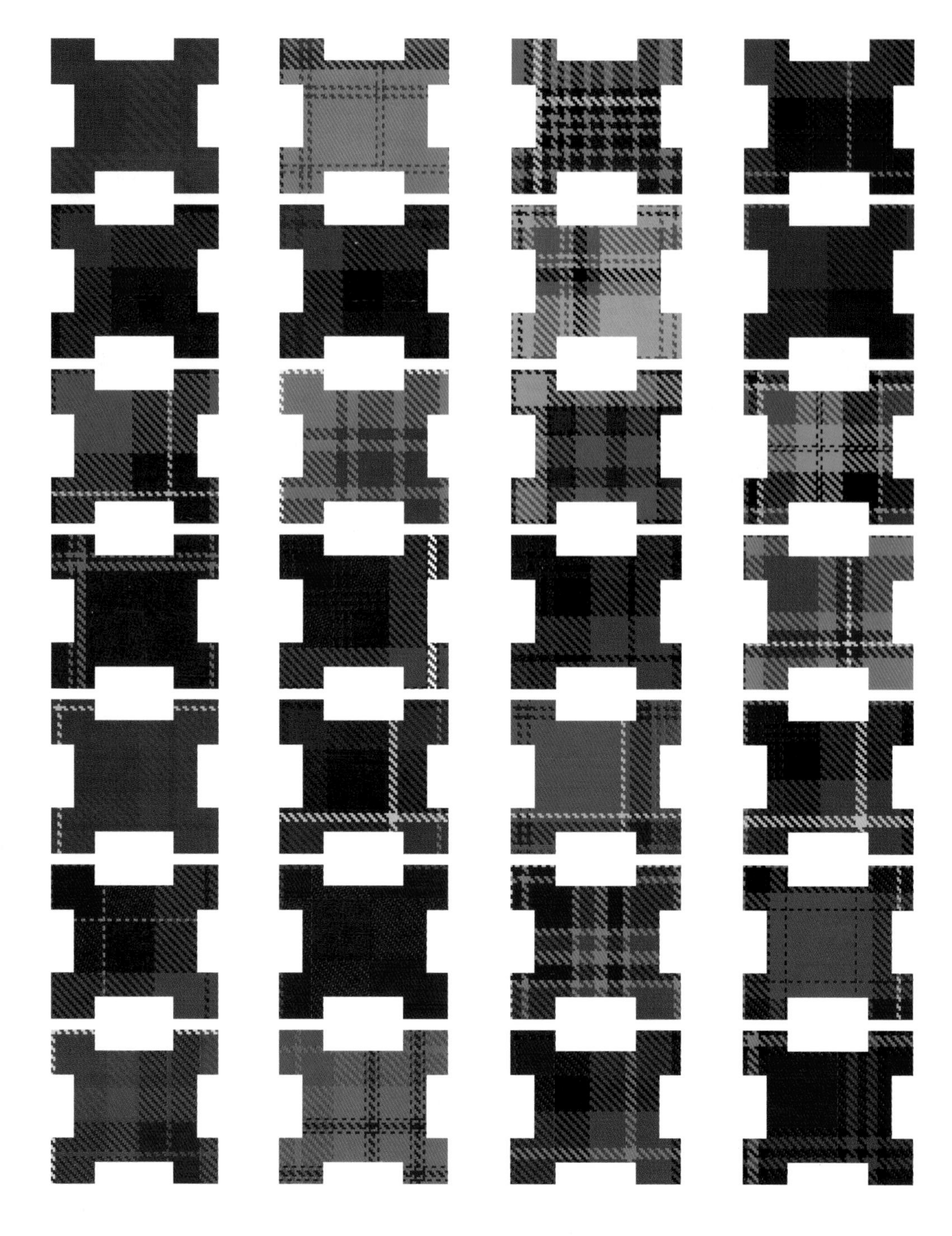

THE HANDBOOK OF

# Clans & Tartans

OF

# Scotland

Maria Costantino

STRATHEARN

D&S Books
Cottage Meadow, Bocombe,
Parkham, Bideford
Devon, England
EX39 5PH

e-mail us at:-
enquiries.dspublishing@care4free.net

This edition printed 2002

ISBN 1-895464-20-X



Creative Director: Sarah King
Editor: Yvonne Worth
Project editor: Judith Millidge
Editorial consultant: Peter Eslea MacDonald
Designer: 2H Design

This edition published by
STRATHEARN BOOKS LIMITED
36, Northline Road
Toronto, On, Canada
MB4 3E2

Printed in China

1 3 5 7 9 10 8 6 4 2

# Contents



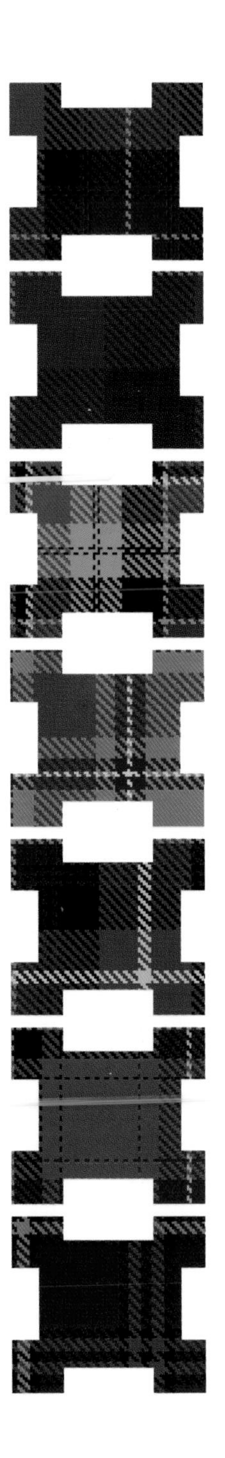

# Introduction – Tartan History

The exact origins of tartan, or *breacan*, as it is called in Gaelic, are obscure. While the use of checks and stripes to make "decorative" textiles is as old as weaving itself, the weaving of different colored yarns of varying thread counts in plain or twill to make multi-colored checks and color blends in such a sophisticated and beautiful way is unique to Scotland.

Today, tartan is possibly the world's most recognised symbol of Scottish national identity. We do know that the word "tartan" is derived from the French word *tiretaine*. This word described a woven cloth of half-wool, half-linen that was popular in the 16th century – a time when France and Scotland had very close ties.

Nevertheless, it was not until the late 18th or early 19th century, when the Scottish clans and families began to adopt particular patterns or color schemes, that tartan became an integral part of clanship. In 1745 when Prince Charles Edward Stewart adopted Highland dress as the uniform for his army, tartan became the visible symbol of Jacobite values – so much so that the following year, after the defeat of the Jacobites at Culloden in 1746, the Disarming Act of 1747 outlawed the wearing of tartan and Highland dress.

There were exceptions in the Disarming Act, however. Prohibition did not extend to clanswomen or to those serving in the British Army. Recruitment of Scottish fighting men began in earnest in 1724 when Field Marshal George Wade was made Commander-in-Chief in Scotland with the specific task of de-militarising the Highlands. Wade formed six 'independent companies' of Highlanders and each one was required to police an area and counter any possible Jacobite trouble. While the recruits were drawn from all parts of the Highlands, in the main they tended to come from clans that supported the government, in particular the Campbells, Munros and Grants.

*Black Watch*

These independent companies wore a Highland dress of belted plaid and when, in 1739, they were formed into a regiment of ten companies, they wore a uniform tartan called the "Government Pattern", a dark green, blue and black tartan. The regiment was called the "Black Watch" – a name recalling the watch or lookouts used by the clans to guard against their livestock being stolen. At this time, all the regiments wore the "Black Watch" tartan, but each was distinguishable by its "facing color", the color of fabric trim on their coat collars and cuffs. With the outbreak of the Seven Years' War in 1756 between England and France, Britain now urgently needed more fighting men and William Pitt, the British Prime Minister, looked to Scotland. Highlanders were recruited into King George II's army as a way of gaining quality soldiers and as a means of quieting "disaffection" among Scots.

*Seaforth Highlanders*

These new Highland regiments continued to wear the "Government Pattern" or "Black Watch" tartan, but to it was added distinguishing lines of red, white and yellow for each regiment. MacLeod's Highlanders, raised in 1778, used red and white lines and was adopted by the Seaforth Highlanders.

The Duke of Gordon chose a yellow stripe for his Fencible regiment raised in 1793, and the next year it was passed to the regiment known as the Gordon Highlanders. Meanwhile, the Argyllshire and Sutherland Highlanders, raised in 1794 and 1800 respectively, wore the Government Pattern unembellished – although the Sutherlands later began using the paler shade of green in the ground color, which today distinguishes them from the very dark green of the Black Watch regiment.

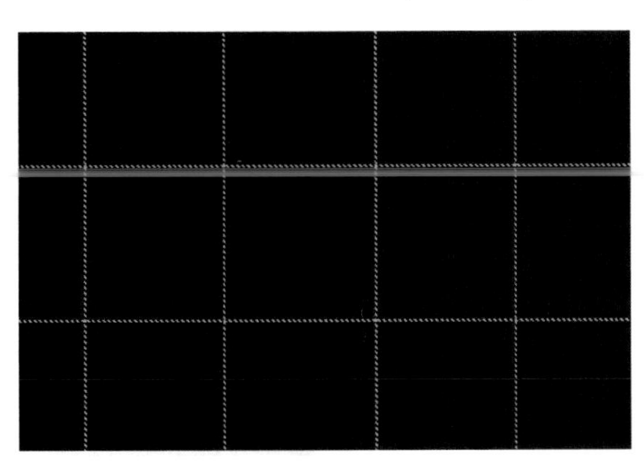

*Gordan Highlanders*

*Argyll and Southern Highlanders*

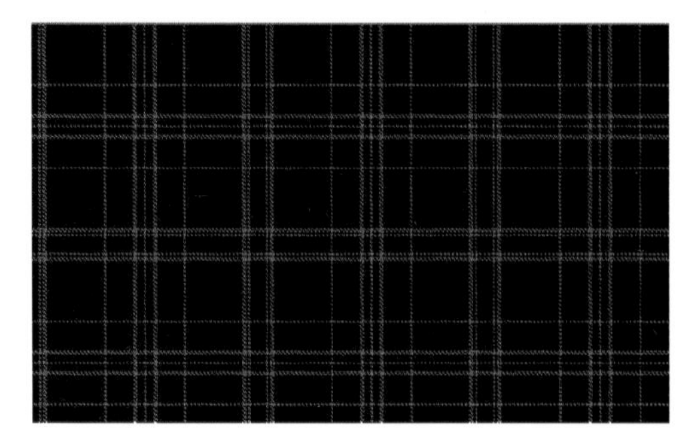

*Cameron Highlanders*

In 1793 the Cameron Highlanders broke with convention completely and invented their own tartan in green, blue and black with red and yellow lines. The Seaforths and Camerons are now combined as the Queen's Own Highlanders.

Highland regiments were successful both at home and abroad: Highland regiments and Highland Emigrant Regiments fought in America and Canada, as well as in India and France. Their reputation not only helped to popularize tartan once again, but also helped to establish the ideal of the tartan clad Highlander as the embodiment of Scotland and heroism.

By the time the Disarming Act was repealed in 1782, an interest in tartan, Highland dress and in Scotland itself was already enjoying a revival. Ladies of fashion adopted feminized versions of the uniforms and soon questions were raised about the authenticity of tartan designs, and, several years later, whether the kilt or "trews" were preferable.

Much of the research into tartans and Highland dress was initiated by the Highland Society of London, which was founded in 1778. The Society's first aim had been to lobby for the repeal of the Disarming Act and for the legal reinstatement of tartan. Once that had been achieved, the Society set about protecting, preserving, and promoting Highland dress, music, language, and literature. In 1815, the Society undertook to collect samples from clans and leading families in order to save old patterns and examples of traditional dye colors. By 1820, the Society had 40 samples, most of which were certified by the clan chiefs with their signature and seal. Throughout the 19th and early 20th centuries, the certified collection continued to grow. Samples were sewn into ledgers and the collection, separated into Highland and Lowland tartans, is now preserved in the Society's archives.

The change in attitude towards tartan was also fostered by writers such as James Macpherson, who published the supposed works of a mythical Irish poet called Ossian. This work of fiction proved so popular that it even became the bedside reading of the Emperor

Napoleon! The popular trend continued in Sir Walter Scott's novels, but tartan's popularity was truly sealed by royal approval. In 1822 George IV paid a state visit to Edinburgh – the first visit to Scotland by the British monarch in over 200 years. Following the king's visit, Wilson's of Bannockburn, Scotland's leading weavers of tartans, could barely cope with the demand and opened a new mill called "The Royal George". For a period, their most popular tartans were 'King George IV' and "Sir Water Scott". Impatient customers demanded tartans, especially new tartans, which were produced to order with names such as "Caledonia" and "Wellington". Setts (the tartan patterns) were enlarged or reduced in scale and in some cases enhanced by thin stripes woven in silk. Later in the19th century, Queen Victoria's well-known love of the Highlands firmly established the character, image and perception of Scotland in the minds of many people, both in Britain and overseas, and the use of tartans spurred a revival within the Scottish textile industry. Under Queen Victoria tartans became internationally popular, as people copied the fashionable monarch in her passion for her highland estates and the "domestic" life she enjoyed there. New, specialized forms of tartans such as "hunting setts" and "dress setts" were developed to suit the different occasions that formed the rituals of upper-class Victorian daily life. New chemical dyes (a product of the Industrial Revolution) produced colors that were more vivid than the "ancient", traditional vegetable dyes.

*Mid-Victorian Highland dress c. 1860.*
*(© 1981 Dr Micheil MacDonald)*

The Queen favored a tartan which was appropriately named "Victoria", a variation of the Royal Stewart, with the broad red bands changed to white, while her husband, Prince Albert, himself designed the sett for the tartan known as "Balmoral", after the Royal family's Scottish home. This tartan, which is not available for sale, is given as a gift to the bride on the occasion of a royal wedding. Parts ofVictoria's beloved Balmoral itself – in particular the Queen's own suite of rooms – were decorated with tartan: the red Royal Stewart and the green Hunting Stewart were used for carpets, while Dress Stewart was used for upholstery and curtains.

At a time when many Scots were leaving their homeland to seek new opportunities in America, Canada, and Australia, tartan became the symbol of their history, culture and national identity. In Canada, for example, Scots continued to show pride in their heritage and many Canadian provinces adopted tartans of their own.

# Tartan Design

Tartan is created by weaving different colored yarns, assembled into sets of various thread counts. Surprisingly few colors are actually required: the subtle variations are, in fact, the result of weaving a few colors in stripes in the "warp" (running lengthways) with the same sequence, width and color in the "weft" (running across). Each section of the design mirrors the section next to it. The resulting pattern is called a "sett" and today a tartan sett is generally classified by the name of a clan or family. The size or scale of the pattern is unimportant. What does matter, however, is the proportion of different colors – the relative widths of the stripes or lines that make up the sett. In tartans, a color appears in its pure, or solid, form and in a blend with each other color. If three colors are used, the result is six "tints". But, however many colors are used, there is never a mix of more than two colors in any part of the weave and, furthermore, two pure colors cannot lie side by side!

## The Weave

*Peter Eslea MacDonald – 'Master Weaver'.*

*(© 1979 Dr Micheil MacDonald)*

Tartans are often mistakenly thought of as squares or checks with lines superimposed on them. Tartans are essentially fabrics woven of simple stripes, but there are remarkably few "simple" schemes of equally spaced and unbroken stripes of a single color. The most outstanding example of this type of tartan is the famous Rob Roy (pictured left). Look closely at the weave of a piece of tartan and you will see how, on the front side of the cloth, the twill effect appears to make diagonal lines from the bottom left to the top right. The threads are woven over two, then under two to create the diagonal rib on the web. The thickness of the thread and the shades of dyes are determined by the weavers. Past methods of hand production, and the use of natural dyestuffs inevitably lead to subtle, yet beautiful, variations in lengths of cloth. With industrialization and, consequently, standardization, thread thickness and color consistency have now become more uniform.

## Hunting, Dress, and District Tartans

When describing tartans, we tend to speak of "ground color" (background color); most tartans fall into either green ground tartans or red ground tartans and many clans use both types, describing them as "hunting" and "dress" setts. Hunting setts are generally in muted colors in order to blend with the colors of the landscape and act as camouflage. Hunting setts are not restricted to the grouse moors, but are often worn as "undress", that is, informal, everyday wear. Dress setts were designed for show – they are popular with Highland dancers and with tourists – and are often in a pattern that features a lot of white. This is because they are believed to be derived from the *arisaid*, a woman's cloak that was made of less expensive, undyed wool. Many of the oldest tartans appear to have been the work of local weavers, and these designs became the patterns now known as "district" patterns.

The Huntly district tartan, from the eastern part of the Central Highlands, dates from the early 18th century and, at this time, was worn by the Gordons, Brodies, Munros and Forbes. Today, the Munro tartan still retains elements of the Huntly design.

*Huntley District*

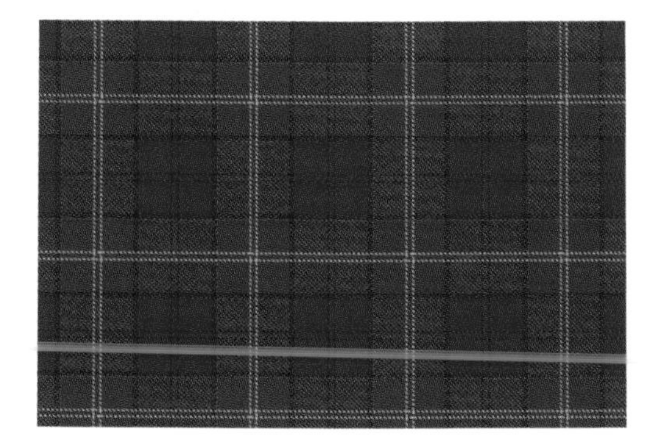

*Lennox*

The Lennox district, near Glasgow, marks the border between the Lowlands and the Highlands. The Lennox tartan was "discovered" in a copy of a 16th-century portrait of the Countess of Lennox, and the Erskines, Maxwells, Chisholms and Wallace clans all have tartans derived from it.

To the north of the Lennox district lies the Glen Orchy district. This district's tartan may well have provided the pattern structure for many of the clan setts in the Central Highlands, as suggested by Blair Urquhart. It is made up of boxes within boxes with dark squares alternating with the open squares of ground color. Clans that have adopted this style of tartan include the MacDonalds of Keppoch, the MacIntyres and the Stewarts of Appin.

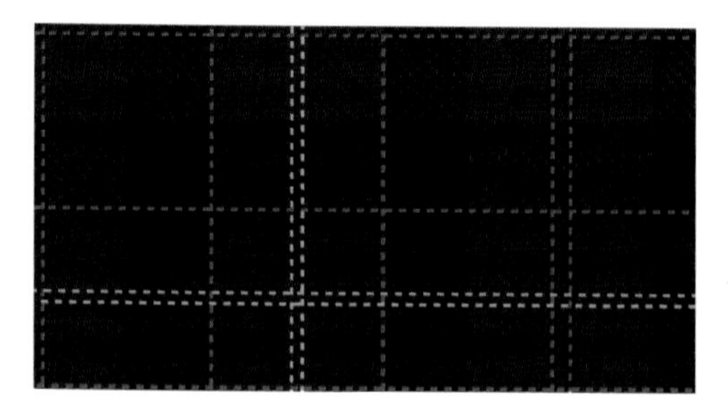

*Lochaber*

The green, black and blue Old Lochaber district tartan from the western part of the Central Highlands appears to have been the basis for the tartans of the Campbells and the MacDonalds. The Old Lochaber was also adopted by the military as the Black Watch.

## Clan Tartans

Tartans of a clan and its main branches are commonly referred to as "clan" tartans, as is determined by the *ceann cinnadh* or clan chief. The clansmen and followers (blood relations and families taking protection from that clan) wear the chief's tartan. The word "clan" or *clanna* simply means "children", i.e. those who have descended from the actual or indeed mythical ancestor from who the community claims descent. The early Scottish clans were essentially tribal organizations whose focus was the clan chief or leader. Today there are around 100 clan chiefs officially recognized by the Lord Lyon, King of Arms.

As with other tribal organizations, clans were free to adopt or recruit new members. Marriages forged links with neighboring tribes or clans, while fostering – the bringing up of the chief's children by favored members of the clan (and in turn their own children by other members of the clan) – cemented incredibly strong ties. It was not unusual for foster brothers to willingly sacrifice themselves in the service of their chief.

Another cohesive bond was in "manrent". This was a bond contracted by the heads of "satellite" families who did not live on the estates of the clan elite, but with whom they were affiliated to safeguard their protection. Some tartans are therefore known as "family" tartans. In its widest sense, the "family" is a group of people that includes all the people affiliated to, or adopted by, a central stem that derived from the founder of the tribe or race.

The Highland Society of London has a collection of tartans where many samples are "certified by the chief" and bear his seal and signature. The Lord Lyon keeps and maintains the Lyon Court Books and the Public Register of All Arms and Bearings. In these are registered those clan and family tartans which appear in the coats of arms, usually as backgrounds to the clan badge. Meanwhile, the task of awarding accreditation status to a newly designed tartan – for a clan, family, district, regiment, corporation or society – is undertaken by the Scottish Tartans Authority and the Scottish Tartans Society.

## Tartans for All!

Everyone is entitled to wear tartan. It is your family name that indicates which tartan you should wear. You can, however, wear any clan tartan that you choose – but you must not claim to be a member of that clan if you are not! If you belong to no particular clan, it is perfectly correct for you to wear a district tartan. Alternatively, you could opt for the "Jacobite" (said to have been derived from a silk scarf made in 1712, possibly in Barcelona!) or the "Strathearn", the name of which is derived from one of the titles of the Duke of Kent, Queen Victoria's father, rather than from the Scottish district itself. You could even commission your own personal tartan! Nevertheless, whichever you choose, remember: never wear the tartans of more than one clan at a time!

*Jacobite*

*Strathearn*

## The Colors

For each tartan illustrated, you will see a color notation. The colors are:

Bk (black)
B (dark blue)
P (purple)
LB or Az (light blue or azure)
G (dark green)
LG (light green)
R (red-scarlet)
Cr (crimson)
Y (yellow)
W (white)
N (grey)
Any other colors are named, for example, maroon.

# Tartan Types and Color Sequence

*Brodie*

There are two types of tartan pattern: Symmetrical and Asymmetrical. The Equal Check is the simplest type and involves only two colors. The finest example of this is the red and black check of the MacGregor tartan, known as the Rob Roy.

In symmetrical tartans, the first and last color is given in the notation in bold type. These are the "pivot" colors on which the design reverses. In the Brodie tartan for example, the threads are counted from the first pivotal color, which is black, for four threads. Then comes red (32 threads), black (16 threads), yellow (2 threads), black (16 threads) and finally, red (4 threads). So the Brodie tartan is notated as: **Bk**4 R32 Bk16 Y2 Bk16 **R**4. The threads are counted in one direction until the other pivotal line is reached, when the sequence is reversed. If you examine a length of Brodie tartan, you will see how the sequence reverses as:

**Bk**4 R32 Bk16 Y2 Bk16 **R**4 Bk16 Y2 Bk16 R32 **Bk**4 R32 Bk16 Y2 Bk16 **R4** Bk16
| *1/2 sett* | *1/2 sett reversed (= full sett)* | *repeat 1st 1/2 sett* | *reverse*
Y2 Bk16 R32 **Bk**2 and so on. *(= 2nd full sett)* |

*Buchanon*

With an asymmetrical tartan, such as the Buchanan Clan tartan (page 34) the full sett is given. The color sequence always starts with the color whose first letter is nearest the beginning of the alphabet. The end threads are not in bold type. This is because when the count reaches the end, the sequence is not reversed, but simply repeated.

There are always exceptions to the rule, however, as in the case of the Campbell of Argyll tartan. The difference here is that two colors – white and yellow – are alternated in an otherwise reversed, symmetrical sequence. In the notation, the colors are shown as W/Y: one color is read in the forwards sequence, the other in the reverse.

A full sett (the sequence of colors read from right to left) is usually between 5 and 7 inches (13 and 18 cms) in width in order to accommodate the kilting (pleats).

## Ancient and Modern Reproduction

Sometimes tartans are described as "Ancient", "Modern", or "Reproduction". These terms don't refer to the age of the pattern, but to the types of dyes that are used. Before the advent of chemical dyes in the mid-19th century, dyers would color their yarn using natural dyes. The resulting colors would vary between individual dyers due to differences in quantities used, the time taken and various other factors. Just like the subtle flavors of different Scotch whiskies, the colors of hand-dyed wool would also show variations. Furthermore, some natural dyestuffs were not lightfast: they faded, rinsed out and changed color over time. When "modern" chemical or "aniline" dyes were introduced, colors became more standardized and more permanent. They also tended to be much darker in tone.

## Recording and Creating Tartan History

As interest grew, and enthusiasm for tartans increased, collections of tartans were formed, such as the one at the Highland Society of London (now housed at the National Museum of Scotland in Edinburgh), and ideas about its origins, history and clan associations were documented. In many instances, there were few "hard facts" and some colorful histories were created that fed both the public's demands and their imagination. *The Vestiarium Scoticum* was published in 1842 by John Sobieski Stolber Stewart Hay and his brother Charles Edward Hay. They claimed that their father was the legitimate son of Bonnie Prince Charlie by his wife, Princess Louisa of Stolberg Gedern. The brothers produced highly plausible work, claiming they had an 18th century manuscript (the *Cromarty Manuscript*) said to have been written by Sir Richard Urquhart around 1721, which itself was based on an earlier, 16th century manuscript. This, they said, gave details of some 75 clan tartans dating from the Middle Ages. From these "descriptions", the "Sobieski Stewarts" as the brothers were known, drew up illustrations of the setts. The so-called "original documents" were never made available for inspection and, despite their many supporters, the brothers were eventually discredited. Nevertheless, many of the designs they "invented" were then adopted and adapted by a number of clans as their tartans.

James Logan published his book, *The Scottish Gael or Celtic Manners, as Preserved among the Highlanders,* in 1831 after five years of research. With help from the Highland Society and William Wilson and Sons, the commercial weavers in Bannockburn, who provided 33 examples of certified tartans of the chiefs and further commercial examples as woven by the firm, Logan produced one of the most authoritative early reference sources for Highland clan tartans.

Between 1845 and 1847 Robert McIan, actor and illustrator, published his drawings of figures in Highland dress in his book, *The Clans of the Scottish Highlands.* James Logan, friend of Robert McIan and fellow tartan enthusiast, provided the text for the book and supplied the patterns for the tartans.

William and Andrew Smith used setts from pattern books provided by William Wilson and Sons and another leading weaving company, Meyer and Mortimer, to illustrate their 1850 publication, *The Authenticated Tartans of the Clans and Families of Scotland.* The Smiths also drew heavily on the findings of a former army outfitter, George Hunter, who, in 1822, had toured the Highlands in search of old examples of tartans.

*MacGregor escort to the 'Honours of Scotland' 1822.*
*(© 1979 Dr Micheil MacDonald)*

James Grant wrote his book, *The Tartans of the Clans of Scotland* in 1886. Grant's illustrations were based on tartans worn at the time, rather than "antique" examples, and contained the first illustration of the "Hunting Stewart". Another author who was active at this time was Henry Whyte. His book, *The Scottish Clans and Their Tartans,* was published in 1891. In 1906 Whyte's book was subsequently enlarged and expanded into two volumes by W. and A. K Johnston, to contain more than 200 tartans – among them many dress and hunting setts illustrated for the first time.

D.W. Stewart's rare and highly collectible, *Old and Rare Scottish Tartans,* was published in 1893. This was a limited edition of 300 copies, each containing 45 examples of tartan with accompanying notes. The examples were woven in silk yarn, carefully selected to obtain the correct color. Continuing his father's scholarly approach, Donald C. Stewart published *The Setts of the Scottish Tartans* in 1950, the first major attempt to record the thread counts and colors of all tartans since Logan published his book in 1831. Pointing out the problems with the earlier literary sources, as well as providing descriptive and historical notes on each tartan, Donald C. Stewart's book is one of the most interesting and accessible texts devoted to tartan.

William Wilson and Sons of Bannockburn were established in *c.*1765 and became one of Scotland's leading commercial weavers, producing tartan cloth for the military regiments. Because the military, women, and the landed gentry were excluded from the ban on wearing tartan imposed in 1746, Wilson's enjoyed a virtual monopoly of tartan production. The most important sources and documents are the company's pattern books kept between *c.*1800–40, which give precise details of thread counts and colors. The Cockburn Collection, at the Mitchell Library in Glasgow, assembled by Sir William Cockburn, consists of 56 samples of tartan supplied by Wilson and Sons. Assembled between 1810 and 1820, the Cockburn Collection is the one of the earliest tartan collections with a known provenance.

# Tartan Glossary

| | |
|---|---|
| **arisaid** | a woman's blanket or shawl |
| **badge** | the clan badge is the heraldic crest of the clan chief surrounded by a "strap and a buckle" which may be worn by clansmen |
| **Black Watch** | "Black" in this sense means "secret" or "undercover" and was a nickname applied to the Independent Companies from around 1700. They "kept watch" on the Jacobite clans' activities |
| ***breacan-an fheileadh*** | Gaelic: "belted plaid". A combination of kilt and plaid made of up to 12 ells (see below) of tartan (6 ells of double tartan) neatly pleated and fastened around the body with a belt. The lower part formed the kilt, while the upper part was fixed to the shoulder by a brooch and hung down the back to make the "plaid". This long piece of plaid could be drawn snugly around the body or over the head to protect the wearer from cold weather. |
| **cadet** | the family descended from the younger sons or daughters of an earlier clan chief |
| **dress tartan** | a tartan where one of the "background" (ground) colors has been changed to white. Used in kilts for Highland dancing |
| **ell** | an ell is an old unit of measurement which could be anywhere from 27–45 inches. The *Scotch Ell* was 37 inches. |
| **fencibles** | short for "defensible", these were companies of regular troops raised for home guard service in 1759, 1778, and 1794 |
| **hard tartan** | a very fine but densely woven tartan produced until the mid-19th century |
| **hunting tartan** | green or subdued colored tartans used for hunting, but more often now used as "undress" or informal, everyday wear |
| **ilk** | as in "of that ilk", this is when a person's name is the same as his or her territorial designation e.g. Moncreiffe of that Ilk |
| **Jacobite** | a supporter of King James VII and II who was deposed in 1689 |
| **Lord Lyon** | the master of the Lyon Court who oversees matters of heraldry and succession in Scotland |
| **philabeg** | (Gaelic, *feileadh beag*, meaning "little plaid" or "little kilt") a kilt made of a six-ell length of single width tartan with no fixed, sewn pleats. This developed into the modern kilt of Highland dress |
| **sept** | most often, a part or branch of a clan. Some clansmen were known by a surname in addition to their clan name. A sept also refers to unrelated families who take protection from a clan |
| **sett** | the pattern of a tartan, the area of the design which is repeated |
| **slughorn** | the "slogan" or warcry of the clan |
| **undress** | informal dress |

# Glossary of Heraldic Terms

## Heraldic Colors

**argent** silver or white
**azure** blue
**blue celeste** sky blue
**gules** red
**murrey** mulberry
**purpure** purple
**sable** black
**vert** green

## Heraldic Terms

**addorsed** back to back
**affrontée** facing the viewer
**antique crown** crown of five or more points
**arms** describes a) the horns, tusks, teeth or talons of a beast when of a different *tincture* from the body, b) wearing armor
**attires** the antlers of a stag
**banded** tied with a band or ribbon
**beaked** when the beaks of birds or creatures is a different *tincture* to its body
**belled** with attached bells
**cabossed** an animal's head depicted *affrontee*, cut off behind the ears with no part of the neck showing
**chapeau** a velvet cap lined with fur
**coronet** a *chapeau* in a gold circlet
**couchant** lying down with its head raised
**couped** cut off cleanly with a straight line
**cubit** a hand and arm *couped* at the elbow
**cutlass** a curved sword like a scimitar
**demi** a human or animal depicted from the waist upwards
**dexter** the right-hand side of shield as held by the bearer, but the left side as seen by the viewer
**displayed** wings outstretched
**dormant** in a sleeping posture
**embowed** bent, or curved
**environed** encircled by
**erased** torn off leaving a jagged edge
**erect** upright

| | |
|---|---|
| **ermine** | white fur with black tails |
| **estoile** | a star with six wavy rays |
| **fess point** | the centre of a shield |
| **fessways** | in a horizontal line across the shield |
| **fleur de lis** | a stylised lily |
| **fructed** | bearing fruit |
| **gorged** | collared |
| **gryphon** | griffin, or winged monster, with the body of an eagle and the back legs of a lion. A male gryphon has no wings but has rays or spikes emerging from the body |
| **guardant** | a beast or monster with its head facing the viewer |
| **hart** | a stag |
| **hilted** | the handle of a sword or dagger when of a different *tincture* to the blade |
| **issuant** | emerging from |
| **jessed** | a falcon with leather straps attached to its legs |
| **langued** | tongued |
| **maned** | the mane of a beast when in a different *tincture* to its body |
| **moor** | a black man |
| **mullet** | a five pointed star (from Fr. *molette* meaning a spur rowel) |
| **naiant** | swimming; a fish shown in a horizontal position |
| **nowed** | tied in a knot |
| **or** | gold |
| **passant** | walking |
| **proper** | depicted in natural colors |
| **rampant** | a beast or monster standing on one hind leg |
| **reguardant** | a beast or monster looking back over its shoulder |
| **segreant** | a *gryphon* in the *rampant* position |
| **sinister** | the left hand side of a shield as held by the bearer, but the right hand side from the viewpoint of the onlooker |
| **skene** | a Highland knife, often depicted as a short sword or dagger |
| **slipped** | flowers and leaves still attached to the stalk |
| **statant** | standing |
| **tinctures** | the metals, furs and colors used in heraldry |
| **tines/tynes** | the branches of a stags' antlers |
| **transfixed** | pierced through |
| **trippant** | a stag or deer when depicted as *passant* |
| **vambraced** | an arm clad in armor |
| **vested** | dressed, or clothed |
| **volant** | flying |

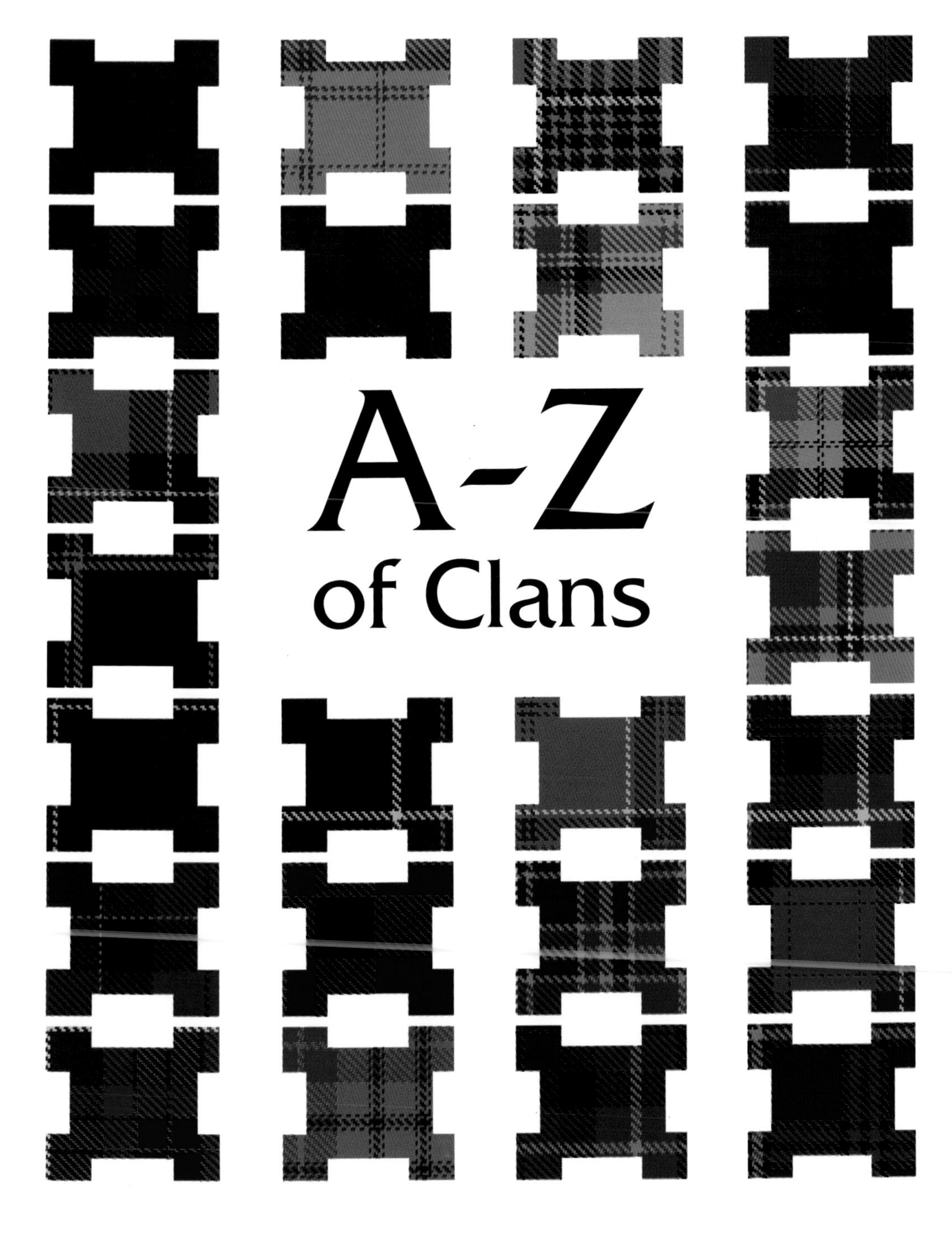

# A-Z of Clans

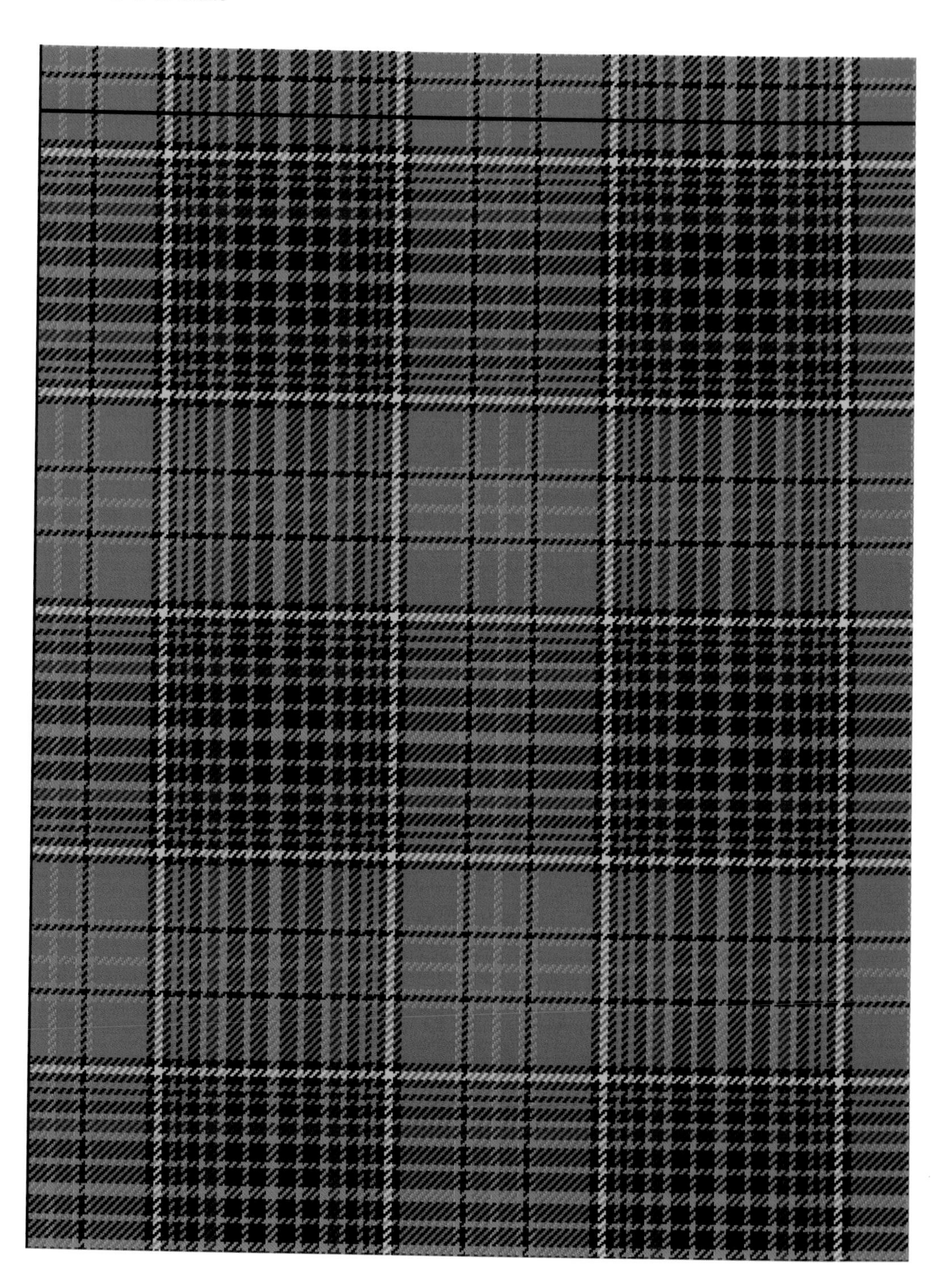

# Anderson

## (MacAndrew)

Earliest known date: 1906
Earliest source: Johnston, 1906
Tartan type: Symmetrical
Sett: **R**6 B12 R2 Bk4 R2 B36 Bk6 W6 Bk6 Y2 Bk2 Y2 Bk8 R2 B8 R6 G12 R4 G12 **R**8

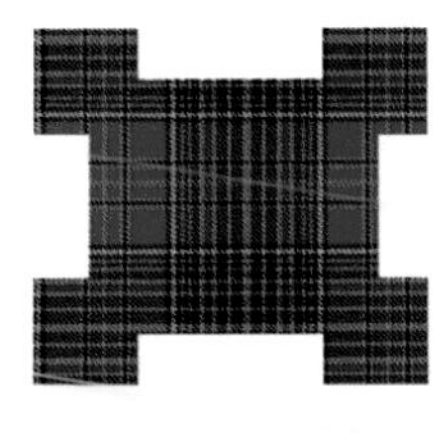

THE GAELIC EQUIVALENT OF ANDERSON is *Gilleaindrias* (Gillanders, or St Andrew's son – St Andrew being the patron saint of Scotland). It appears that the descendants of MacGillandrish over the course of time had their name "anglicized" to MacAndrew and, in the Highlands, it is by this name that the Andersons are called. An early notable MacAndrew was Iain beag MacAindrea (Little John MacAndrew) of Dalnahatnich in Duthil. In 1670, Little John took part in one of the last *creach* or cattle-lifting expeditions. The *creach* had been a ritualistic "rite of passage" whereby the young men of a clan demonstrated their manhood by stealing livestock from neighboring clan territory. By the mid 17th century, the *creach* had largely disappeared, replaced by the *spreidh* – plundering by groups who returned the lifted animals after they received a *tascal* (information money as to the livestock's whereabouts) and a guarantee that they would not be prosecuted!

The most prominent branches of the family have been the Andersons of Dowhill, the Andersons of Wester Ardbreck in Banffshire, and the Andersons, lairds of Candacraig in Strathdon. Since the 1400s, however, the Andersons have been associated with the Confederation of Clans and regarded as a Clan Chattan (see page 40). Although a coat of arms was granted to "Anderson of that Ilk" in the 16th century, this particular family has not been identified since no actual place known as "Anderson" ever existed!

The elaborate Anderson family tartan can be traced back to W. and A.K. Johnston's *The Tartans of the Clans and Septs of Scotland*, published in 1906, but there have been several variations, in particular in the color of the ground. As well as grey, the ground color has been rendered as pale blue or turquoise.

# Armstrong

Earliest known date: 1842
Source: *The Vestiarium Scoticum*, 1842
Tartan type: Symmetrical
Sett: **G**4 Bk2 G60 Bk24 B4 Bk2 B2 Bk2 B24 **R**6
Clan motto: *Invictus maneo* ("I remain unvanquished")
Clan crest: An arm from the shoulder, armed Proper

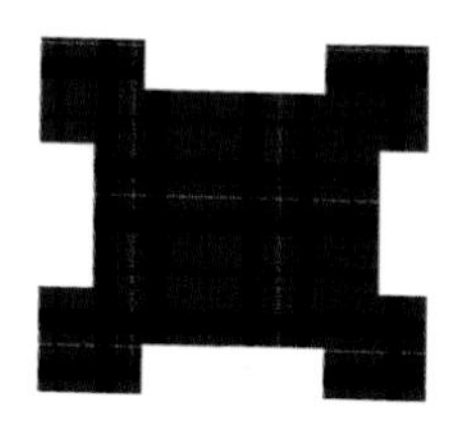

THE ARMSTRONGS WERE A POWERFUL FAMILY who were much respected and feared in Northumbria, England. According to legend, the first Armstrong was Siward Beorn ("Sword Warrior") also called Siward Digry ("Sword Strong Arm"). He was a nephew of King Cnut, the Danish-born king of England from 1016 until 1035. By 1376, the Armstrongs had extended their influence into Scotland, establishing the seat of the clan chief at Mangerton, in Liddesdale, which forms the southern part of Roxburghshire. The clan grew to such a strength that by 1528 it was said they could put 3,000 horsemen into a battlefield. This power was seen as so threatening to James V that in 1530, according to tradition, the king tricked John Armstrong of Gilnockie into a meeting near Harwick at which the unsuspecting laird was arrested and hanged. In return, the Armstrongs refused to support James' invasion of England.

The Union of the Crowns in 1603 ended the Anglo-Scottish border wars and, by 1610, the last Armstrong laird had been hanged and the families scattered. Since that time there has been no Armstrong chief. but in its place, an active clan association that organized the first gathering of Armstrongs for 400 years in 1979. Recent famous Armstrongs have included the arctic explorer, Alexander Armstrong, and, the first man on the moon, Neil Armstrong. The Armstrong clan tartan is a traditional, symmetrical design of green, black and blue, with a red stripe on the blue.

Surnames with possible associations: Fairbairn, Nixon

# Baird

Earliest known date: 1906
Source: Johnston, 1906
Tartan type: Symmetrical
Sett: **P**6 G2 P2 G16 Bk16 B16 Bk4 **B**6
Clan motto: *Dominus fecit* ("The Lord made this")
Clan crest: A gryphon's head erased Proper

IT IS SAID THAT THE FIRST BAIRD saved the life of the king, William I the Lion (1165–1214), from an attack by a wild boar. While the name Baird originated from "bard" meaning poet, it also seems to be territorial, derived from lands held by the family near Biggar in Lanarkshire. During the reign of Alexander III (1249–86) the Bairds increased the landholdings in the region but, by the end of the century, the family of Baird of Kyp had sworn submission and allegiance to Edward I of England. Consequently, the principal Baird family became that which held land of Auchmedden in Aberdeenshire. Their influence was strengthened by marriage into the powerful Keith family, and eventually the Auchmedden lands passed into the hands of the earls of Aberdeen. According to legend, a pair of eagles that had regularly nested on Auchmedden crags left the area, thus fulfilling the ancient prophesy that "There shall be an eagle in the craig while there is a Baird in Auchmedden". When Lord Haddow, the eldest son of the Earl of Aberdeen, married a daughter of William Baird of Newbyth, the eagles promptly returned! Famous members of the Baird clan include the pioneer of television, John Logie Baird.

The symmetrical clan tartan was first recorded in 1906. In this, and in an early 20th century sample from the Highland Society in London, the triple stripes are woven in red. Today, however, they are generally woven in purple.

# Barclay

Earliest known date: 1842
Source: *The Vestiarium Scoticum*, 1842
Tartan type: Symmetrical
Sett: **R**2 G32 B32 **G**2
Clan motto: *Aut agere aut mori* ("Either to do or die")
Clan crest: A hand holding a dagger Proper (on a chapeau Azure doubled Ermine)

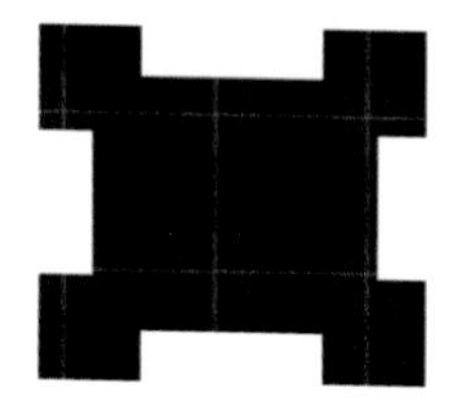

The Barclays claim descent from the house of Berkeley, of Berkeley Castle in Gloucestershire, who settled in England following the Norman Conquest. Originally, the name was "de Berchelai" and in the Domesday Book, the family is mentioned as owning land between the rivers Wye and Usk. John de Berchelai arrived in Scotland in 1067 in the retinue of Margaret, the sister of the Saxon Edgar the Aetheling. When Margaret married the Scottish king, Malcolm III, she gave land to her supporters, with John de Berchelai receiving Towie. The Barclays grew in power, lands and prestige: Sir Walter de Berkeley was Chamberlain of Scotland under William the Lion in 1165, while in the early 14th century, Sir David Barclay was a chief supporter of Robert I (the Bruce). In the 17th century Colonel David Barclay, 1st Earl of Urie and a professional soldier, was converted to the Society of Friends (Quakers). His son Robert Barclay published *An Apology for the true Christian Divinity as the same held forth and preached by the people called in scorn Quakers* (1675), while his grandson David Barclay of Cheapside, London was the founder of Barclays Bank. Overseas, John and Peter Barclay, who were silk merchants in Banff, settled in Livonia on the Baltic Sea coast in 1621. From this branch of the family descended Field Marshal Michael Andreas Barclay de Tollie, commander of the Russian Army which defeated Napoleon in 1812 and who was created a prince by the Tsar.

The Barclays have no "regular" tartan, although the green hunting version is most associated with the clan. Based on an earlier hunting sett published in 1842 in the *Vestiarium Scoticum*, the blue was significantly darker than the green. A second, yellow tartan, which serves as the dress Barclay tartan, was published in 1906 in the *Tartans of the Clans and Septs of Scotland*.

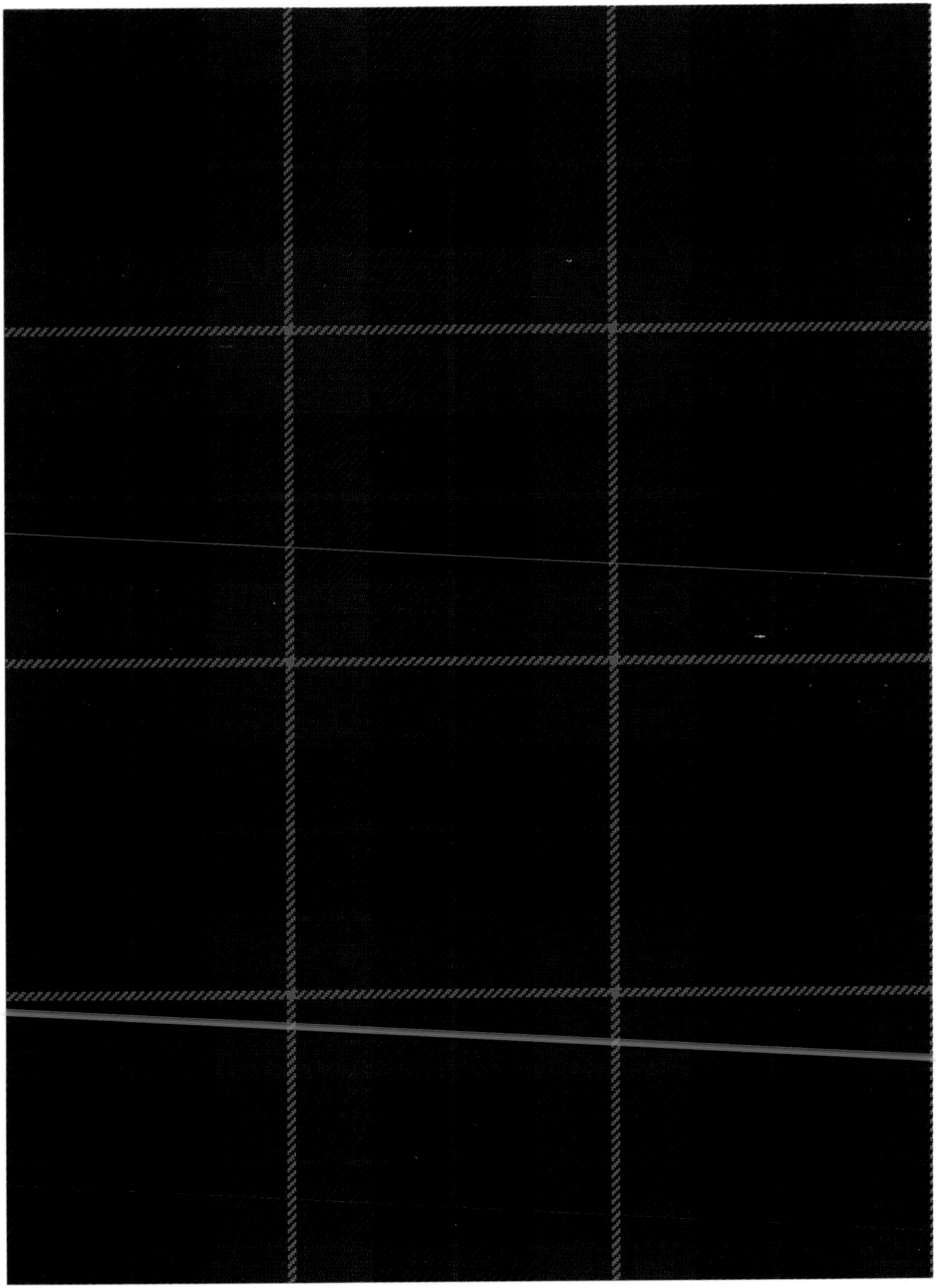

# Brodie

Earliest known date: 1842
Earliest source: *The Vestiarium Scoticum*, 1842
Tartan type: Symmetrical
Sett: **Bk**4 R32 Bk16 Y2 Bk16 **R**4
Clan motto: "Unite"
Clan crest: A right hand holding a bunch of arrows all Proper
Badge: Periwinkle

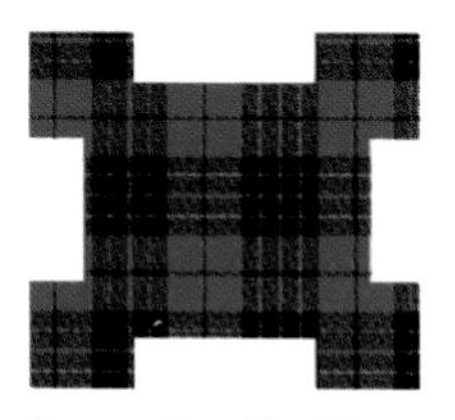

THE CLAN NAME IS DERIVED FROM BRODIE (Gaelic, *brothaach*), a local place name of lands near Forres, Morayshire. Michael Brodie of Brodie received a charter from Robert I (the Bruce) confirming ownership of the lands. Many family documents disappeared or were destroyed, however, when Lord Lewis Gordon, 3rd Marquis of Huntly, burnt Brodie House in 1645. Nevertheless, the Brodies were a prominent force in Moray: Alexander Brodie of Brodie (1617–79) was a fierce supporter of the reformed religion and attacked Elgin Cathedral in 1640, destroying its carvings and paintings which he considered idolatrous. In 1649, he negotiated with the exiled Charles II for his return to Scotland and, following the defeat of Royalist forces at Worcester in 1651, Brodie was summoned by Oliver Cromwell to consider a union between Scotland and England. Alexander (born in 1697) was appointed Lord Lyon, King of Arms of Scotland in 1727, and was Lyon during the Jacobite rebellion of 1745.

The origins of the Brodie tartan are difficult to ascertain. W. & A. Smith's book *Authenticated Tartans of the Clans and Families of Scotland* (1850) is the earliest source for the Brodie tartan. They based their authentication of 69 tartans on the findings of George Hunter, a former army outfitter, who in 1822 toured the Highlands in search of old tartans. D.W. Stewart in *Old and Rare Tartans of Scotland* (1893) also traces the tartan to the beginning of the 19th century, but also states that, around this time, the Brodies in Aberdeenshire wore the Huntly district tartan.

Surnames with possible connections: Bryde

# Bruce

Earliest known date: 1842
Earliest source: *The Vestiarium Scoticum*, 1842
Tartan type: Symmetrical
Sett: **W/Y**2 R16 G4 R4 G12 **R**2
Clan motto: *Fuimus* ("We have been")
Clan crest: A lion statant Azure armed and langued Gules
Badge: Rosemary

The Scottish king, Robert I the Bruce, belonged to the Norman French family of De Bruis. His ancestor, Robert de Bruis, came to England with William the Conqueror in 1066 and was awarded land in Yorkshire, while his son was given the Lordship of Annandale. A second Robert de Brus became a companion in arms to King David I of Scotland, but when he refused to support the king's invasion of England, he surrendered his holdings in Annandale to his second son (also Robert) and joined the English forces. Indeed, after the defeat of the Scots at the battle of the Standard in 1138, de Brus took his own son prisoner!

It was Robert, the 5th Lord of Annandale (d.1245) who laid the foundations of the royal house of Bruce when he married Isobel, the great-granddaughter of King David I. In 1255, their son, Robert de Bruce, was made one of the Regents of the Kingdom of Scotland and guardian of Alexander III. In 1290, he claimed the crown of Scotland but was overruled by Edward I who awarded the crown to John Balliol. Balliol's defeat at the battle of Dunbar in 1296 saw the rule of Scotland shared by the Bruces and the powerful Comyn family. In 1306 hoping to negotiate a compromise, Robert the Bruce (1274–1329) met John Comyn at Dumfries. An argument erupted and Bruce murdered his rival. Within a week, Bruce was crowned king at Scone and his power finally cemented in the decisive victory at Bannockburn in 1314.

The design of the Bruce clan tartan comes from *The Vestiarium Scoticum*. Although doubt has been cast on the authenticity of the *Vestiarium*, the sett, which has alternating yellow and white lines, was approved by the clan chief Lord Bruce, Earl of Elgin, in 1967.

Surnames with possible associations: Carlyle, Randolf, Stenhouse

# Buchanan

Earliest known date: 1845-7

Earliest source: MacIan 1845-7

Tartan type: Asymmetrical

Sett: Bk2 Y12 Bk2 B8 Bk2 G12 B8 G12 Bk2 B8 Bk2 R16 W2 R16 Bk2 B8 Bk2 Y12

Clan motto: *Clarior hinc honos* ("Hence the brighter honor")

Clan crest: A dexter hand holding up a ducal cap (Proper), tufted on top with a rose Gules, within two laurel branches in orle (also Proper)

Badge: *Dearc bhraoileag* (Bilberry) or *Darag* (Oak)

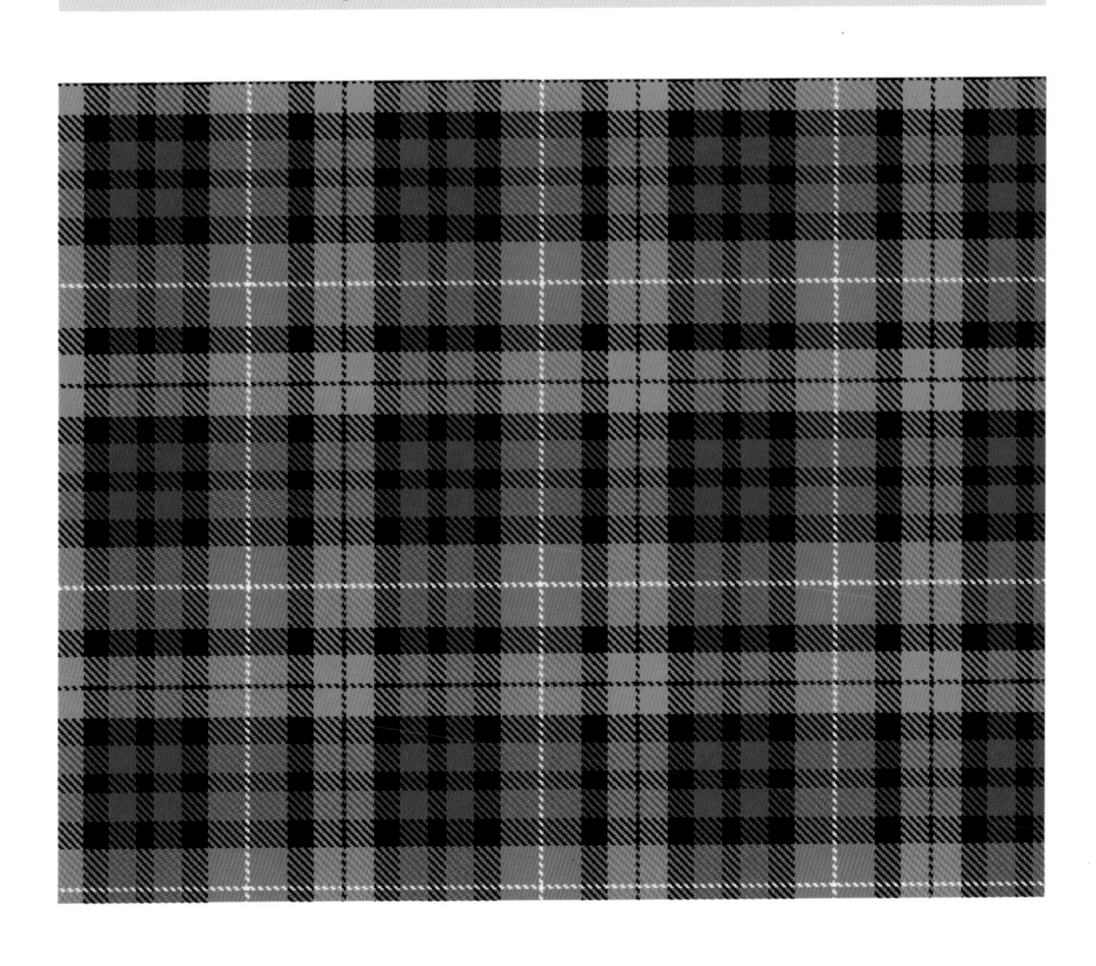

The name Buchanan is derived from the Gaelic ecclesiastical term *buth chanain* which means "the canon's seat". It seems that an ancient Buchanan may have been a clergyman in the service of the ancient Celtic Church. Gilbert, who also took the Buchanan name, acquired the Buchanan lands in Stirlingshire from the Earl of Lennox in the middle of the 13th century. In 1282, Maurice of Buchanan received a charter confirming him a baron of the lands. He also held the small island of Clarinch in Loch Lomond, the name of which became the clan's *slughorn* (slogan, or warcry): "Clar Innis". The Buchanans were supporters of Robert the Bruce during the War of Independence. Later Alexander Buchanan (d.1424) fought with the French against Henry V of England. Walter Buchanan married Isabel, the only daughter of Murdoch, Duke of Albany and Regent of Scotland. When Murdoch was beheaded by his cousin James I in 1425, the Buchanans became the nearest relatives to this branch of the royal family. The fortunes of the Buchanans later waned, however: in 1682 John Buchanan, 22nd (and last) laird, sold the ancient lands to pay off huge debts. The lands are now owned by the Duke of Montrose.

Although there has not been a recognized clan chief since the late 17th century, one James Buchanan did become the 15th President of the United States of America from 1857–61. The Buchanan tartan is one of the most popular (and the most irregular) tartans in use. There is much debate as to who was responsible for altering an earlier symmetrical design, described by Logan in 1831, to the unusual asymmetrical sett first illustrated by MacIan and which appeared in *The Clans of the Scottish Highlands* (1845-7).

Surnames with possible associations: Colman, Cormack, Cousland, Donle(a)vy, Dove, Dow(e), Gibb, Gilbert(son), Harper(son), Lennie/y, Macaldonich, Macandeoir, Maca(u)s(e)lan(d)(e), Maccalman, Maccalmon(d)(t), Maccasland, Macchruiter, Maccolman, Maccormack, Maccubbin, Macdonlevy, Macgilbert, Macinally, Macindoe, Mackinley, Macmaster, Macmaurice, Macmurchie(y), Macnuyer, Macwhirter, Masterson, Morris, Richardson, Rusk(in), Spittal, Watt, Yule

# Cameron

Earliest known date: 1842
Earliest source: *The Vestiarium Scoticum*, 1842
Tartan type: Symmetrical Sett: **Y**2 R32 G12 R4 G12 **R**4
Clan motto: *Aonaibh re chéile* ("Unite")
Clan crest: A sheaf of five arrows points upward Proper tied with a band Gules
Badge: *Darag* (Oak) or *Dearca fithitch* (Crowberry)

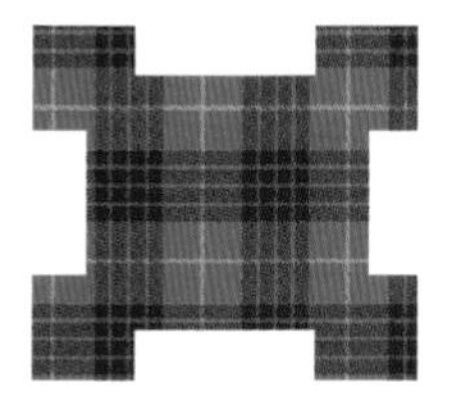

Some scholars say that the Camerons are descended from a son of Camchron, a king of Denmark, while others maintain that the first true clan chief, Donald Dubh (born *c.*1400), was descended from a medieval family in Fife, the Cameron of Ballegarno. Whatever his origins, Donald was an astute leader who united a number of tribes to form the Clan Cameron. In 1528 Ewen Macallan, took the title "Cameron of Lochiel", which has remained the chief's title ever since.

The oldest Cameron taartan is the chief's own "Cameron of Lochiel", authenticated in a posthumous portrait of the 19th chief, Donald "The Gentle Lochiel". Painted by George Chalmers in 1764, (after the chief had died in exile in France in 1748 and the tartan had been banned as a result of the 1745 uprising) the portrait of the chief and his tartan hangs at the clan seat at Achnacarry, in Lochaber. Two other Cameron tartans are in use: The Clan Cameron was first illustrated in *The Vestiarium Scoticum* (1842) but only came into wide use in the late 19th century. The Cameron of Erracht tartan, once used as the hunting Cameron, is now the official regimental tartan of the Queen's Own Cameron Highlanders. The Cameron Highlanders (or 79th) were first raised by Allan Cameron of Erracht in 1793.

Surnames with possible associations: Clark(e), Clarkson, Clerk, Lonie, Macallan, Machlerich, Macclery, Macildowie, Mackail, Macmartin, Maconie, Macourlic, Maculric, Macvail, Macwalrick, Martin, Paul, Sorely

# Campbell

Earliest known date: Not before 1810 as Campbell
Earliest source: Cockburn Collection, 1810–20
Tartan type: Symmetrical
Setts:
Campbell of Argyll: **B**2 Bk2 B16 G16 Bk2 W/Y4 Bk2 G16 Bk16 B2 Bk2 B2 Bk2 **B**16
Campbell of Bredalbane: **B**2 Bk2 B16 Bk16 Y2 G28 Y2 Bk16 B2 Bk2 B2 Bk2 **B**16
Campbell of Cawdor: **Az**4 Bk2 G16 Bk16 B16 Bk2 **R**4
Clan Campbell crest: A boar's head fessways erased Or, armed Argent, langued Gules
Clan motto: *Ne Obliviscaris* ("Do not forget")
Badge: *Roid* (Wild Myrtle) or *Grarbhag an t-sleibhe* (Fir Club Moss)

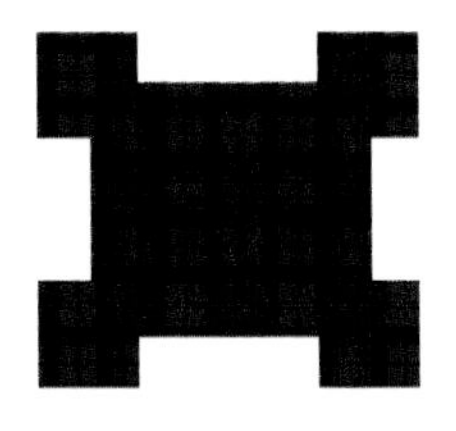

The great Clan Duibhne, or Campbell, is said to have been founded by Diarmid O'Duibhne, but it was Eva O'Duibhne, the heiress of the line, who carried the chiefship of her tribe and who married the first Campbell. The main house is Campbell of Argyll, the founder of which was Cailean Mor who died in 1294, and from whom successive chiefs of the Clan take the patronymic MacCailean Mor. In 1445, Sir Duncan Campbell of Loch Awe was made Lord Campbell, and his grandson became the Earl of Argyll. In 1703, the Campbells were elevated to a dukedom, with the hereditary offices of Lord Justice General and Admirals of the Western Coasts and Isles of Scotland. Another Cailean (or Colin) founded the family line of Campbell of Cawdor, while Black Colin of Glenochry, the second son of Sir Duncan of Loch Awe, founded the line of Campbells of Bredalbane. There are also several "cadets" of the house, such as Campbell of Glenlyon, and of Barcaldine.

The tartan worn by the MacCailein Mor, the Chief of the Campbells, his family, and most of the principal Campbell families in Argyll, is a plain green, black and blue sett, and this is now the official tartan of all the Campbells. This tartan, woven in darker shades, is also called the 42nd, the Government, Military, Sutherland, or Black Watch. In the 18th century, the Scottish weavers Wilson of Bannockburn used this sett as the background and added stripes of different colors to distinguish the various Campbell lines and regiments. The Campbells of Argyll added yellow and white; the Campbells of Breadalbane, of Cawdor and of Loudoun added further color variations and may have their origins in the setts used by military regiments such as the Breadalbane Fencibles of 1793 and the Loudon Highlanders raised at the time of the '45 and disbanded in 1748.

Surnames with possible associations: Burn(e)s, Caddell, Conochie, Denoon, Denune, Fisher, Hastings, Haw(e)s, Hawson, Lorne, Loudon, Maccarter, Macdermid, Macdiarmid, Mackellar, Mackelvie, Macoran, Macowen, Mactavish, Macure, Pinkerton, Tawesson, Torry, Ure

# Chattan

Earliest known date: 1816
Earliest source: Logan, 1831
Tartan type: Symmetrical
Clan crest: A catt salient Proper
Clan motto: "Touch not the catt but a glove"
Badge: *Lus nan cnaimhseag* (Red Whortleberry)

The Clan Chattan is a confederation of clans in Lochaber, Strathnairn and Badenoch, and comes under Mackintosh hegemony. Before the 14th century, the Clan Chattan seems to have been a "conventional" clan, descended from their 13th-century ancestor, Gillechattan Mor. "Gillechattan" means "St Cattan's gillie", that is, at his birth he was placed under the special protection of the saint. "Cattan" means "little cat" and the wild cat is the heraldic beast of the Clan Chattan. As other clans settled in the districts and intermarried with them, they also joined the confederation. In addition to the descendants of the original clan (the Cattanachs, MacPhersons, MacBeans, and MacPhails), the Clan Chattan confederation has members made up of the Mackintosh and their cadet branches (Farquarsons, Shaws, MacThomases, MacCombies) and families not originally related by blood (Davidsons, MacPhails, MacAndrews, Gows, Clarks, Gillespies, Nobles, MacHardy, MacKilligins, and Ritchie – into which pop superstar Madonna married!)

During the Jacobite risings of 1715 and 1745, the Clan Chattan supported the Stewarts and suffered in consequence. The confederation was split by feuds among the major families to secure what remained of power, but the Mackintosh chiefs continued to be the "captains" of the clan until 1947, when Duncan Alexander Mackintosh or Torcastle was recognized by the Lord Lyon as the Chief of Clan Chattan in his own right. He had his own tartan, called the "Finzean Fancy", but containing an extra white line. A Clan Chattan society preserves and publicizes the history and contemporary activities of the Clan worldwide.

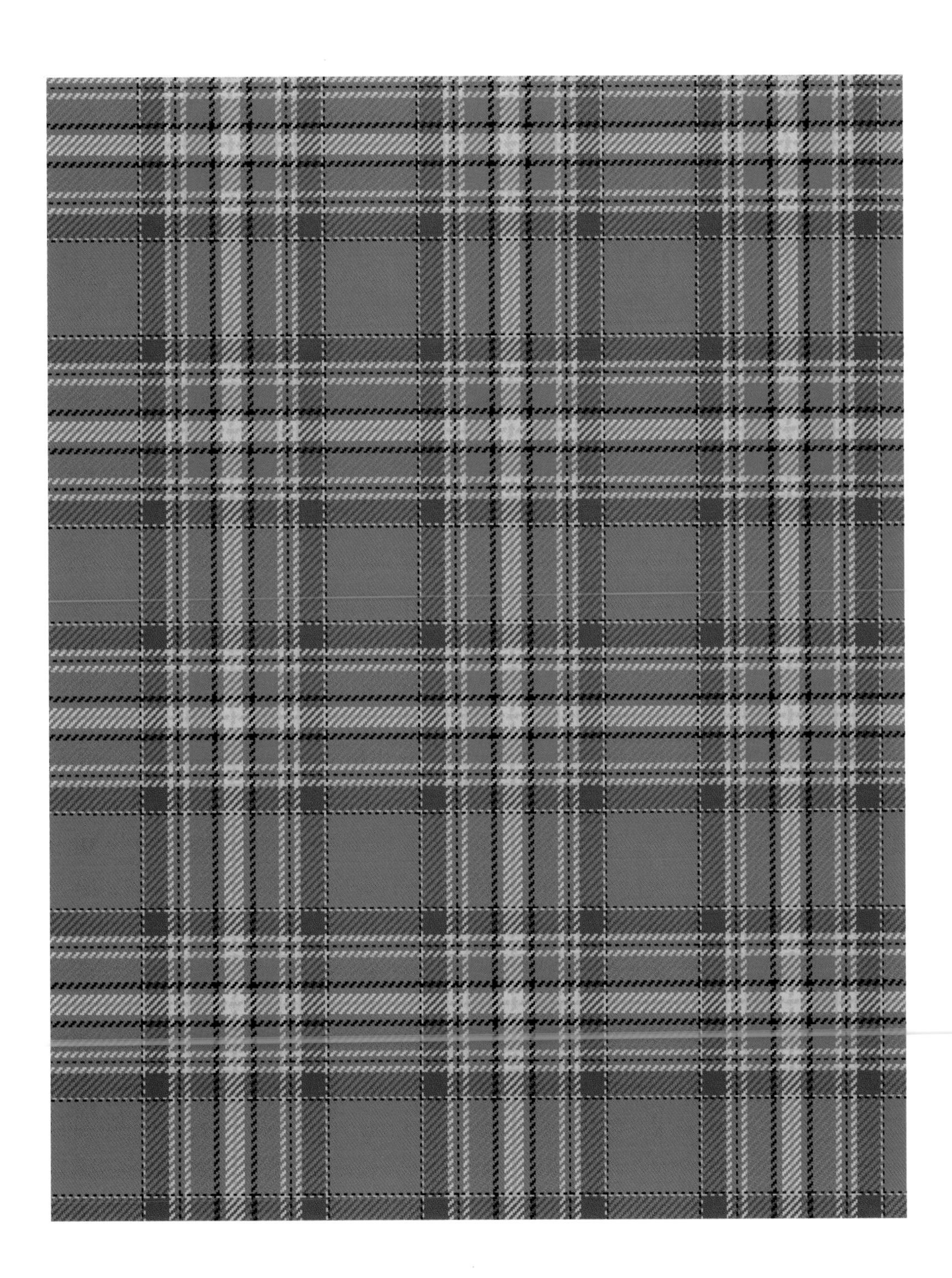

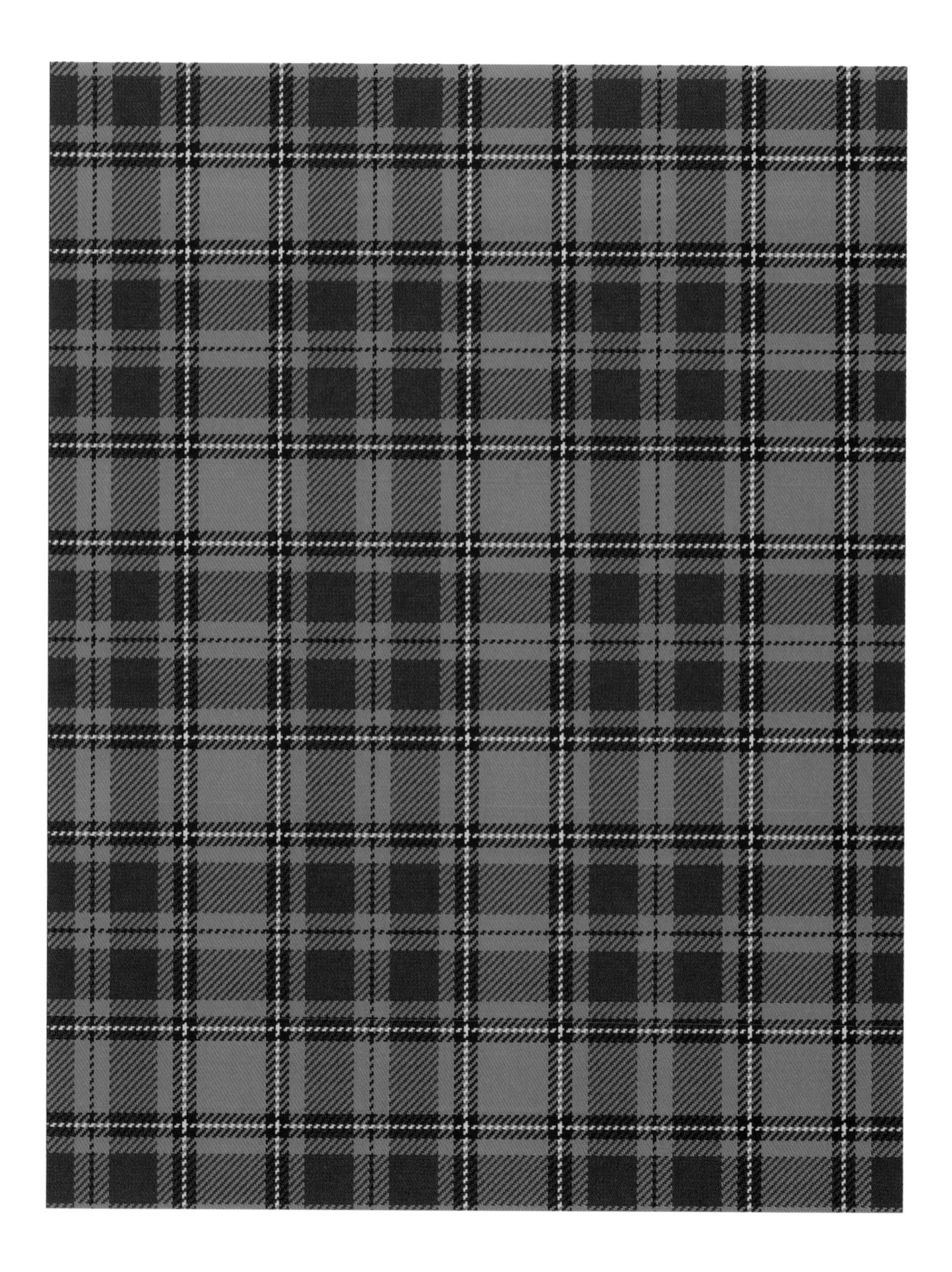

# Chisholm

Earliest known date: 1842
Earliest source: *The Vestiarium Scoticum*, 1842
Tartan type: Symmetrical
Sett: **R**24 B4 W2 B4 R6 G16 R6 **B**2
Clan crest: A dexter hand holding a dagger erect Proper, the point thereof transfixing a boar's head erased Or
Clan motto: *Feros ferio* ("I am fierce with the fierce")
Badge: *Raineach* (Fern)

The Chisholms were first recorded in Roxburghshire, in the Borders in the mid-13th century. Of Norman French origin, the name was originally de Cheselhelme. The Ragman Rolls record John de Cheselhelme of Roxburghshire in 1296, whose seal was a boar's head (this remains the clan's principal device to this day). Tradition has it that two Chisholm brothers saved the life of the king from an attack by a wild boar. As their reward, the family were granted lands in Inverness-shire. The family grew in strength and prestige in the north when, in 1359, Sir Robert de Chisholme was made Constable of Urquhart Castle on the shores of Loch Ness and his son, Alexander, married Margaret, the heiress to Erchless Castle and lands in Strathglass.

Adherents to the Jacobite cause in 1715, the family forfeited their estates. A pardon was granted in 1727 and much of the land regained, but in 1745 when Bonnie Prince Charlie raised his father's standard, Roderick, a son of the Chisholm chief, led a battalion for the Jacobite cause. Of the Chisholms who went into battle at Culloden, fewer than 50 survived. Mass emigration to America emptied Chisholm lands of their tenants during the 18th century, and the direct Chisholm line died out with Alexander, the 23rd chief, in 1793. The chieftanship passed to a half-brother, William. The clan headquarters are at Cnoc-an-Fhurain, Barcaldine, Argyll and there is a sample of the Clan Chisholm tartan (derived from the Black Watch sett) and Chisholm hunting tartan in the collection of the Highland Society in London. The most frequently seen Chisholm tartan is that described in 1842 in the *Vestiarium Scoticum*, although in 1831 Logan described a version with the white lines centered on the outer blue stripes.

# Colquhoun

Earliest known date: *c.*1810–20
Earliest source: Cockburn Collection, 1810–20
Tartan type: Symmetrical
Sett: **B**2 Bk2 B16 Bk16 W2 G16 **R**4
Clan crest: A hart's head couped Gules, attired Argent
Clan motto: *Si je puis* ("If I can")
Badge: *Caltuinn* (Hazel)

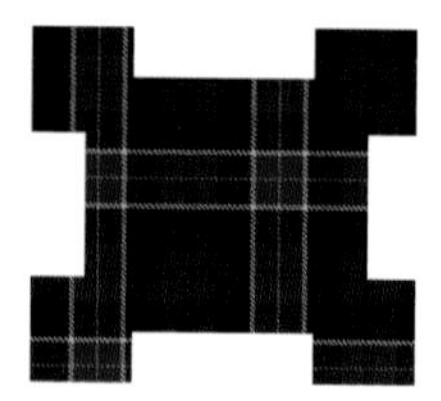

The Clan Colquhoun's lands are on the shores of Loch Lomond. The founder of the family was Humphrey de Kilpatrick or Kirkpatrick, who was granted the lands of Colquhoun from the Earl of Lennox during the reign of Alexander II (1214–49). Ingram, the son of Humphrey Kilpatrick, was the first to assume the name of Colquhoun. Around 1368, the lands of Luss, from which the chiefs now take their territorial designation (as Colquhoun of Luss), were acquired when Sir Robert married "The Fair Maid of Luss", the heiress of the Lord Of Luss. Rising in power, the Colquhouns were to become governors of Dumbarton Castle and the controllers of the castle of Camstradden.

In 1632, the Colquhoun estates were forfeited when Sir John, the 11th Laird of Luss, was accused of using witchcraft in order to abscond with his sister-in-law. After much negotiation, Sir John's son, Humphrey, recovered the Colquhoun estates in 1646. Humphrey had no male heirs so he applied to the Crown for a patent to allow the title to pass on his death to the male issue of his daughter's husband, James Grant of Pluscardine. This was on the proviso that any heirs adopted the name and Arms of Colquhoun and that the estates of Colquhoun and Grant were never joined. Thus, James Grant succeeded as Sir James Colquhoun. When James' elder brother died without an heir, James inherited the Grant estates and reverted to that name. James' son, also called James, became Chief of Colquhoun and built the grand Rossdhu House in Luss, Dunbartonshire, which remains the seat of the Colquhoun chiefs. The Clan Colquhoun tartan as it currently appears was certified by the chief with his seal and signature in around 1816 and appears in Wilson of Bannockburn's pattern book from 1819. *The Vestiarium Scoticum*, however, shows an erroneous pattern with the white stripe next to the blue.

Surnames with possible associations: Cowan, King, Macachounich, Macmanus

# Crawford

Earliest known date: 1842
Earliest source: *The Vestiarium Scoticum*
Tartan type: Symmetrical
Sett: **Cr**12 W4 Cr60 G24 Cr6 G24 **Cr**6
Clan crest: A stag's head erased Gules, between the attires a cross crosslet fitchée Sable.
Clan motto: *Tutum te robore reddam* ("I will give you safety by strength")
Badge: *Bosca* (Boxwood)

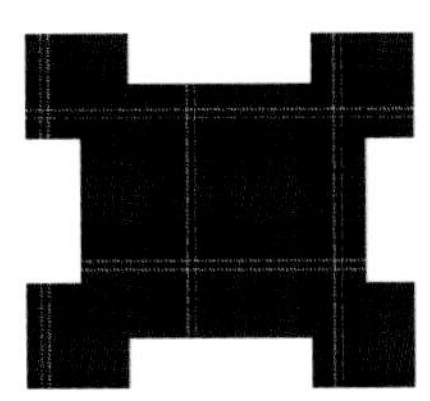

The name Crawford, or Crawfurd, is believed to be Norman French in origin and was derived from the Barony of Crawford in Upper Clydesdale, Lanarkshire. In 1248, Sir John Crawford of that Ilk died: the elder of his two daughters married Archibald de Douglas, and the younger married David Lindsay, the ancestor of the Earls of Crawford. In 1296, Sir Reginald Crawford was created the Sheriff of Ayr. He was murdered by the English at a banquet there the following year. Sir Reginald's sister, Margaret, married Sir Malcolm Wallace of Ellerlie and became the mother of the great Scottish patriot, William Wallace. The Sheriff of Ayr's family however, produced the two main branches of the family who were styled "of Auchinames" (a title granted by Robert the Bruce in 1320), and "of Craufurdland" (a title conferred by Robert III in 1391 on Ardoch, the 6th laird). Sir William Crawford of Craufurdland, who was knighted by James I, fought with the Scots in the service of the French king, Charles VII at Creyult, Burgundy, in 1423. Later, in 1513, a Craufurdland followed James IV into battle at Flodden, where he perished, along with many other Scottish nobles. The Castle of Craufurdland was much extended in the 17th century by the 16th laird, and it remains the family seat today.

Despite the family's long history, the Crawford Clan tartan first appeared sometime between 1829 and 1842. It was first recorded in *The Vestiarium Scoticum* in 1842, which describes the green next to the crimson line as being the color of a "tender ash tree", with the rest of the green being "grass-green".

# Cumming, or Comyn

## (also Cumin)

Earliest known date: 1850

Earliest source: Smith, 1850 (for sett shown)

Tartan type: Symmetrical

Sett: **Bk**4 R36 G12 R6 G18 W2 G18 **R**6

Clan crest: A lion rampant Or, in his dexter paw a dagger Proper.

Clan motto: "Courage"

Badge: *Luis Mhic Cuimin* (Cumin), but more often, Wheat

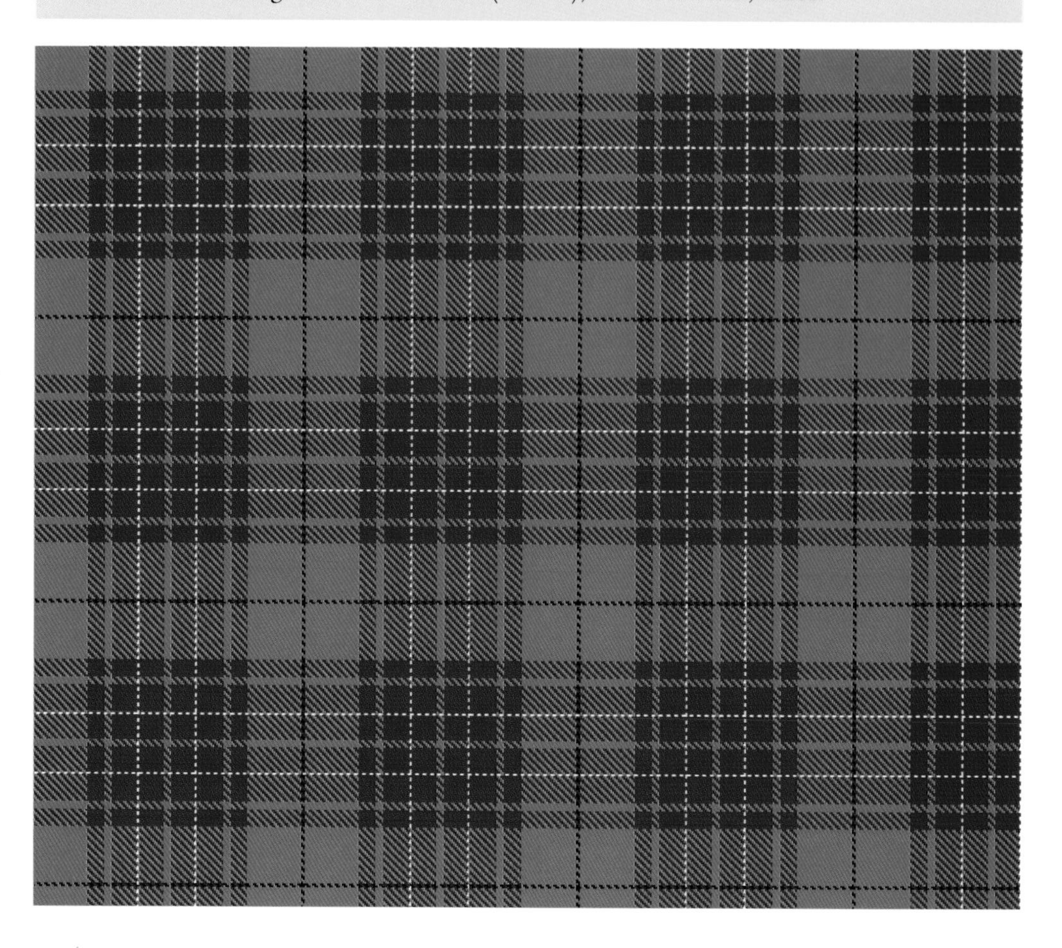

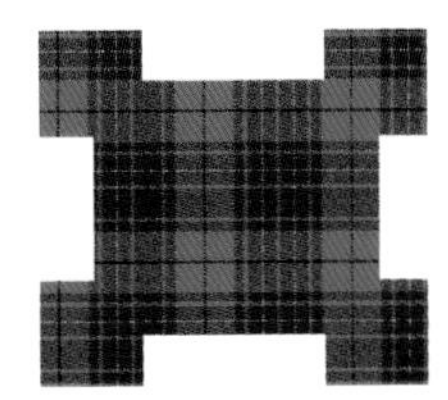

The Comyns were, along with the Bruces, one-time competitors for the Crown of Scotland. The name is believed to derive from Comines, near Lisle in northern France, from where Robert de Comyn, a companion of William the Conqueror in 1066, is thought to have originated. Comyn was created Earl of Northumberland in 1069 and his grandson, William, arrived in Scotland with King David, who awarded him lands in Roxburghshire. William married the granddaughter of King Donald Bane (later Donald III, who was the son of Duncan I) and they had a son, also named William, who became Earl of Buchan. He fathered Sir John "the Red" Comyn, Lord of Badencoh, the chief of the clan that by now comprized three earldoms (Monteith, Menteith and Atholl, and Buchan) and 32 Knights of the Name.

On the death of Alexander III, two Comyns, both direct descendants of Duncan I, were appointed to the council of six guardians of Scotland. They were Alexander Comyn, Earl of Buchan, and John "the Black" Comyn, Lord of Badenoch. In 1290, the child-queen Margaret "the Maid of Norway" died and among the claimants to the throne were the two Comyn guardians, Robert Bruce (grandfather of the future king) and John Bailliol, (brother-in-law to "Black John"). Edward I of England was called on to decide who should reign and he chose Bailliol. Conflict soon broke out, with claimants taking sides and changing allegiances in the struggle to win the throne and to break free of English domination. In 1306, Robert the Bruce met with John "the Red" Comyn in Greyfriars Church in Dumfries in the hope of negotiating a compromise, but an argument erupted and Comyn was killed, leaving Bruce to establish his position as king. In the conflicts that followed, the Bradenoch Comyns were removed from the centre of Scottish politics. In their place, new branches grew and the name was restyled as Cumming with the chiefly line running through the Cummings of Altyre.

There was once some confusion regarding the tartan of the Cummings: in *The Clans of the Scottish Highlands* (1845-7) Logan designated it as "MacAuly" and MacIan illustrated it as such. In 1850 W. & A. Smith, however, showed the current Cumming tartan, which, they said, had the approval of the clan chief.

Surnames with possible associations: Comine, Macniven, Niven, Russell

# Davidson

Earliest known date: 1822
Earliest source: D.W. Stewart, 1893
Tartan type: Symmetrical
Sett: **R**2 B12 G2 B2 G12 Bk2 G12 Bk2 G2 Bk12 **R**2
Clan crest: A stag's head erased Proper
Clan motto: *Sapienter si sincere* ("Wisely if sincerely")
Badge: *Lus nan cnaimhseag* (Red Whortleberry)

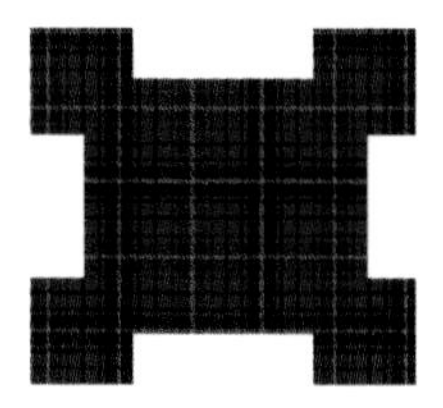

Sometime before 1350, the Davidson clan associated themselves with, and took the protection of, William Mackintosh of Mackintosh, and, since that time, they have been considered a sept of the Clan Chattan. The first known leader was David Dhu of Invernahaven. His mother was Slane Mackintosh, the daughter of the 6th Mackintosh chief, and his father Donald, the grandson of the Comyn murdered by Robert the Bruce. Because the name of Comyn was proscribed, the clan became known as Clann Da'idh or Clan Dhai. David Dhu and the Davidsons took part in two notable battles: Invernahaven (1370) and North Inch of Perth (1396). In the first, the Mackintoshes, with their Clan Chattan supporters, the Davidsons and Macphersons, opposed the Camerons who had invaded Badenoch. However, a dispute arose between the Davidsons and Macphersons over who should lead. The Mackintoshes supported the Davidsons, and, feeling slighted the Macphersons left the battlefield. The Camerons, however, exploited their enemies' confusion and, in the ensuing battle, all but wiped out the Davidsons. Following defeat once more at North Inch, it is said that the family of the Davidson chief moved north, where it gave rise to the Davidsons of Cantray (in Inverness) and Tulloch (in Ross-shire), through whom the chiefship passed.

In 1909, the Clan Dhai, or Clan Davidson Association, was formed to unite Davidsons throughout the world. The clan tartan used today omits the white stripe of an earlier sett from 1822 that is preserved in the Highland Society of London and in the Moy Hall Collection kept by Mackintosh of Mackintosh at Moy Hall, near Inverness. The clan also has a Half Davidson (a reduced pattern) and a Double Davidson.

Surnames with possible connections: Davie, Davis, Davison, Dawson, Day, Dean, Dow, Kay, MacDade, MacDaid, MacDavid

# Douglas

Earliest known date: c.1830

Earliest source: Logan, 1831

Tartan type: Symmetrical

Sett: **Bk**4 Az4 G16 B16 **W**2

Clan crest: On a Chapeau Gules furred Ermine, a salamander Vert encircled with flames of fire Proper

Clan motto: *Jamais arrière* ("Never behind")

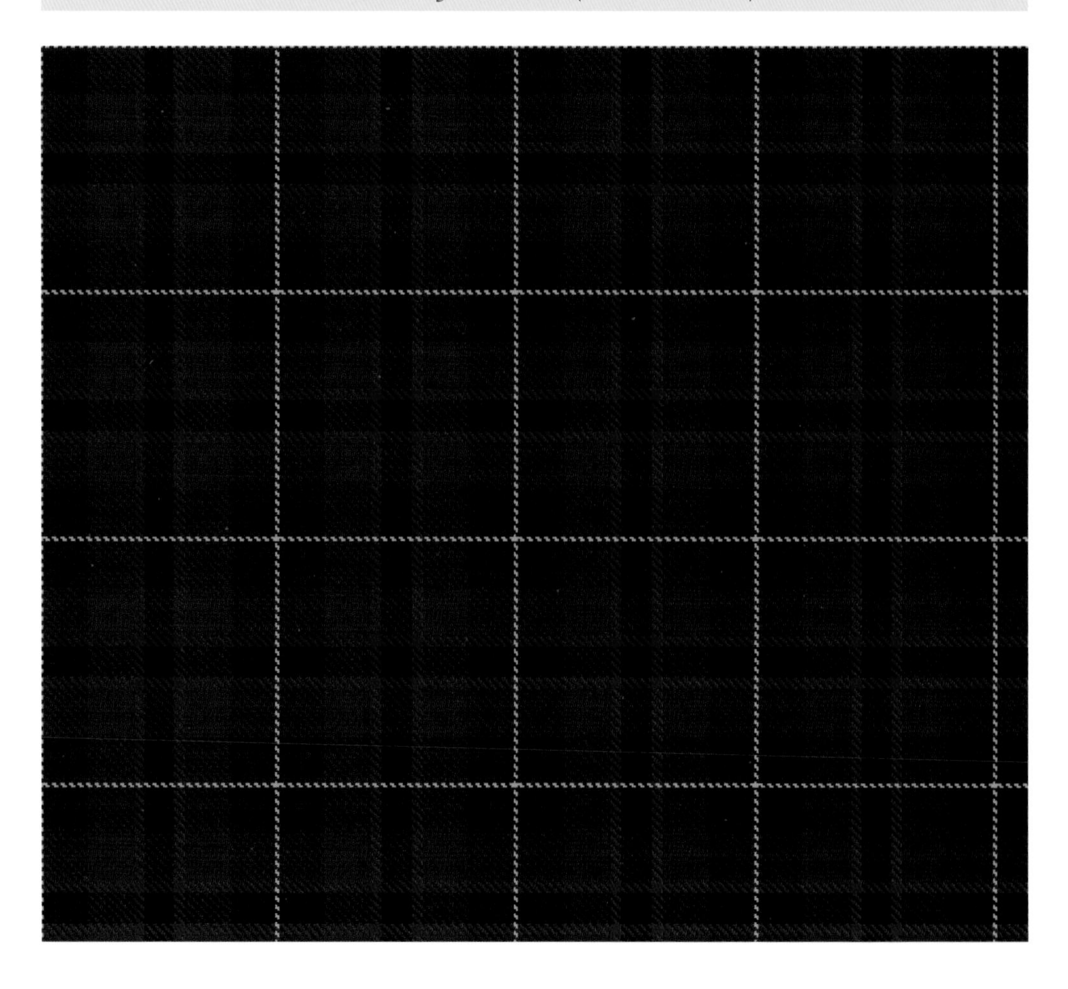

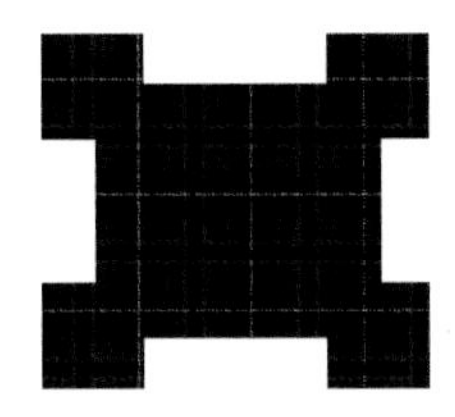

William de Dufglas, who lived between 1174 and 1199, was the first recorded Douglas. His name appeared as a witness to a charter from the Bishop of Glasgow to the monks of Kelso. His descendant, Sir William "le Hardi" Douglas, was governor of Berwick in 1296 and was taken prisoner by the English when the town fell in that year. He was released when he accepted Edward I's claim as ruler of Scotland, but he later joined William Wallace in the struggle for Scottish independence. Le Hardi's son, known as "Good Sir James", was the founder of the "Black Douglases" and one of Robert the Bruce's leading captains in the War of Independence. On his way to the Holy Land during the Crusades in 1330, Good Sir James died in Spain fighting the Moors, and the Douglas estate was settled on his nephew, Sir William, in 1343. Later, in 1357, this Sir William was made the Earl of Home and, by marriage, became the Earl of Mar. While a grandson became the progenitor of the Marquises of Queensberry – who gave their name to the rules of boxing – an illegitimate grandson, Archibald "The Grim", became the 3rd Earl and strengthened the family's power by marrying his son to Princess Margaret, daughter of Robert III. Such power was seen as a threat to national stability: the 6th Earl (who was married to the widowed Queen Margaret Tudor) and his brother were assassinated in 1440. The 9th Earl avoided such a fate but died without an heir, and the line of "Black Douglases" ended with him in 1491.

The first of the "Red Douglases" was George, 11th Earl of Angus and 1st Marquis of Douglas. He married a Stewart princess and, once again, the Douglas star was in ascendance. In 1660 William, the 2nd Marquis became, through marriage, the Duke of Hamilton, and the titles of Marquis of Douglas, Earl of Angus and many others passed to him. Since then the eldest son and heir of the Duke of Hamilton is always known as the Marquis of Douglas and Clydesdale. Around 1830 James Logan received a list of tartans from Wilson, the weavers in Bannockburn, stating that "no. 148" had been sold as the Douglas tartan for some considerable time. In addition to the green and blue Douglas, there is also a black and grey sett, which first appeared in *The Vestiarium Scoticum* in 1842.

Surnames with possible associations: Drysdale, Lockerbie, Morton

# Drummond

Earliest known date: 1746
Earliest source (recorded): Logan 1831
Tartan type: Symmetrical
Sett: **R**72 W2 B6 Y2 G32 R16 B6 Az4 W2
Clan crest: On a crest coronet Or, a goshawk, wings displayed Proper, armed and belled Or, jessed Gules.
Clan motto: *Virtutem cornat honos* ("Honor crowns virtue")
Badge: *Cuileann* (Holly)

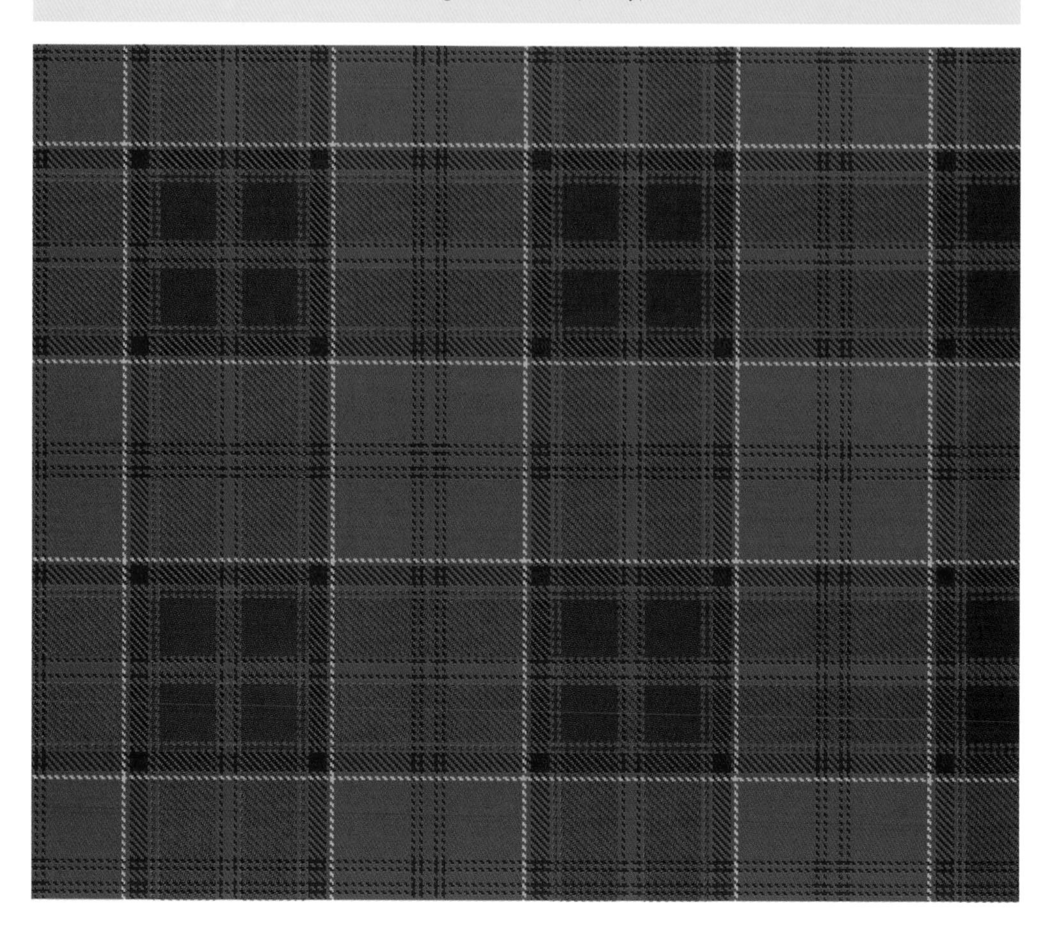

The Drummond Clan name is derived from a territory, the lands of Drymen or Drummond in Stirlingshire, the name of which in Gaelic is *dromainn*, meaning "a ridge of high ground". Legend has it that the first noble to settle the lands of Drymen was a Hungarian who fled to Scotland in 1067 from the invasion of William the Conqueror. The first chief to appear in written records was Malcolm Beg, a steward of the earldom of Strathearn in 1225. It was Malcolm's son, Sir Malcolm, who first took the name of Drummond.

The clan were fierce supporters of Bruce and Scottish independence: at Bannockburn in 1314, Sir Malcolm covered the battlefield with caltrops, or spikes, which disabled much of the English cavalry. Such caltrops appear on the coat of arms of the Chief of Clan Drummond and his motto "Gang warily" (Go carefully) also allude to them. His son, another Malcolm, was the father of Margaret, who later became the queen of David II. Sir John Drummond was made Lord Drummond in 1488, a title still held today by present chiefs. James, the 4th Lord Drummond was created Earl of Perth in 1605.

The Drummonds remained firm supporters of the Stewart kings: James, the 4th Earl, was appointed Lord High Chancellor of Scotland in 1684. When he was exiled for declaring his Catholic faith, the exiled Scottish king, James VII, summoned him to France and made him the Duke of Perth. James, the 2nd Duke, was among the first to join the Jacobite rising in 1715, while the 3rd Duke joined Bonnie Prince Charlie on his arrival in Perth in 1745 and fought at Culloden. After the defeat of the Jacobite forces however, the duke was forced to flee: he died *en route* to France in 1746, and his estates and titles were forfeited to the English Crown. In 1853, an Act of Parliament restored George Drummond (Duc de Melfort, Comte de Laussane and Baron of Valrose) to the title of 14th Earl of Perth. The 16th Earl, Eric, was celebrated as the first Secretary General of the League of Nations.

Most Drummonds now wear the tartan also known as Grant, while the Drummonds of Strathallen (a line which opened to succession to the house of Perth in 1902) wore the Ogilvie as their tartan. The pattern known as Drummond of Perth, of which there is a sample dating from 1816 in the Highland Society of London, is based on a tartan which is said to have been worn by Bonnie Prince Charlie as a cloak during the '45.

Surnames with possible associations: Brewer, Doig, Grewar, MacGrewar, Gruer, MacGrowther, MacGruder, MacGruther, MacRobert

# Dunbar

Earliest known date: 1842
Earliest source: *The Vestiarium Scoticum*, 1842
Tartan type: Symmetrical
Sett: **R**8 Bk2 R56 Bk16 G42 **R**12
Clan motto: *In promptu* ("In readiness")
Clan crest: A horse's head Argent, bridled and reined Gules

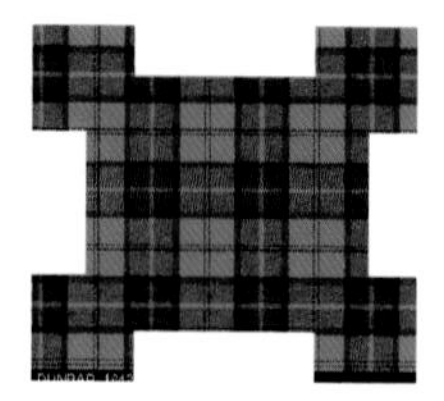

The Dunbars were a powerful Lowland family who claimed descent from King Malcolm I. Malcolm's son Gospatric was created Earl of Northumbria by William the Conqueror in 1067, but in 1072, he was deprived of the lands and fled north to Dunbar where he was given lands by Malcolm III and his son became the Earl of Dunbar. His descendant, Patrick, the 8th Earl, known as "Black Beard", was one of the competitors for the crown of Scotland at Berwick in 1291, but withdrew his claim and submitted to Edward I of England. His son, Patrick, also favored the English and sheltered the English King Edward II at Dunbar Castle following his flight from the battlefield at Bannockburn in 1314.

By the late 14th century, the Dunbars held vast estates and great power that were coveted by none other than James I, who imprisoned George, the 11th Earl, on fabricated charges of treason in order to seize his estates. The last earl died in England in 1455, but the family had established a number of branches, in particular the Dunbars of Mochrum (to which the present Dunbar chief, Sir Jean Dunbar of Mochrum, who lives in Florida, USA, belongs) and of Westfield, Durn, Both and Hemprigg. All five branches are baronetcies. Two of the most famous Dunbars were Gavin Dunbar, Archbishop of Glasgow and Chancellor of Scotland during the reign of James V (r.1513–42), and William Dunbar, born around 1460, one of Scotland's most famous poets. The Dunbar tartan first appeared in *The Vestiarium Scoticum* in 1842, but Wilson and Sons in Bannockburn also wove a Dunbar tartan in around 1840, although whether this was a family or a district sett is unclear.

# Dundas

Earliest known date: 1842
Source: *The Vestiarium Scoticum*, 1842
Tartan type: Symmetrical
Sett: **Bk**4 G4 R2 G48 Bk24 B32 **Bk**8
Clan crest: A lion's head affrontee, looking through a bush of oak Proper
Clan motto: *Essayez* ("Try")
Badge: Bilberry

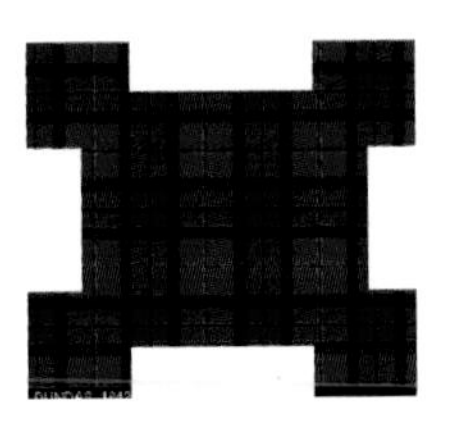

The earliest reliable written source which records the founder of the clan, Serle de Dundas, dates from the reign of King William I the Lion (1165–1214), while the name Dundas itself is said to be derived from lands on the southern shores of the Forth. In 1296, Saer de Dundas allied with the English king, Edward I. His successor Sir Hugh, however, fought with Wallace in the defense of Scotland, and the next chief, Sir George was a firm friend of Robert the Bruce and is reputed to have died fighting for the Scottish king David II in 1332. Sir Archibald, 12th of Dundas, was a favorite of James III and ambassador to England. The king had intended to reward Archibald for his good service by making him an earl, but the king died before the honor could be bestowed. James IV made recompense by giving Dundas the island of Inchgarvie with the right to build a castle. George, the 18th Laird, was a staunch Presbyterian who supported the Covenant and was in charge of the defense of Linlithgowshire against Oliver Cromwell's forces. The direct line, however, expired with his grandson Ralph, 20th Laird, but the principal branches of the family by now extended to the Dundas of Blair Castle, Arniston, Duddingston and Fingask.

Members of the Dundas family played a vital role in restoring the Highland way of life after the penalties imposed as a result of the '45. In 1784, Henry Dundas, 1st Viscount Melville and a distinguished politician, introduced a bill to Parliament to restore the estates forfeited to the Crown after the uprising. The "authority" for the Dundas Clan tartan is *The Vestiarium Scoticum* of 1842. The design, with its green, blue and black background (with two red stripes on the green), may be derived from traditional Highland military tartans.

# Eliot/Elliot

Earliest known date: *c.*1906

Source: Johnston, 1906

Tartan type: Symmetrical

Sett: **R**2 B6 Maroon8 **B**32

Clan crest: A hand couped at the wrist in armour holding a cutlass in bend Proper

Clan motto: *Fortiter et recte* ("Boldly and rightly")

Badge: White Hawthorn

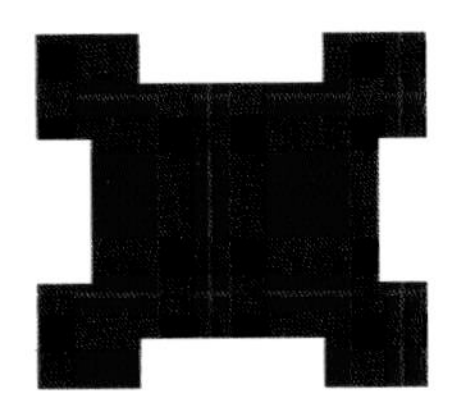

Originally called Ellot, this great Border clan came from Angus but moved to Teviotdale during the reign of Robert the Bruce (r.1306–29). According to a family story, one of the most powerful nobles in Scotland, William Soulis, Lord of Liddesdale, had been convicted of treason against Bruce and had his lands forfeited. In order to secure the region, Bruce gave these lands to trusted clans, among them the Ellots. In the 15th century, the Ellots' name changed once more. It was now Elwalde, or Elwold. Robert Elwold, the chief of the clan in the second half of the century, was Captain of Hermitage Castle, while his son, Robert Elliot of Redheugh, the 13th chief, fell at Flodden in 1513 alongside the Scottish king James IV and many other Scottish nobles. The last of the line was Robert Eliot of Redheugh who in 1624, was accused of conspiring against the Duke of Buccleuch.

By this time however, the Union of the Crowns in 1603 had already marked the beginning of the end for the Border clans: *reiving* (stealing, or plundering, such as the "traditional" activity of the *creach* or cattle lifting) was punished by execution. At the same time, many Borderers took the opportunity to start a new life in Ulster during the period known as the "Plantation", when much of this Province of Northern Ireland was colonized. With the Redheugh line extinct, the Eliot leadership passed in 1673 to a descendant, Sir Gilbert Eliot of Stobbs, near Hawick in Roxburghshire, 1st Baronet of Nova Scotia. The present chief is Margaret Eliot of that Ilk.

Meanwhile, in 1703, another branch of the Eliots acquired lands in Minto. Sir Gilbert Eliot, 1st Earl of Minto was a diplomat in Vienna and Viceroy of Corsica, while the 4th Earl became Viceroy of India in 1813. Although there is no very early record of the Eliot tartan, it is nonetheless unique in its coloring, being an attractive blue and maroon.

# Erskine

Earliest known date: 1842
Earliest source: *The Vestiarium Scoticum*, 1842
Tartan type: Symmetrical
Sett: **R**8 G2 R56 G48 R2 **G**12
Clan crest: On a chapeau Gules furred Ermine, a hand holding up a skene in pale Argent, hilted and pommelled Or.
Clan motto: *Je pense plus* ("I think more")
Badge: Red Rose

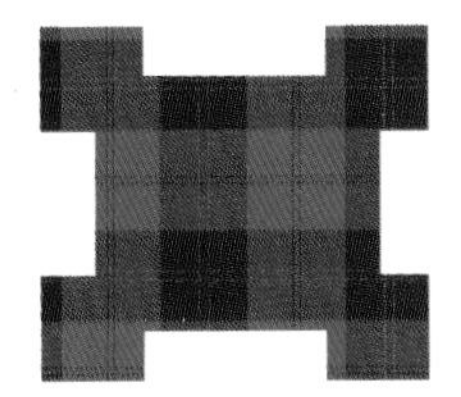

The Erskines derived their name from lands in Renfrewshire, south of the River Clyde, which were held by Henry, Baron of Erskine in the reign of Alexander II (r.1214–49). The Erskines became staunch supporters of the Bruce family – the families were related by marriage – while David II (r.1329–71) appointed Sir Robert de Erskine Constable and Keeper of the strategically important royal castle at Stirling, an office that today is still held by the Erskine chief. In the 15th century, Robert, Lord Erskine made claim to the title of Ear of Mar by right of descent. The king, however, refused to grant the title, claiming it belonged to the Crown because the last Earl of Mar, Alexander (d.1435) had been a Stewart. In spite of this dispute with the king, the Erskines did not lose royal favor: they became guardians to the young James IV and five further generations of royalty.

In 1497, the 3rd Lord Esrkine built the huge tower at Alloa, which would be the seat of Erskine chiefs for 300 years and where Mary, Queen of Scots would spend the first five years of her life. It was Mary who eventually gave Lord Erskine the title Earl of Mar, but without its earlier precedence.

The 6th Earl, John, who was born in 1675, was known as "Bobbing John" on account of his ability to shift political allegiance according to his needs for advancement or plain survival! Accepting the Hanoverian succession, Bobbing John attended court in London to find he was not given the post of Secretary of State for Scotland. Seeing this as an insult, he returned to his lands, called out his clansmen and all loyal Stewart supporters, and with an army of over 10,000 under the banner of the "Old Pretender" James VIII, engaged the royal forces led by the Duke of Argyll at Sheriffmuir in November 1715. The rising failed and Mar fled to France, forfeiting his lands and his titles. In 1824 however, the Erskine title was restored and the earldom of Kellie (a title bestowed on a younger son of the chiefly line in 1619), passed to the Erskine chief in 1835, so that today's chiefs are known as the Earls of Mar and Kellie.

The Erskine tartan first appeared in *The Vestiarium Scoticum* in 1842. Similar tartans were ascribed to both the Ramsays and Cunninghams – names used by some of the scattered MacGregors when their own name was proscribed between 1563 and 1775 – and appear to be derived from the old black and red MacGregor tartan. This somewhat tenuous connection with the MacGregors, does not however, explain the origin of the tartan ascribed to the Erskines.

# Farquharson

Earliest known date: 1774 (alleged dated samples)

Earliest source: *c.*1816, certified samples in the Highland Society. Earliest recorded source: Wilson's Pattern Books, 1819

Tartan type: Symmetrical

Sett: **R**4 B8 Bk2 B2 Bk2 B2 Bk16 G16 Y4 G16 Bk16 B16 Bk2 **R**4

Clan crest: On a chapeau Gules furred Ermine, a demi-lion Gules holding in his dexter paw a sword Proper

Clan motto: *Fide et fortitudine* ("By fidelity and strength")

Badge: Scots Fir

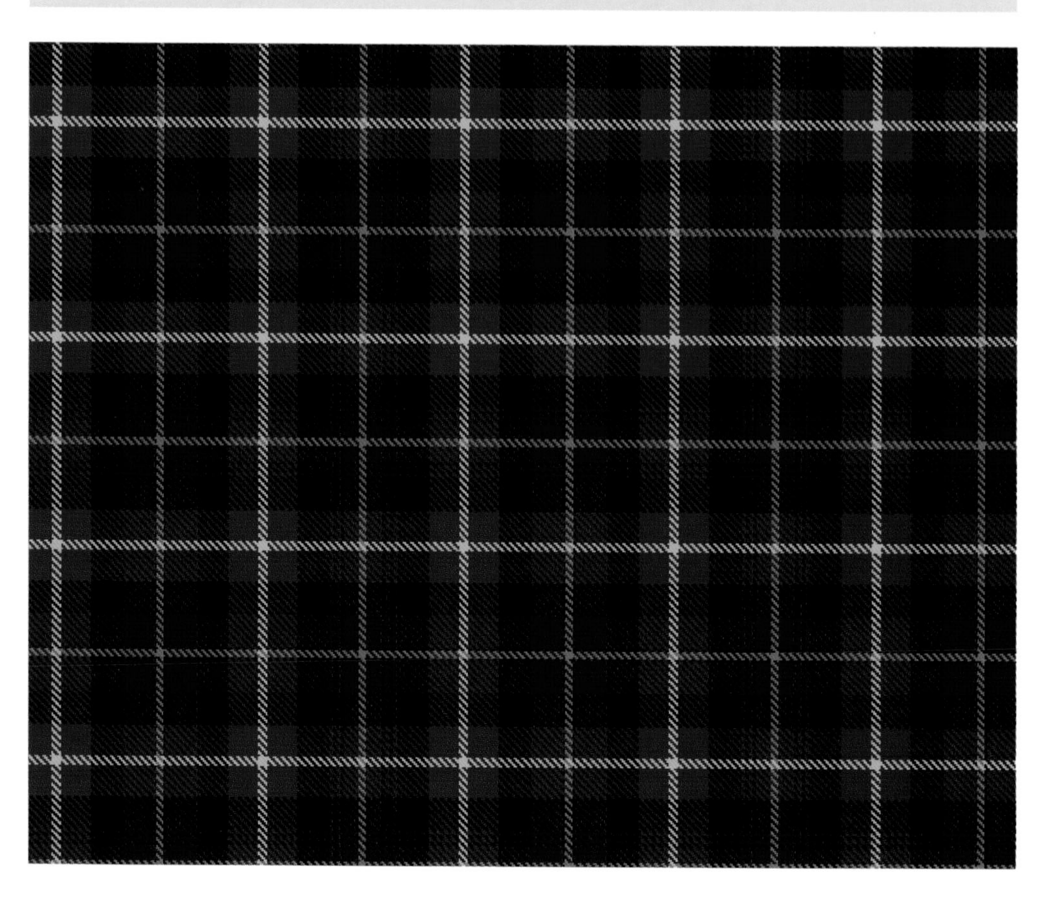

The Clan Farquharson is descended from Farquhar, the fourth son of Alexander Cier (Shaw) of Rothiemurchus, a branch of the Clan Chattan, who controled the Braes of Mar near the source of the River Dee in Aberdeenshire. Farquhar's son Donald married Isobel Stewart, the heiress of Invercauld and their son, Finlay Mor, (in Gaelic: *MacFionlaigh Mor*) became the real progenitor of the Clan Farquharson. He was the royal standard bearer at the battle of Pinkie, where he died in 1547 and, from him, and then on, the Farquharsons were termed "Clann Fionnlaigh", or descendants of Finlay.

Finlay's nine sons from two marriages ensured the clan's growth in strength and importance: the main branches of the name and clan have included Monaltrie, Whitehouse, Haughton, Breda, Allargue, Inverey, Tullochy, Allanquoich, Broughdearg, Achriachan, and Finzean. Yet, the Farquharsons were not as numerous as some of their neighbors and they joined the Clan Chattan confederation. They did, however, still have a fierce, fighting reputation: Donald Farquharson of Monaltrie fought with Montrose in 1644 and the family later supported Charles II; John Farquharson of Inverey (d.1698) – known as the "Black Colonel" – was a famous Jacobite who supported James VII and torched Braemar Castle. John Farquarson of Invercauld, with four officers and 140 men joined the Clan Chattan regiment in the 1715 Rising and was taken prisoner by the English. At Culloden, the Farquharsons were supporters of Bonnie Prince Charlie. Led by the "Baron Ban", Francis Farquharson of Monaltrie, the clan mustered 300 men and fought in the center of the front line. The Baron Ban was captured and condemned to death at the Tower of London, but was reprieved at the last minute.

When James Farquharson of Invercauld, clan chief for 56 years, died without a male heir in 1850, the chiefship passed to his daughter Catherine. Her husband, James Ross, took the Farquharson name and the chiefship passed through them to the present chief, Alwyn Compton Farquharson of Invercauld. The Farquharson tartan, based on the Black Watch, was first published in Logan's *Scottish Gael* in 1831 (which used Wilson and Son's pattern books from 1819 as the source). Yet, a sample in the Highland Collection bearing the seal of Farquharson of Finzean dates from around 1816. Even earlier samples, said to be from 1774, were exhibited in 1930 at the Highland Exhibition in Inverness. The description that Logan gave in 1831 – of the yellow line centered on each band of green, and the red line on each band of blue – does conform to the earlier samples.

Surnames with possible associations: Barrie, Bowman, Brebner, Christie, Coutts, Findlay, Findlayson, Finlay, Finlayson, Hardie, Hardy, Kerracher, MacCaig, MacCartney, MacCuaig, MacEarachar, MacFarquhar, MacHardie, MacHardie, MacKerchar, MacKerracher, MacKindlay, Reoch, Riach, Tawse

# Fergusson

Earliest known date: 1831
Earliest source: Logan, 1831
Tartan type: Symmetrical
Sett: **G**4 B24 R2 Bk24 G24 **Bk**4
Clan crest: Upon a chapeau Gules furred Ermine, a bee on a thistle Proper
Clan motto: *Dulcius ex asperis* ("Sweetness after difficulties")
Badge: *Aithean* (Poplar)

The Gaelic patronym, *MacFhaerghuis*, is translated often as either "Son of the Angry" or "Son of the Proud". Several distinct families bear this name, although efforts have been made to find a common ancestor! In Argyllshire, the ancient home of the Clann Fhearghuis of Stra-chur, claim descent from Fergus Mor mac Erc, an early king of the Scots of Dalriada who brought the Stone of Scone to Scotland. In Ayrshire, and Dumfries and Galloway, Fergussons claim descent from Fergus, Prince of Galloway who was alive during the reigns of David I (r.1124–53) and Malcolm IV "the Maiden" (r.1153–65). These may account for the "proud" epithet, while the "angry" may well have originated with the Fergussons of Dunfallandry in Atholl, who claim their noble ancestor was Adam, son of Fergus, known as "Adam na canabaig" (Adam of the pavilion). He had lands in Perthshire granted by Bailiol and Bruce. As well as barony in Atholl, Adam gained another by murdering Baron Maol of Dunfallandry, then marrying his own son to the Maol heiress. In Carrick, the Fergussons of Kilkerran claim descent from Fergus, son of Fergus, who received a charter from Robert I the Bruce (r.1306–29). While the Kilkerran Fergussons were recognized as the principal house by the 17th century, it was only in 1950 that this was formally adjudged by the Lyon Court.

The Fergusson tartan was first published in Logan's book in 1831. Logan gave two thread counts to the red stripe and this was the version approved by the Clan Society. This is a slight variation on the version approved by the Clan Fergusson chief in 1977 (with a slightly wider red stripe). The tartan is called the Fergusson of Balquidder in order to distinguish it from the tartan known as Fergusson of Atholl, which contains a white stripe and the MacLaren tartan, which is a Fergusson of Atholl design but with a yellow stripe.

Surnames with possible associations: Fergus, Ferries, MacAdie, MacKerras, MacKersey

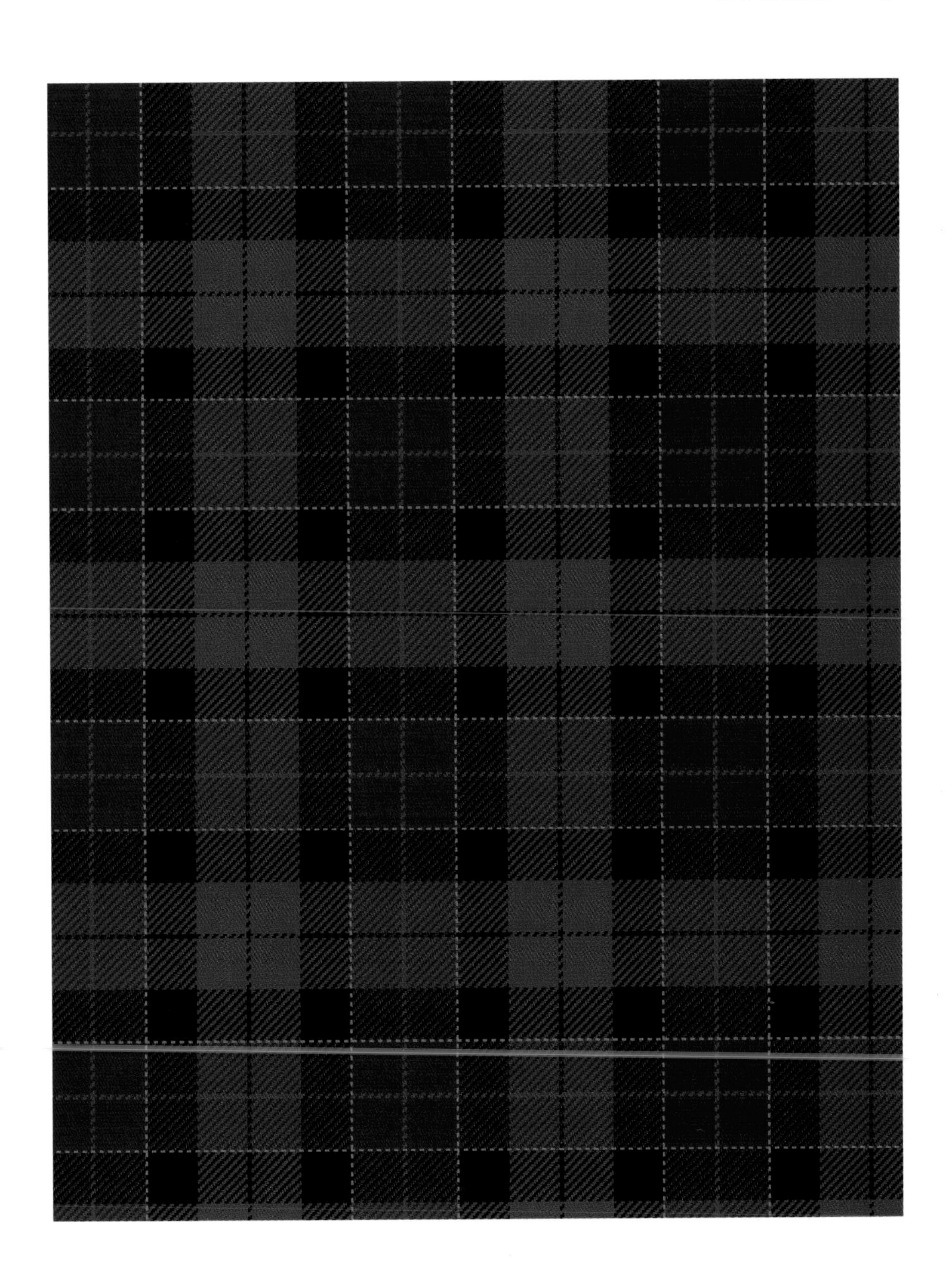

# Forbes

Earliest known date: *c.*1819

Earliest source: Wilson and Son's pattern books, 1819

Tartan type: Symmetrical

Sett: **B**16 Bk2 B4 Bk2 B4 Bk12 G16 Bk2 W4 Bk2 G16 Bk12 B16 Bk2 **B**4

Clan crest: A stag's head attired with ten tines Proper

Clan motto: "Grace me guide"

Badge: *Bealaidh* (broom)

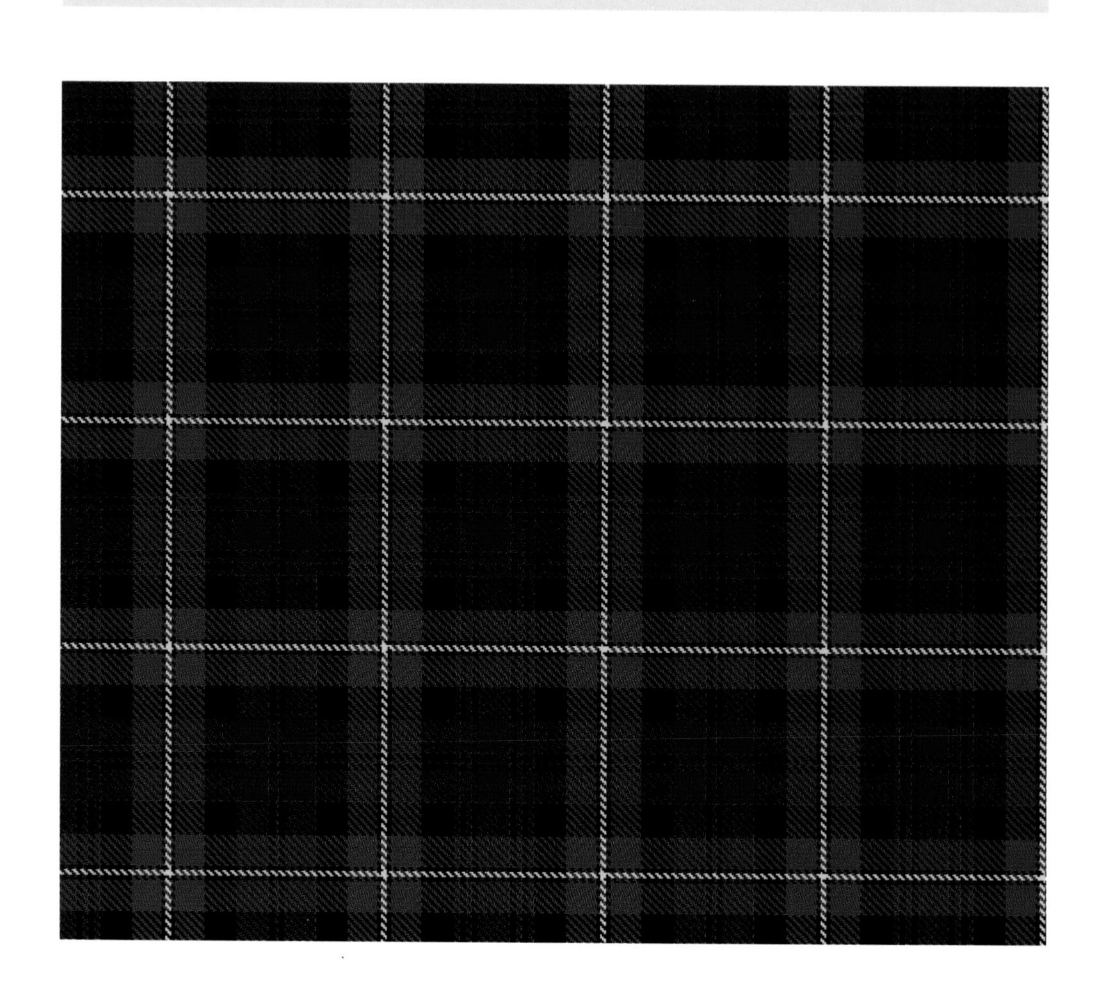

The lands in northeast Scotland which spread from mountainous Aberdeenshire to coastal Banff were said to have been uninhabitable because of ferocious bears, until the founder of the clan, Oconochar, killed them and took possession of the land. In 1271, Alexander III granted a charter conferring the feudal tenancy of these lands on Duncan Forbes, the reigning chief of the Clan Forbes. The ancient seat was the fortress of Drumminor on the northern slope of the Braes o' Forbes. Today, it is the Castle Forbes, Donside, Aberdeenshire. Built in 1815 by James Ochoncar, 17th Lord Forbes, his descendants still live there.

The Forbes grew in power in the 14th century. The colorfully named John Forbes of the Black Lips (d.1406) had four sons: the eldest, Sir Alexander who fought against the invasion led by Donald of the Isles in 1411, was created Lord Forbes in around 1444; Sir William was the progenitor of the Forbes of Pitsligo; Sir John, the ancestor of the Forbes of Polquhoun, and, Sir Alistair of Brux founded the lines of Forbes of Shellater and of Inverarnon. Grandsons of the 1st Lord Forbes also founded the houses of Forbes of Corsindae and Monymusk, and the baronetcy of Craigevar. In 1582, James VI reconfirmed lairdship of the clan lands in the Forbes, but constant feuding with the Gordons had caused so much debt that much of the Forbes land were sold. Nevertheless, the Forbes title has been handed down through successive generations.

In 1701 on the union roll, Forbes was the premier lordship of Scotland, a precedence that is still held today. Legend has it that a Miss Forbes designed the Forbes tartan in 1822, for the Forbes of Pitsligo. She was responsible for changing the yellow line of the regimental Gordon tartan to a white line. This tartan, which is still in use today, did, however, appear earlier (in 1819), in Wilson and Son's pattern book. Because Miss Forbes' sett is easily confused with the Lamont tartan – the only difference is that the white lines in the Lamont do not have black guards (edges) – a second, different sett, (known as Forbes Ancient) has also been registered with the Lord Lyon.

Surnames with possible associations: Berry, Boyes, Michie, Walters

# Fraser

Earliest known date: 1816

Earliest source: *The Vestiarium Scoticum*, 1842

Tartan type: Symmetrical

Sett: **W**2 R24 G12 R2 B12 **R**2

Clan crest: On a mount a flourish of strawberries leaved and fructed Proper

Clan motto: "All my hope is in God"

Badges: *Iubhar* (yew), *fraise* (Fr: strawberry)

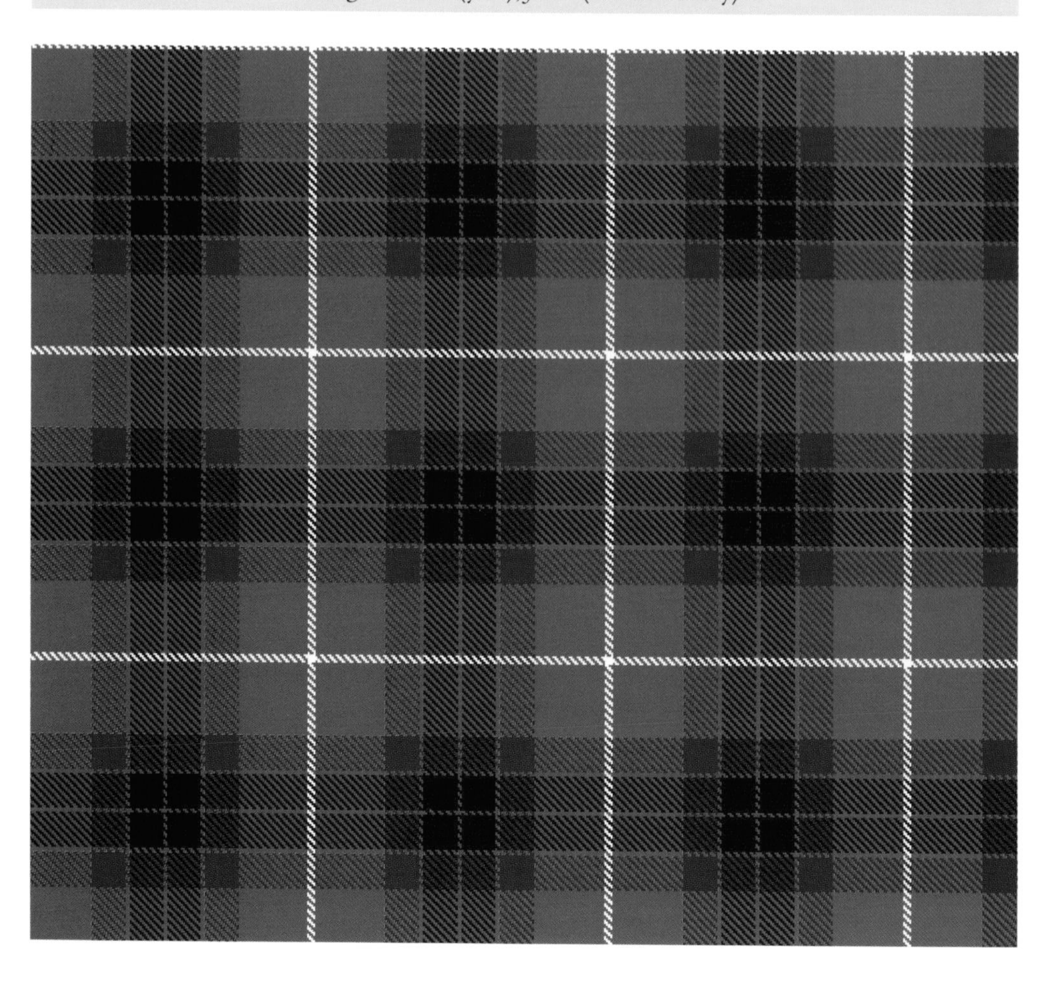

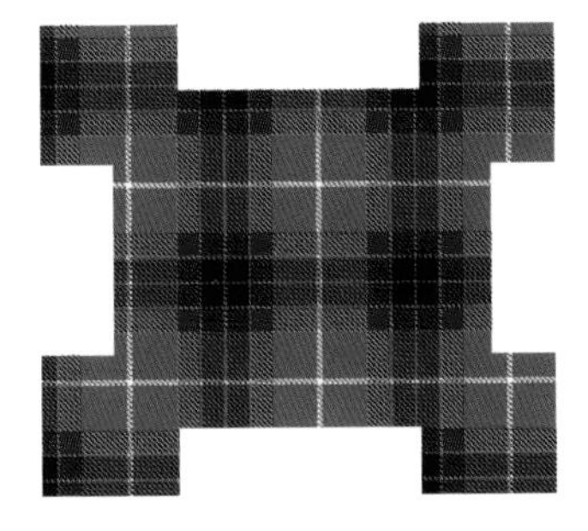

The name Fraser appears to be French in origin: it was possibly "Fresel",the exact meaning of which is uncertain, but seems to be connected to a pun on the the Fraser coat of arms which contains a strawberry plant – in French, strawberry is *fraise*. In the 11th century there was a noble family in Anjou, France, called Frezel, who gave their name to the Seigneurie of Freselière. In the following century many of the sons of Norman lords were invited to settle in Scotland and one Simon Fraser is noted as holding lands at Keith in East Lothian and in 1160 as giving the Church of Keith to the Abbey of Kelso. The lands were called Simon Keith after him and, since then, the name Simon has been a favorite with Frasers in Scotland. The Clan Fraser of Lovat call their chief in Gaelic *Mac Shimi*, the "son of Simon". Through marriage, these Frasers gained land in Lovat, as well as in Stratherrick and Glenelg. Simon Fraser, 11th Lord Lovat was created a duke, but was beheaded as a Jacobite in 1747 at the Tower of London. His eldest son, General Simon Fraser of Lovat, raised the Fraser Highlanders and was their commander at the capture of Quebec. The youngest son, Colonel Archibald, raised the Fraser Fencibles to counter the French invasion threat and went on to urge Parliament to repeal the laws banning the wearing of Highland dress.

A second branch of the Fraser family became the Sheriffs of Peebles and acquired Oliver Castle on the River Tweed through marriage to the Oliver heiress. The most famous member of this family was Sir Simon Fraser. He fought with Wallace and Froissart's *Chronicles* mentions that he defeated the English three times in one day at Rosslyn in 1302. Captured by the English after supporting Robert the Bruce, Fraser was executed in London in a most gruesome manner by "hanging, drawing and quartering".

Other Fraser kinsmen were more fortunate: Sir Alexander Fraser was Chamberlain of Scotland and hero at Bannockburn. He married Mary, Robert the Bruce's sister – a former prisoner of the English, who had been kept in cage in public view! These were the ancestors of the Frasers of Philorth – now Lords Saltoun – granted the right by James VI to have their own University at Fraserburgh – a right that still exists, even though the actual university was jealously undermined by nearby Aberdeen University.

*Fraser Hunting*

Another Fraser, this time the descendant of a younger son of the 2nd Lord Lovat, was Simon Fraser of Culbokie, from a branch that styled themselves "MacHuisdean". He was an explorer of Canada and, in 1964, the Simon Fraser University in British Columbia was named after him. Although doubt has been cast on whether it really is a Fraser tartan, the most popular Fraser tartan is the one described in *The Vestiarium Scoticum* in 1842. There are also other Fraser tartans: the Clan Fraser (described by Logan in 1831); the Fraser of Lovat in the Certified Tartans Register; a Fraser Regimental tartan in the Highland Society collection and a Hunting Fraser. This last tartan uses brown in place of the red and alternate white and red lines centered on the ground color.

Surnames with possible associations (Clan Fraser): Cowie, Frew, Frissell, Frizell, MacGruer, MacImmey, MacKim, MacKimmie, MacSymon, Oliver
(Fraser of Lovat): MacShimes, MacSimon, Sim, Sime, Simon, Simpson, Simson

# Gordon

Earliest known date: 1794
Earliest source: Wilson and Son's pattern book, 1819
Tartan type: Symmetrical
Sett: **B**24 Bk4 B4 Bk4 B4 Bk24 G24 Y4 G24 Bk24 B22 Bk4 **B**4
Clan crest: Issuant from a crest coronet Or a stag's head affrontée Proper attired with ten tines Or
Clan motto: *Bydand* ("Remaining")
Badge: *Iadh-shlat* (Ivy)

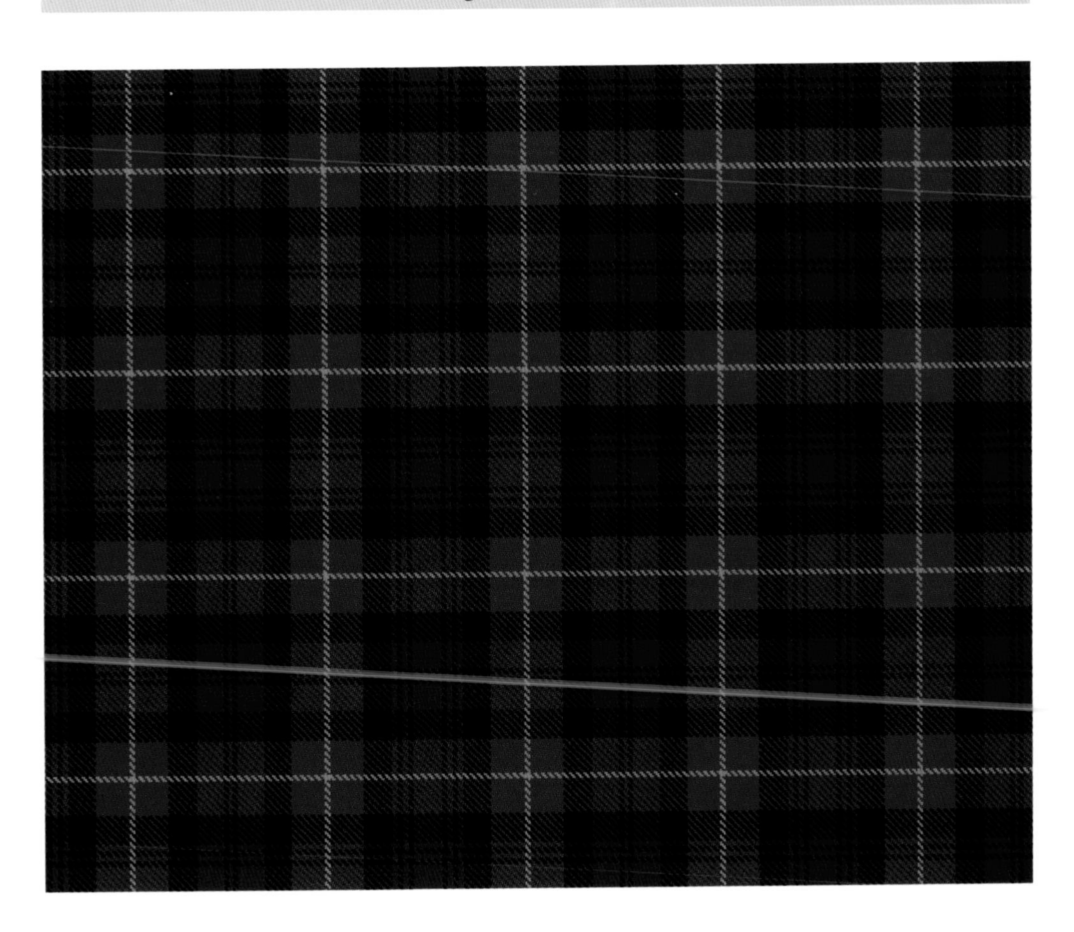

One of the great families of north-east Scotland, the Gordons first appear under that name in the 12th century – when surnames were first being adopted – as holding the lands of Gordon in Berwickshire. The place name seems to be local and is derived from *gor din*, meaning a hill fort in ancient British. Richard, Baron of Gordon in 1150, granted land to the monks of St Mary of Kelso. In 1320, Sir Adam was the Scottish ambassador who petitioned the Pope to remove the excommunication placed on Robert the Bruce after he had murdered John Comyn in 1306. For services rendered, Robert the Bruce gave Sir Adam, Lord of Gordon, large areas of former Clan MacDuff territory that had been forfeited, as well as the Lordship of Strathbogie in Aberdeenshire. This was "renamed" Huntly by the Gordons.

In 1436, Sir Alexander Gordon was created Lord Gordon, and his son made the Earl of Huntly. The Gordons were soon involved in a power struggle between the king and the Clan Douglas: Huntly was for the king, but as he moved his troops south, the Earl of Moray, a Douglas ally, invaded Gordon lands and burned Huntly Castle. The Gordons returned to their devastated lands, rallied their forces, defeated the Douglases and built a brand new castle on the ruins of the old that rivalled the other great houses of the kingdom.

George, the 4th Earl of Huntly, was Chancellor of Scotland in 1547 and a close confidant of the regent, Mary of Guise (mother of Mary, Queen of Scots). In 1599, the 6th Earl of Huntly was created Marquis. His son, George, the 2nd Marquis was a royalist supporter in the Civil War. Captured at Strathdon in 1647, he was executed by the Covenanters at Edinburgh two years later. He is reputed to have declared: "You may take my head from my shoulders, but not my heart from my king". In 1651, the Gordon estates and titles were restored to the family and, in 1684, Lord Louis Gordon, 4th Marquis of Huntly, was made Duke of Gordon by Charles II. The Gordons fought on both sides during the Jacobite risings of 1715 and 1745. The 2nd Duke of Gordon followed the standard of the "Old Pretender" at the battle of Sheriffmuir in 1715. While the 3rd Duke remained loyal to the Hanoverians when Prince Charles Edward Stewart reasserted his father's claim in 1745, the duke's brother raised a regiment to fight for the Stewart cause.

The two regiments known as the "Gordon Highlanders" were raised by this clan: the 81st

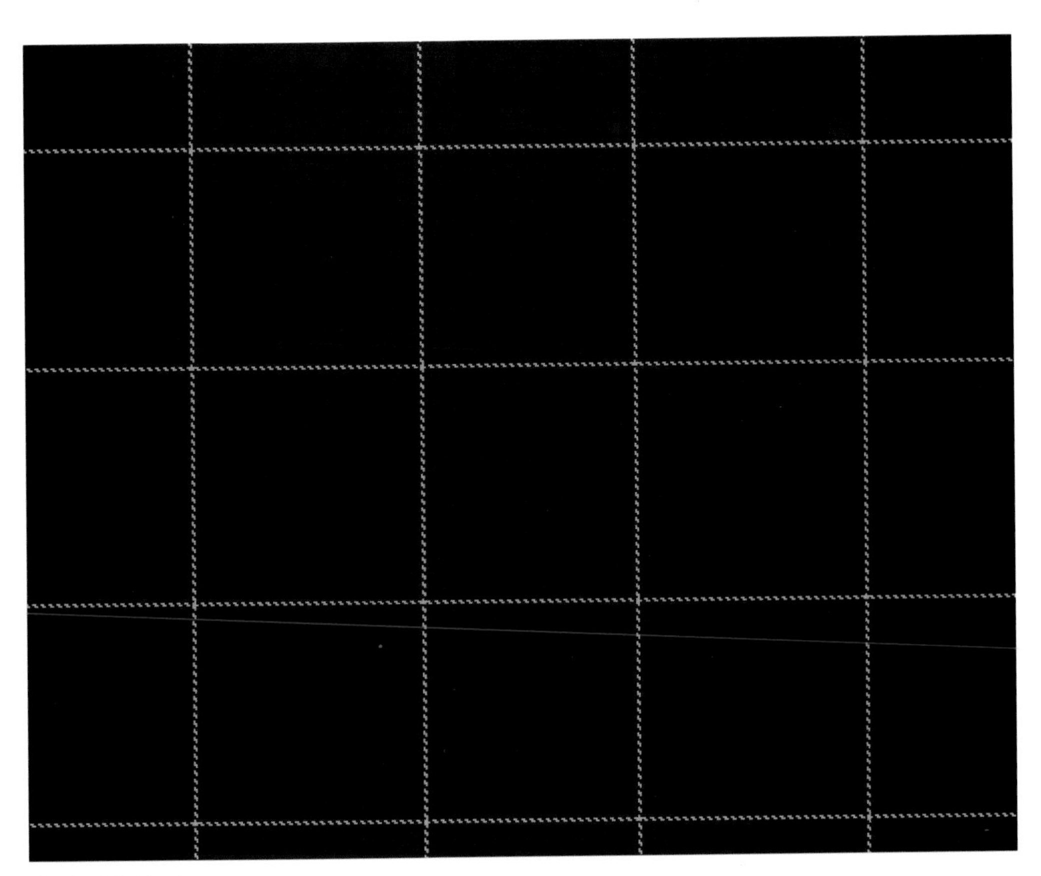

*Gordon Highlanders*

was raised in 1777 (disbanded in 1783) and the 92nd, or Gordon Highlanders, in 1794. Wilson of Bannockburn's agent produced samples of Black Watch tartan for the duke – although some say it was at Jane, the Duchess of Gordon's request – with one, two and three yellow stripes added to the sett. The duke chose the single stripe to create the new regimental tartan for the 92nd Gordon Highlanders, which was subsequently adopted by the Clan Gordon, while the Huntly tartan was used as the full dress tartan.

Surnames with possible associations: Addison, Adie, Aitcheson, Aitken, Barrie, Cullen, Eadie, Edie, Geddes, Huntly, Milne, Todd

# Graham

Earliest known dates: Graham of Mentieth clan tartan: 1816
Graham of Montrose clan tartan: 1810–20
Earliest sources: Mentieth: Logan, 1831
Montrose: Cockburn Collection, 1810–20
Tartan types: Symmetrical
Sett: Mentieth : **Bk**2 Smalt24 Bk24 G2 Az4 **G**32
Montrose: **Bk**2 B8 Bk8 G8 W2 G8 **BK**8
Clan crest: A falcon Proper, beaked and armed Or, killing a stork Argent, armed Gules.
Clan motto: *Ne oublie* ("Do not forget")
Badge: *Buaaidh-chraobh* (Laurel)

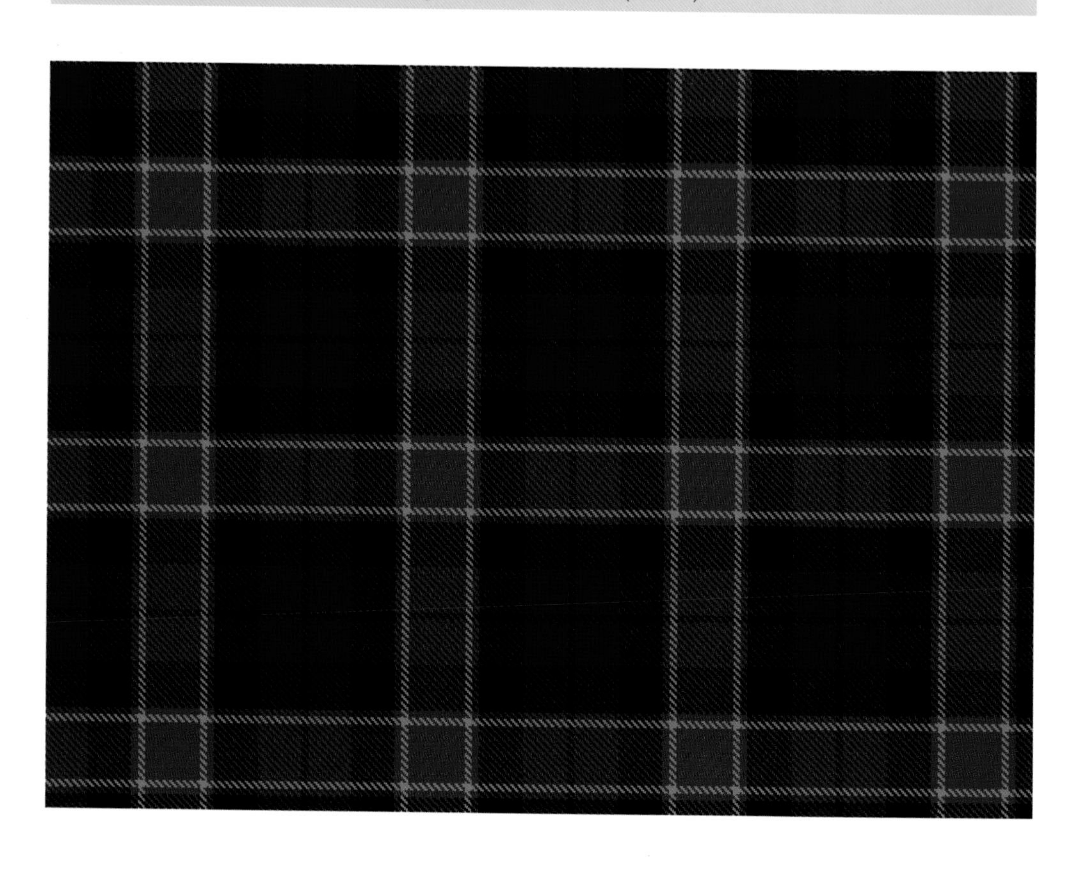

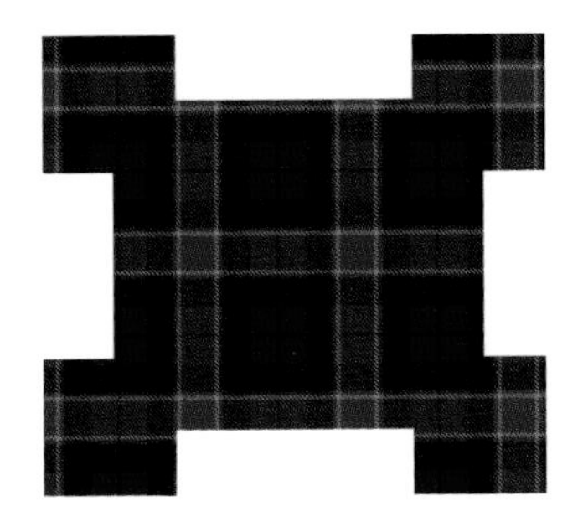

For more than 900 years, the name Graham has been notable in Scottish history, although originally, the family were of Anglo-French extraction. The name was derived from the lordship of an English manor, the "grey home" – or Greagham as it was called in the Domesday Book. The first record of a Graham in Scotland is of William de Graham, in the 12th century. A companion of David I, Graham personally witnessed the king's charter founding the Abbey of Holyroodhouse in 1128. From William de Graham's eldest son Peter, the Grahams of Dalkieth and Eskdale descended, although the direct line ended in 1341. Peter's younger brother, Alan de Graham, founded the great house of Graham of Montrose. Sir Patrick de Graham, who died in 1296, had married into the family of the earls of Strathearn, and was granted lands in the Highlands at Loch Arklet and on the banks of Loch Lomond. His son exchanged some of his estates wanted by Robert the Bruce for lands at Montrose in Angus.

In 1445, Patrick, at that time the Graham chief, became a peer as Lord Graham. He exchanged the Highland lands at Lochs Arklet and Lomond for lands held by the Buchanan chief near Mugdoch. Meanwhile, the chief's half-brother, Patrick Graham, Earl Palatine of Strathearn, who had married King Robert II's granddaughter, was killed by the Drummonds in 1413 and left his infant son and heir in the guardianship of his younger brother, Sir Robert Graham of Kinpont. In 1427, James I seized the infant's rich earldom, giving him instead the Highland parish of Aberfoyle and part of the Port of Menteith, along with the tile of Earl of Menteith. James then sent the child as a hostage to England where he was imprisoned in Pontefract Castle for the next 26 years.

The Menteith Grahams managed to hold on to their Highland territory until 1680 when William Graham, childless and debt ridden, made over the lands of his inheritance to his chief, Graham, 3rd Marquis of Montrose – who had already regained the original Graham lands at Loch Lomond as well as all of the bankrupt Buchanan chief's estates! From then one, each Marquis of Montrose was styled in Gaelic *An Greumach Mor* – the "Great Graham". Logan described the Graham of Menteith Clan tartan as having a broad, "smalt" colored stripe. Smalt was a coloring agent derived from blue glass and which was used to color other vitreous materials. The closest color description would be "cobalt blue". An early sample of Graham of

*Graham of Montrose*

Menteith tartan dating from the original certified tartans of 1816 is in the Highland Society collection. The certification seals on this sample were, however, illegible and moth damaged. A sample of the Graham of Montrose tartan, which is also in the Society's collection, does retain the signature and seal of the clan chief from around 1816. This tartan is also worn by 205 (Scottish) Field Hospital Royal Army Medical Corps (Volunteers).

Surnames with possible associations: Airth, Bonar, Bontein, Bontine, Buntain, Bunten, Buntine, Haddon, Howe, Howie, MacGilvernock, MacGrime

# Grant

Earliest known date: 1819

Earliest source: Wilson, 1819

Tartan type: Symmetrical

Sett: **R**12 B2 R4 B4 R64 Az2 R4 B16 R4 G4 R4 G48 R4 B4 **R**12

Clan crest: A burning hill Proper

Clan motto: "Stand Fast"

Badge: *Giuthus* (Pine)

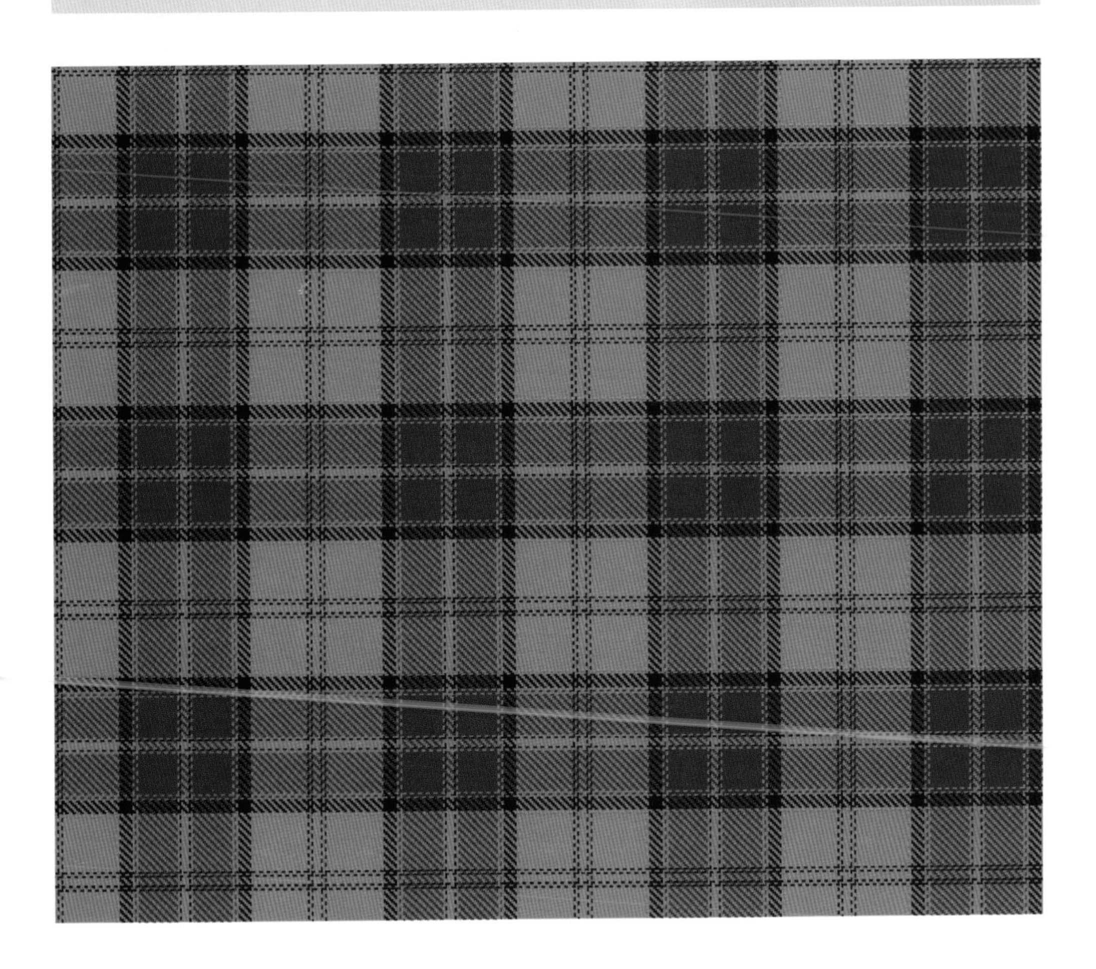

While some Grants claim the clan is part of the Siol Alpin – the Highland clans whose chiefs are said to descend from the 9th century King Alpin, father of Kenneth MacAlpin, King of the Scots – the surname Grant may well be derived from Anglo-Norman French *Le Grand* meaning "big".

In 1246, William le Grant was the lord of a manor in Nottinghamshire, England. His wife Mary was an heiress of the Bisset family, which held large estates in Aird and in Stratherrick, where the Grants first appear in the Scottish Highlands. One of William's two sons, Sir Lawrence de Grant, became Sheriff of Inverness in 1258, and gradually, the Grants became the ruling clan in Glenmoriston and Glenurquhart to the west of Stratherrick, and in Strathspey to the east. Sir Ian Grant, who was also Sheriff of Inverness in 1434, was the first chief of the Clan Grant from whom an uninterrupted line can be deduced. Through his marriage to Maude, daughter and heiress of Gilbert of Glencarnie, Grant acquired the principal holdings in Strathspey. The Glencarnies were a younger branch of the earls of Strathearn and held Kinveachy, which passed to Maude.

Today, Kinveachy is the home of the descendants of the Grants of Grant although the chief's stronghold was at Castle Grant, formerly called Castle Freuchie: until they became known as the Lairds of Grant in the 16th century, the clan was styled as Grant of Freuchie. In 1493, the lands had been elected into the Barony of Freuchie, then, in 1694, it became the Regality of Grant with the Castletown of Freuchie renamed, replanned and rebuilt in 1766 as Grantown-on-Spey. The Regality was a semi-independent state: the Grant chiefs were responsible for law enforcement, the courts, prisons, the municipal systems, weights and measures, and even had the right to hold a council or "petty (little) parliament". The Regality, awarded to the Grants for their support of William III, was abolished in 1747, along with their rights to "home rule".

The Grant's general support of the Hanoverian succession (although some individual Grants were Jacobite supporters) saved the clan from much of the persecution inflicted on other Highland clans following the 1715 and 1745 Jacobite risings. The Grant lands however, were eventually lost: in 1811, Sir Lewis Grant of Grant inherited the Ogilvie earldoms of Seafield and Findlater to become the 5th Earl of Seafield – and the 27th chief of Clan Grant. A long dispute with his brothers ensued, which resulted in the estates being disentailed (they could not be passed along the line of heirs). Consequently, the chief of the Clan Grant was no longer the

*Black Watch*

Earl of Seafield (although this title can pass along the female line). However, the chief of Clan Grant still retains the independent peerage created in 1817 with the title Lord of Strathspey. In peace, it would seem that the Grants could wear any tartan they chose! In the ten Grant portraits from Cullen House, in north-east Scotland, painted by Richard Waitt at the beginning of the 18th century no two tartans are alike – even the sitter's costumes are made of different pieces of tartan! Today, the usual design for the Clan Grant tartan is the one described by Logan in 1831, who had obtained many of his specimens from the weavers William Wilson & Sons of Bannockburn. Wilson's pattern books of 1819 and 1847 gave precise details of both colours and threads for many tartans. For undress, from their early association with the regiment, the Black Watch is worn.

Surnames with possible associations: Gilroy, Suttie

# Gunn

Earliest known date: *c.*1815
Earliest source: Cockburn Collection, 1810–20
Tartan type: Symmetrical
Sett: **R**4 G24 Bk24 G2 B24 **G**4
Clan crest: A dexter hand wielding a sword in bend Proper
Clan motto: *Aut pax aut bellum* ("Either peace or war")
Badge: *Aitionn* (Juniper) or *Lus nan laoch* (Roseroot)

Surnames with possible associations: Enrick, Galie, Gaunson, MacComas, MacCorkill, MacCorkle, MacIan, MacKames, MacKeamish, MacKean, MacManus, MacRob, MacWilliam, Nelson, Robinson, Robison, Robson, Ronald, Ronaldson, Sandison, Swan, Swanson, Will, Williamson, Wilson

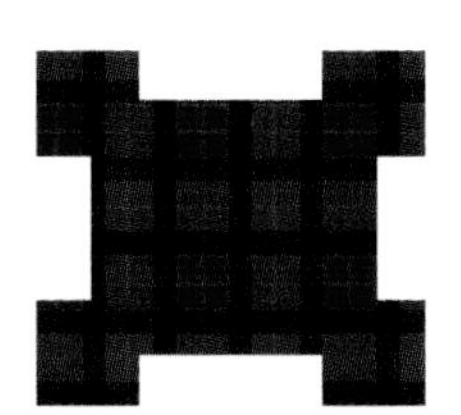

The Gunn name was derived from the Norse word *gunnr* – war! The 1st chief of Clan Gunn was George, Crowner (Coroner) of Caithness in 1464, whose chiefly title in Gaelic was *Mac Sheumais Chataich*, but it seems he was wore widely known as *Am Braisdeach Mor* "the great brooch-wearer" on account of his badge of office as Coroner.

The homelands of the Gunns in Scotland were in the highland regions of Caithness, particularly in the 30-mile long Gunn's Glen or Glenn na Guineach, on the Sutherland border. Consequently, the Gunn's lands formed a sort of "buffer zone" between the territories of the rival earls of Caithness and Sutherland. From around 1426, the Gunn's themselves had been locked in fierce conflict with the Clan Keith, who, from their castle at Ackergill, challenged the Gunn chiefs for power in the region. The Gunns repeatedly raided Keith territory, but were defeated in battle in 1438 at Tannach Moor near Wick and again in 1484, at Strathmore, near Dirlot. A well-known tale tells of how both the Gunns and the Keiths, seeking reconciliation, agreed to meet in the chapel of St Tyer near Wick. Each was to bring 12 horses – but the devious Keiths had two men on each horse! Outnumbered, the Gunns – including the Coroner-Chief and four of his sons – were slain, and his great brooch of office stolen. The next century saw allegiances shifting: in 1582, the Gunns were supported by the Earl of Caithness against the Mackays and in 1585, against the Earl of Sutherland. In 1586, however, Caithness and Sutherland were allied together against the Gunns. Meanwhile, the Gunns had strengthened ties with the Mackays through marriage.

While the chiefly line of the Gunns was that of Killearnan, there were two other important branches with chieftains of note: the "Robson" Gunns of Braemore, descended from Robert, one of the younger sons of "Coroner" George, and the Bregaul Gunns of Dale, descended from "Coroner" George's third son, John. In September 1821, George Gunn, the 10th Mac Sheumais Chataich presided over a special meeting at Thurso to form a clan society, the Loyal and United Benevolent Society of the Clan Gunn. Each member was required to attend an annual meeting wearing a coat of tartan belonging to the clan. Since the death of the 110th Chief, who died without an heir, the Clan Gunn has been led by a commander appointed by the Lord Lyon while the Lyon Court seeks to establish representation to the chief's bloodline. The Clan Gunn tartan contained in the Cockburn Collection is one of the oldest specimens available. While Logan recorded a sett in 1831, Donald C. Stewart noted that a specimen from around 1815 had a "light" shade of green, while the blue was "quite dark". Today, the central blue stripes are often reproduced in very dark blue – almost black – which gives the impression of four, equally dark-toned stripes.

# Hamilton

Earliest known date: 1842

Earliest source: *The Vestiarium Scoticum*, 1842

Tartan type: Symmetrical

Sett: **W**2 R18 B12 R2 **B**12

Clan crest: In a ducal coronet an oak tree fructed and penetrated transversely in the main stem by a frame saw Proper, the frame Or.

Clan motto:"Through"

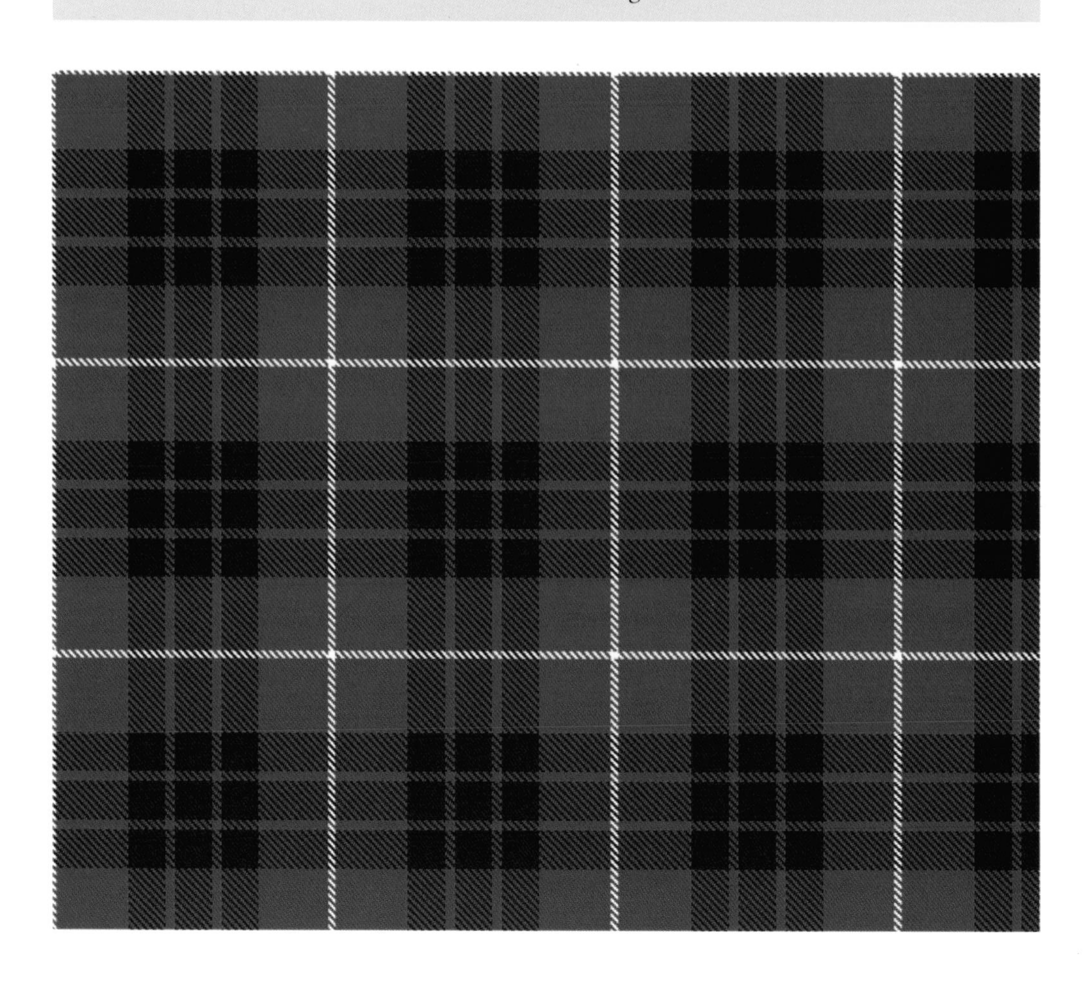

The ancestor of the Hamiltons was Sir Walter fitz Gilbert (i.e. Walter son of Gilbert) of Hameldone who appears in a charter to the monastery at Paisley in around 1294 as holding lands in Renfrewshire. As a reward for his support to Robert the Bruce, Sir Walter was given the lands of Dalserf that had been forfeited by the Comyns, along with the barony of Cadzow (now called the town of Hamilton). In 1445, James, 6th Lord of Cadzow, was created Lord Hamilton and he brought the Hamiltons to the Highlands by his marriage in around 1474 to Princess Mary of Scotland, sister of James III. Mary was a young widow with a son from her first marriage to Lord Boyd, while Hamilton was an elderly widower. In 1484, Mary's eldet son was murdered by the Montgomereys and her heir became her second son by her marriage to Hamilton. Significantly, throughout the 16th and 17th centuries, the Hamilton chiefs would often be the nearest heirs presumptive to the throne of Scotland. In 1503 James, 2nd Lord Hamilton, was also made Earl of Arran and given the island. The 2nd Earl of Arran was Regent of Scotland for the infant Mary Queen of Scots. In order to secure his own claim to the throne, the earl proposed to marry his son to the child queen. In the end, Mary married the French dauphin, and Arran was exiled for five years after openly opposing the widowed Mary's marriage to Lord Darnley in 1561. Nevertheless, the earl remained faithful to Mary: after she had escaped from Loch Leven, the ill-fated queen stayed at Cadzow Castle in 1568.

In 1599, John, the 4th Earl of Arran, was made the Marquis of Hamilton. His brother Claude, was made Lord Paisley in 1587 and, later, Lord Abercorn. This branch of the Hamiltons also prospered, and were made dukes in 1868. In 1643, James, the 3rd Marquis of Hamilton was made 1st Duke of Hamilton. At Cadzow, overhanging the River Clyde, Anne, the daughter of the 1st Duke of Hamilton, began the magnificent Hamilton Palace in the late 17th century. Subsequent dukes enlarged the palace and built the hunting lodge called Chatelherault, now part of the public park. Although demolished due to mining subsidence, the palace's famous herd of semi-wild white cattle still remains, and is thought to be descended from aurochs, the extinct wild European ox. The Hamilton family seat is now at Lennoxlove, near Haddington.

There is no evidence of a Hamilton tartan prior to the publication in 1842 of *The Vestiarium Scoticum* and it is now thought that the actual design was the work of Allan Hay (alias Charles Edward Stewart) who prepared the illustrations for his brother, John Sobieski Stolber Stewart Hay's text. Nevertheless, the Hamilton Red Clan tartan, like many other setts devised by the brothers, was popular enough to be successfully adopted as the clan's tartan.

# Hay (and Leith)

Earliest known date: 1810–20

Earliest source: Cockburn Collection, 1810–20

Tartan type: Symmetrical

Sett: **Bk**6 R2 Y2 Bk4 R32 G4 R2 Y2 R4 G30 W2 Bk30 R2 P30 R4 Y2 R2 P4 R32 Bk4 Y2 R2 **Bk**6

Clan crest: Issuing out of a crest coronet a falcon volant Proper, armed, jessed and belled Or.

Clan motto: *Serva jugum* ("Keep the yoke")

Badge: Mistletoe

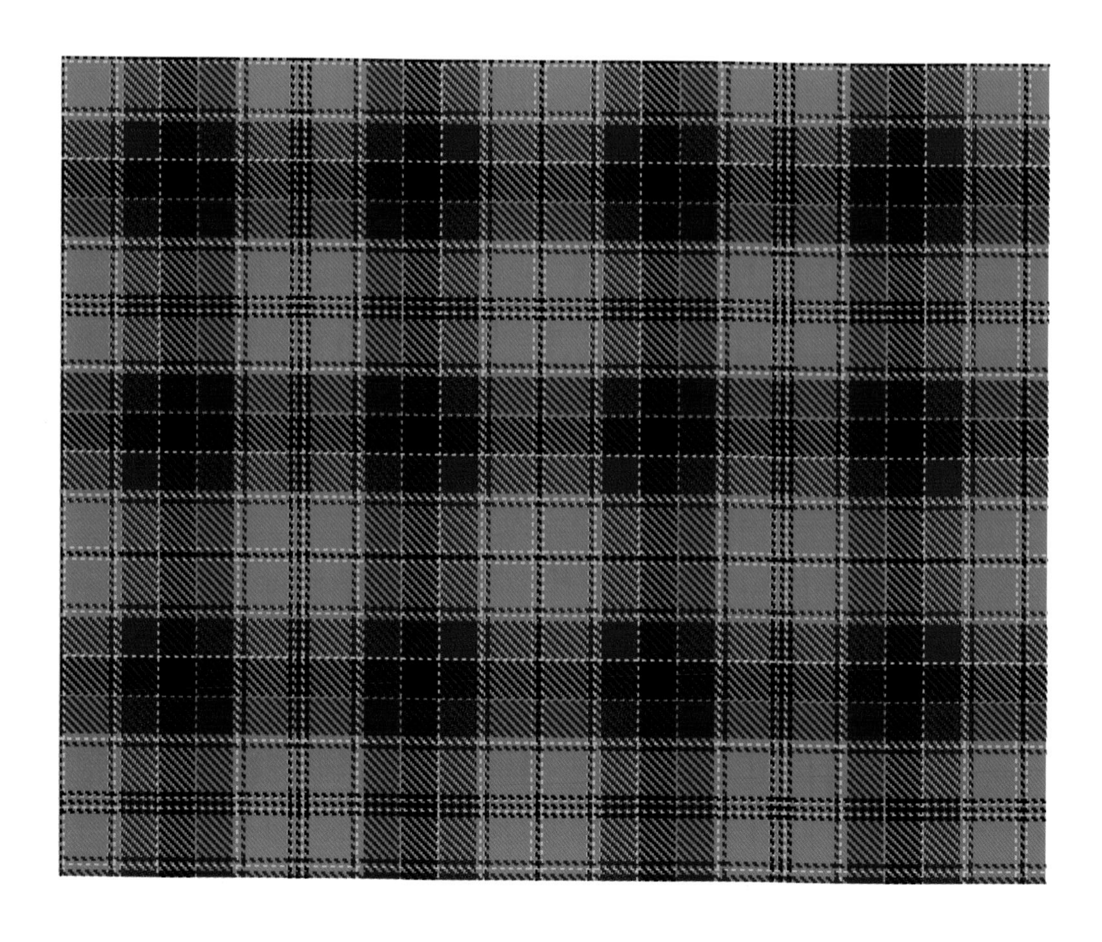

The surname Hay, which is the family name of the Earls of Erroll, is derived from La Haye in Normandy. A family of Norman princes, who arrived with William the Conqueror in England in 1066, brought it to Britain. The first Hay in Scotland was the first Baron, William de Haya (the charter-Latin form of de la Haye) who was at the Scottish court in around 1160. William was given the lands of Erroll in Perthshire in 1172, and was made an ambassador to England in 1199. The Hay's fortunes however were firmly established by Sir Gilbert Hay, 5th Baron of Erroll and Sheriff of Perth. He was one of Robert the Bruce's most effective supporters and as a reward for his loyalty, Bruce gave him the Regality of Slains on the coast of Buchan and made him the hereditary Constable of Scotland after the battle of Bannockburn in 1314. The post meant that Hay was commander of the royal bodyguard with responsibility for the king's personal safety, a "martial judge" in the royal household and court, and the Ceremonial Commander-in-Chief of the whole Scottish army. This dignity is still enjoyed, giving present Hay chiefs precedence in Scotland over every other hereditary honor apart from the royal family itself.

Sir Thomas Hay, 7th Baron, married Elizabeth, the daughter of King Robert II. The Hays of Delgatie descend from their second son, Sir Gilbert of Dronlaw, whose castle near Turriff is now the clan center. Francis Hay, the 9th Earl of Erroll, was a leading figure in the counter-reformation. With other Catholic nobles, Hay entered a secret treaty with Philip II of Spain to depose Queen Elizabeth I and put James VI (to be converted to Catholicism) on the throne of a united Catholic Britain. James VI, however, felt obliged to perform some act of remonstration, and personally blew up Slains Castle in 1595, since which time it has remained a ruin. Undaunted, Hay returned from a brief spell in exile, returned to Scotland – and to royal favor – and built a new castle further north at Bowness on Cruden Bay, now also in ruins.

In the 18th century, the Hays remained loyal to the Stewart cause and came out in both Jacobite risings of 1715 and 1745, but, on the death of the 13th Earl's sister in 1758, the title passed to a great-nephew, James Boyd. As well as the earldom, James also assumed the surname of Hay, along with the chiefship of the clan. The 19th Earl, William Hay, founded the fishing village of Port Erroll, while in 1950, Diana, Countess of Erroll (who moved into a wooden house built on the ruins of "Old" Slains in 1960), founded the Clan Hay Society. Two tartans

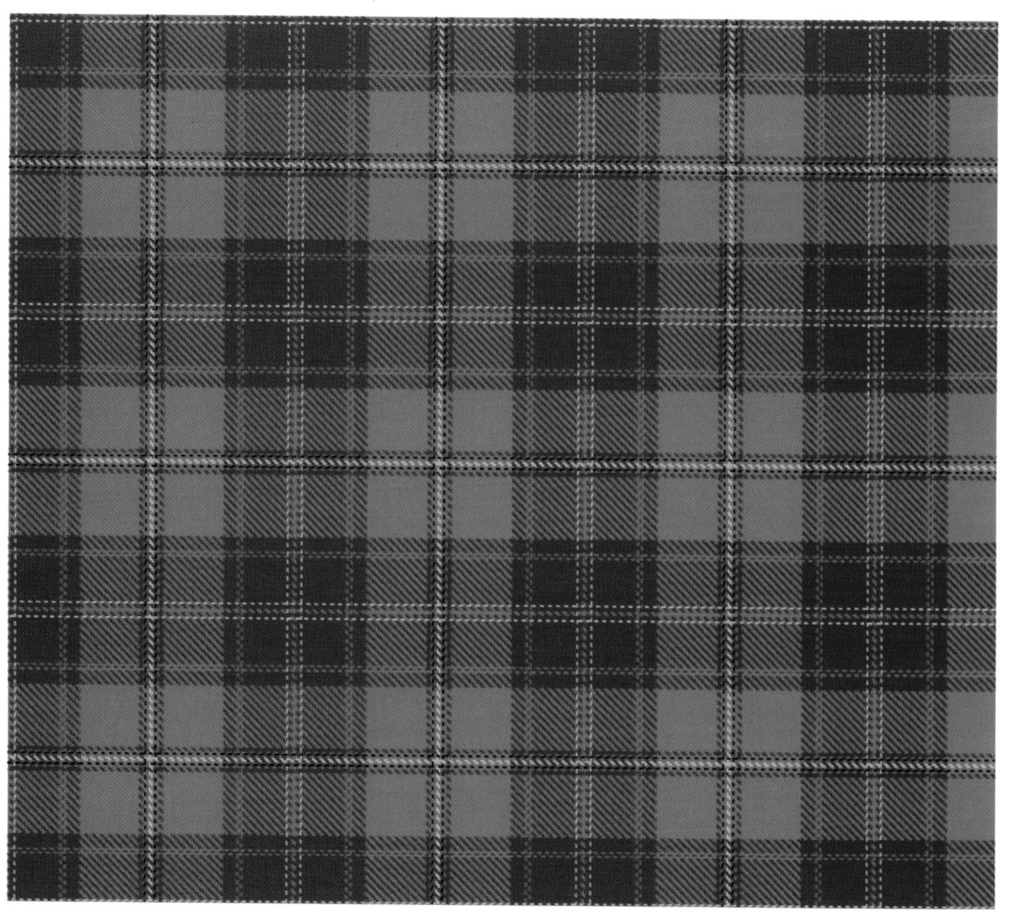

*Hay*

bear the Hay name: the most elaborate, with a repeat pattern occupying 13 inches, is called "Hay and Leith" from the Cockburn Collection. The name was given by Logan in his book, presumably because it was also in use by the family of Leith-Hays whose home was at Leith Hall, near Huntly – the two families may have been connected by marriage. The second sett, which does not contain purple, but has wider white and black stripes, was shown in *The Vestiarium Scoticum* in 1842.

Surnames with possible associations: Arrol, Constable, Gifford

# Henderson

Earliest known date: 1906

Earliest source: Johnston, 1906

Tartan type: Symmetrical

Sett: **Y**2 K12 G8 K2 G32 B2 G8 B12 **W**2

Clan crest: A cubit arm Proper the hand holding an estoile Or surmounted by a crescent Azure

Clan motto: *Sola virtus nobilat* ("Virtue alone ennobles")

Badge: *Canach* (Cottongrass)

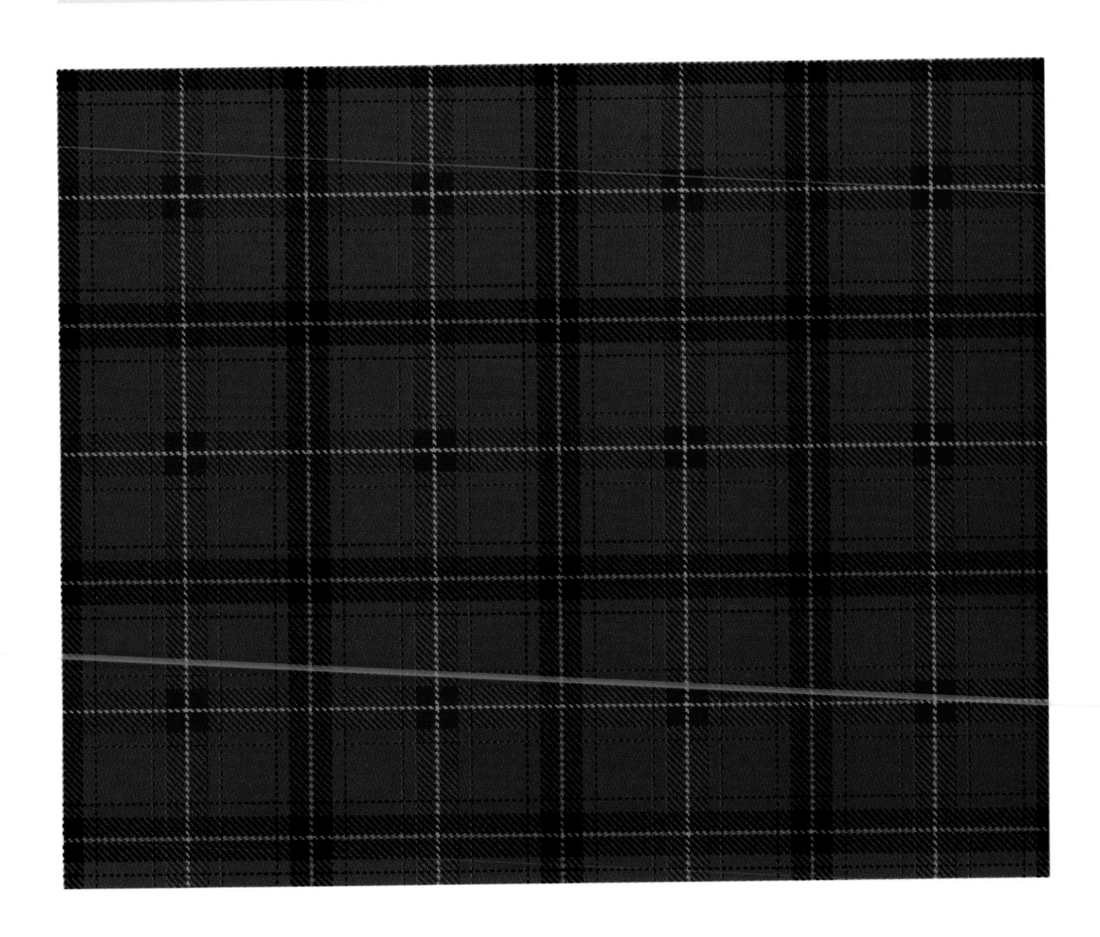

The Hendersons claim descent from a Pictish prince called Eanruig Mor Mac Righ Neachtan – "Big Henry, son of King Nectan". According to tradition, the chiefs of the clan held their seats at Callart, on the northern side of Loch Leven. The direct line of these "Hendersons of Glencoe" ended when the last chief Dugall MacEanruig (Dugall MacKendrick – the Gaelic form of the name Henderson) produced an heiress who, as "Heretrix of the clan", passed the chiefship to her son (by her lover Angus Og of Islay), Iain Fraoch ("Heather John") who was, consequently, a MacDonald. His son, known by the local people as Iain Abrach (John of Lochaber), became the first MacIain of Glencoe and, from then on, the patronymic MacIain would designate the MacDonald chief of Glencoe. Iain Froach, possibly in recognition of his maternal lineage, appointed Hendersons as his bodyguards and until the death of the last MacIain chief, Hendersons were traditionally given the honor of the "first lift" of the chief's coffin on its way to burial.

Other Hendersons were to be found in the far north of Scotland as well as in the Borders where the name is simply a variant of "sons of Henry" and is often found in the form "Henryson". The Hendersons of Caithness are descended from Hendry, the son of George Gunn the Coroner (see Clan Gunn, page 82) and they wear the Clan Gunn tartan. The Hendersons of Fordell are descended from James Henderson who was Lord Advocate in around 1494. He came from Dumfriesshire, acquired lands of Fordell in Fife and built the castle there. The most famous of these Hendersons was Alexander, born around 1583, who was a leading voice in the Scottish Reformation. He opposed Charles I's attempts to reform the Church of Scotland and introduce the "new" prayer book, and, with Johnston of Warriston, drafted the National Covenant which was sworn in Greyfriars Churchyard in Edinburgh in 1637. Alexander was buried in the same churchyard, where there is a monument to him.

Fordell became the title of the Lowland chiefs and it is from this family that the current Henderson Chief is descended. The Henderson Clan tartan was recorded by W. and A.K. Johnston in 1906. It is similar to the Davidson tartan (see page 50) in that it has the main band of pattern in black and blue placed on a green ground. Since the Davidsons formed part of the Clan Chattan, while the Hendersons were associated with the Gunns and MacDonalds, there is nothing common in their clan histories to explain the similarities in tartans. Donald C. Stewart contends that the earlier Davidson tartan (from 1822) was the basis for the Henderson tartan.

*Davidson*

# Home

Earliest known date: 1842

Earliest source: *The Vestiarium Scoticum*, 1842

Tartan type: Symmetrical

Sett: **B**6 G4 B48 Bk16 R2 Bk4 R2 **Bk**56

Clan crest: On a cap of maintenance Proper, a lion's head erased Argent

Clan motto (and *slughorn* ): "A Home, A Home, A Home"

Badge: *Bealaidgh* (Broom)

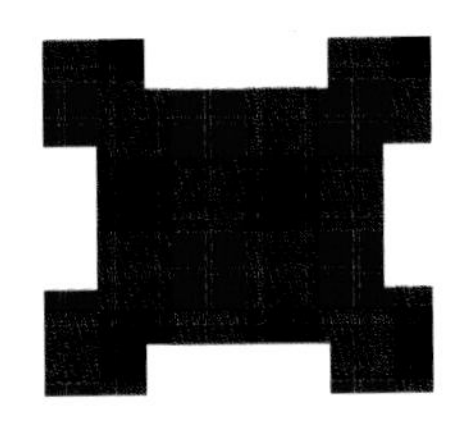

The powerful Border family of Home (pronounced Hume) are said to be descendants of the Saxon princes of Northumberland. Patrick, the second son of Cospatrick, Earl of Dunbar is regarded as the founder of the family while the first recorded ancestor was Aldan de Home (*c.* 1172) who took his name from his landholdings in Berwickshire. His descendant, Sir Thomas Home married an heiress of Dunglass and had two sons: David Home of Wedderburn the ancestor of the Earls of Marchmont, and, Sir Alexander of Dunglass, a great soldier who fought at the battle of Homildon in 1402, and was killed fighting in France at Verneuil in 1424.

Sir Alexander had three sons: from the youngest descend the Homes of Spott; from the middle son descend the Homes of Tyninghame and Ninewells. The eldest son (also called Alexander) carried on the family line and his son – another Sir Alexander – was made Lord Home in 1473. Lord Home joined the rebellion against James III that ended with the king's defeat at Sauchieburn, yet he did find favor with James IV. Alexander, 3rd Lord, was the Royal Cupbearer, Great Chamberlain of Scotland, Warden of the Marches and a counsellor to the Queen Regent,. But when the Regency was transferred to the Duke of Albany, the fortunes of the Homes declined: Lord Home was arrested, tried for treason and he – along with his brother – were executed in 1516. Alexander, the 5th Lord, was also a victim of shifting allegiances in the complex political world during the reign of Mary, Queen of Scots. Home supported the Queen's marriage to Bothwell, but then led his troops against her at the battle of Langside in 1568 and imprisoned the queen at Loch Leven. Home was later arrested and convicted of treason – but against the young James VI! Because of failing health, Lord Home was released from Edinburgh Castle but he died soon after. Alexander, 6th Lord was surprisingly, a favorite with James VI and, in 1605, he was elevated to the title Earl of Home. When the 2nd Earl of Home died without issue, the titles passed to a distant cousin, Sir James Home of Coldingknows.

In the 20th century, the Homes came to pubic prominence once more: the 14th Earl disclaimed his hereditary peerage for his own lifetime in order to become prime minister as Sir Alec Douglas Home. The family seat is the Border estate of Hirsel in Berwickshire, from which Sir Alec named his life peerage, as Lord Home of the Hirsel. The Home tartan, like many of the other Lowland tartans, first appeared in *The Vestiarium Scoticum*. Since these Lowland tartans were "devised" by the *Vestiarium's* authors, it is not surprising that there are marked similarities between them: Donald C. Stewart points out that although it is in different colors, the Home tartan has the same scheme as a tartan called the Gray Douglas.

Surnames with possible associations: Eaton, Greenlaw, Lansdale

# Innes (of Moray)

Earliest known date: 1938

Earliest source: Sir Thomas Innes of Learney, *Tartans of the Clans and Families of Scotland*, 1938

Tartan type: Symmetrical

Sett: **LB14** Bk48 R8 Bk8 R8 Bk8 R48 Y8 R12 B24 R12 Bk8 G40 Bk8 R12 **W4**

Clan crest: A boar's head eraser Proper

Clan motto: "Be traist"

Badge: Bulrush

The Clan Innes of Moray (not to be confused with the Clan MacInnes of western Scotland, see page 154) is said to descend from Berowald, a Flemish nobleman who was granted a barony by Malcolm IV in 1160. The title included lands along the coast between Spey and Lossie. In 1226, Alexander II granted a charter confirming the title and lands to Berowald's grandson, Walter, who assumed the surname of Innes. In 1579, the Privy Council recognized the Inneses as a "clan". "Good Sir Robert" (1364–81), the 8th Laird of Innes, had three sons: Sir Alexander who married the heiress of Aberchirder, succeeded as 9th Laird; John, who became the Bishop of Moray, and, George, who became the head of the Scottish Order of Trinitarian Friars.

The 10th Laird, Walter (d.1454) was chief for 42 years, while the 11th:Laird, "Ill Sir Robert" – a name given to him on account of his wicked ways rather than his poor health – fought under the Earl of Huntly at the battle of Brechin in 1452, and finally made amends for his sins in life by founding the order of Greyfriars in Elgin. James, the 12th chief, was an armor-bearer to James III and lavishly entertained James IV at the Castle of Innes in 1490. The 20th chief, Sir Robert, was a prominent Covenanter and was created a baronet in 1625. He built Innes House in 1640 from the proceeds of the sale of the Aberchider estates and raised a regiment to fight the cause of Charles II. James, the 3rd Baronet, married Lady Margaret Ker: through her came the dukedom of Roxburghe to which Sir James Innes, the 6th Baronet and 25th chief succeeded as the 5th Duke in 1805.

One of the descendants of Walter Innes of Innerlackie – the 2nd son of "Ill Sir Robert Innes", – was Sir Thomas Innes of Learney, the author of *The Tartans of the Clan and Families of Scotland* in 1938. Sir Thomas Innes, was one of Scotland's foremost experts on heraldry and from 1945 to 1969, he was Lord Lyon, King of Arms. His son, Sir Malcolm Innes of Edingight, shared his father's passion for Scottish history and was appointed Lord Lyon in 1981. Sir Thomas included the red Innes of Moray sett in his book, and clearly distinguishes it from the green MacInness Clan Tartan (see page 154).

Surnames with possible associations: Dinnes, Ennis, Innie, Thain, Wilson

# Johnston

Earliest known date: 1842

Earliest source: *The Vestiarium Scoticum*, 1842

Tartan type: Symmetrical

Sett: **Y**6 G4 Bk2 G60 B48 Bk4 B4 **Bk**4

Clan crest: A winged spur Or

Clan motto: *Nunquam non paratus* ("Never unprepared")

Badge: Red Hawthorn

The Johnstons were a powerful border clan whose origins date back to an early 13th century. knight, Sir Gilbert de Johnstoun. His grandson, Sir John, a knight of Dumfries, appeared in the Ragman Rolls of 1296 as having sworn his loyalty to Edward I. Sir John's son Adam was Laird of Johnston around 1413 and was the ancestor of the Johnstons of Newbie, Mylnefield and Galabank. John married twice: his first wife bore him a son, also Adam, the ancestor of the Johnstons of Westerhall; his second wife bore him Sir Gilbert, ancestor of the Johnstons of Elphinstone. Both sons took the Royalist side in the struggles between James II and the Douglases and were important in the suppression of the rebellion against the Crown. The Johnstons, whose stronghold was Lochwood Tower, near Beattock, were also involved in long-running and deadly feud with the Maxwells. Lord Maxwell, one of the most powerful men in the region, burned Lochwood Tower, but was killed in 1593, along with many of his men at the battle of Dryfe Sands near Lockerbie. At a meeting in 1608 to end the feud, Johnston was killed by the 9th Lord Maxwell, who was himself executed for this crime in 1614.

In the following years, the Johnston star was in ascendancy: Sir James of Johnston was created Lord Johnston of Lochwood in 1633, and then in 1643, the Earl of Hartfell, a title which was given to him and his male heirs only. As reward for his loyal support for the royalist cause, Charles II created Johnston the Earl of Annandale and Hartfell and a charter in 1662 made the land into a territorial earldom entailed to male heirs – or to female ones should he have no sons. In 1701 William, the 3rd Earl of Hartfell and 2nd Earl of Annandale, was elevated to the rank of marquis. In 1792, on the death of George, the 3rd – and last – Marquis, the titles became dormant and the estates passed to a grandnephew, James, 3rd Earl of Hopetoun.

Throughout the 19th century, several attempts were made to revive the Annandale titles, but it was only in 1982 that the Lord Lyon recognised Major Percy Johnston of Annandale and of that Ilk as baron of the lands of the earldom of Annandale and Hartfell and the lordship of Johnston. The case proceeded to the House of Lords who found in favor of the Major's son, Patrick, now the Earl of Annandale and Hartfell and Chief of the name and arms of Johnston. The tartan of this great clan did not have a name prior to the publication of *The Vestiarium Scoticum* in 1842. It is possible that it came from the Johnstons of Aberdeenshire, in the north of Scotland, who descended from Stephen Johnston and his wife Margaret, the daughter and heiress of Sir Andrew Garioch. They obtained the lands of Johnston, which gave the name to their descendants whose family seat is at Caskieben, Blackburn. Unlike the Border clan of Johnstons of Annandale, the Johnstons of Caskieben are not allowed the title "of that Ilk".

Surnames with possible associations: Rome

# Keith (and Austin)

Earliest known date: 1819

Earliest source: Wilson and Son's pattern book, 1819

Tartan type: Symmetrical

Sett: **Bk**4 G18 B8 Bk8 **B**8

Clan crest: Out of a crest coronet Or, a roebuck's head Proper, attired Or

Clan motto: *Vertas vinci* ("Truth conquers")

Badge: White Rose

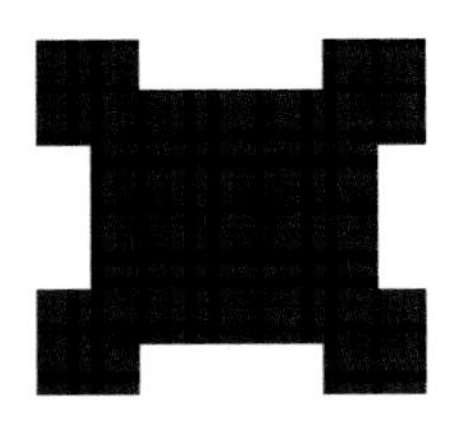

The Keiths, the hereditary Marischals of Scotland, are descended from Hervey Keith, who received a charter from David I granting him the lands of Keth (Keith) in about 1150. Robert de Keth succeeded to the office of Marischal in 1294, but was imprisoned by the English until 1303. The following year he was one of Edward's four Deputy Wardens of Scotland but at Christmas 1308, Sir Robert de Keth joined the cause of Robert the Bruce. For his support, Keth was rewarded with a grant of the Royal Forest of Kintore, Aberdeenshire, where the Marischal built his castle. In 1324, Robert the Bruce made the office of Marischal hereditary in Sir Robert's family. Sir Robert went on to command the Scots cavalry at Bannockburn. where he played a decisive role in the defeat of the English and was rewarded with the forfeited Comyn estates in Buchan. His great-grandson, Sir William founded the tower of Dunottar Castle, near Stonehaven, while in turn, his son, Sir Robert, was elevated to the peerage as Lord Keith. William, 2nd Lord Keith was created Earl Marischal in 1458.

The 3rd Earl, known as "William of the Tower", was a distinguished statesman – in spite of his life in seclusion at Dunottar. It was said that his estates lay in so many counties he could travel from Berwick to John O'Groats eating each meal and sleeping each night in his own lands! William, the 6th Earl, was a Covenanter and, after the coronation of Charles II at Scone in 1651, he was imprisoned in the Tower of London until the Restoration of the Monarchy in 1660 because he and his brother John had "rescued" the Scottish Crown Jewels from Cromwell's occupation and hidden them at Dunottar Castle. When Charles II was restored, John was made Earl of Kintore, and became a Privy Councillor and, later, Lord Privy Seal.

George, the 9th Earl, supported the Jacobite cause in 1745 and, for this, the Keiths forfeited their lands, castles and titles. George and his brother, Field Marshal James Keith left for the continent: the earl became a close friend of Frederick the Great, while James became one of Prussia's leading generals. On the earl's death in 1778, the chiefship passed to Keith of Ravelston. His nephew was dubbed Knight Marischal for George IV's state visit to Edinburgh in 1822. Since this line expired, the Keith-Marischals have been represented by the Keith-Falconers, the earls of Kintore, whose seat is at Keith Hall, Aberdeenshire. The clan tartan, known as Keith and Austin is the pattern recorded by Wilson and Sons of Bannockburn in 1819 as "No. 75, or Austin". According to D.W. Stewart, the firm of Romane and Paterson had supplied the tartan from the early years of the 19th century to various families of Keiths and Austins, including the Keith-Falconers, the earls of Kintore.

Surnames with possible associations: Austin, Dickson, Dixon, Harvey

# Kennedy

Earliest known date: 1845

Earliest source: MacIan illustration, 1845

Tartan type: Symmetrical

Sett: **R**4 G48 B8 Bk6 B6 Bk6 B6 Bk6 B8 G24 Cr2 G4 Cr2 G6 Y2 G4 **Bk**4

Clan crest: A dolphin naiant Proper

Clan motto: *Avise la fin* ("Consider the end")

The Kennedys, (whose name in Gaelic was *Cinneidigh*, meaning "ugly" or "grim-faced") claim descent from ancient lords of Galloway. In the early part of the reign of William the Lion (1165–1214) Gilbert Mac Kenedi was a witness to a charter of lands in Carrick to the Abbey at Melrose, while under Alexander II (1214–49), Gillespie Kenedi was named as the seneschal (a steward in charge of medieval princely court) of Carrick. The Kennedys had a blood kinship with the earls of Carrick: John Kennedy of Dunure was married to Mary de Carrick. He supported Robert the Bruce in the War of Independence and was recognized by Robert II in 1372 as Chief of the Kennedys. His grandson, Sir Gilbert Kennedy of Dunure married Princess Mary, daughter of Robert III, and their son Gilbert was one of the six Regents of Scotland during the minority of the child-king James III. Sir Gilbert was created Lord Kennedy around 1457. His younger brother James became Bishop of St Andrews and the founder of the famous University of St Andrews. The 3rd Lord Kennedy was created Earl of Cassillis (in Ayrshire) in 1509. He died at Flodden, and the 2nd Earl was assassinated in 1527 by Sir Hew Campbell of Loudon. Gilbert, the 3rd Earl, fared no better: he was poisoned at Dieppe for protecting the Scottish royal succession of Mary, Queen of Scots. John, the 4th Earl, is remembered for having "roasted the Abbot of Crossraguel", while Lady Jean Hamilton, wife of the 6th Earl – a zealous Protestant and supporter of Parliament during the Civil War – was reputed to be the lover of the gypsy Sir John Faa!

With the death of the 8th Earl without heir, the House of Lords settled the Kennedy succession on Sir Thomas Kennedy of Culzean as the 9th Earl. His brother, David, the 10th Earl, commissioned Robert Adam to build the castle at Culzean, and when hel died, the title passed to Captain Archibald Kennedy in America. A distinguished naval officer, Archibald also owned part of New York City. Attempting to remain neutral in the American War of Independence, Archibald ended up being mistrusted by both sides. Eventually, his New York properties – including No.1 Broadway – were confiscated by George Washington. Archibald's son became the 12th Earl and through his friendship with the Duke of Clarence, became Marquis of Ailsa in 1806. The Kennedys' seat remains at Cassillis and at Culzean Castle.

The colorful history of the Kennedys is matched by their tartan: a single red stripe in scarlet, two fine lines in crimson, and a yellow stripe on a green ground with black and blue. D.W. Stewart maintains that the Kennedys in Carrick adopted this tartan in the 18th century as a symbol of their Jacobite sympathies – even though wearing tartan in the Scottish Lowlands at this time would have been regarded as extremely provocative.

Surnames with possible associations: Cassels

# Kerr

Earliest known date: 1842

Earliest source: *The Vestiarium Scoticum*, 1842

Tartan type: Symmetrical

Sett: **Bk**8 R4 Bk2 R56 Bk28 G6 Bk2 G4 Bk2 **G**40

Clan crest: The sun in splendour Or

Clan motto: *Seo sed serio* ("Late but in earnest")

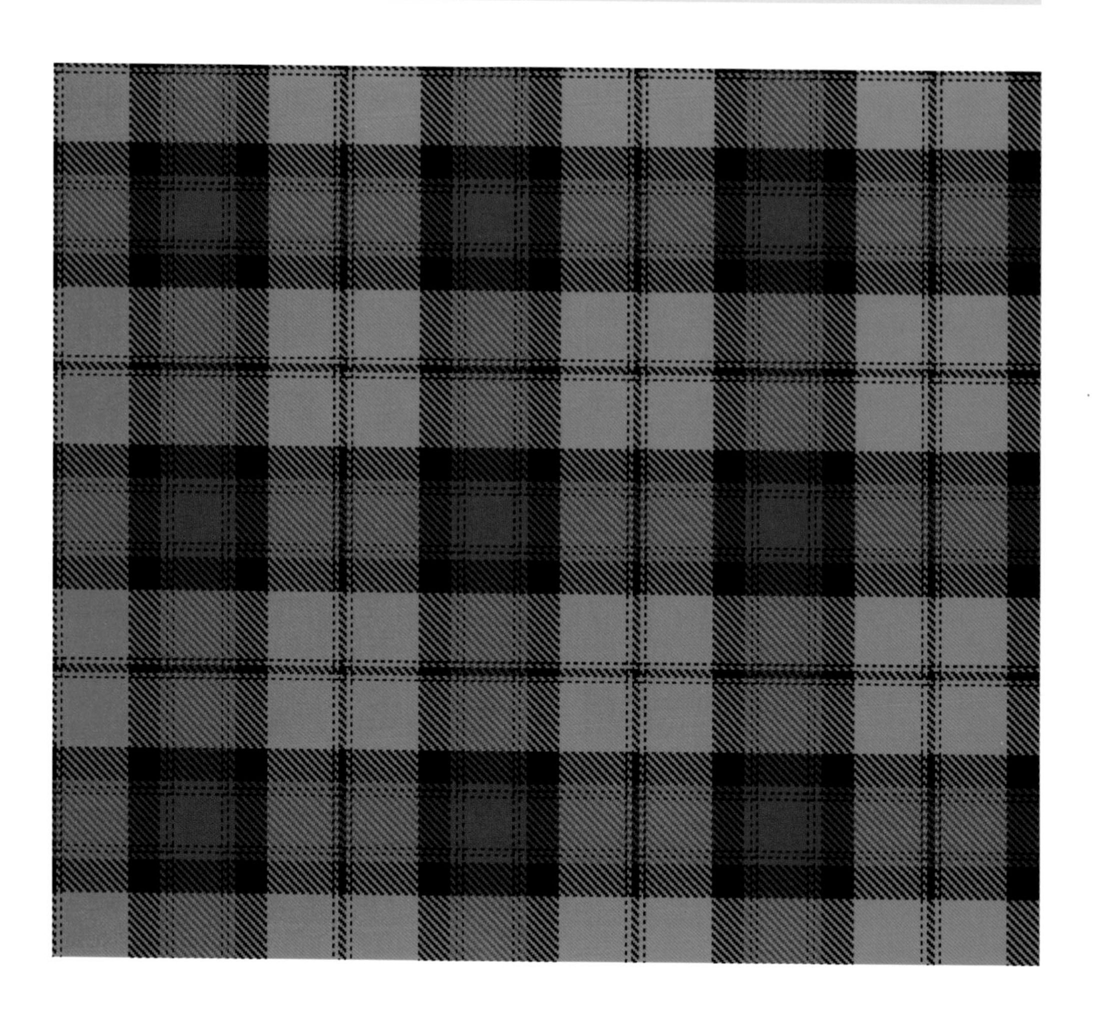

The Kerrs of the Scottish Border are of Norman-French descent. Their name has been rendered in a number of forms such as Ker, Carr, Carre but is ultimately derived from the Norse *kjrr* meaning "marsh dweller". The Kerrs came to Scotland from the Norse settlements in Normandy, on the French coast. The first Kerr on record in Scotland is John Ker of Swinhope who lived during the reign of William the Lion (r.1165–1214).

The Kerrs divided into two main branches, which by tradition are said to descend from the brothers Ralph and John who settled near Jedburgh in 1330. The Kerrs of Cessford are descended from John Kerr of Altonburn, the younger son; his descendant, Andrew Kerr of Altonburn, became Baron of Cessford in 1467. From the elder brother Ralph, the Kerrs of Ferniehurst claim descent as well as the chiefship of the Kerrs: Margaret Kerr, the heiress of the house married Thomas, the third son of Andrew Kerr of Altonburn, Baron of Cessford. Their son, Sir Andrew Kerr of Ferniehurst, was granted a royal charter to the barony of Oxnam and was appointed Warden of the Middle March in 1502. When the English besieged Kerr's Ferniehurst Castle in 1523, they claimed that it was defended by spirits and "fearful sights" – including the devil himself! Sir John Kerr, the next laird, recovered Ferniehurst Castle from the English and his successor, Sir Thomas Kerr, was an ardent supporter of Mary, Queen of Scots; in 1662, Sir Thomas' son, Sir Andrew, was created Lord Jedburgh.

Two further peerages came to the Kerr family: Robert Kerr of Woodhead and Ancrum, who was descended from a younger son of the first Sir Andrew Kerr of Ferniehurst, was created Earl of Ancrum in 1633, while Sir William Kerr, son of the Earl of Ancrum, was created the Earl of Lothian. The Earl of Lothian's son, Robert, was elevated to marquis in 1701 and succeeded to the earldom of Ancrum.

While Ferniehurst Castle continues to belong to the chiefs of the Kerrs, the seat is the mansion house of Mount Teviot, in Ancrum. Like many other Borders tartans, the origin of the Kerr tartan is unknown and it first appeared in *The Vestiarium Scoticum* along with dubious claims to antiquity. Donald C. Stewart noted that the Kerr tartan was reminiscent of the Stewart of Atholl tartan, a drawing of which was prepared for the *Vestiarium* but was not published.

Surnames with possible associations: Carr, Caw, Cessford

# Lamont

Earliest known date: *c.*1810–20
Earliest source: Cockburn Collection, 1810–20
Tartan type: Symmetrical
Sett: **B**6 Bk2 B2 Bk2 B2 Bk8 G8 W2 G8 Bk8 B8 Bk2 **B**2
Clan crest: A dexter hand couped at the wrist Proper
Clan motto: *Ne parcas nec spernas* ("Neither spare nor dispose")
Badge: *Craobh-ubhal fhiadhain* (Crab-apple tree)

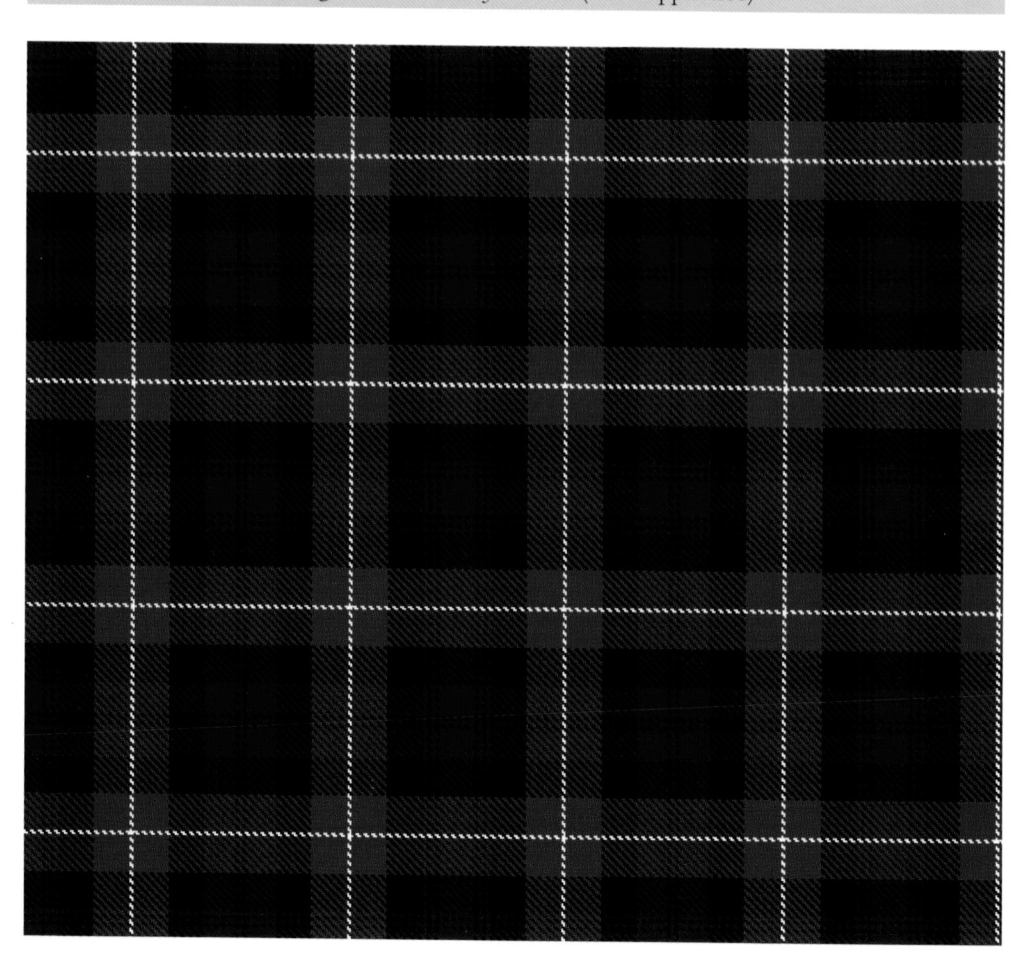

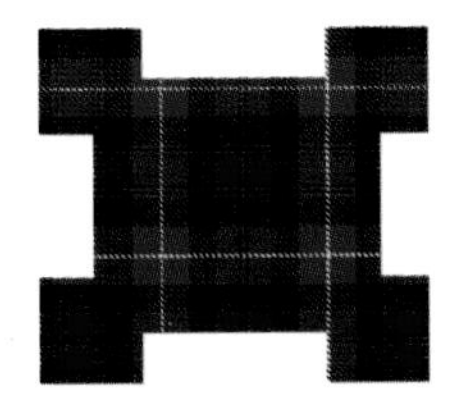

At one time in south Argyll, the chiefs of the Lamonts were called "Mac Laomain Mor Chomhail Uile" – "The Great MacLamont of all Cowal". While some maintain the Lamonts have a Norman-French heritage, it is more likely that they originated in Ulster and descended from a son of the O'Neill princes of Tyrone. The first chief of the Clan Lamont of whom there is historical evidence is Ferchar, who lived around 1200. It was Ferchar's grandson, Laumun, who first used the name, which has since become hereditary. Laumun is recorded in 1238 as granting lands at Kilmun (together with the church of Kilfinan) to the monks of Paisley. These grants were confirmed in 1270 and again in 1295, by Malcolm, son of Laumun. In 1456, John Lamond is recorded as the baillie of Cowal, but later that century, the direct line of the chiefs died out and representation passed to the Lamonts of Inveryne at Toward Castle, who later styled themselves "Lamont of Lamont".

In 1643, Sir James Lamont of Lamont, chief of the clan, declared for the Royalist cause, which brought the Lamonts into direct confrontation with their powerful Campbell neighbors. Around 1646, the Lamont lands were ravaged by the Campbells. Sir James carefully negotiated a written peace treaty securing the safety of the Lamonts by handing over the castles of Toward and Ascog. Nevertheless, Sir James was imprisoned in a dungeon at Dunstaffnage for five years – without a change of clothes! The castles were ruined, and about 200 of the clanspeople – men, women and children – were taken as prisoners by the Campbells to Dunoon and then massacred at the Gallowhill. In 1906, a memorial to mark this event was erected by the Clan Lamont Society. In 1646, Ard Lamont became the seat of the Lamont chiefs until it, and the last of the clan lands, were sold in 1893 by the 21st chief, John Henry Lamont of Lamont. While the clan Lamont chiefship passed to the Monydrain branch of the Lamonts overseas in Australia, in Scotland, Sir Norman Lamont, 2nd Baronet and 15th Laird of Knockdow, left his estate in trust as a home for the clan.

Given thel influence exerted over the Lamonts by the Campbells, it is not surprising that the Lamont tartan is like the tartan known as Campbell of Argyll (page 38) – except that the lines on the green ground are of white. The Lamont Clan tartan, of which there is a certified sample dated 1817 in the Collection of the Highland Society, is also almost identical to the Forbes tartan (page 68) except that the white lines in the Lamont tartan do not have black guards.

Surnames with possible associations: Blake, Brown, Burdon, Clement, Lamb, Lambie, Lammond, Lamondson, Landers, Lemond, Limond, Limont, Lucas, Luke, MacAlduie, MacClymont, MacGilledon, MacGilliegowie, MacIlwhom, MacIlzegowie, MacLucas, MacLymont, MacPatrick, MacPhorich, Meikleham, Patrick, Toward, Towart, Turner, White, Whyte

# Leslie

Earliest known date: 1850 Earliest source: Smith/Smibert, 1850

Tartan type: Symmetrical

Sett: **R**4 B16 Bk16 W2 G16 **Bk**2

Clan crest: A demi griffin Proper, baked, armed and winged Or

Clan motto: Grip fast

Badge: Rue

The name Leslie is derived from lands of the same name in Aberdeenshire and the first Leslie on record was Bartolf of Leslie, a noble who came to Scotland in the retinue of Edgar the Aetheling, brother-in-law of king Malcolm III (r.1057–93). The king appointed Bartolf Governor of Edinburgh Castle and awarded him lands in Fife, Angus, the Mearns and Aberdeenshire, while his son, Malcolm, was made the Constable of the Royal Castle of Inverury by David II. In 1282, Sir Norman Leslie acquired the lands of Fythkil, in Fife, which would thereafter be called Leslie. George Leslie, made Lord Leslie of Leven in 1445, with the lands united into the barony of Ballinbreich, was later (c.1458) created the 1st Earl of Rothes by James II. William, the 3rd Earl, died at Flodden, while George, the 4th Earl, died mysteriously – along with the Earl of Cassillis (see Clan Kennedy, page 00) – at Dieppe, France returning from the wedding of Mary, Queen of Scots to the French Dauphin in 1558.

A loyal Royalist, John, the 7th Earl of Rothes, carried the Sword of State at the coronation of Charles II at Scone in 1651, and in 1680 was made the Duke of Rothes. A distinguished statesman, he was also a supporter of the ruthless policy to suppress by force the extreme Protestant movement who met in secret, illegal gatherings called conventicles. When he died without a male heir, the dukedom also ended, but under the terms of an earlier charter, the earldom could be passed through the female line and was subsequently preserved. Consequently, the duke's daughter became Countess, and her eldest son, John, became the 8th Earl of Rothes.

The 9th Earl supported the Hanoverian succession and in 1715 commanded a regiment at the battle of Sheriffmuir against the Jacobite rebels. He also sold much of the Rothes estates – although Leslie House, near Fife, remained the seat of the earls until 1926 when it, too, was finally sold.

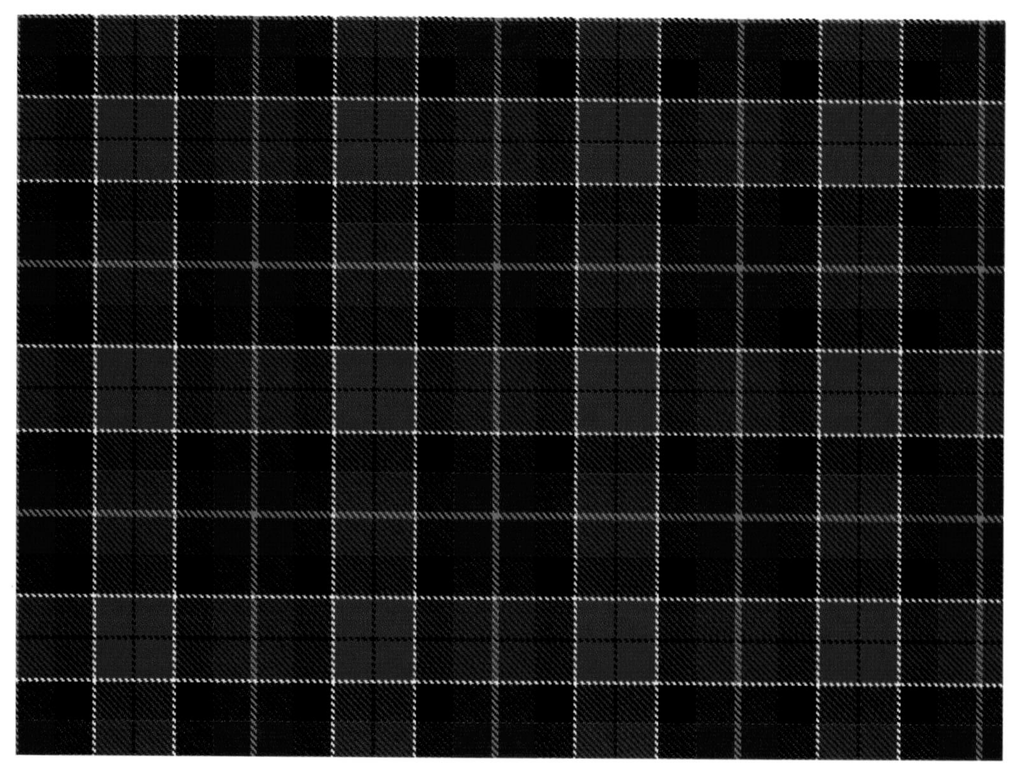

*Leslie Hunting*

A famous branch of the Leslies is the Leslies of Balquhain in Aberdeenshire. They descend from Sir George Leslie who was granted the Balquhain estate by David II in 1340. Sir Andrew, the 3rd Baron, feuded with the Clan Forbes who burnt down Balquhain Castle. Sir William, the 7th Baron, rebuilt it in the early 16th century, and it remains in the Leslie family to this day. The Leslie hunting tartan is said to have been worn by George, 14th Earl of Rothes, who died in 1841. This is the darker – and the older – of two tartans that were shown by the Smith brothers in 1850, but they did not call it "Hunting". The second tartan, the predominantly red "Dress Leslie" tartan can be dated to 1842, when it first appeared in *The Vestiarium Scoticum*.

Surnames with possible associations: Bartholomew, Lang

# Lindsay

Earliest known date: 1842

Earliest source: *The Vestiarium Scoticum*, 1842

Tartan type: Symmetrical

Sett: **Cr**6 B4 Cr48 B16 G4 B4 G4 B4 **G**40

Clan crest: Issuing from an antique ducal coronet Or, the head, neck and wings of a swan Proper.

Clan motto: *Endure fort* ("Endure boldly")

Badges: Rue, and Lime Tree

The name Lindsay is derived from "Lindsey" – the "island of the linden, or lime tree" – where they held the manor of Fordington, south of the River Humber in East Yorkshire. In 1120, Sir Walter de Lindsay was a member of Prince David's council in Lothian and, when David became king, the Lindsays sat as barons in the Scottish parliaments from 1147.

William de Lindsay, Baron of Luffness held huge estates in Crawford, Clydesdale, as well as the Highland district of Glenesk (through his marriage to the heiress of the Stirlings of Edzell) and around two-thirds of the whole county of Angus! This land would soon become known as the Land of the Lindsays. His son, Sir David, was the ancestor of the Lindsay barons of Lamberton in Berwickshire, and held lands in the Lake District, England. He gained the admiration of the English king, Richard II, at the tournament for the Feast of St George at London Bridge in 1390 and in 1398, and was created Earl of Crawford and Admiral of Scotland in 1403.

On her journey north to overthrow the powerful Gordons, Mary, Queen of Scots held a Privy Council at the Lindsay stronghold of Edzell Castle. Sir David Lindsay of Edzell, son of the 9th Earl of Crawford, built the mansion attached to the tower of the castle in 1580. In 1604, by now a judge and bearer of the title of Lord Edzell, he added the magnificent pleasure gardens laid out in heraldic designs and surrounded by garden walls that cunningly incorporated gun loops for defence in their design. Lord Edzell's son, David Lindsay of Edzell, later fell into disfavor at Court, however, when he accidentally killed his uncle, Lord Spynie. Edzell became a Covenanter and, by 1645, the Glenesk lands had been ravaged. In 1715, David Lindsay of Edzell, last Baron of Glenesk was obliged to sell the highland estates to pay off debts. The title of Earl of Lindsay, however, remained in the family until the 19th century, when it passed to Alexander, 6th Earl of Balcarres, 23rd Earl of Crawford.

The Lindsays of Balcarres were descended from a younger son, the 9th Earl of Crawford. They earned an earldom for supporting Charles I during the Civil War and the Lindsay chiefs are now styled as earls of Crawford and Balcarres. As well as being brave soldiers, the Lindsays also distinguished themselves in the arts and sciences: Lady Anne Lindsay, born around 1750, was the composer of the song "Auld Robin Gray". The 26th Earl was President of the Royal Astronomical Society who gave his observatory at Dunnecht in Aberdeenshire to the nation.

The Lindsay tartan is instantly recognizable by its rich crimson color. The tartan first appeared in 1842, in *The Vestiarium Scoticum* and its scheme is like the Stewart of Atholl except that the black in this tartan is rendered in the Lindsay tartan in dark blue.

Surnames with possible associations: Cobb, Deuchar, Downie, Summers

# Livingstone

Earliest known date: unknown
Earliest source: D.C. Stewart, 1950
Tartan type: Symmetrical
Sett: **R**16 G4 R40 G32 R8 Bk2 R4 Bk2 R8 **G**24
Clan crest: A demi savage, wreathed abouth the head and middle with laurel, on his dexter shoulder a club, in his sinister hand a serpent nowed all Proper.
Clan motto: *Si je puis* ("If I can")

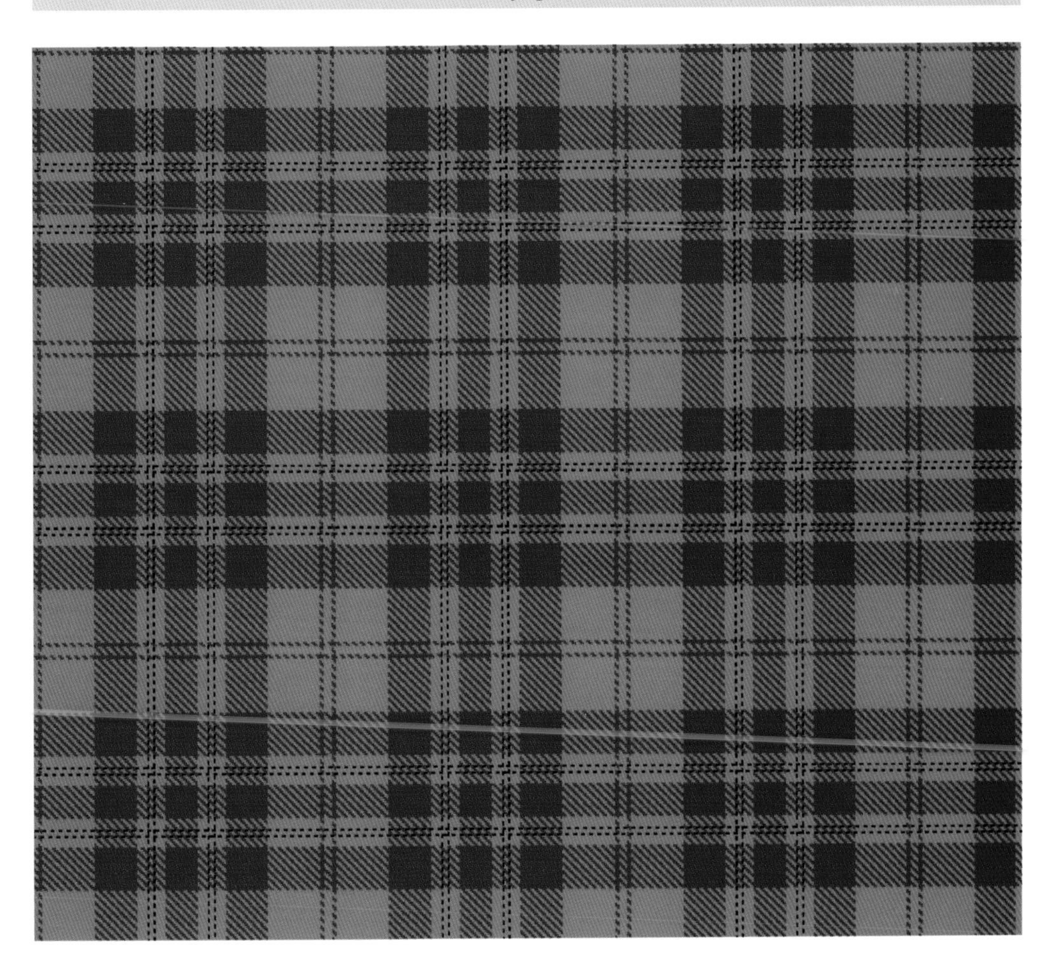

The Lowland house of Livingstone probably derived its name from their lands of Leving's-ton in West Lothian. A Saxon called Leving or Leuing settled in Scotland during the reign of Edgar (1097–1107) and his grandson is named in a charter of William the Lion (1165–1214) as Livingstone. Sir Archibald de Livingstone swore fealty to Edward I in 1296, and his grandson, Sir William, accompanied David II on his invasion of England in 1346 but was taken prisoner at Durham. For his part in negotiating the release of the Scottish king, Sir William was granted the barony of Callendar, in Stirlingshire. Sir Alexander Livingstone of Callender, who died about 1450, was one of the guardians of the infant king James II – a post he extorted from the king's mother while she was his virtual prisoner at Stirling Castle! In the 1440s the Livingstones were also responsible for persuading the Earl of Douglas and his brother to Edinburgh Castle on the grounds of a possible reconciliation. Instead, the Douglases were seized and executed, but in revenge, Sir Alexander Livingstone was imprisoned and one of his younger sons was killed. Sir James Livingstone, his eldest son, was raised to the peerage as Lord Livingstone in 1458. However, when he died in *c.*1467, the title passed to his nephew, John.

The 5th Lord Livingstone was one of the guardians of Mary, Queen of Scots during her childhood. He accompanied the young queen to France where he died. He was succeeded by his son William, also a fierce supporter of Mary, who fought for her at the battle of Langside in 1568. His son, Alexander, 7th Lord Livingstone, was created Earl of Linlithgow in 1600. The family's loyalty to the crown in the Civil War led to their estates suffering at the hands of Cromwell's forces. Later, as punishment for their support of the Jacobite cause and for their part in the 1715 Rising, the titles were forfeited.

The "Highland Livingstones" have a different origin: called in Gaelic Mac-an-leigh meaning "son of the physician", from which we get the surname MacLeay. The Mac-an-leighs of Appin, who took the Anglicized version of the name, styled themselves the Barons of Bachuil. They are the keepers of the *bacalum*, or pastoral staff of St Molaug (d.592), known as the *Bachuil Mor* or Great Staff. At Hogmany the barons filled a vessel with spring water, which was then stirred with the holy relic. The water was decanted into bottles and distributed to Livingstone relatives in the belief that it would guard against misfortunes in the coming year. The famous missionary and African explorer, Dr David Livingstone was descended from this branch.

*Livingstone/MacLay*

The origins of the Livingstone tartan are unknown: the early texts such as *The Vestiarium Scoticum* make no mention of it. It is similar to the Stewart of Appin tartan (page 244) with whom the Livingstones were associated, and, there is also an alternative Livingstone/MacLeay tartan which is a variation on the MacLaine of Lochbuie sett (page 171).

# Logan (or MacLennan)

Earliest known date: 1831
Earliest source: Logan, 1831
Tartan type: Symmetrical
Sett: **Y**4 Bk2 R2 G32 Bk24 B32 R4 B4 R4 B6 **R**12
Clan crest: A demi-piper all proper, garbed in the tartan of the Clan MacLennan
Clan motto: *Dum spiro spero* ("While I breathe I hope")
Badge: *Conasg* (Furze)

Modern scholars maintain that Logan (or possibly Lobban) was an alternative name for MacLennan, rather than a separate clan which shared a tartan. Lobban is a Morayshire name: one William Lobane appears in 1564 as a tenant in Drumderfit.

The MacLennans were at one time numerous in Kintail, Ross-shire. At the battle of Auldern in 1645, Ruaridh – the six-foot tall, red-bearded MacLennan chief – was killed fighting to the last as part of the Earl of Seaforth's Covenanter force. The traditional (and more colorful) account of the origin of the connection between Logan and MacLennan begins with a feud between the Frasers and Logans, with the latter defeated at the battle of Drumderfit, near Kessock Ferry. Their leader, Gilligorm Logan, was killed in battle and his pregnant wife carried off by the Frasers. (A wooden effigy of Gilligorm taken from his tomb was preserved in the House of Drumderfit until it was destroyed by fire after the Rising of 1715.) Gilligorm's posthumous son was born among the Frasers and it is said his back was broken to stop him growing up strong and avenging his father's death. This son was called Crotair MacGilligorm (the "Hump-backed son of Gilligorm"). He took Holy Orders and moved to the West Coast where he built churches at Kilmuir in Skye and in Glenelg. Following ancient Celtic practice (rather than the decree from Rome making priests celibate) Crotair married and had a son called Gille Fhinnein or "Follower of St Finnan". His descendants were said to take this new name, which eventually became known as MacLennan.

James Logan first described the Logan/MacLennan tartan in 1831 and in the 19th century, Wilson and Sons of Bannockburn produced a range of popular Logan tartans including "Dark" (black in place of blue), "Light" (with pink stripes) and with a yellow stripe. The Logans also have a second tartan, which has also been known as "Skene" and "Rose".

Surnames with possible associations: Loban, Lobban

# MacAlister

Earliest known date: 1816

Earliest source: Smith, 1850

Tartan type: Symmetrical

Sett: **R**16 LG2 DG4 R4 Az2 R2 W2 R2 Az2 R4 DG6 R2 W2 R12 Az2 R2 DG24 R2 Az2 R32 Az2 R2 DG24 R2 Az2 R12 W2 R2 B8 R2 W2 R4 DG6 LG2 R4 LG2 DG6 R6 W2 R2 B4 R2 W2 **R**16

Clan crest: A dexter arm in armour erect, the hand holding a dagger in pale all Proper

Clan motto: *Fortiter* ("Boldly")

Badge: *Fraoch gorm* (Common heath)

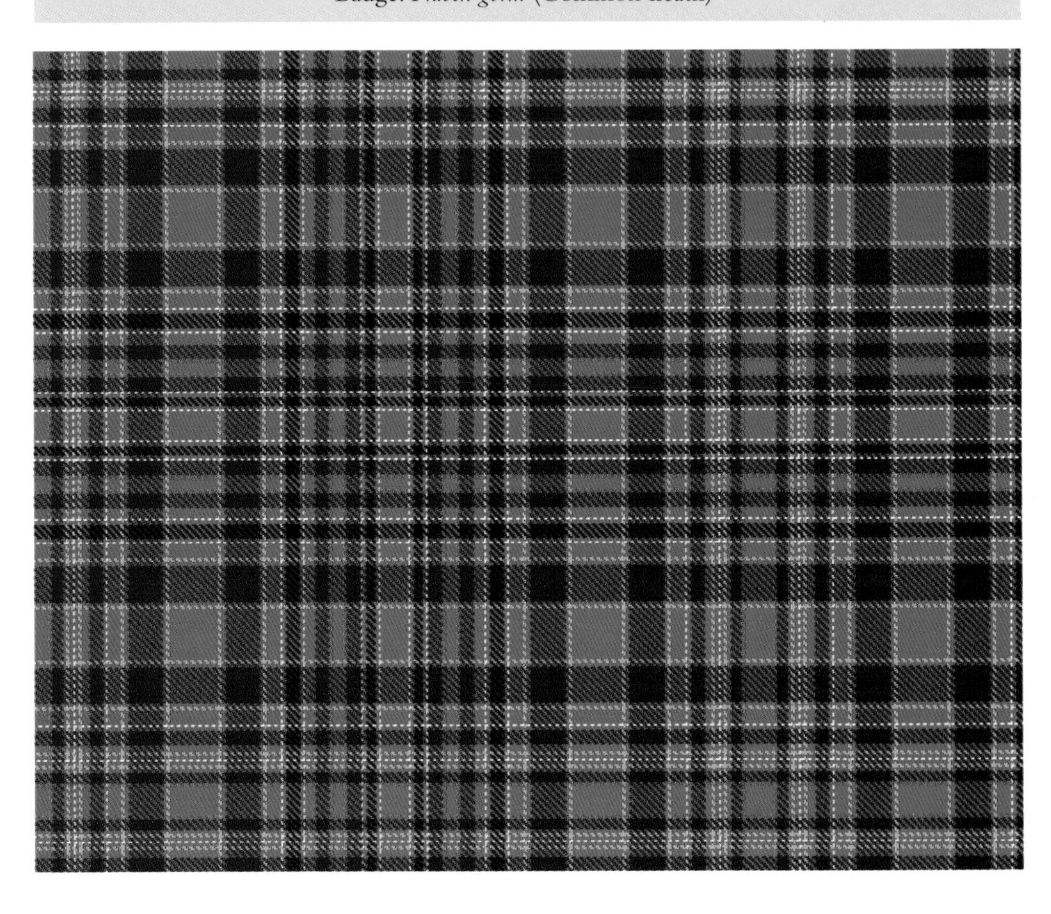

MacAlister means "Son of Alasdair" (the Gaelic for "Alexander"). Although there is doubt as to the exact origins of this clan, the accepted view is that it branched off from the main Clan Donald stem in the early 13th century and that they are descended from Alasdair Mor, second son of Donald, Lord of the Isles and the younger brother of Angus Mor.

Alasdair Mor was slain in battle in 1299 against Alasdair MacDougall, Lord of Lorn. In 1366, Ranald, son of Alexander appears as chief of the Clan Alister with residence in Kintyre. Around this time, the MacAlisters were also in Stirlingshire and, in subsequent centuries, their surname became anglicized into the Lowland version "Alexander". By the 16th century, they held the lands of Menstrie; these Alexanders became viscounts in 163) and the earls of Stirling (from 1633 to 1739) as well as viscounts of Canada. From this branch of the MacAlisters, the Alexander earls of Caledon claim descent.

Charles MacAlister was appointed Steward of Kintyre by James III in 1481 and at the same time received a grant of lands in the area. Charles was succeeded by his son John, who styled himself as John of Lowb. Lowb – now rendered as Loup – is derived from the Gaelic *lub*, meaning a curve or a bend, and describes the shoreline which bounded the clan lands. During the 15th and 16th centuries, members of the clan obtained lands in Bute and Arran where their descendant continue to live. Nevertheless, although the Clan MacAlister were influential, they were not as numerous as other clans and therefore, to secure their position and territory, they were obliged to enter alliances with other clans and families. Consequently, in the second half of the 16th century, a new branch of Clan MacAlister, the Tarberts came into existence. (A *tarbert* or drawboat, is a place where the Vikings dragged boats across land on rollers. This particular tarbert, between the Loup and Loch Fyne, had been secured by King Magnus Bare-Legs of Norway in 1093. He agreed with King Malcolm Creann-mor of Scotland that, while the mainland was Scottish, the test of what were Norwegian lands was whether a ship with its rudder in position could sail around it. Magnus craftily "won" the Kintyre peninsula by having his own boat dragged across dry land – with himself at the helm!)

In 1591, Godfrey MacAlister of Loup received a charter from the Earl of Argyll making the heads of this house the hereditary Constables of Tarbert Castle. In 1602, Archibald MacAlister, heir to Tarbert, was denounced as a rebel after leading a raid on the island of Bute. Found guilty of treason, Archibald was sent to the Tollbooth prison in Edinburgh and was hanged. Eventually the Kintyre estates were sold off and today, Glenbarr Abbey is the Clan MacAlasdair center.

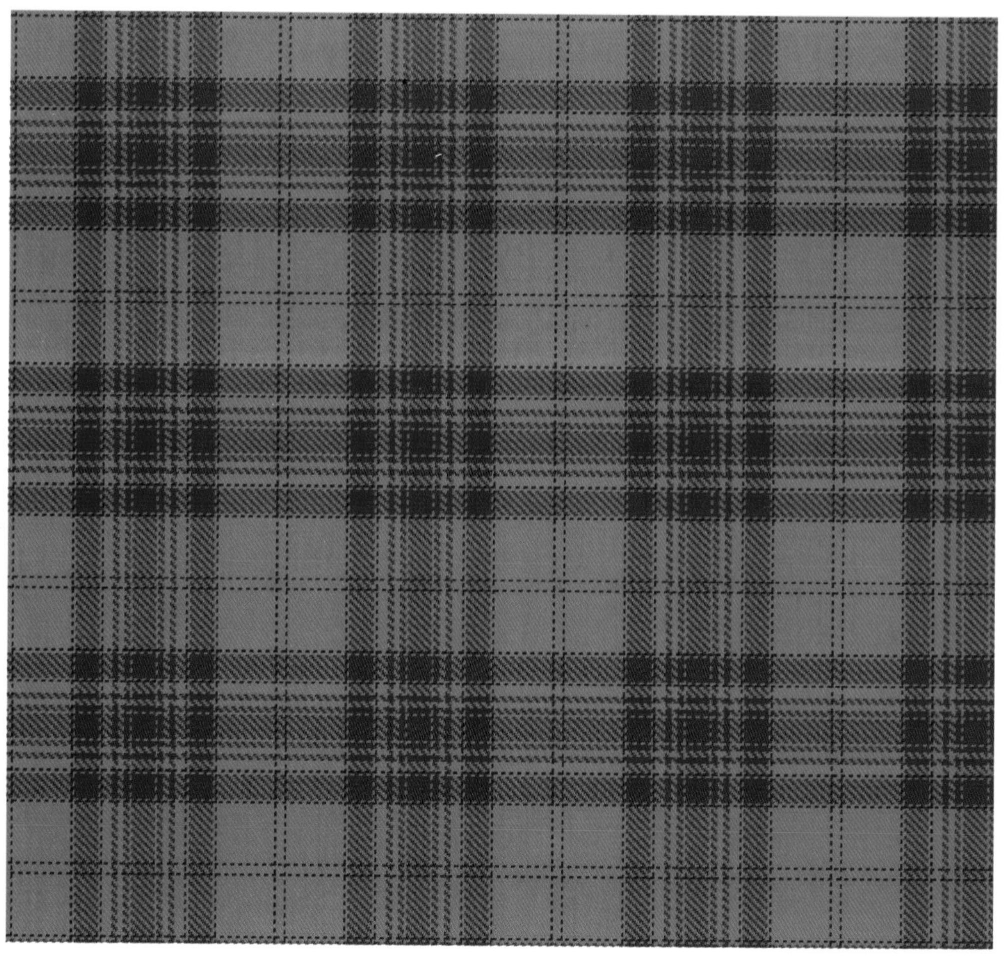

*MacAlister of Glenbarr*

A version of the MacAlister tartan similar to this – with its complex sett – was certified by the MacAlister chief in 1816. It belongs to the MacDonald group of tartans, and resembles the MacDonald of Staffa tartan – which corresponds to the ancient heritage of the MacAlisters. A second tartan, the MacAlister of Glenbarr Clan Tartan, has been adopted by MacAlister Societies in the USA and Australia.

Surnames with possible associations: Alexander, Allison, Saunders

# MacArthur

Earliest known date: 1842

Earliest source: *The Vestiarium Scoticum*, 1842

Tartan type: Symmetrical

Sett: **Y**6 G60 Bk24 G12 **Bk**64

Clan crest: Two laurel branches in orle Porper

Clan motto: *Fide et opera* ("Fidelity and labor")

Badge: Roid (Wild myrtle) and *Garbhag an t-sleibhe* (Fir Club moss)

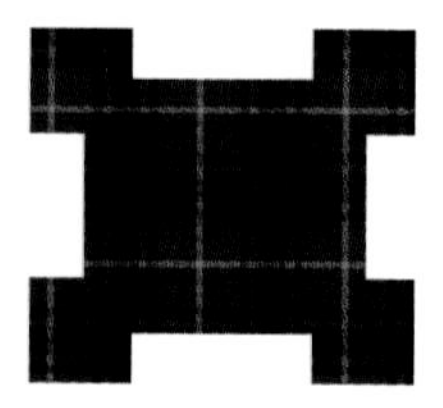

One of the oldest clans in Argyll, the Clan MacArthur, or *Clann Artair-na-tir-a-chladich-ile* (Clan Arthur of the shore-land) had their lands on the shores of Loch Awe, which they had held since Celtic times. Staunch supporters of Robert the Bruce in the struggle for an independent Scotland, their chief Mac-ic-Artair (Son of Arthur) was rewarded with grants of lands that had been forfeited by the MacDougalls who had opposed Bruce. A century later, however, the influential position and the lands held by the MacArthurs were lost when the chief Iain MacArthur of Tirracladich was beheaded for treason by James I in 1427. While these MacArthurs were never to recover their power, their descendants dispersed. Some of the MacArthurs settled on Skye where they established a famous piping school and became hereditary pipers to the MacDonalds of Sleate. Another branch of the clan, the MacArthurs of Proiag, became armorers to the MacDonalds of Islay.

The Clan MacArthur does not, at present, have a chief: chiefship is deemed to lie in the line of the MacArthurs of Proaig in Islay. Instead, the Lord Lyon appointed James MacArthur of Milton at Dunoon as commander of the clan in 1991. Many of the MacArthurs of Milton – several of whom fought on both sides during the Jacobite risings – left Scotland after the battle of Culloden in 1746. Some settled in the West Indies, others in Australia, Canada, and the USA. John MacArthur helped to establish the woollen industry in Australia by cross-breeding Irish and Bengal sheep and later introducing Merino sheep from South Africa. One MacArthur emigrated from Glasgow and arrived in America in 1840. His son, Arthur MacArthur, was a lieutenant general in the Union Army during the Civil War, while his grandson was surely the most famous "son of Arthur", General Douglas MacArthur, the US military commander in the Pacific during World War II. Because of their links with the MacDonalds, the MacArthur Clan tartan shares the same basic form as the MacDonald Lord of the Isles sett (page 133). The tartan was first recorded in 1842 in *The Vestiarium Scoticum*.

Surnames with possible associations: Arthur

# MacAulay

Earliest known date: 1886
Earliest source: Grant, 1886
Tartan type: Symmetrical
Sett: **Bk**4 R32 G12 R6 G16 **W**2
Clan crest: A boot couped at the ankle thereon a spur Proper
Clan motto: *Dulce ericulum* ("Danger is sweet")
Badge: *Muileag* (Cranberry) and *Giuths* (Pine tree)

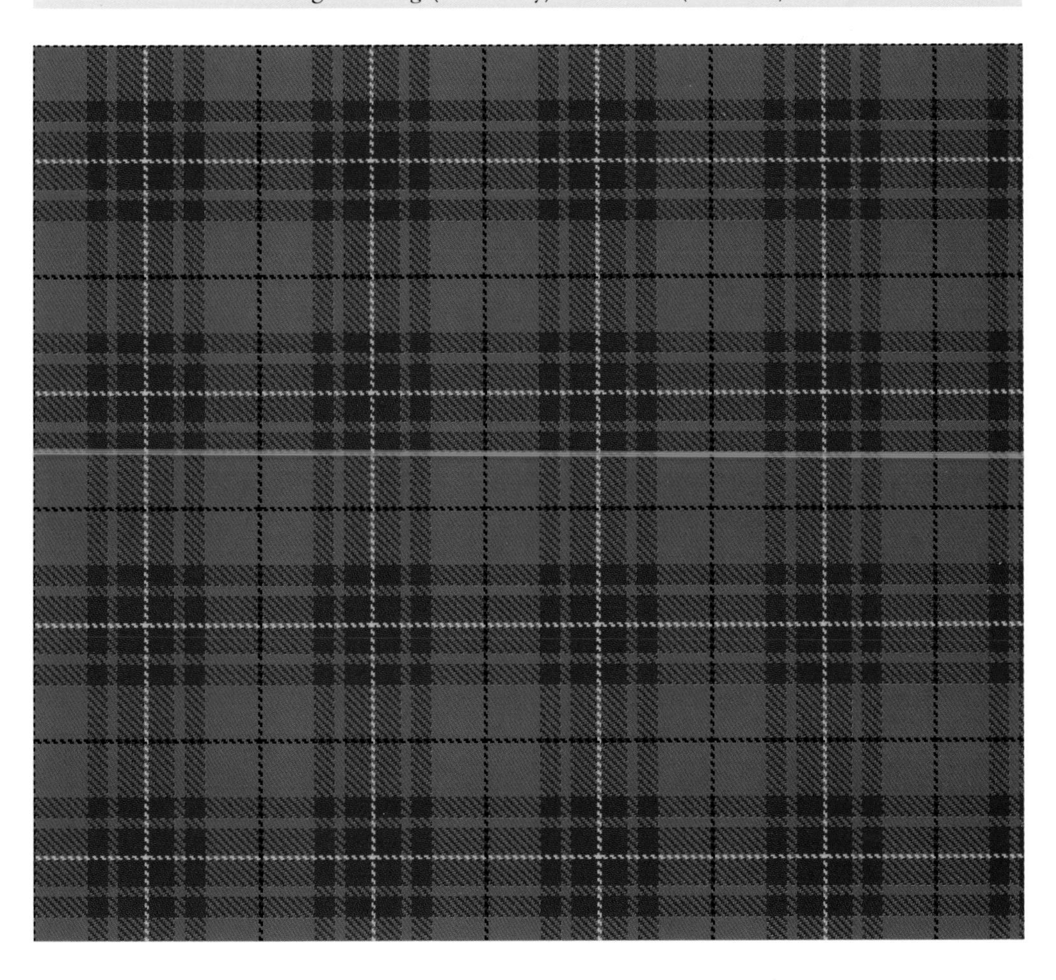

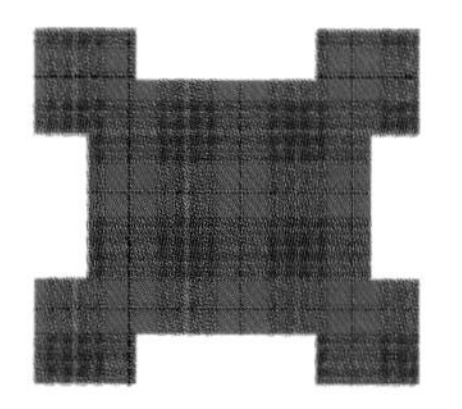

There have been two clans which shared the name MacAulay: the MacAulays of Ardincaple in Dunbartonshire and the MacAulays of Lewis, but there is no connection between the two. The MacAulays of Ardincaple are often said to be the descendants of Siol Alpin (from whom the MacGregors also descend). Others maintain that these MacAulays stemmed from Amalghaidh, a younger son of the Earl of Lennox. In 1587, Sir Aulay MacAulay of Ardincaple appeared in the Roll of Landlords and Baillies in the Highlands and Isles as one of the principal vassals of the Earl of Lennox: whether blood relations or not, the MacGregors and MacAulays were closely connected. In 1591, in a bond between the two families, MacAulay acknowledged MacGregor of Glen Strae as his superior and agreed to pay tributes in cattle. Yet, the MacAulays were quick to denounce any relationship with the MacGregors when the latter family was declared outlaw and, in 1610, the Laird of Ardincaple pledged a surety for the good behavior of his clan. The fortunes of the clan, however went into decline and the last portions of the clan lands passed out of the hand of the 12th chief in 1767, when Ardincaple was sold to the Duke of Argyll.

The MacAulays of Lewis claim Norse descent as their name means simply "son of Olaf". The first recorded MacAulay of Lewis was Donald Cam (Donald One-Eye) in 1610. His son, Angus of Brenish, fought for Charles I in the Civil War and was killed at the battle of Auldearn in 1645. He was succeeded by his son Dugald Fear Bhrenis and from him was descended Thomas, Lord Macaulay [*sic*], the politician, poet, essayist, and historian whose most well known works are *A History of England* and *Lays of Ancient Rome*. A Member of Parliament from 1830–56, Macaulay was raised to the peerage in 1857.

The MacAulay tartan is close in design to the MacGregor tartan (page 151). Logan first recorded a MacAulay tartan and his description was of a complete repeat of the design. In 1881, a shorter version, shown here, was published by C.N. M'Intyre North in *Book of the Club of True Highlanders*, the count for which was evidently given to him by Logan. However, it could be that the difference in the "long" and "short" versions of four lines of color was simply because of an error, overlooked during copying. But because the shortened version resembles the MacGregor tartan (with whom the MacAulays of Ardincaple had links), the design was adopted as the clan tartan.

Surnames with possible associations: MacPhedron, MacPheidiran

# MacCallum (Malcolm)

Earliest date: c.1893 (MacCallum) 1850 (Malcolm)
Earliest source: D.W. Stewart, 1893 (MacCallum); Smith, 1850 (Malcolm)
Tartan type: MacCallum: Symmetrical Malcolm: Assymetrical
Sett: MacCallum **Bk**2 B12 Bk12 G8 Az2 Bk4 **G**16
Malcolm: B2 R2 B12 Bk12 G12 Bk2 Y2 Az2 Bk2 G12 Bk12 B12 R2
Clan crest A tower Argent, window and port Azure
Clan motto: *In ardua tendit* ("He attempted difficult things")
Badge: Rowan (Mountain Ash) berries.

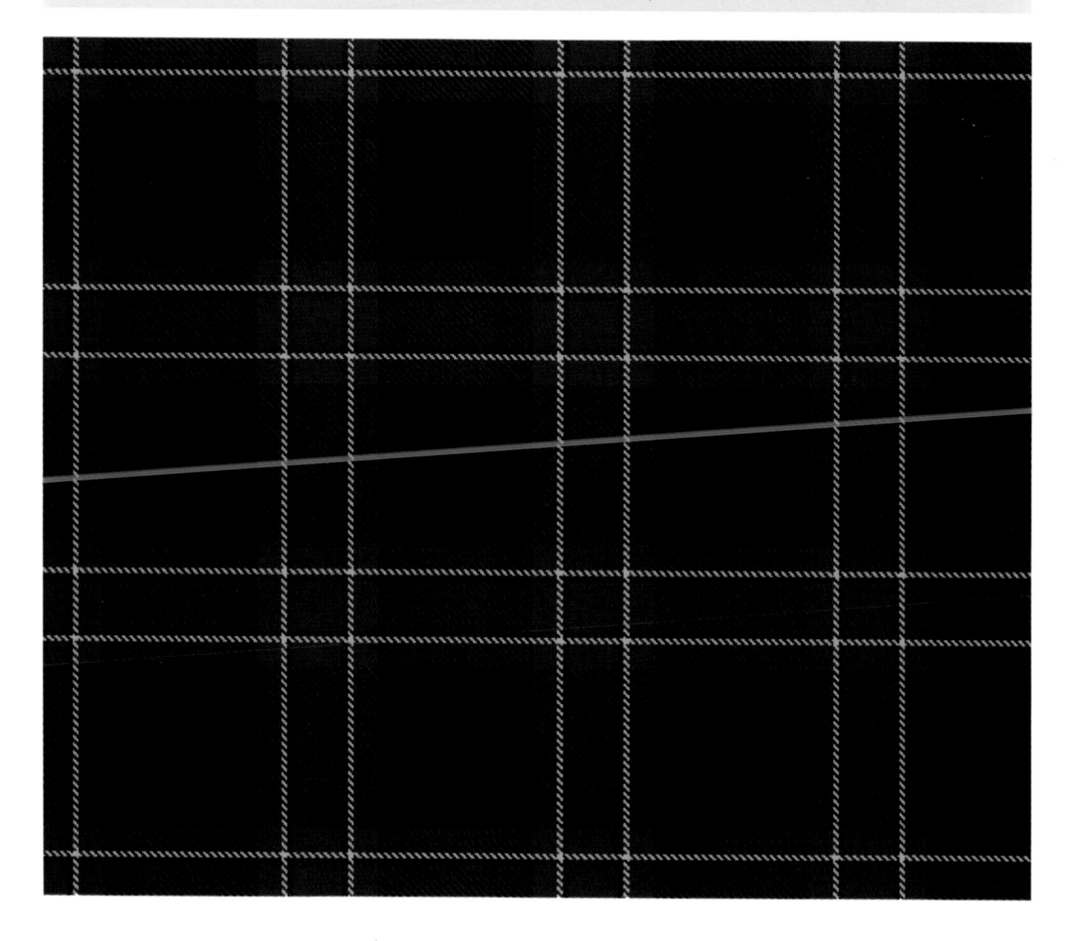

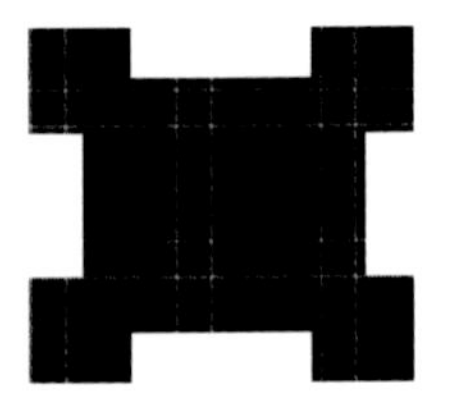

The MacCallums derive their name from *Mac Ghille Chaluim* or "son of the follower of Columba" and is often Anglicized as Malcolm, which itself is derived from the Gaelic *Maol Chaluim*. Maol means "shaven-head" – synonymous for "monk" so the name also means a follower of St Columba. The clan settled in Lorn, Argyllshire with the clan headquarters at Colgin, a few miles from Oban. Legend states that three sons of the chief family of Colgin decided to leave home, so their father prepared horses with panniers for each of them. Each of the sons was sent on his way and told to set up home on the spot where his panniers fells from his horse. One son's panniers fell off before he had even left his father's land so he remained at home. Another's fell at Glenetive, while the third brother's fell off at Kilmartin, Argyllshire. In reality, Ronald MacCallum of Corbarron was made Constable of Craignish Castle in 1414, while Donald MacGilespie Vich O'Challum received a charter for the lands of Portalloch in Kilmartin from Duncan Campbell of Duntrune in 1562 and eventually the MacCallums acquired Duntrune Castle itself, which today remains the clan chief's seat. Zachary, the 5th Laird of Portalloch also inherited the estates of Corbarron.

Over the years the name MacCallum became anglicized as Malcolm. However, in 1770, the name Malcolm – as distinct from MacCallum – was established when Dugald MacCallum, 9th chief of Portalloch changed the family name to Malcolm for, it is said, "aesthetic reasons". John Malcolm, 15th Laird of Portalloch who succeeded 1893 was created Baron Malcolm of Portalloch in 1896, but the title became extinct when he died without an heir. The chiefship passed first to his brother Edward, and then to his nephew Sir Ian Zachary Malcolm, 17th Laird. He was married to Jeanne Langtry, the daughter of the famous actress Lillie Langtry.

Although the name Malcolm is a "variation" on the MacCallum name, it is now usual practice to distinguish the MacCallum and the Malcolm tartans. Sir Iain approved the "old" MacCallum tartan described by D.W. Stewart in 1893. According to Stewart, the family had lost trace of the original sett: the tartan was "recreated" from the various (and varying) memories and accounts of elderly inhabitants in Argyllshire. A second tartan, the Malcolm, was recorded in 1850 by the Smiths. This is asymmetrical containing a light blue line followed by a yellow line always in the same order.

Surnames with possible associations: Malcolmson

# MacDonald

Eariest known date: *c.*1810–20
Earliest source: Cockburn Collection, 1810–20
Tartan type: Symmetrical
Sett: **G**16 R2 G4 R6 G24 Bk24 R2 B24 R6 B4 R2 **B**16
Clan crest: On a crest coronet Or, a hand in armour fessways couped at the elbow Proper holding a cross crosslet fitchee Gules
Clan motto: *Per mare per terras* ("By sea and by land")
Badge: Heather

The oldest and the most famous of all the Scottish clans, the Clan MacDonald derives its name from its ancestor, Donald of Islay, whose grandfather, Ranald mac Somerled, was King of the Isles and Lord of Argyll and Kintyre from 1164 to 1207. When Somerled died, his vast kingdom was divided between his sons: Dugall got Lorne, Mull and Jura; Angus received Arran, Bute and Garmoran; Reginald – Donald of Islay's father – received Islay and Kintyre. Each successive Lord of the Isles descended from Donald would bear the Gaelic title *Mac Dhomhnuill* "the Son of Donald", but MacDonald was not used as an ordinary surname by the family or their clansmen until the 16th century. The earlier surname "of the Isles" or even simply "Isles" was used, while cadets were called by their patronymic or even by their nickname. Nevertheless, all would refer to themselves as a *Domhnullach* – "one of the Clan Donald".

When Donald died sometime around 1269, he was succeeded by Angus Mor who, with his uncle Ruari, fought alongside Alexander III against Norway over the sovereignty of the Hebrides. Angus's son, Angus Og, supported Robert the Bruce and led his clansmen at the battle of Bannockburn in 1314. Og was rewarded with grants of lands in the west Highlands and Islands where he maintained an independent principality. He was succeeded by his son John "the Good" of Islay, who, from 1353, assumed the title Lord of the Isles. His first marriage to Amy MacRuairdh produced a son, Ranald, who became the ancestor of the Clanranalds (page 128), while a second marriage to Princess Margaret, daughter of Robert II, gave another son Donald, who became Lord of the Isles and Chief of the Clan Donald.

The power of the MacDonalds reached its peak under John, 10th Lord of the Isles and Earl

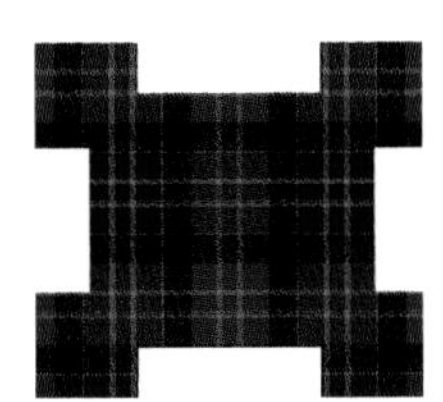

of Ross. He entered the Treaty of Ardtonish with Henry VI of England in 1462, agreeing to accept the English king as sovereign once James IV was defeated. James invaded the isles in 1463 and stripped John of his titles.

The Clan Donald was then divided into more or less independent branches: Clanranald, Sleate, the earls of Antrim, the MacIains of Ardnamurchan, the MacDonalds of Glencoe, the MacDonalds of Dunnyveg and the Glens, and the MacDonnells of Glenagarry and of Keppoch. These branches were regarded as separate clans until 1660, when Charles II restored the Name and Chiefship to Aeneas MacDonald of Glengarry with succession limited to his male heirs. This line expired in 1680, and soon afterwards Sir James MacDonald of Sleate on Skye, was recognized by Parliament as Laird of MacDonald. The lands were later erected into barony and the MacDonalds were made lords (1776). The 3rd Lord MacDonald settled the chiefship and peerage on his younger son and a private Act of Parliament in 1847 confirmed the succession. For decades, a dispute over the legitimacy of this succession raged between the Lords MacDonald and the MacDonalds of Sleate (see page 131). It was finally settled in 1947, when the Lord Lyon recognized Alexander Godfrey (formerly of Sleate) as 7th Lord MacDonald of MacDonald, High Chief of the Name and of all Clan Donald.

Surnames with possible associations: Alexander, Allan, Allanson, Balloch, Beath, Begg, Bowie, Burk, Colson, Connall, Connell, Coull, Coulson, Crombie, Crum, Donaldson, Donillson, Galt, Gilbride, Gill, Gorrie, Gowan, Gowrie, Hawthorn, Hewitson, Hewitt, Howison, Hudson, Hutchenson, Hutcheson, Hutchinson, Hutchison, Isles, Jeffrey, Kean, Keene, Kellie, Kinnell, Leitch, MacAchaillis, MacAllan, MacBeath, MacBurie, MacCaishe, MacCall, MacCaul, MacCluskie, MacCodrum, MacConnell, MacCook, MacCosram, MacCrain, MacCrindle, MacCririe, MacCuish, MacCutcheon, MacDaniell, MacDrain, MacEachern, MacElheran, MacGill, MacGillivantic, MacGorrie, MacGorry, MacGoun, MacGowan, MacHugh, MacHutcheon, MacIleach, MacIlrevie, MacIlwraith, MacKeachan, MacKellaachie, MacKellaig, MacKelloch, MacKiggan, MacKillop, MacKinnell, MacLairish, MacLardie, MacLarty, MacLaverty, MacLeverty, MacPhillip, MacQuistan, MacRorie, MacRory, MacRuer, MacRurie, MacRury, MacSwan, MacSween, MacWhannell, Mark, Martin, My, Murdoch, Murdoson, Norie, Park, Paton, Philipson, Purcell, Revie, Ronald, Ronaldson, Rorison, Sanderson, Shannon, Sporran, Whannell, Wheelan, Wilkie, Wilkinson

# MacDonald of Clanranald

Earliest known date: 1816

Earliest source: Wilson, 1819

Tarta type: Symmetrical

Sett: **G**16 R2 G4 R6 G24 W2 Bk24 R2 B24 R6 B4 R2 **B**16

Clan crest: A triple-towered castle Argent, masoned Sable, and issuing from the center tower a dexter arm in armour embowed grasping a sword all Proper

Clan motto: "My hope is constant in thee"

Badge: *Fraoch* (Common heath)

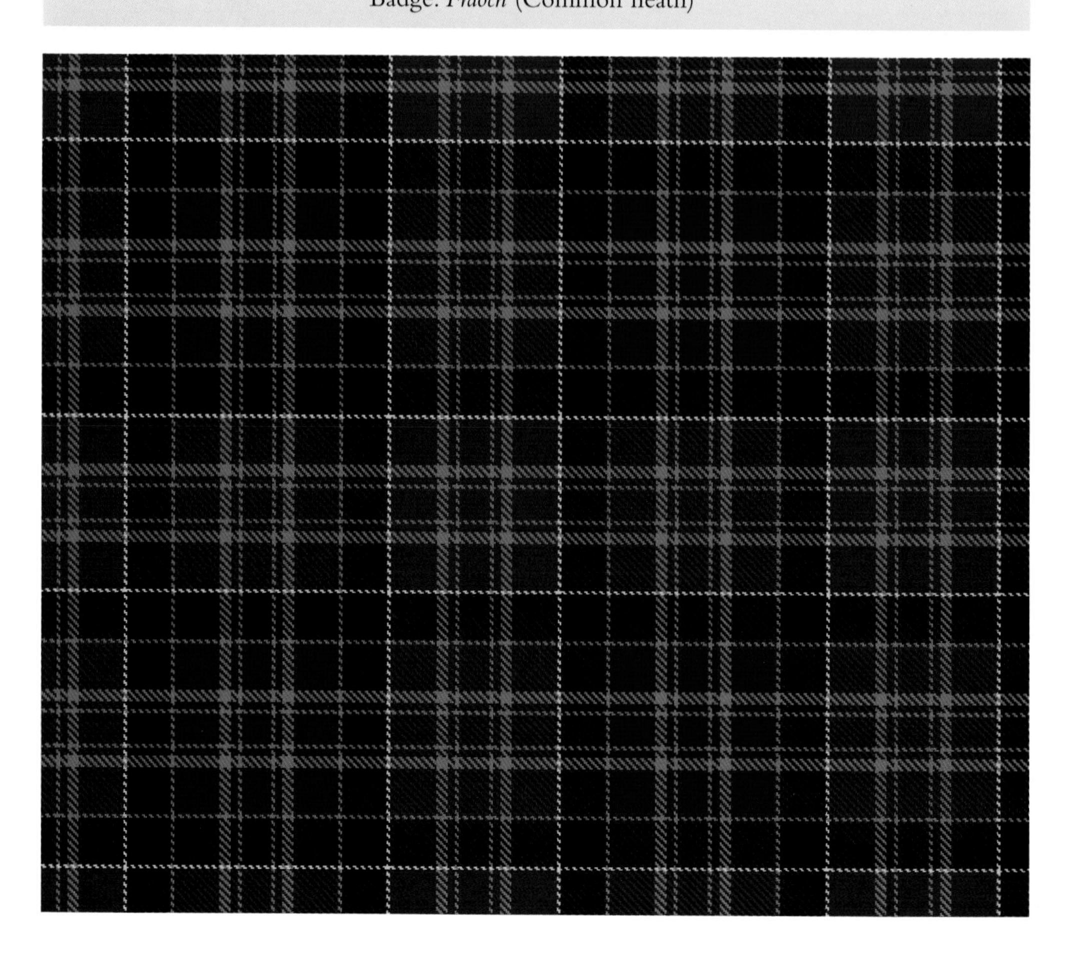

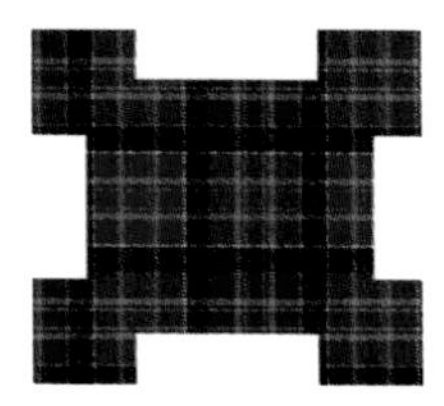

By his first marriage to Amy MacRuairidh, John, the 7th Lord of the Isles, had a son called Ranald, and from him both the Houses of Glengarry and of Clanranald are descended. Although Ranald was technically the eldest and should have succeeded his father as Lord of the Isles, this title was passed to his younger half brother Donald, who was born to John's second wife, the Stewart Princess Margaret. In return for being passed over as chief, Ranald was given the greater part of the MacRuarirdh inheritance brought into the family by his mother.

Ranald himself had five sons: Allan of Clanranald; Donald, who founded the line of Glengarry; Alasdair Crarrach "The Warty"; Angus of Morar, and, Dugall of Sunart. The 6th Chief of Clanranald, Dugall, was evidently such a cruel man that he was killed by his own clanspeople. He was succeeded by his uncle, Alistair Allanson, who died in 1530, and his son, John of Moydart, who styled himself Mac Mhic Ailein, was then invested as chief at the family seat of Castle Tirrim. When James V annulled all the charters given to clan chiefs, John led his clan in open rebellion and was imprisoned by the king. A power struggle bagan as John's right to the chiefship and the estates was challenged by Ranald Gallda, the son of Alan MacRuairidh, the 5th Chief of Clanranald (1481–1509). When James V died in 1542, the Earl of Arran, acting as Regent for Mary, Queen of Scots, released the imprisoned chief – part of Arran's ploy to counter the power of the Duke of Argyll. The struggle ended at the battle of Blarnaleine in 1544 where Ranald fell. John was later recognized by the Crown as the rightful Chief of Clanranald. After his death in 1584, he was succeeded by his son Alan, whose own son, Donald, the 10th Chief, was knighted by James VI.

John, the 11th of Clanranald was a firm supporter of Charles I and played a part in Montrose's victory at Inverlochy in 1645. Alan, 13th of Clanranald, supported the Jacobite cause. He was made Lord Clanranald, but was killed in battle at Sheriffmuir in 1715, and the chiefship passed to his brother Ranald who was forced to spend most of his life in exile in France. He died at the Jacobite Court at St Germain in Paris in 1725, and the succession passed to his cousin Donald, 15th of Clanranald. It was his grandson Ranald, the 17th, known as "Young Clanranald" who led the clan out in support of Bonnie Prince Charlie, but after Culloden he was forced to flee to France. He returned to Scotland in 1754, and the line of succession continued through him until 1944 when the chiefship or captaincy passed to the heirs of Alexander of Boisdale, a younger brother of the "Young Clanranald".

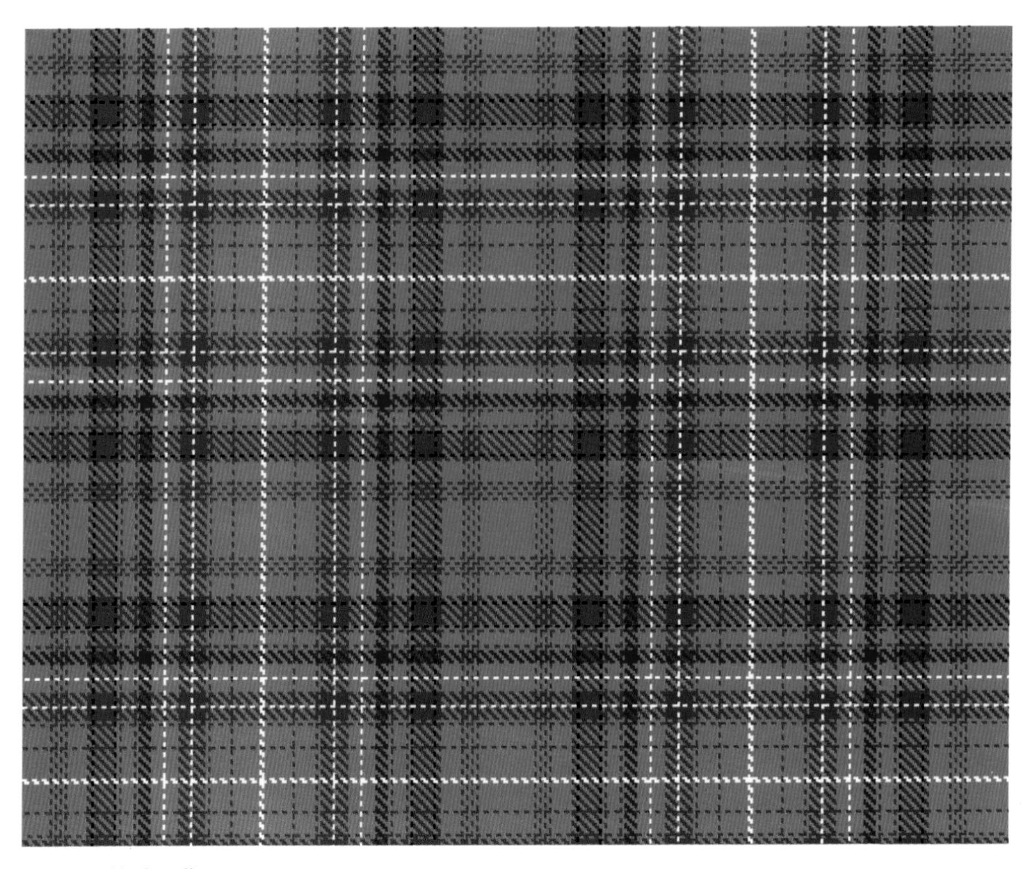

*MacDonald of Staffa*

There is a certified example of the Clanranald tartan in the Collection of the Highland Society, which dates from around 1816. It was later described by the Smith brothers in 1850 as a Clan MacDonald tartan with the addition of the two white stripes. Until recently, the various branches of the Clan Donald were regarded as independent clans in their own right. Clanranald maintains its own chief and its own tartan, but there are other branches associated with the MacDonalds. The MacDonalds of Staffa, who also have a clan tartan, are in fact, a cadet branch (a family descended from the younger sons or daughters of an earlier chief) of the Clanranald.

Surnames with possible associations: MacEachen, MacEachin, MacGeachie, MacGeachin, MacKechnie, MacKeochan, MacKichan, MacMurrich, MacVarish, MacVurie

# MacDonald of Sleate

Earliest known date: 1750
Earliest source: Armadale Castle portrait
Tartan type: Symmetrical
Sett: Original count: **Bk**4 R36 G4 R10 **G**32
Clan crest: A hand in armour fesswise holding cross crosslet fitchee Gules
Clan motto: *Per mare per terras* ("By sea and by land")
Badge: *Fraoch* (Heath)

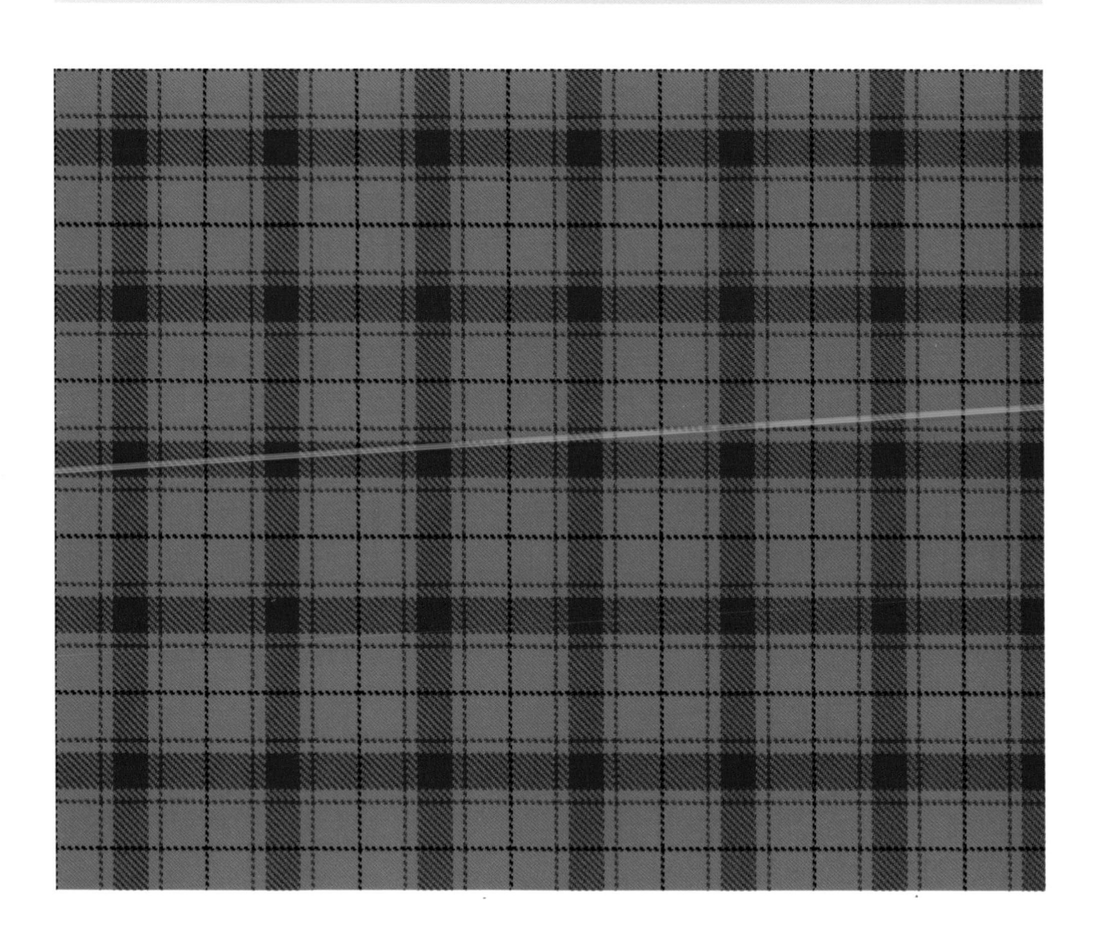

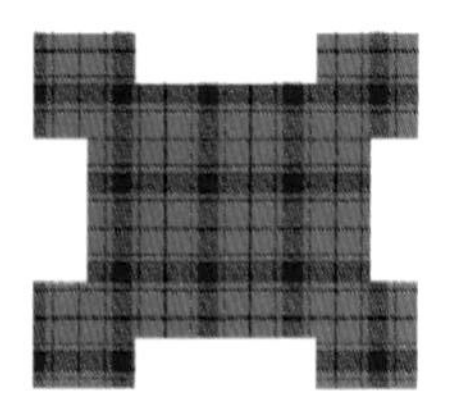

The MacDonalds of Sleate, one of the independent branches of the Clan Donald and with its own chief, are descended from Usidein, or Hugh, the younger son of Alexander, Earl of Ross and Lord of the Isles, who died in 1449. Known in Gaelic as *Clann Usidein*, or the "Children of Hugh", their earliest place of residence was the stronghold fort of Dunskaich, to the south of Sleate. Hugh, the 1st Chief of Sleate, married three times and was succeeded by his son John (d.1502). John was succeeded by his brother, Donald Gallach. Donald's mother was Elizabeth Gunn, the daughter of the Coroner of Caithness – "Gallach" means "native of Caithness", hence Donald's name.

Donald was murdered in 1506 by his half-brother, but was succeeded by his son Donald Grumach, who was proclaimed chief of all Clan Donald around 1518. He, in turn, was succeeded by his eldest son Donald Gorm. Donald Gorm attempted to restore the ancient Lordship of the Isles, which had been forfeited in 1495. He proclaimed himself Chief and Lord of the Isles and, in 1539, led his men in the siege against the Mackenzie's Eilandonan Castle in Kintail, which was being held by Duncan MacRae. With his troops under fire from the castle, Donald Gorm was shot in the leg by an arrow and died from his blood loss. The feud with the Mackenzies was not, however, ended until the Council of Perth in 1539.

Donald Gorm was succeeded by his son Donald, known as Domhnull Gorm Sasunnach, or "Son of Donald Gorm the Sasunnach" (southerner, or English) because he spent much of his early life across the border. His son and successor, Donald Gorm Mor was invited, along with his Clanranald kinsmen, to meet Lord Ochiltree, the king"s representative in 1608 to discuss the royal policy on the isles. The meeting was a trap and Donald Gorm Mor was imprisoned in Blackness Castle until he agreed to submit to the king's wishes. He died in 1616 without an heir and was succeeded by his nephew Sir Donald MacDonald, later 1st Baronet of Sleate and supporter of the royalist cause in the Civil War. Sir Donald, 4th Baronet Sleate, supported the Stewart cause and led his clansmen at Killicrankie and Sheriffmuir in 1715, but, despite his Jacobite sympathies, did not join in the 1745 Rising. Consequently, the Sleate estates were never forfeited.

Sir Alexander, 9th Baronet was created Lord MacDonald in 1796. His grandson, Godfrey, married Louisa, the daughter of the Duke of Gloucester (the brother of King George III). The only problem was that his marriage, while legal in Scotland, was not legally recognized in England until 1803! Consequently, Lord MacDonald's eldest son was legitimate in Scotland but illegitimate in England. It was decided that he should change his name to Bosville and he inherited his mother's vast estates. The second son, born after the marriage was recognized in England, would succeed to the Chiefship of Clan Donald and the peerage. This was formalized by a private Act of Parliament in 1847. However, in 1910, Alexander Bosville, grandson of Lord MacDonald's eldest son obtained a Declarator of Legitimacy confirming that his grandfather was, in fact, legitimate and that he was entitled to resume the name MacDonald (albeit Bosville-MacDonald) and the baronetcy of Sleate. He thus became 14th Baronet and Chief and Chief of the Family of MacDonald of Sleate, and the 22nd Chief of Clan Uisdein. Lord MacDonald remained Chief of the Name and the MacDonald of MacDonald.

The MacDonald of Sleate tartan was evidently manufactured early in the 19th century. It was called "MacDonald of Sleate, Lord of the Isles" by the Smiths in 1850, but it seems that this was an incorrectly rendered version of the MacDonald tartan that appears in a portrait at Armadale Castle. In this portrait, the tartan has a black line as shown here. This was omitted in *The Vestiarium Scoticum* in 1842, and it seems that, from then on, either by mistake or by design, it became customary to produce the tartan in red and green alone.

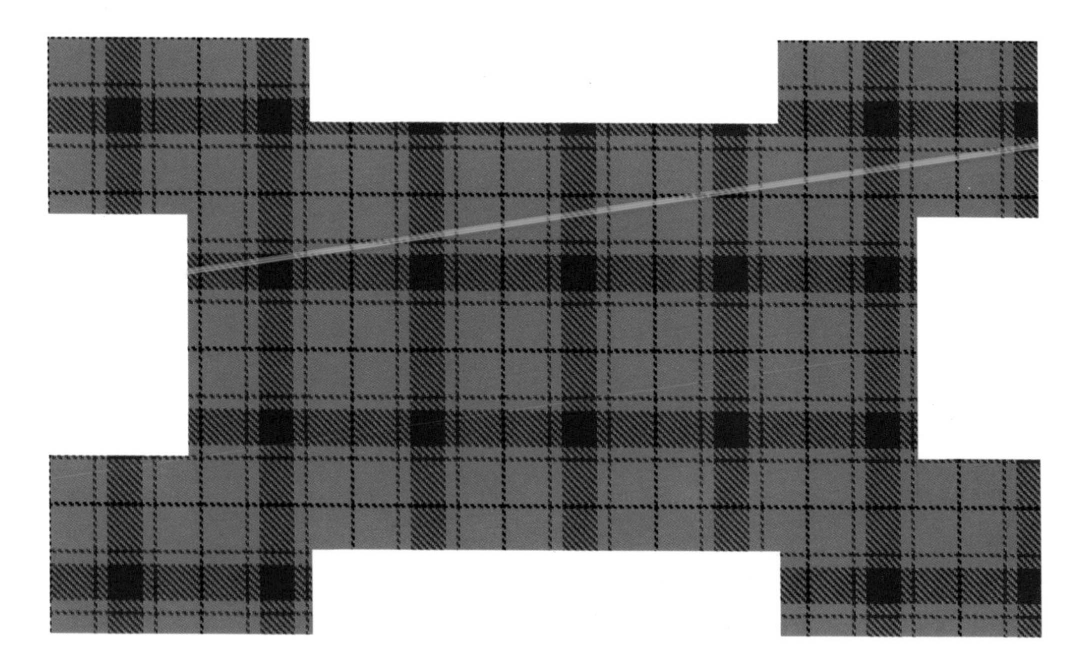

# MacDonell of Glengarry

Earliest known date: 1850
Earliest source: Smith, 1850
Tartan type: Symmetrical
Sett: **B**16 R2 B4 R6 B24 R2 Bk24 G24 R6 G4 R2 G8 **W**2
Clan crest: A raven Proper perching on a rock Azure
Clan motto and *slughorn* (slogan, or warcry): *Craig an Fhithich* ("The rock of the raven")
Badge: *Fraoch gorm* (Common heath)

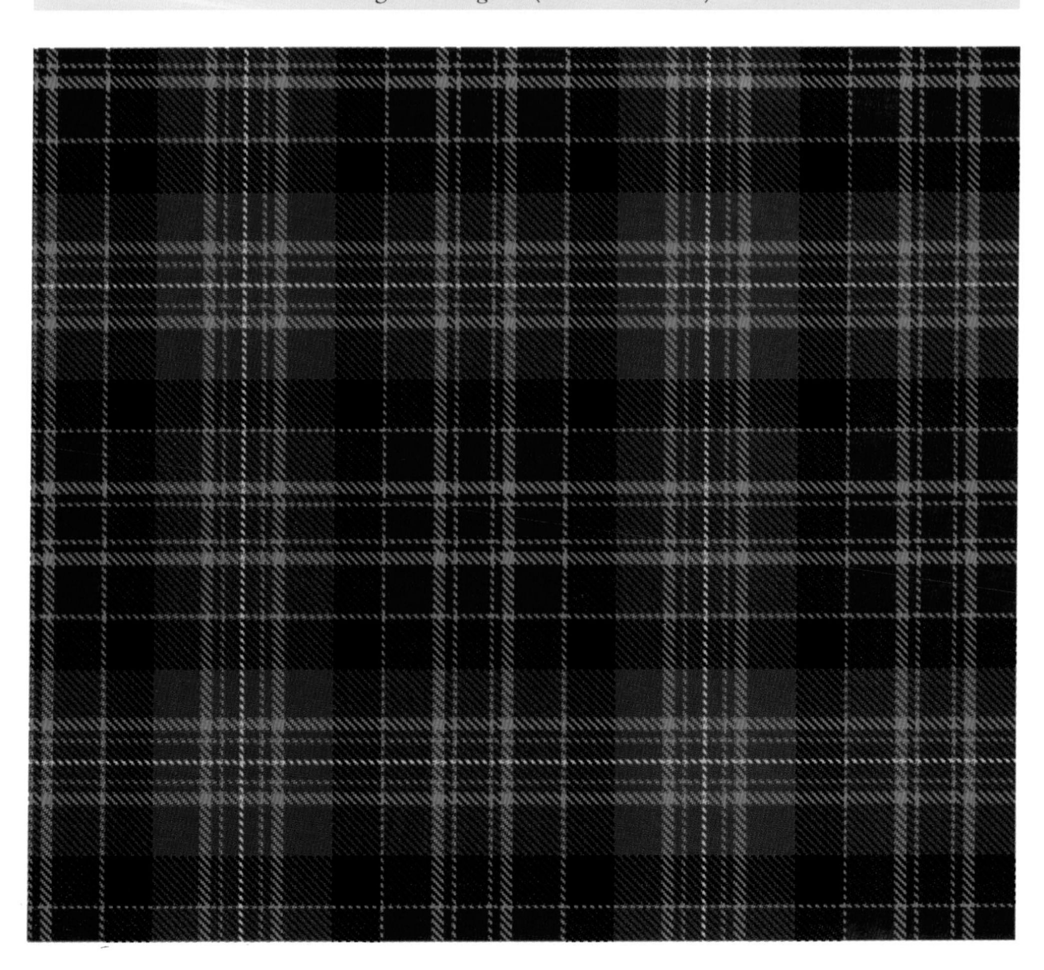

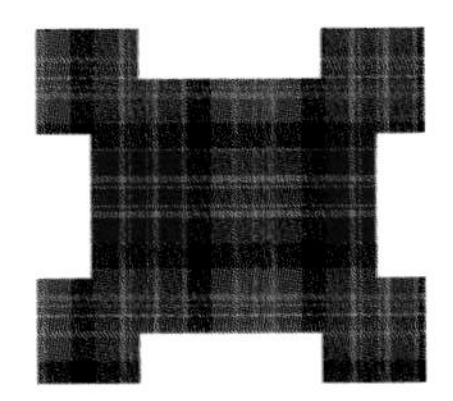

The MacDonells of Glengarry are descended from Ranald, the eldest son of John, 7th Lord of the Isles. Ranald had five sons: one became the founder of the MacDonalds of Clanranald, another, Donald, became the founder of the MacDonells of Glengarry, although most historians say that the true founder of the line and first chief was Donald's son, Alexander. In 1539, Alister MacDonell, the 6th Chief, received a royal charter for the lands of Glengarry and Morar, the Castle of Strome and a large proportion of lands of Lochalsh, Lochcarron and Lochbroon. Despite these grants of land from the Crown, Glengarry's fealty lay in the more ancient ties with his kinsman Donald Gorm of Sleate (see page 132) whom he supported in his claims to reclaim the Lordship of the Isles. After Donald Gorm died while besieging Eileandonan Castle, Glengarry was imprisoned in Edinburgh Castle where he remained until King James V's death in 1542. Alister was succeed by his son Angus MacAlister MacDonell in 1560, who in turn was succeeded by his son Donald, 8th Chief of Glengarry, reputed to have lived for 100 years! His lands were erected into a free barony in 1627 – even though in 1609 he had failed to appear before the mighty Privy Council to answer charges that he was harboring fugitives from the isles and was denounced as a rebel!

Angus, the 9th Chief, fought for Charles I at Inverlochy and for Charles II at Worcester. Cromwell seized his estates, but following the Restoration, they were returned and he was made Lord MacDonell and Aros. When he died without an heir, the peerage ended and the chiefship passed to Archibald, the son of his uncle, Donald Gorm MacDonell of Scotus. A supporter of the Stewart cause, the 11th Chief, Alister MacDonell, was ennobled by King James VIII in 1716; the 12th chief was powerful enough to put 500 clansmen in the field of battle in 1746, while the 13th chief was captured *en route* from France by the English as he attempted to join the '45. He was imprisoned in the Tower of London until 1747.

Colonel Alister MacDonell (1771–1828), the 15th Chief, is possibly the most well known: he was the friend of Sir Walter Scot and the subject of Sir Henry Raeburn's magnificent portrait. He was the last Highland chief to wear the Highland dress *at all times* and was invariably accompanied by a group of retainers dressed likewise. When he died, his son and successor was obliged to sell the Glengarry estates – except for the ruined castle at Invergarry overlooking Loch Oich – before emigrating to New Zealand.

The MacDonell of Glengarry tartan is the basic MacDonald sett, but with the addition of one white stripe. Raeburn's portrait does not show the Glengarry tartan accurately: D.C. Stewart described it as a "blend of Glengarry and Old Stewart". There is, however, a certified sample in the Highland Society's collection, but there is doubt over whether the thread counts of the contemporary weave match this specimen.

# MacDonell of Keppoch

Earliest known date: 1893
Earliest source: D.W. Stewart, 1893
Tartan type: Symmetrical
Sett: **G**4 R4 B2 R48 B12 R6 G24 R8 **B**2
Clan crest: A dexter hand fessways couped at the wrist, grasping a cross crosslet
Clan motto and *slughorn* (slogan or warcry): *Dia is Naomh Aindrea* ("God and St Andrew")
Badge: *Fraoch* (Heath)

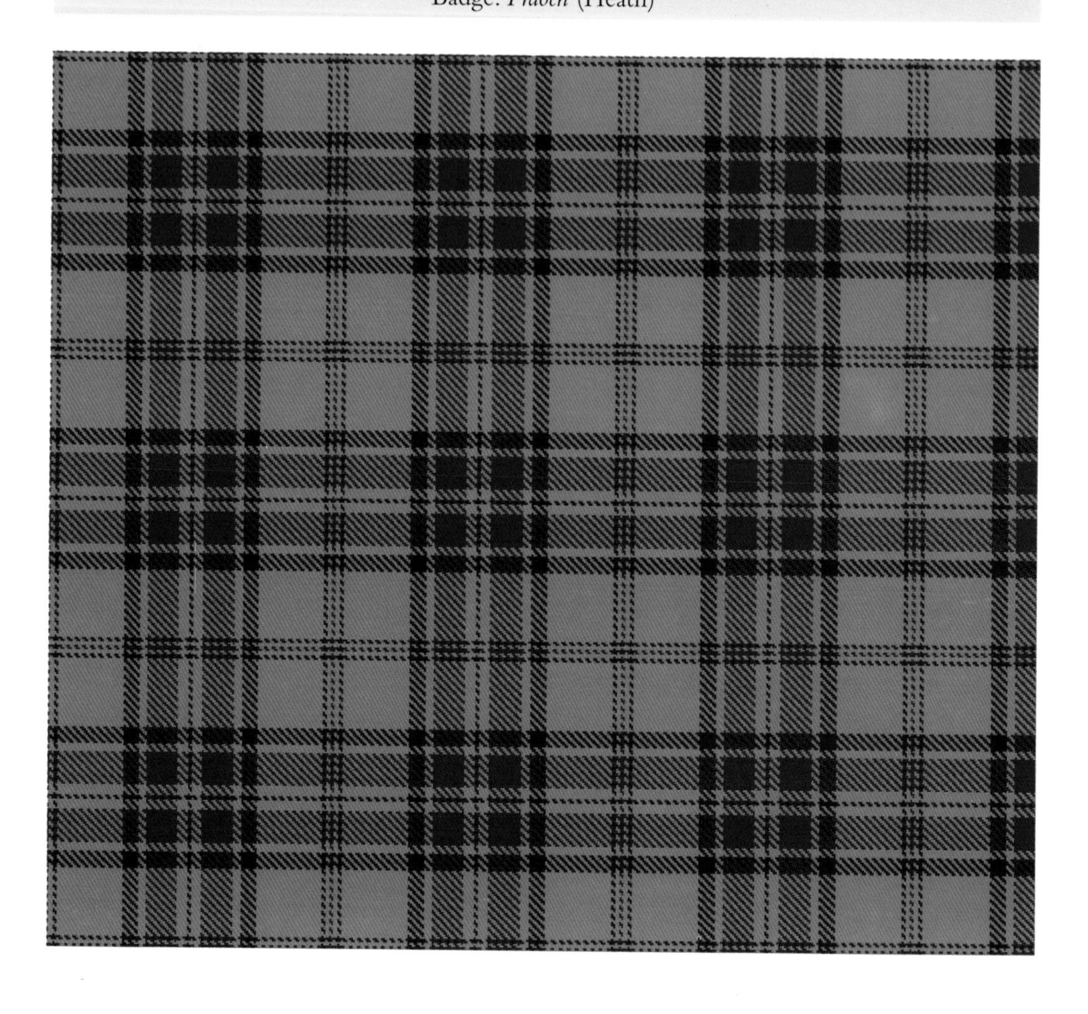

The MacDonells of Keppoch on the mainland of Scotland are descended from Alasdair *Carrach* "The Warty" MacDonell, the third son of John, 7th Lord of the Isles and his wife Princess Margaret, daughter of Robert II. His son, Angus, 2nd of Keppoch, supported the MacDonald chief, the 10th Lord of the Isles. For his loyalty to his MacDonald kinsman, MacDonell forfeited the Lordship of Lochaber to the Crown. Donald Glas MacDonell, 6th Chief built the old Castle of Keppoch. His son Ranald, fought at the battle of Blarnaleine in 1544. Three years later, he was taken prisoner by the Earl of Huntly and beheaded. He was succeeded by his sons Alexander and Ranald Og as 8th and 9th chiefs respectively, and then by Alistair nan Cleas, son of Ranald Og, who became the 10th Chief of Keppoch. From one of his sons are descended the Canadian line of MacDonells, the "Seigneurs of Rigaud" in Quebec. A third son of Ranald Og, called Alister Buidhe murdered his nephew (the 12th Chief) and became the 13th Chief of Keppoch. From him was descended Colonel MacDonell, 15th of Keppoch who fought for the Jacobite cause at Sheriffmuir in 1715. His son and successor was an early supporter of Prince Charles. He fell at Culloden and his natural son Angus became the captain of the branch until his half-brother Ranald came of age. Ranald tried in vain to recover the forfeited Keppoch lands and eventually, when his great-grandson Donald Nicholas MacDonell died in 1899, the direct line of the chiefs of Keppoch became extinct.

Today, the Clan MacDonell of Keppoch is without a chief, although the Canadian branch of the family is represented by a Seigneur. D.C. Stewart describes three tartans as MacDonell of Keppoch: one was copied by his father D.W. Stewart in 1898 from a "relic of the '45" – a plaid supposedly given to Keppoch by Prince Charles Edward Stewart. The same origin is given for a second tartan illustrated by MacIan. If this is to be believed then the prince must have handed out numerous plaids to his followers! The third tartan, and the one in use today, departs from the expected MacDonald sett and is more like the Clan MacKintosh sett. This departure does support the theory that tartan design was based less on clan affiliations and more on territorial origin – especially since the neighboring MacDonells and the MacKintoshes were feuding for nearly 200 years.

# MacDougall

Earliest known date: *c.*1815

Earliest source: Collection of the Highland Society

Tartan type: Symmetrical

Sett: (Smith's count:)**Az**2 Cr4 W2 R2 G12 R4 G2 R4 B6 Cr4 W2 R2 W2 Cr4 G6 R6 G6 R2 B2 R12 Cr4 W2 R4 **Az**2

Clan crest: On a chapeau Gules furred Ermine, a dexter arm in armour embowd fessways couped Proper, holding a cross crosslet fitchee erect Gules

Clan motto: *Buaidh no bas* ("Victory or death")

Badge: *Fraoch dearg* (Bell Heath)

The Gaelic *Dubh-Gall* means "Black Foreigner" and was used to describe the raiders of Ireland and the Hebrides. In time, it came to be used as the first name, the modern form of which is Dougall or Dougald. As a surname, MacDougall means "Son of Dougall" and the clan chief is known as MacDougall of MacDougall. The clan appears to have taken its name from Dougall, one of the sons of Somerled, King of the South Isles and Lord of Lorn, and Raghnild, the daughter of King Olaf of the Isle of Man. After Somerled's death in 1164, Dougall inherited most of Argyll and Lorn, as well as a number of islands including Mull, Jura, Tiree, Coll, Scarba and Lismore. Dougalls' son, Duncan mac Dougall, Lord of Lorn built several castles: Dunstaffnage (which later passed to the Campbells) and Dunollie, in Oban Bay which, although is in ruins, is still the seat of the chief today.

It must be remembered that the MacDougall lands in the Hebrides were not part of Scotland, but formed part of Norway until around 1266. The 3rd MacDougall chief, Eoghan or Ewan of Argyll, tried vainly to keep on good terms with the ever-expanding kingdom of Scotland and the now declining power of Norway. In 1263, Ewan was forced to choose: he opted to join Scotland after asking permission from the Norwegian king and surrendering his Hebridean lands back to him. This evidently was no great loss since, by the time Ewan's son, Alasdair of Argyll, Lord of Lorn, became the 4th MacDougall chief, he was one of the most powerful barons in the kingdom and was created a sheriff to govern his estates on behalf of the Crown. Such influence in Argyll inevitably attracted hostility: in 1294, John "The Lame" MacDougall led his clan against the Campbells at the Path of Lorn between Loch Avich and Scammadale. Furthermore, because of marriage ties with the Comyns – the 4th Chief had married a sister of "Black Comyn" whose son "Red Comyn" was a rival for the throne of Scotland – the MacDougalls came into direct conflict with Robert the Bruce.

In 1309, Bruce led an army into Argyll against the MacDougalls. At the Pass of Brander, John the Lame led a failed ambush of 2,000 MacDougalls. Forced to flee, John was eventually captured by Bruce and died a prisoner on Lochleven. After Bruce's triumph, the MacDougall lands were forfeited and most of them passed to their old enemies, the Campbells. The MacDougall fortunes were improved when David II restored to the MacDougalls the Lordship of Lorn after Ewan, the 6th Chief married a grand-daughter of Robert the Bruce. Royalist supporters in the Civil War, the MacDougall lands were once more forfeited and not returned

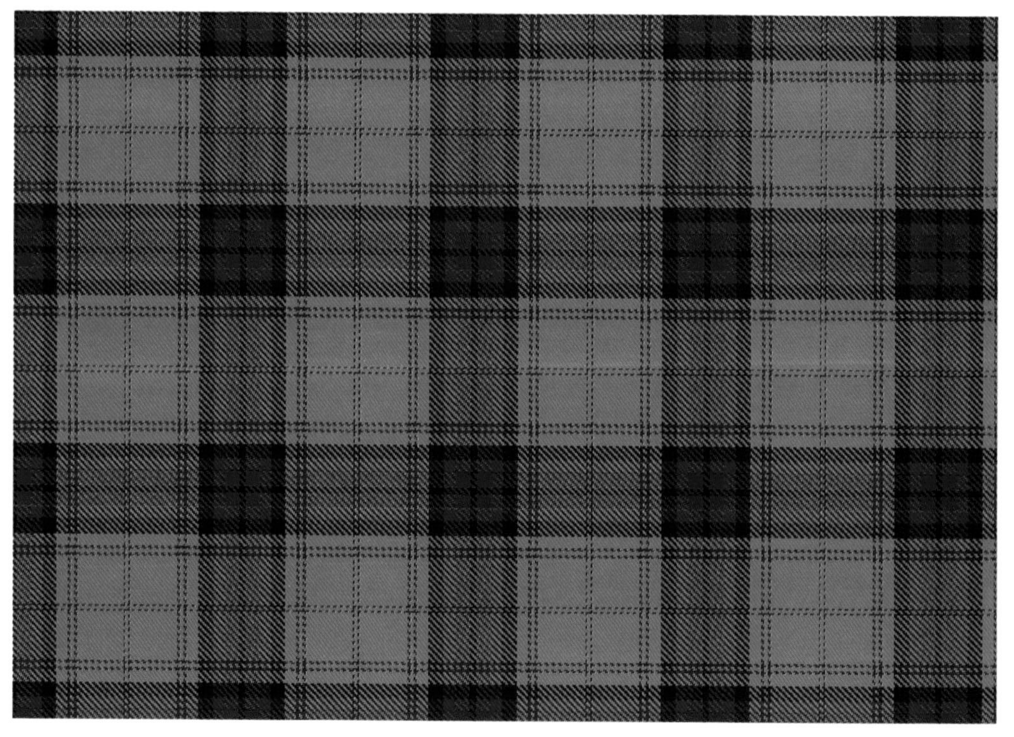

*MacDougall – Vestiarium*

until the Restoration of the monarchy in 1660. In 1715, they were supporters of the Stewart cause and Iain Ciar, 22nd chief, fought at Sheriffmuir. Forced into exile he eventually returned to Scotland as a fugitive until he was pardoned in 1727. While his son Alexander was a Jacobite supporter, he did not join the '45.

The Highland Society of London has a sample of MacDougall tartan certified by the chief and dating from around 1815. The Paton Collection, also has a specimen dating from around 1830. The MacDougall tartan is a complex sett: while Logan gave a thread count for the design in 1831, it appears that weavers have continued to remain in doubt about the details. Logan's count did not have white lines; Smibert's version of 1850 used no crimson but included both white and pale blue; The Smith's (1850) showed crimson and more white lines, while in Grant's version (1886), the white lines were changed to pale blue.

Surnames with possible associations: MacConacher, MacCowan, MacLintock, MacLucas, MacLugash, MacLulich, MacNamell, MacCoull, MacCowl, MacOwl

# MacDuff

Earliest known date: 1810–20

Earliest source: Cockburn, 1810

Tartan type: Symmetrical

Sett: **R**8 Bk2 R8 G12 Bk8 Az6 **R**16

Clan crest: A demi-lion Gules holding in the dexter paw a broadsword erected in pale Proper, hilted and pommelled Or

Clan motto: *Deus juvat* ("God helps")

Badge: *Bosca* (boxwood) and *Lus nan cnaimhseag* (Red Whortleberry)

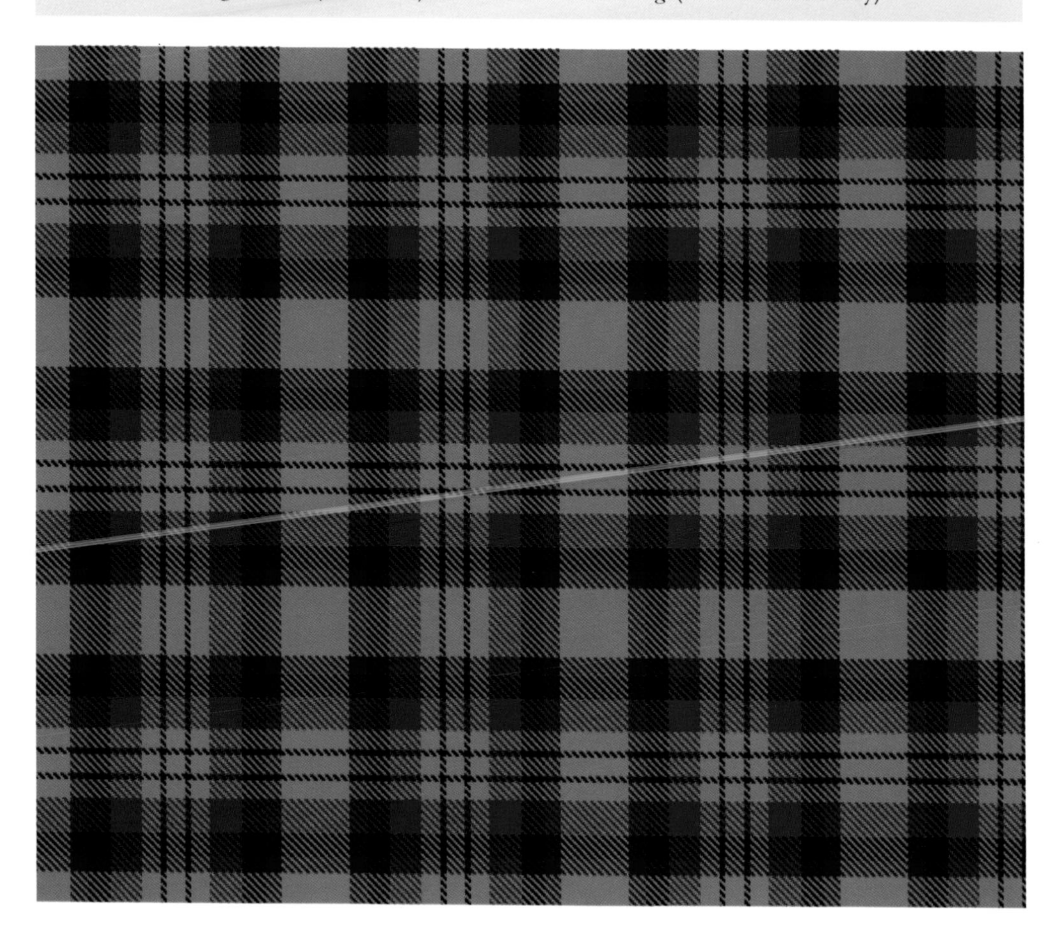

The main power of the clan was in Fife and MacDuff is the patronymic of the first Celtic earls of Fife. The MacDuffs claim descent from the royal Scottish-Pictish line through Queen Gruoch, whose second husband was Macbeth. When Macbeth died, Malcolm III seized the throne. Malcolm's son, Aedh, or Aethelred was barred from the throne on account of being an abbot, although his younger brothers became kings Edgar, Alexander I and David I. However, Aedh's religious office did not prevent him from marrying Queen Grouch's grand-daughter. He was then created Earl of Fife and hereditary abbot of Abernethy before dying in about 1128.

By now the MacDuffs were the premier clan and its chief the most important man in the land after the king. Above all, the chief had the right to enthrone the king on the Stone of Destiny at Scone. After Edward I took the Stone to Westminster (1306), Robert the Bruce underwent a second coronation in order to be crowned by a member of the Clan MacDuff. (Isabel, Duncan MacDuff's sister, was kept prisoner in a cage in public view at Berwick Castle by the English as a reprisal for this act!) When Duncan, the 11th Earl of Fife, died *c.*1353 leaving only a daughter, the direct line of the Celtic earls of Fife ended. The earldom passed to Robert Stewart, the Duke of Albany and Regent of Scotland. Claiming descent from the earls of Fife (without any supporting evidence), in 1404 David Duff received a charter from Robert III for the lands of Muldavit in Banffshire. Although this was sold by John Duff in 1626, his half-brother Adam Duff of Clunybeg began to acquire great wealth himself and his son, Alexander, acquired large areas of lands in north-eastern Scotland during the 17th and 18th centuries. His descendant, William Duff of Braco, MP for Banff county, was made Lord Braco in 1725, and in 1759 was made Viscount MacDuff and Earl of Fife. Alexander, the 6th Earl, was created Duke of Fife in 1889 when he married Princess Louise, daughter of King Edward VII.

A sample of the MacDuff tartan, certified by the chief in *c.*1816 is in the Cockburn Collection, and the sett was first published by Logan in 1831. In 1898, D.W. Stewart noted that the tartan was the Royal Stewart without the yellow and white lines and added that whether this was because the MacDuff tartan was the basis of the Royal Stewart, or because of the MacDuff earls' of Fife relationship with the Scottish crown, is unknown.

Surnames with possible associations: Fife, Fyfe, Kilgour, Spence

# MacEwan

Earliest known date: 1906
Earliest source: Johnston, 1906
Tartan type: Symmetrical
Sett: **Y/R**4 Bk2 G24 Bk24 B24 Bk2 **B**4
Clan crest: A trunk of an oak tree sprouting Proper
Clan motto: *Reviresco* ("I grow strong again")

In Gaelic, the MacEwans are called *Clann Eoghain na h-Oitrich* – the "MacEwans of Otter". On a rocky point on the coast of Lochfyne was the *Caisteal Mhic Eoghain* – MacEwan's castle. Closely allied with the MacLachlans, the Lamonts and the MacNeills, by the 12th century, the MacEwans held substantial land in Cowal. The earliest chief appears to have been around in the 13th century. In the next century, around 1315, the chiefship was held by Gillespie of Otter, who was succeeded by Swene, the 9th and last Otter chief. In 1431–32, Swene was granted a barony for the lands of Otter by James I, which he in turn granted to Duncan, the son of Alexander Campbell of Lochow. Consequently, the barony and estates passed to the Campbells and from then on, the MacEwans became dependants of the Campbells or "broken" (clanless).

By 1598, many MacEwans were supporting themselves by robbery while others sought new alliances, either seeking protection from MacLachlan of MacLachlan or as the subjects of the Earl of Argyll. Some MacEwans joined the Campbells of Craignish, while other founded colonies in the Lennox county of Dumbartonshire. Yet, true to their clan motto, some MacEwans grew strong again – particularly in the south-west of Scotland where they made their home at Bardrocht in Ayrshire. Nevertheless, the MacEwans are still without a chief. There is, however, an active clan association. Because of their historical associations, it is not surprising that the MacEwan tartan resembles a Campbell tartan (called the Campbell of Loudon) but replaces the white line in the Campbell for a red one.

Surnames with possible associations: MacCune

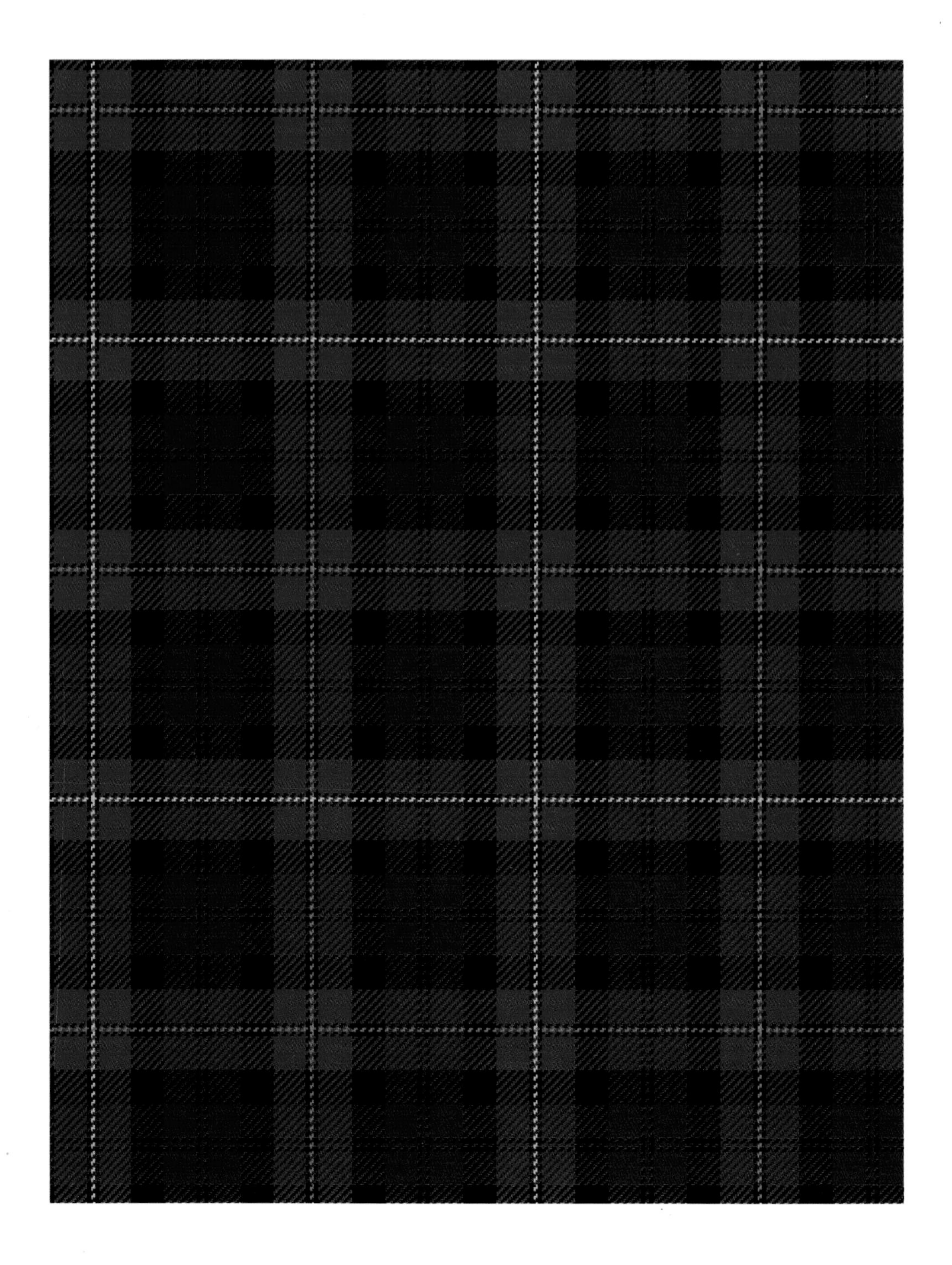

# MacFarlane

Earliest known date: 1819

Earliest source: Wilson, 1819

Tartan type: Symmetrical

Sett: **R**84 Bk2 G24 W4 R6 Bk2 R6 W4 G4 P24 Bk8 R6 W8 **G**6

Clan crest: A demi-savage brandishing in his dexter hand a broadsword Proper and pointing with his sinister hand to an Imperial Crown Or on a wreath.

Clan motto: "This I'll defend"

Badge: *Muileag* (Cranberry) and *Oireag* or *Foighreag* (Cloudberry)

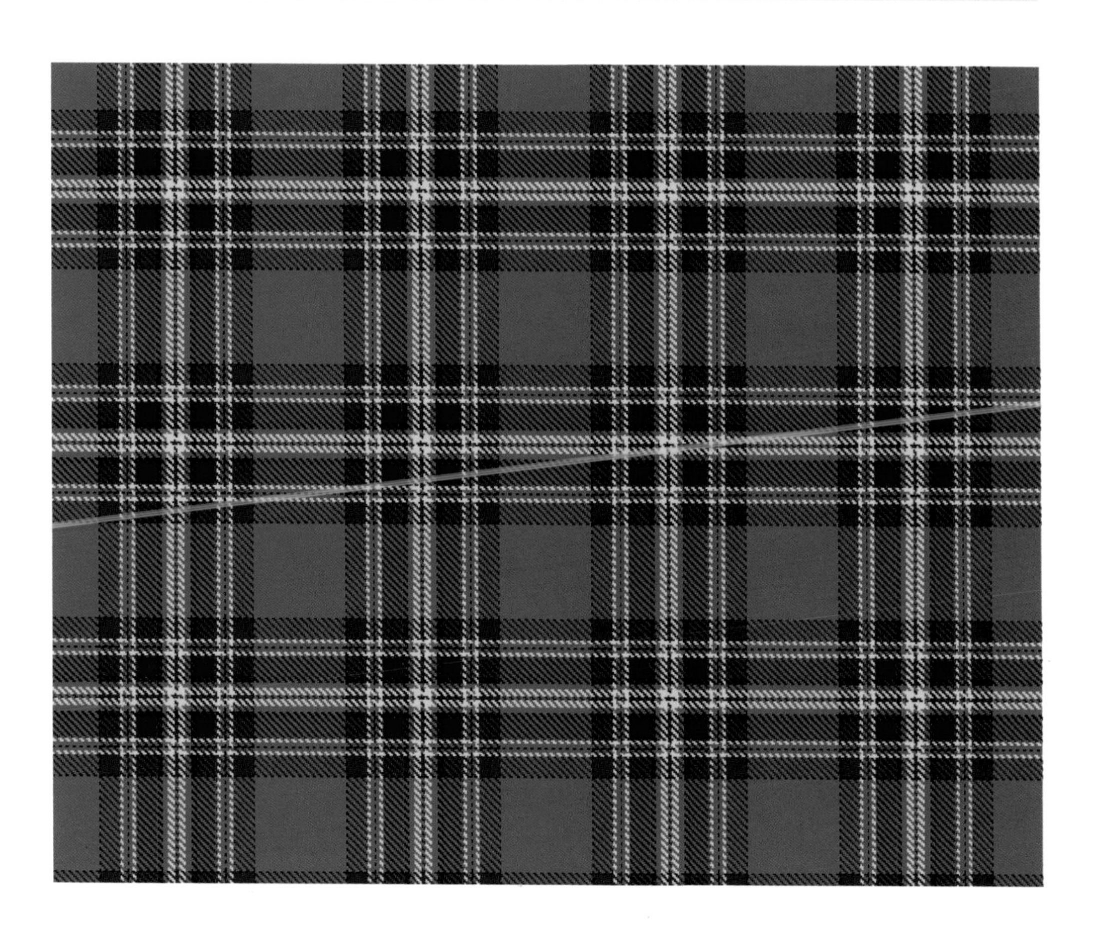

The name MacFarlane comes from the Gaelic *Mac Pharlain*, meaning "son of Parlan"; they are descended from a younger son of Alwyn, Earl of Lennox from *c.* 1180–1225. Malduin, gave sanctuary to Robert the Bruce when he was forced to flee through Loch Lomondside to safety.

In 1420, Iain MacPharlain was granted a charter confirming the lands of Arrochar. When, in 1425, Duncan, the last Celtic Earl of Lennox, had his head hacked off by James I (because James hated the earl's late son-in-law, the Regent Albany), the MacFarlane chiefs claimed the chiefship of the Lennox clan since they were also heirs descended from the old earls. Although the MacFarlanes had a valid claim, the earldom was given to John Stewart, Lord Darnley. MacFarlane opposition to this was eventually overcome when Andrew MacFarlane, 10th chief, married one of Lord Darnley's daughters. Andrew's son, Sir Iain, fell at Flodden in 1513, and later, in 1547, the MacFarlanes opposed the invading English at the battle of Pinkie where Duncan, 13th chief, and his brother were both killed. After the murder of their kinsman Lord Darnley, who was the second husband of Mary, Queen of Scots, the MacFarlane chief called out 300 clansmen against the queen at the battle of Langside in 1568. The victory here secured the crown for the infant James VI – which is also alluded to in the clan's arms.

The MacFarlanes were loyal to the crown and consequently declared for Charles I and fought at Inverlochy in 1645. When Cromwell's forces invaded Scotland, Walter MacFarlane, 16th chief, held out against the Roundheads even though his island castle of Inveruglas in Loch Lomond was burnt to the ground. The chief's "old" house at Arrochar was replaced by a new one by the 20th Chief, Walter MacFarlane (d.1767). It had been prophesied earlier that a black swan would settle among the white birds of the MacFarlanes and that when it did, the chiefs would lose their lands. In 1785, the Arrochar lands were sold to pay of debts and the last MacFarlane chief emigrated to America. The direct male line of MacFarlane chiefs ended with William MacFarlane, 25th of that Ilk who died in 1886. In 1912, the MacFarlane Society was established in Glasgow. The complex pattern and colors of the MacFarlane tartan were derived from a woven silk sash dated 1822 that is in the collection of the Scottish Tartan Society and was recorded by Logan in 1831. However, earlier in 1819, Wilson & Sons of Bannockburn had also produced a MacFarlane tartan sett, but with purple in place of the blue.

Surnames with possible associations: Allan, Allanson, Bartholomew, Bryce, Caw, Griesck, Gruamach, Kinnieson, Knox, MacAindra, MacAllan, MacCaa, MacCause, MacCaw, MacCondy, MacEoin, MacErracher, MacGaw, MacGeoch, MacInstalker, MacIock, MacJames, MacNair, MacNeur, MacNiter, MacRob, MacRobb, MacWalter, MacWilliam, Miller, Monach, Parlane, Robb, Stalker, Weaver, Webster, Wylie

# MacFie/MacPhee

Earliest known date: 1906
Earliest source: Johnston, 1906
Tartan type: Symmetrical
Sett: **W/Y**2 R24 G4 R2 **G**32
Clan crest: A demi-lion rampant Proper
Clan motto: *Pro rege* ("For the king")
Badge: *Darag* (Oak) and *Dearca fithich* (Crowberry)

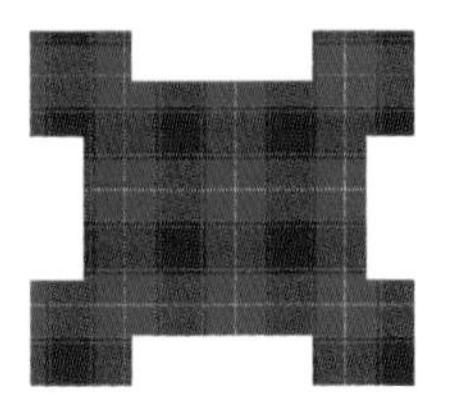

In Gaelic, the name MacFie is written as *Maca'phi*, while in its English form it is usually MacFie, MacPhee or Macafie. The name is in fact one of the oldest forms of MacDuffy, from *Mac Dhuibhshith*, meaning "son of the Black one of Peace", or "son of the Black Elf". The exact origins of the name are obscure: there does seem to have been a family on South Uist in the Hebrides (the MacDuffies or MacFies were also a Hebridean clan) known as *Dhub-sidh* (Black Fairy) who were said to have been able to communicate with the fairy world. However, legend states that the MacFies are descended from a sea-woman – a mermaid, perhaps – who was prevented from returning to her watery home!

The chiefs of the clan were the MacFies of Colonsay, the hereditary keepers of the records of the Lords of the Isles. The island of Colonsay was later passed to the MacDonalds and the Campbells and then on to the MacNeills. In 1463, MacFie of Colonsay appears as a Member of the Council of the Isles that advised the MacDonald rulers. When James IV decided to wrest power from the MacDonalds and their supporters and bring the islands under royal control, the MacFies sided with the MacDonalds and, in 1531, a MacFie of Colonsay was cited for treason. In 1615, now allied to the MacDonalds of Islay, Malcolm MacFie of Colonsay joined in the rebellion against the Earl of Argyll, the king's representative, but MacFie was betrayed by the Campbells (to whom Islay had been promised) to the chief of Clan Donald South, Colkitto, who handed MacFie over to the earl. In 1623, Colkitto murdered Malcolm MacFie – who was hiding under a pile of seaweed – and seized Colonsay for himself. The MacFies were now dispossessed. Many went to the mainland and settled in Lochaber. Colonsay eventually passed to the Duke of Argyll, who exchanged it (along with Oronsay) for Crerar with Donald MacNeill, whose descendents would become ennobled as Lord Colonsay.

In the middle of the 19th century, Ewan MacPhee became famous as the last Scottish outlaw: a sheep stealer who lived in rough and ready conditions on Eileen Mhic Phee in Loch Quoich, MacFie became something of a local celebrity, and sustained his family on gifts from well-wishers and neighbors. The present chief Sandy MacPhie, lives in Queensland, Australia. In 1991, he approved the MacFie tartan, which is a variation of the red MacDonald, that appeared in W. and A.K Johnston's *The Tartans of the Clans and Septs* of Scotland in 1906.

Surnames with possible associations: Duffie, Duffy, Fee, MacGuffie, MacHaffie

# MacGillivray

Earliest known date: 1831

Earliest source: Logan, 1831

Tartan type: Symmetrical

Sett: **R**8 Az2 B2 R64 Az4 R4 B24 R4 G32 R8 Az2 R8 **B**4

Clan crest: A mountain-cat sejant guardant Proper, his dexter forepaw on the ground, his sinister forepaw in a guardant posture and his tail reflexed under his sinister paw.

Clan motto: "Touch not this cat"

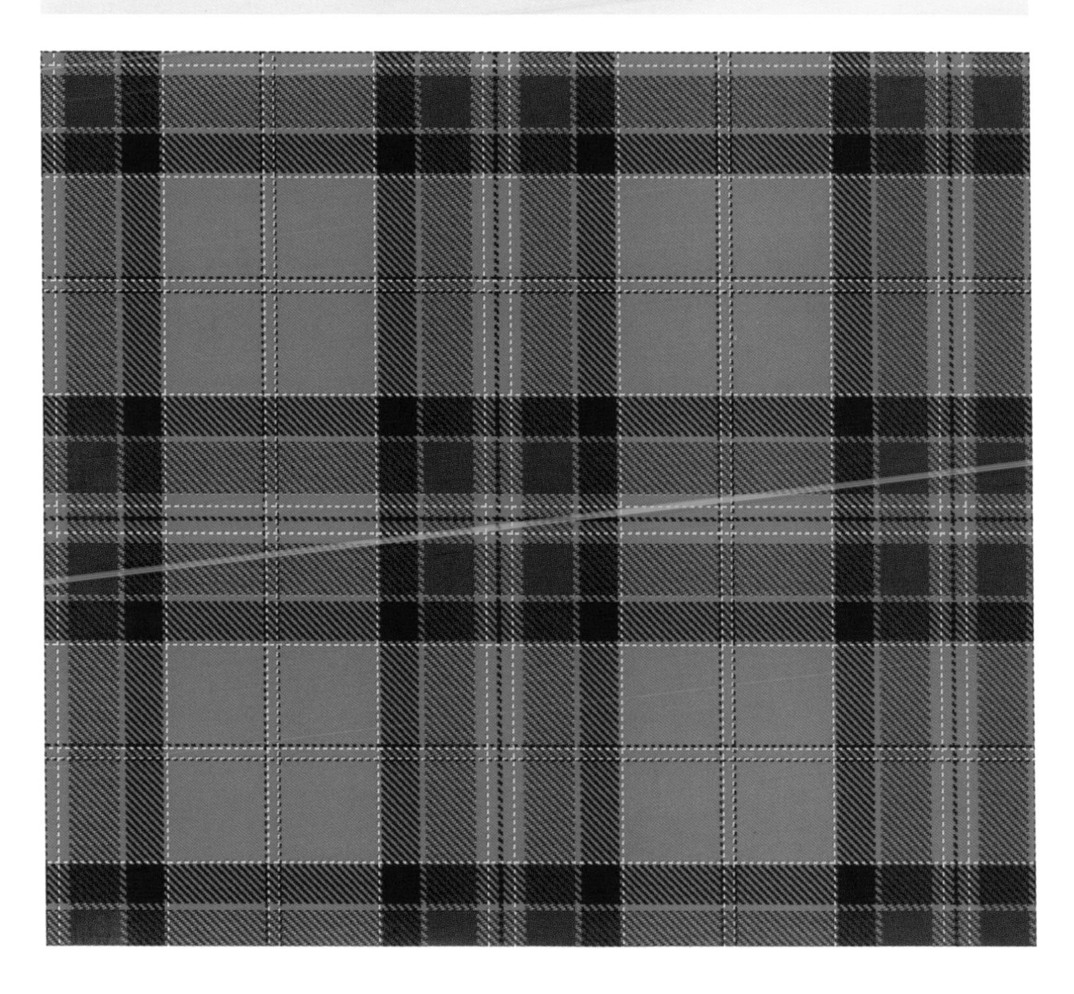

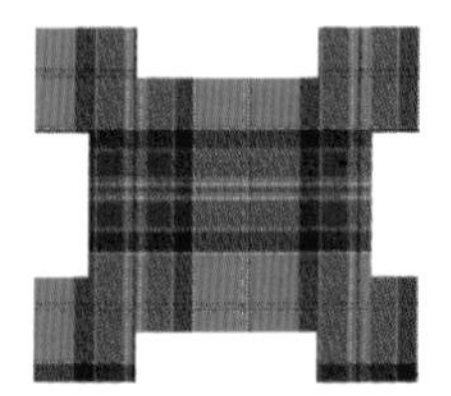

Known in Gaelic as *Clann Mhic Gillebhrath* ("Clan of the Son of the servant of judgement"), the MacGillivrays are one of the oldest septs of the Clan Chattan. According to the Croy manuscript, in 1268 Gillivray, the progenitor of the clan, placed himself under the protection "for posterity" of Farquhard MacKintosh, 5th of MacKintosh (d.1274). By the process of adoption under Celtic Law, Gillivray became part of that clan and later, through MacKintosh's inheritances, into the Clan Chattan.

It seems that the MacGillivrays originally came from the west coast of Scotland – possibly from Mull – before settling at Dunmaglass where, in 1500, Duncan MacGillivray was recorded as living. In 1609, when the Clan Chattan Bond of Union was signed, the MacGillivray chief was a minor, so the bond was signed by Malcolm of Dalcrombie and Duncan MacFarquhar of Dunmaglass on his behalf. Like the majority of Clan Chattan families, the MacGillivrays were staunch Jacobites and in 1715, the Laird and his brother were Captain and Lieutenant respectively in the Clan Chattan Regiment. The clan was also called out in 1745, and were led by their chief, Alexander. He died on the battlefield at a well, which still bears his name.

After Culloden, many of the MacGillivrays emigrated abroad: William MacGillivray was a successful trader in Canada and later became head of the Canadian Northwest Company and, in keeping with the ancient name as "servant of judgement", a member of the Legislative Council of Lower Canada. When John Lachlan MacGillivray of Dunmaglass died in 1852, he left £40,000, his estates and a year's free rent to all his tenants. The MacGillivray estates were consequently dispersed, and finally sold in 1890. The last MacGillivray chief is believed to have died in Canada.

Although there are several active clan societies around the world and a Clan Commander appointed by the Lord Lyon, no one has yet established his rights to the MacGillivray chiefly arms. D.C. Stewart in 1950 described the MacGillivray clan tartan as a "characteristic Clan Chattan tartan" and noted that the same light blue lines were common to the tartans of neighboring clans in Strathnairn and Morvern.

Surnames with possible associations: Gilroy, MacGillivour, MacGilroy, MacGilvra, MacGilvray, Milroy

# MacGregor

Earliest known date: 1810-20

Earliest source: Cockburn Collection, 1810–20

Tartan type: Clan tartan: Symmetrical

Sett: **R**72 G36 R8 G12 Bk2 **W**4

"Rob Roy" (undress tartan): Simple check of equal quantities of red and black.

Clan crest: A lion's head erased Proper, crowned with an antique crown Or

Clan motto: *'S rioghal mo dhream* ("My race is royal")

Badge: *Giuthas* (Scots Pine tree)

The motto of the Clan MacGregor tells of their royal descent, from Gregor, the brother of Kenneth MacAlpin, King of Scotland (843–60). The original home of the MacGregors was Glenstrae – the "three glens" of the rivers Orchy, Strae and Lochy, and out into Glengyle and Roro.

The first chief appears to have been Gregor "of the golden bridles", who refused to submit to any other clan and continued to defend the ancestral territory by the sword – even though, technically, the family line ended with a childless daughter of Gregor's uncle, Iain of Glenorchy, who was married to a Campbell. Gregor's own son, Iain Camm "the One-Eyed" of Glenochry (d.1390), became the 2nd Chief of Clan Gregor. However, Robert the Bruce granted the barony of Loch Awe – which included most of the MacGregor lands – to the chief of the Campbells and the MacGregors were forced to retreat deeper into their lands until eventually they were restricted to Glenstrae. In 1519, Ian of Glenstrae died without a direct heir. The Campbells managed to establish Eian, head of the Clan Dughail Ciar, as their own choice as chief of the Clan Gregor – especially since Eian was married to Campbell of Glenorchy's daughter. The now disinherited line of MacGregors, led by Gregor Roy MacGregor, continued to wage war against the Campbells. An outlaw for ten years, MacGregor was eventually captured and killed by the Campbells in 1570.

In 1603, James VI declared the whole Clan Gregor outlaw and the use of the name MacGregor was proscribed under penalty of death. Clan MacGregor was broken and the scattered clansmen, forced to take new names, became known as the "Children of the Mist". Rob Roy MacGregor, born in 1671, the younger son of MacGregor of Glengyle, was immortalized – and romaticized – as the eponymous hero of Sir Walter Scott's novel. Although he acted as a maverick, in 1715 Rob Roy rallied to the Jacobite cause. Following the battle of Sherriffmuir, however, he returned to his robber ways. He died in 1734 and is buried in the churchyard at Balquhidder. In 1774, the laws proscribing the Clan Gregor were repealed and General John MacGregor-Murray of Lanrick (a MacGregor descended from Duncan MacGregor of Ardchoille of the disinherited line who died in 1552), was declared the head of the "Children of the Mist" and the rightful chief of the Clan Gregor.

A sample of the MacGregor Clan tartan is in the Cockburn Collection and dates from around 1810–20; the same pattern was used by Wilson's in their pattern book of 1819 under the name "MacGregor Murray". The tartan was also one of only a handful of authentically recorded patterns in *The Vestiarium Scoticum*. A second pattern of equal red and black check is

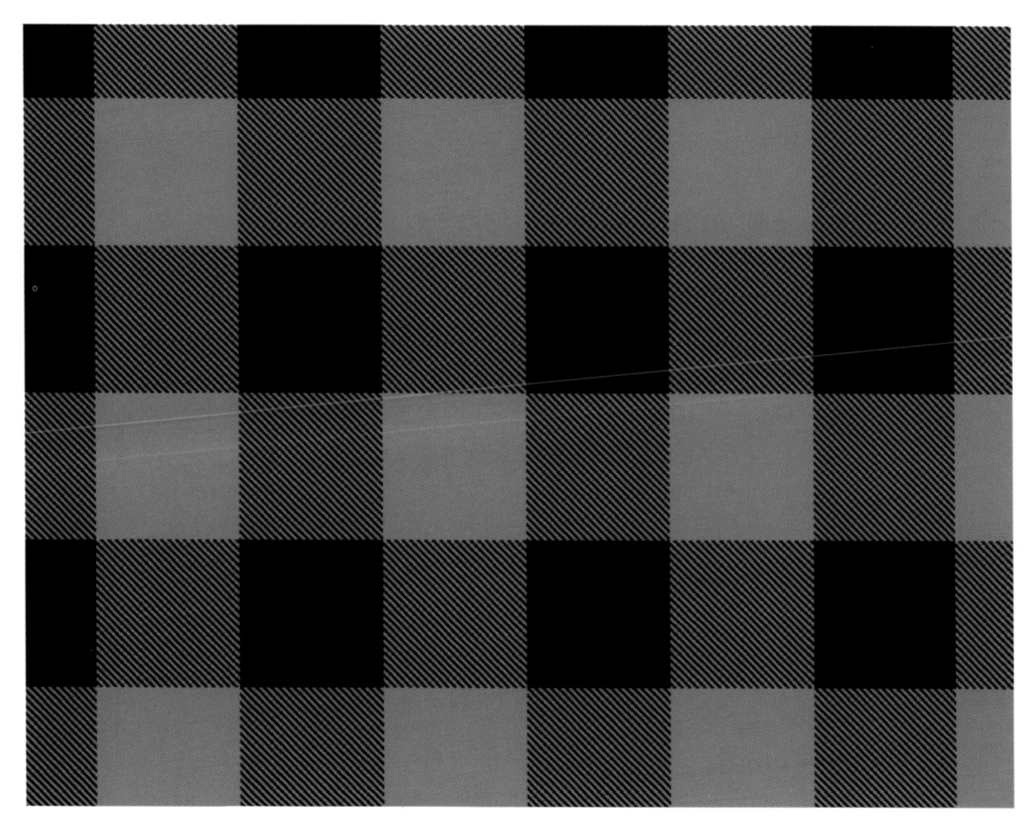

*MacGregor - Rob Roy*

known as the "Rob Roy". Although there are several portraits all reputed to be of Rob Roy, in none does he wear this pattern! In the Highland Society Collection from around 1816–17, there is a sample of "Rob Roy" certified by John MacGregor-Murray, but labelled simply as the "MacGregor Tartan for undress ordinary clothing". Nevertheless, the name Rob Roy seems to have become forever attached to this pattern.

Surnames with possible associations: Black, Bowers, Bowmaker, Brewer, Caird, Dochart, Docharty, Gregorson, Gregory, Greig, Grier, Gruer, Leckie, Lecky, MacAdam, MacAra, MacAree, MacCrouther, MacGrewar, MacGrowther, MacGruder, MacGruther, MacIlduy, MacLeister, MacLiver, MacNee, MacNie, MacNish, MacPetrie, Neish, Nish, Peterkin, Petrie, Skinner, Stringer, White, Whyte

# MacInnes

Earliest known date: 1908
Earliest source: Frank Adams *The Clans, Septs and Regiments of the Scottish Highlands, 1908*
Tartan type: Symmetrical
Sett: **Y**4 Bk24 G4 Bk4 G4 Bk4 G32 Bk6 Az6 Bk6 B24 G12 **R**4
Clan crest: A sinister arm from the shoulder close attired in the tartan of the Clan Aonghais, cuff flashes yellow with three butons Or, grasping a bow Vert, stringed Gules
Clan motto: *Ghift dhe Agus n righ* ("By grace of God and king")
Badge: *Cuileann* (Holly)

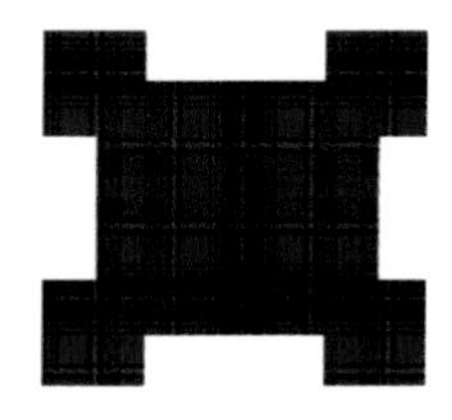

The name MacInnes is derived from the Gaelic *Mac Aonghias* which means "son of Angus". They are said to have been the original inhabitants of Ardnamurchan and Morvern, which was then conquered by Alexander II. Claiming descent from the early rulers of the region and from the Lords of Lorn, the MacInnes were later to come under the control of the Campbells who secured power over much of the region.

The last MacInnes chief was murdered at Ardtornish in 1390 and part of the clan became identified with the Campbells of Craignish, while others, under Neil an Bogha, are said to have become hereditary bowmen to the MacKinnons on the isle of Skye. This is alluded to in the most widely used crest of the MacInnes name. It seems however, that some of the MacInneses managed to recover some of their possessions as the MacInnes in Morvern appeared later Constables of the castle at Kinlochaline. They were governing it on behalf of the Sir Rorie MacKenzie of Tarbat, the "Tutor of Kintail" when it was besieged and burnt by Alister MacColla MacDonald, known as Colkitto – meaning "sinister" or, "left-handed" – in 1645 when he was fighting for Charles I. In the 17th and 18th centuries, the Kinlochaline branch of the MacInnes followed the Campbells in their support of the Hanoverian succession to the throne. Another branch, however, supported Stewart of Ardsheal in 1745. Like many other families, during the late 18th and 19th centuries, the MacInnes emigrated abroad, and can be found across the English-speaking world.

Surnames with possible associations: MacCanish, MacCansh, MacMaster

# MacIntyre

Earlies known date: 1850 Earliest source: Smith, 1850
Tartan type: Symmetrical
Sett: **Az**2 R4 G4 R8 B32 R4 G2 R8 B2 R4 G32 R8 B4 R4 **Az**2
Clan crest: A dexter hand holding a dagger in pale Proper
Clan motto: *Per ardua* ("Through difficulties")
Badge: *Fraoch gorm* (Common heath)

A tale dates the origins of the Clan MacIntyre to the 12th century when Somerled was establishing his lordship over the Western Isles. Somerled's nephew, MacArill, had promised to help his uncle win the hand of the daughter of King Olaf of Norway and he drilled holes in the hull of the king's boat, which he only repaired when Olaf agreed to the marriage. Consequently, MacArill became known as "the carpenter" and was in his uncle's good books.

MacArill's descendants, the MacIntyres – or as they are called in Gaelic, *Clann-an-t-Saor* ("Children of the Carpenter"), are said to have come from the Hebrides to Lorn in around 1360 in a ship with a white cow and settled in Glen Noe in Argyll. The chiefs appear to have been Foresters to the MacDougall and then the Stewart Lords of Lorn and maintained this position under the Campbells in return for the annual payment in summer of snowball (only obtainable with great difficulty from a very high mountain!) and a fatted white calf. This rent remained fixed until the 18th century when Campbell of Bredalbane encouraged the MacIntyre tenant of Glen Noe to translate the payment into cash: soon the rent was increased to such a great amount that the MacIntyres could no longer pay and the 4th Chief Duncan MacIntyre was forced to leave the ancient homelands for America in 1783. He died in 1792, but left descendants in New York.

Little is known of early "pre-modern" chiefs: the first that is recorded with any accuracy was Duncan, who died in 1695. He led the MacIntyres at Inverlochy in 1645 when the Campbells were routed by Montrose. James, the 3rd Chief, was born sometime around 1727. Although a supporter of Bonnie Prince Charlie, he did not join in the rising of 1745 – although many of his clansmen did; he fought under Stewart of Appin at Culloden and later sought protection from the Clan Chattan. In 1991, James Wallace MacIntyre of Glencoe, the 9th Chief of the Clan MacIntyre, was formally recognized by the Lord Lyon and admitted to the Standing Council of Scottish Chiefs. The MacIntyre clan tartan is also known as the Glennorchy District Tartan. In 1850, the Smith brothers described a tartan, which they called "MacIntyre of Whitehouse", while James Grant in 1886 took his thread count from a tartan published earlier in *The Vestiarium Scoticum* in 1842. The Smith's sett is the one most often available today – even though it is different to the sett officially recorded by the Lord Lyon.

Surnames with possible associations: MacTear, Tyre, Wright

# MacKay

Earliest known date: 1816

Earliest source: Logan, 1831

Tartan type: Symmetrical

Sett: **Bk**6 G28 Bk28 G4 G(v.dk green)28 **G**6

Clan crest: A dexter arm erect couped at the elbow the hand grasping a dagger also erect all Proper

Clan motto: *Manu forti* ("By a stong hand")

Badge: Great Bulrush

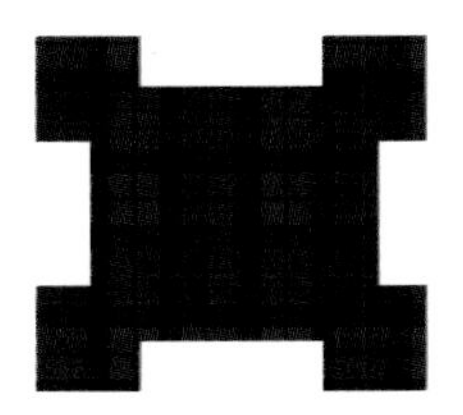

In Gaelic the name MacKay is *Mac Aoidh*. In ancient times it was spelled "Aed", the Gaelic for "fire", but the Old Scots sometimes wrote it as "Ed" "Eth" or "Heth" and in charter-Latin, it became "Odo". By the 16th century, "Aoidh" had become anglicized as "Hugh". The name came from the ancient Celtic royal house: Aoidh, or Hugh, was the abbot of Dunkeld, 1st Earl of Fife, and the elder brother of Alexander I and David I (Aoidh's clerical post meant he was barred from the throne). He married the granddaughter of Queen Gruoch (Macbeth's wife, heiress of Moray and the royal line of King Duff who was slain in 967).

After Aoidh's death around 1130, the Moraymen, led by Angus, King of Moray and Malcolm MacAoidh, tried to seize the Scottish throne from King David I. They were defeated and Angus was killed, but the struggle was continued by Malcolm MacAedh until his son Donald MacAedh was captured in 1156. MacAedh became reconciled with the Scottish king and was made Earl of Ross (northern Moray) before his death in 1168. MacAedh's grandson made one further attempt to seize the throne when Alexander II was crowned, but he was caught and beheaded and the earldom of Ross was forfeited. Malcolm's son-in-law Harald, however, was the Earl of Caithness: at that time Strathnaver and Sutherland both belonged to him, and it was in Strathnaver, the Duthaich Mhic Aoidh (MacKay country) in the far north that the MacKays appear in force in the late 13th century. By the time of Angus Dubh MacAedh, who married the sister of Donald, Lord of the Isles in 1415, the MacKay chiefs could call out 4,000 men from their lands at Strathnaver.

In 1529, Donald MacKay of Strathnaver had his lands erected into the barony of Farr. His son, and the next chief, Iye Dhu MacKay, forfeited the barony amidst the turmoil of Mary, Queen of Scots' reign, but it was recovered by his son, Huistean Dhu MacKay. He married the daughter of the Earl of Sutherland, once their feuding neighbors, but on whom the MacKays were to soon become dependent. Many of the MacKay chiefs became mercenaries on the Continent: the MacKay regiment under the command of Donald MacKay was famous through Europe during the Thirty Years War (1618–48). Donald was created baronet of Nova Scotia in 1627 and later made Lord Reay. He fought for Charles I in the Civil War and their home, the House of Tongue on the Strathnaver coast, was burnt in 1656 by Cromwell's forces, but rebuilt in 1678. Lord Reay, however, went into exile. The family eventually settled in Holland where they prospered: in 1822, Barthold MacKay was made Baron MacKay van Ophemert and, in 1881, his son, Donald James MacKay, succeeded a distant cousin to become 10th Lord Reay in

*MacKay*

the United Kingdom and Chief of the Clan MacKay. By this time, however, the House of Tongue and the MacKay estates – virtually the entire northwestern corner of Britain – had been sold to their Sutherland kinsmen to pay off huge debts.

A certified sample of the MacKay clan tartan dates from 1816 in the collection of the Highland Society. While Wilson's of Bannockburn recorded the sett in 1819 with the blue altered to purple, in 1831 Logan described the color as "corbeau", which is in fact a very dark green. D. W. Stewart noted that the MacKay tartan was similar in all but color to that of their neighbors, the Clan Gunn's and, instead of emphasizing clan associations, today's researchers are focusing more on the geographical, or territorial, sources for clan tartan designs.

Surnames with possible associations: Bain, MacCay, MacCrie, MacGhee, MacGhie, MacQuoid, MacVail, Morgan, Pollard, Polson, Scobie

# MacKenzie

Earliest known date: 1778

Earliest source: Wilson's pattern book, 1819

Tartan type: Symmetrical

Sett: **B**24 Bk4 B4 Bk4 B4 Bk24 G24 Bk2 W4 Bk2 G24 Bk24 B24 Bk2 **R**4

Clan crest: A mount in flames Proper

Clan motto: *Luceo non uro* ("I shine, not burn")

Badge: *Cuileann* (Holly)

Little is known of the early history of the chiefs of the Clan MacKenzie: in 1450 the genealogy of the clan chiefs was given as "Murdoch, son of Kenneth, son of John, son of Kenneth, son of Angus, son of Christian, son of Adam, son of Gilleoin-Oig of the Aird" (who seems to have been alive at the beginning of the 12th century and belonged to a branch of the ancient royal house of Lorn). We do know that the name MacKenzie comes from the Old Gaelic *Mac Cainnigh*, or "son of Coinneach". Cainnigh, which means "bright one" or "fair one", has long been anglicized as "Kenneth". Until the 18th century, MacKenzie was always pronounced as "MacKingie".

By around 1267, the MacKenzies were settled at Eileandonoan, the castle at Loch Duich in Kintail. Alexander "Ionraech", the first chief of whom there is any real evidence, a young man at this time, was summoned to meet King James I in 1427. He died in 1488, having been rewarded in 1463 by James III with a royal charter for lands at Kintail after leading the MacKenzies against the rebellious Earl of Ross. In 1508, the Kintail lands were erected into a free barony. His grandson, John, followed James IV to Flodden with a number of his clan and narrowly escaped being taken prisoner.

By the beginning of the 17th century, MacKenzie lands stretched as far as the Outer Hebrides and included Lochalsh and the isle of Lewis. In 1609, Kenneth MacKenzie was created Lord MacKenzie of Kintail (from whom descended the MacKenzies of Pluscarden and Lochslinn); his brother Sir Roderick of Coigach, became the ancestor of the earls of Cromartie, while Colin, Lord MacKenzie's eldest son, was made the Earl of Seaforth in 1623. This title was passed to half-brother, George, 2nd Earl, who supported the reformed church and signed the National Covenant in 1638. After the execution of Charles I, Seaforth joined Charles II in Holland. Kenneth, 3rd Earl of Seaforth was also a Cavalier: Cromwell seized his estates but awarded an allowance to Seaforth's wife, Countess Isabel MacKenzie of Tarbat.

Kenneth, the 4th Earl, continued to support the Stewarts: he followed James VII to Ireland and France and was made Marquis of Seaforth. William, the 5th Earl, was charged with treason for his part in the rising of 1715, however, and his title forfeited. His grandson, Kenneth, Lord Fortrose, regained the title from the Crown in 1771. In gratitude, in 1778 he and the Clan MacKenzie raised the Ross-shire Regiment (the 78th), a force of 1,000 to serve in India.

The MacKenzie clan tartan was also the regimental tartan of the Seaforth Highlanders (the

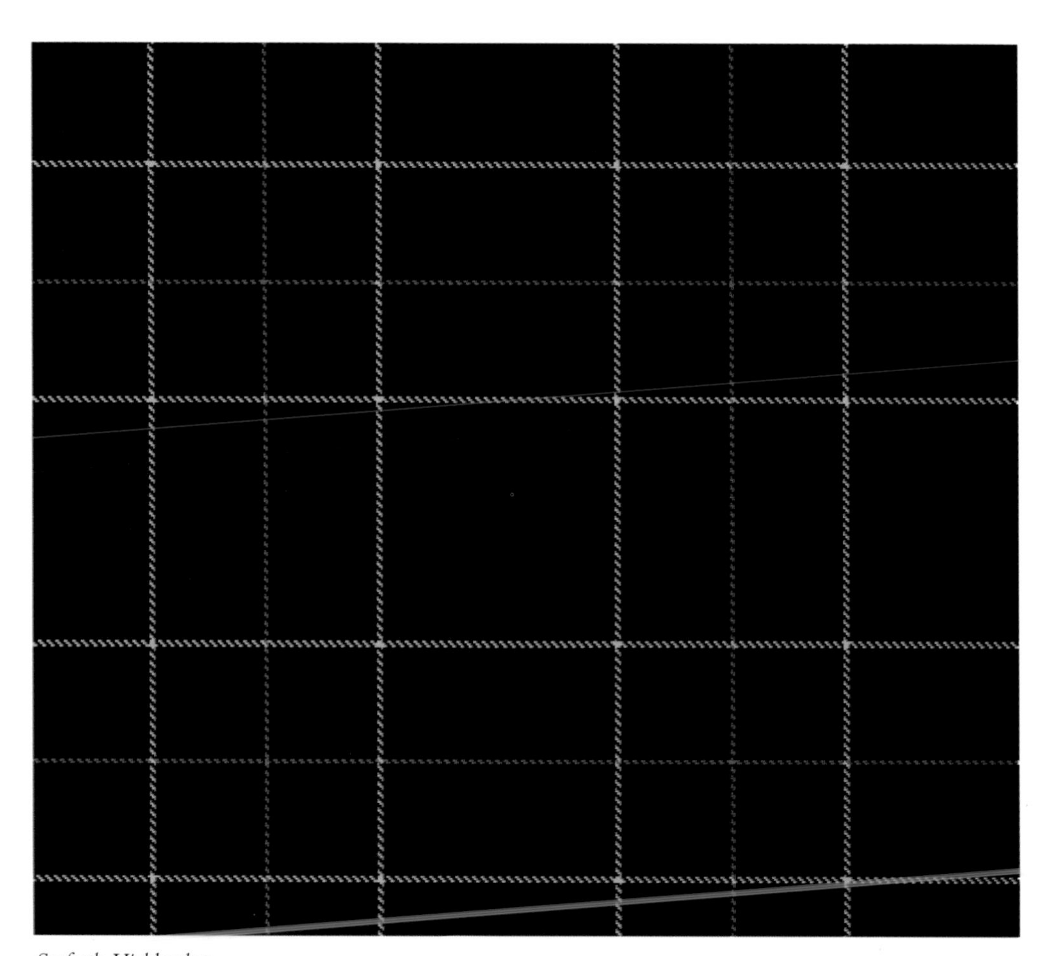

*Seaforth Highlanders*

Seaforth Highlanders are now united with the Cameron and Gordon Highlanders as "The Highlanders" and use the MacKenzie in trews). Whether the MacKenzies had a different tartan prior to 1778 is not known. Wilson's pattern book records the various widths and weights of cloth – officers' kilts were generally made of finer wool than those worn by other ranks.

Surnames with possible associations: Charles, Kenneth, Kennethson, MacBeolain, MacConnach, MacMurchie, MacMurchy, MacVanish, MacVinish, Smart

# MacKinnon

Earliest known date: 1810
Earliest source: Cockburn, 1810-20
Tartan type: Symmetrical
Sett: **W**4 R8 Az4 G16 R32 G4 B8 R4 G32 R12 B4 G4 R6 **Az**4
Clan crest: A boar's head erased and holding in its mouth the shank of a deer all Proper
Clan motto: *Audentes fortuna juvat* ("Fortune aids the brave")
Badge: *Giuthas* (Pine Tree)

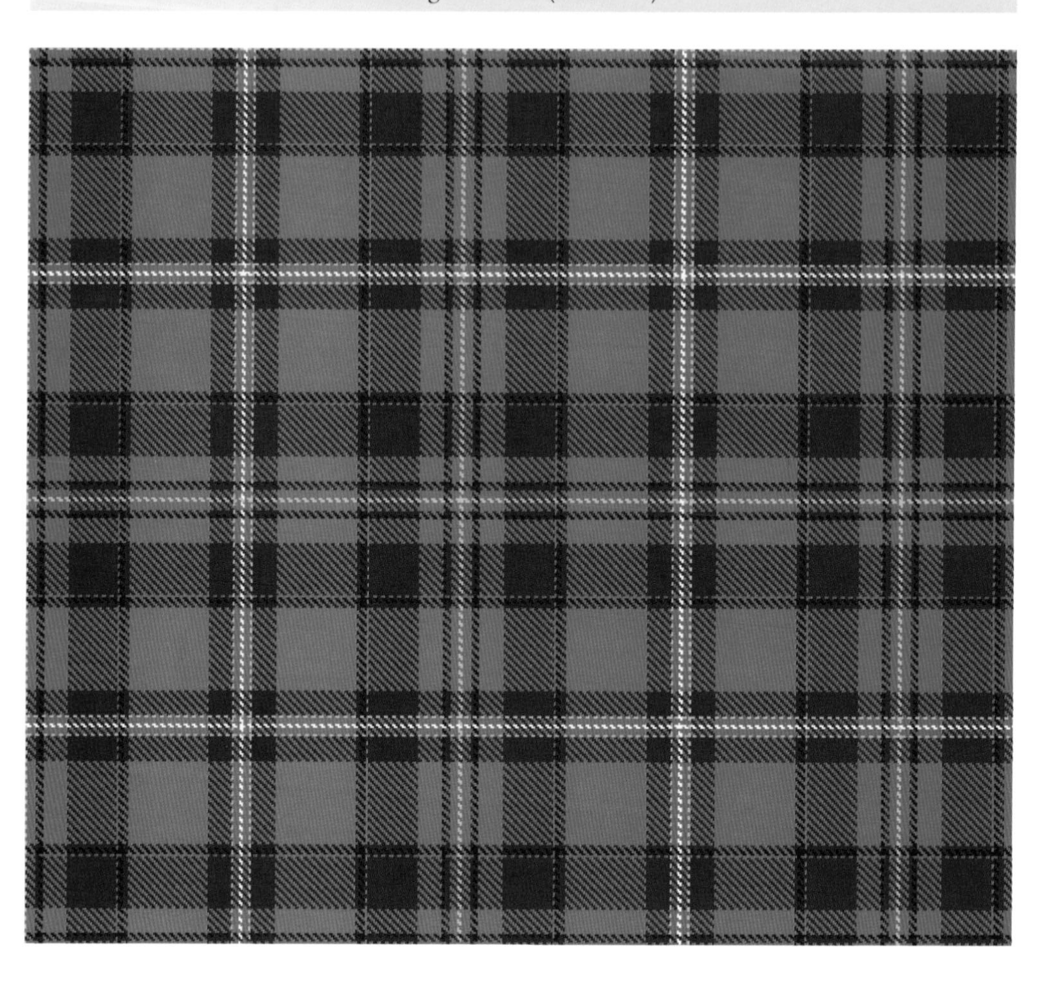

The MacKinnons claim descent from Fingon, a younger son of Kenneth MacAlpin, King of the Scots. Their plant badge, the pine, is a reference to their links with the "Clan Alpin". The original home of the Clan MacKinnon was at Mull, where they held lands under the Lord of the Isles. By 1594, they also held lands in Strathardal, Skye, with the chief's castles of Dunakin by Kyle Akin and Dunringill, and, later, a house at Kilmorie. One branch of the family were also hereditary abbots of Iona: Iain MacKinnon, the 9th chief who died in 1500, was also Bishop of the Isles – his magnificent tomb effigy can be seen in Iona Cathedral.

In 1606, James VI planned to wrest power from the ancient island chiefs in order to bring them under royal rule. In 1609 Lachlan MacKinnon was forced to submit to the king, which severely restricted his powers. Despite this, the MacKinnons remained loyal to the Stewarts and fought in Montrose's army at Inverlochy in 1645 and in 1651, Laclan Mor raised a regiment and fought at Worcester, where he was knighted on the battlefield by Charles II. The clan remained loyal in the next century, although the MacKinnon chief was declared forfeit after Sheriffmuir in 1715. After Culloden, the MacKinnon chief Iain Og hid Prince Charles Edward in a cave and smuggled him to Mallaig. When Iain Og died in 1756, he was succeeded by his son, Charles, but by now the MacKinnon estates were in such debt that they were eventually sold in 1791. Charles left a son, John, the last chief of the line, who died in 1808. The chiefship then passed to William MacKinnon MP in 1811, a descendant from the second son of Lachlan Mor who had emigrated to the West Indies.

The MacKinnon tartan has undergone various alterations over time, but the tartan approved by the chief and used today returns to the form of the earliest example from c.1816 in the collection of the Highland Society with azure blue stripes. In 1831, Logan had recorded these stripes in white; the Smiths (1850) recorded them as crimson; MacIan (1847) as black and white, and Grant(1886) as black!

Surnames with possible associations: MacKinney, MacKinven, MacMorran, Morren

# MacKintosh

Earliest known date: 1816
Earliest source: Collection of the Highland Society, 1816
Tartan type: Symmetrical
Sett: **R**48 B12 R6 G24 R8 **B**2
Clan crest: A mountain cat salient guardant Proper
Clan motto: "Touch not the cat but a glove"
Badge: *Lus nam braoileag* (Red Whortleberry)

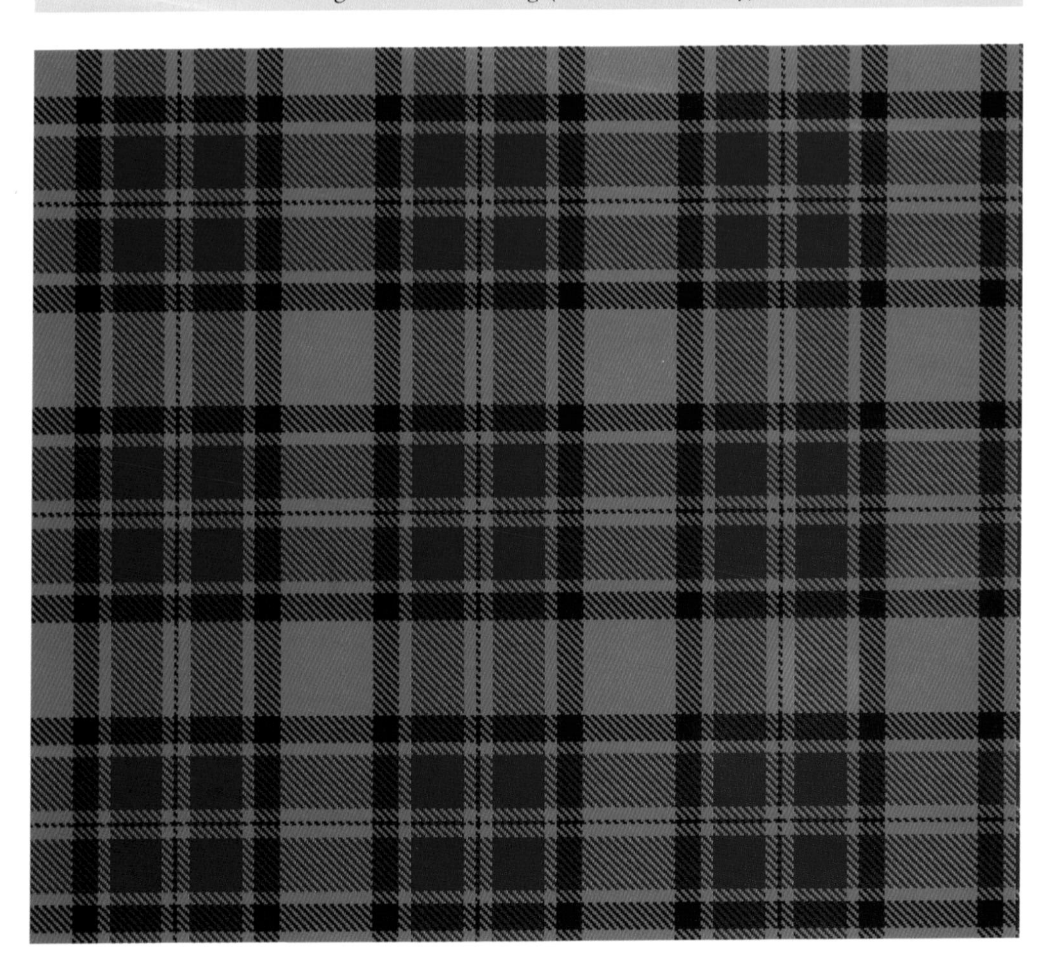

MacKintosh – or more properly "Macintosh" – is from the old Gaelic *Mac an Toisich* which means "son of the leader, or chief". According to tradition, the founder of the clan was Shaw, the younger son of Duncan MacDuff, the ancestor of the Earls of Fife. Around 1163, he was made Constable of Inverness Castle and granted lands in the Findhorn valley, Farquhar, the 5th chief, led the clan against the army of King Haakon of Norway at the battle of Largs in 1263. After his death in a duel in 1265, his infant son Angus was brought up by his uncle, Alexander of Islay, Lord of the Isles, who arranged his marriage to Eva, the daughter of Dougall Dal, chief of Clan Chattan in Lochaber. The Clan Chattan, which developed into a clan confederation, was generally led by MacKintosh chiefs.

The first truly powerful MacKintosh chief was Malcolm, the 8th chief (1430–64). Under him MacKintosh lands stretched from Petty to Lochaber. His son Duncan made the fortunate marriage to Flora, daughter of the Earl of Ross and Lord of the Isles. William, the 16th chief, was found guilty of conspiring to kill Huntly, the Lord Lieutenant of the North, and was executed at Strathbogie in 1550. For the next 200 years, the Mackintoshes feuded with the Camerons, the MacDonells of Keppoch, and the Gordons. The last clan battle was fought against the MacDonells at Muroy and, in 1672, Lachlan, Chief from 1660, was declared Chief of Clan Chattan by Lord Lyon, King of Arms.

The MacKintoshes supported the royalist cause and fought under Montrose for Charles I. In 1715 they remained loyal to the Stewart cause: Lachlan MacKintosh led 800 clansmen out to battle and was rewarded with the title of Lord MacKintosh. After the defeat of the Jacobites at the battle of Preston, many MacKintosh clansmen were deported to the Americas. Lord MacKintosh died childless in 1731 and the chiefship passed to William of Daviot as 22nd chief. His brother Angus, 23rd chief was a supporter of the Hanoverian king, George, and a captain in the Black Watch Regiment when Prince Charles Edward Stewart landed in Scotland in 1745. In his absence, his wife, who became known as "Colonel Anne", led the Clan MacKintosh in support of Prince Charlie. Colonel Anne's strategy won the Jacobites the engagement known as the "Rout of Moy". In 1746, when the prince stayed at Moy, a force of 1,500 government troops was sent to capture him. They were deceived by five of Colonel Anne's servants into believing that they were in the middle of the entire Jacobite army and promptly fled!

When Alfred Donald, the 28th Chief of the Name of Mackintosh (and 29th Chief of Clan Chattan), died in 1938, the chiefship was settled on his cousin, Rear-Admiral Lachlan

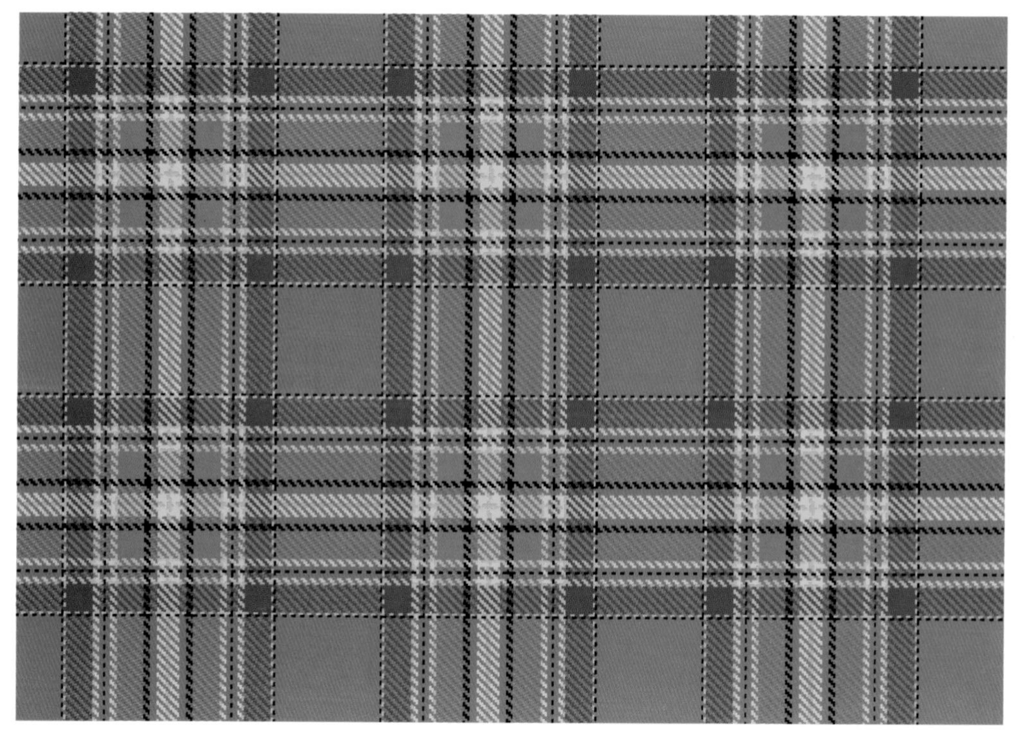

*Clan Chattan*

MacKintosh of MacKintosh, while the chiefship of the Clan Chattan passed to Alfred Donald's grand-daughter. However, when she married and no longer bore the name of the stem family of Clan Chattan, the chiefship of this clan was passed to Duncan Alexander MacKintosh of MacKintosh-Torcastle and Clan Chattan who lived in Rhodesia (now Zimbabwe), although the seat of the MacKintosh chiefs remained at Moy Hall in Inverness-shire.

A certified sample of the MacKintosh tartan dating from 1816 and bearing the signature of the chief can be found in the Collection of the Highland Society. Logan published the tartan in 1831 and possibly knew of the earlier specimen. Logan also wrote that the chief wore a tartan of a "very showy pattern", which was registered in 1947 as "Clan Chattan (Chief)".

Surnames with possible associations: Ayson, Dallas, Doles, Elder, Esson, Hardie, Hardy, Maccartney, MacConchy, MacGlashan, MacKeggie, MacKieson, MacRitchie, Niven, Noble, Ritchie, Smith, Tarrill, Thain, Tosh

# MacLachlan

Earliest known date: 1831

Earliest source: Logan, 1831

Tartan type: Symmetrical

Sett: **R**32 Bk4 R4 Bk4 R4 Bk32 B32 G6 B32 Bk32 R32 Bk4 **R**4

Clan crest: Issuant from a crest coronet of three strawberry leaves Or a castle set on a rock all Proper

Clan motto: *Fortis et fidus* ("Brave and strong")

Badge *Caorunn* (Mountain Ash, Rowan)

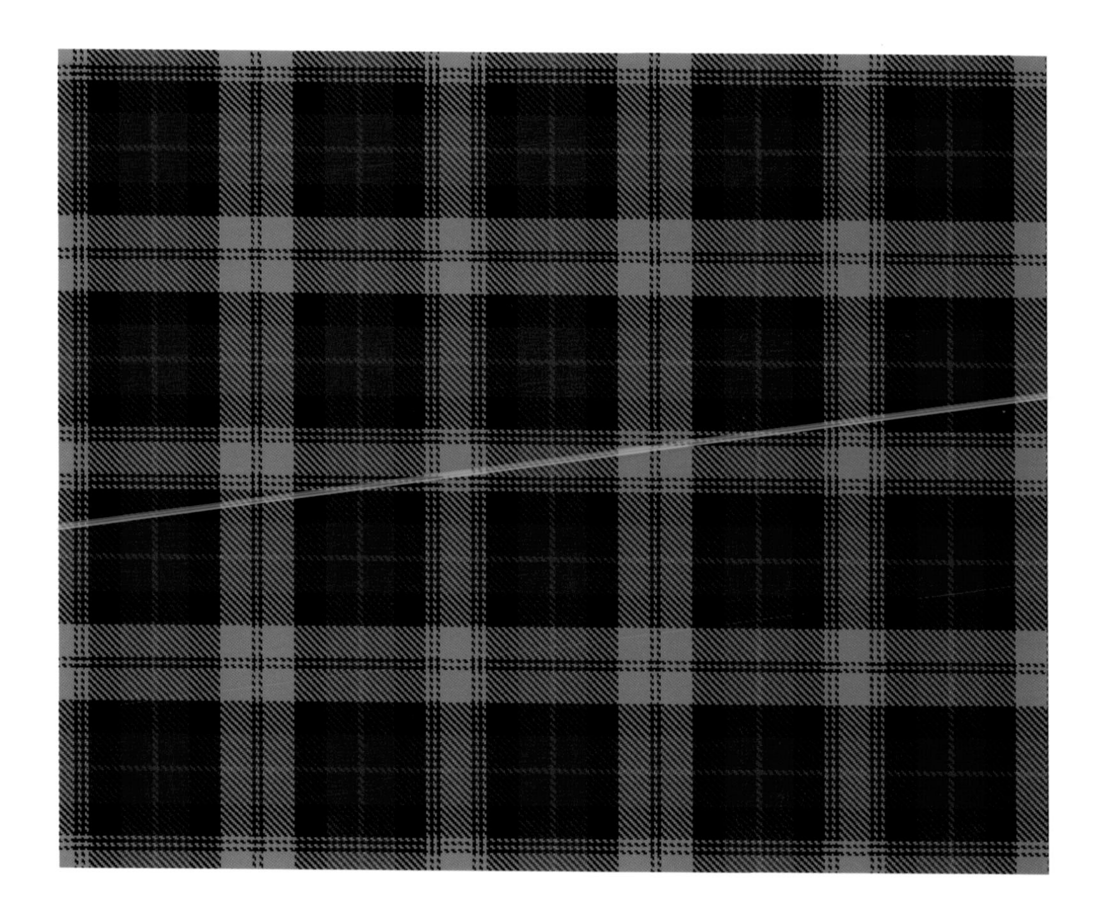

The MacLachlans take their name from Lachlan Mor, a chief who lived by Loch Fyne in the 13th century and after whom is named the barony of Strathlachan, the Castle Lachla, seat of the MacLachlans of MacLachlan, close to where the River Lachlan flows into Lachlan Bay! Lachlan Mor himself was part of the great dynastic family of King Niall of the North of Ireland, who were the rulers of Ulster.

In 1292, Gillespie MacLachlan was one of the 12 barons whose lands were formed into the sheriffdom of Argyll. Gillespie supported Robert the Bruce and attended the first Scottish Parliament held at St Andrews in 1308. When Lachlan Og became the MacLachlan chief in around 1582, he was obliged to resign some of his lands to the Lamont chief because his kinsman Lachlan MacLachlan of Dunnamuck had killed Robert Lamont of Silvercraigs.

Lachlan Og led the Clan Lachlan in the 7th Earl of Argyll's campaign in 1615 against the MacDonalds of Islay and in 1633 (although he had already received a charter from the Scottish king, James VI, for his lands in 1591) procurred an Act of Parliament under Charles I confirming him as "Laird of MacLachlan". In 1646, during the Civil War, the Maclachlans took the opportunity of settling old scores and rivalries in the massacre of the Lamonts. In this they were led, surprisingly, by the Reverend Colin MacLachlan! In 1656, however, Lachlan MacLachlan of that Ilk received a commission from Oliver Cromwell, the Lord Protector, to be Justice of the Peace in Argyllshire. His son Archibald, who became the 15th chief, received a charter following the Restoration of the monarchy, erecting the lands of Strathlachlan into a barony. In the next century, the MacLachlans were loyal Jacobites: Lachlan MacLachlan, 16th chief, signed the Address of Welcome to the Old Chevalier, King James VIII Stewart, (the Old Pretender) on his landing in Scotland. It is said that, because of this, Campbell of Ardkinglas followed the MacLachlan "like a sleuthhound" for five years and shot him dead in 1719. Undeterred, the MacLachlans again supported the cause in the 1745 Rising under Prince Charles Edward Stewart (the Young Pretender). The 17th Chief led 300 of his clansmen at Culloden and was killed by a cannon shot.

After the '45, the MacLachlan were declared forfeit for treason: but, because the estates had been "made over" to the 18th chief more than ten years earlier, they escaped untouched – although Castle Lachlan was burnt down in 1746. A new mansion house, the present Castle Lachlan was built in the 19th century in sight of the ruins of the old stronghold. The present form of the MacLachlan tartan can only be traced as far back as 1831,(although it may in fact be older) and is the version recorded by Logan.

Surnames with possible associations: Ewing, Gilchrist,Lauchlan, MacLaghlan

# MacLaine of Lochbuie

Earliest known date; 1810

Earliest source: Cockburn, 1810-20

Tartan type: Symmetrical

Sett: **R**64 G16 Az8 **Y**2

Clan crest: A branch of laurel and a branch of cypress in saltire surmounted of a battle-axe in pale all Proper

Clan motto: *Vicere vel mori* ("To conquer or die")

Badge: Blaeberry

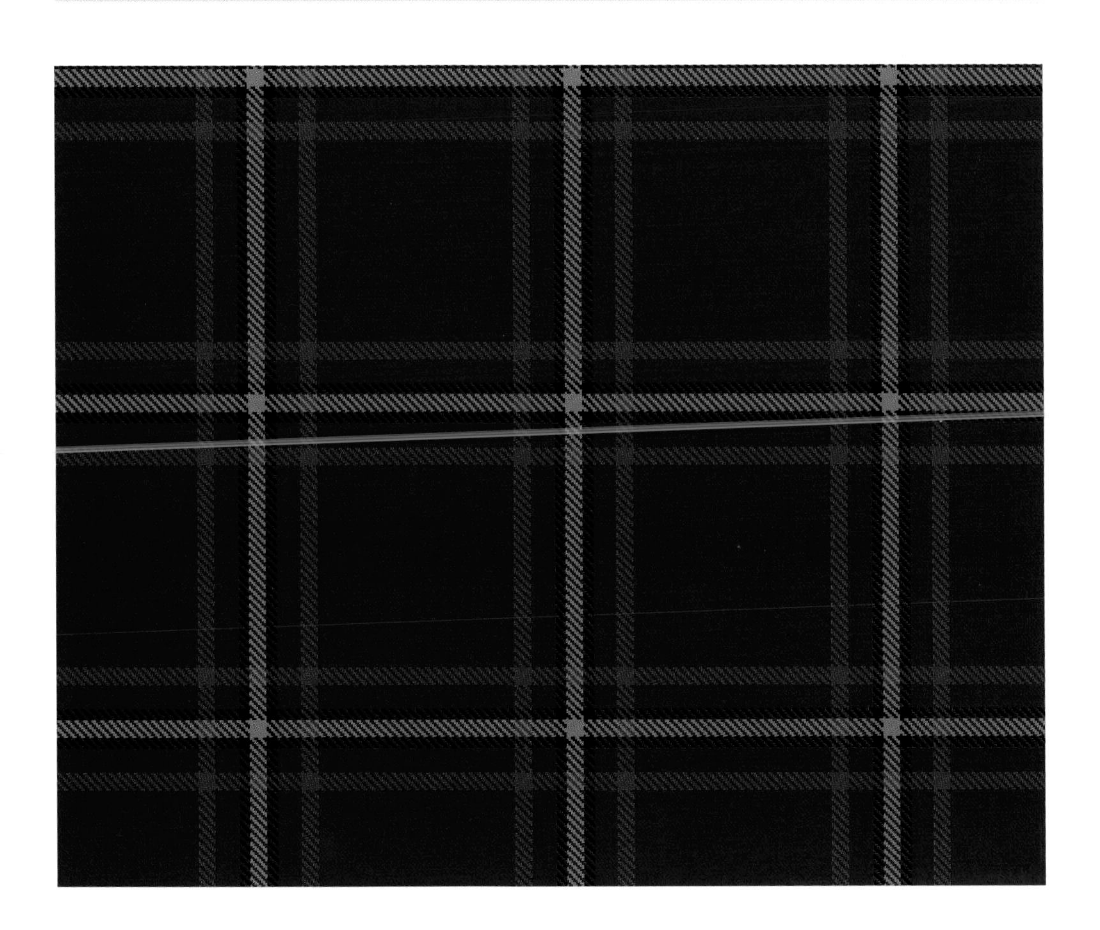

The MacLaines of Lochbuie (as well as the MacLeans of Duart, see page 176) are descended from Gillean Na Tuaidh (Gillean of the Battle-axe, whose weapon appears in the clan crest) a 13th century warrior who held lands in Morven and Mull. Gillean and his sons fought at the battle of Largs in 1263 against the Norwegian king Haakon IV and ended the Norse rule over the Hebrides. Gillean's great-great-grandson, Iain Dhu, settled in Mull and was the father of Eachainn Reaganach (Hector the Stern), who received the lands of Lochbuie from John, 1st Lord of the Isles in around 1350 and built his castle at the head of the loch.

Hector had several sons: Tearlach (Charles) was the ancestor of the Clan Thearlaich of Dochgarroch (known as the MacLeans of the North), but the second chief of Lochbuie was Hector's son, Murdoch Roy. The 5th chief, John Og of Lochbuie died in around 1494 and was succeeded by his son, Murchadh Gearr (Murdoch the Short), but his uncle, Murdoch of Scallasdale seized the estate for himself. Murdoch Gearr fled to Ireland but, supported by a strong force, he soon returned. According to legend, he made himself known to his childhood nurse who then helped him regain possession of the Castle of Lochbuie. Shortly afterwards he defeated his uncle in battle at Grulin. John Mor, the 7th chief, was famed as a swordsman, and his son, Hector, was the first chief to adopt the spelling of the name "MacLaine". Murdoch, the 10th chief, was a royalist supporter and fought with Montrose in 1645. For this he subsequently forfeited his lands, which were not restored until 1661. Hector MacLaine of Lochbuie, the 12th chief, fought victoriously in the first Jacobite battle of James VII's campaign at Knockbreck in Badenoch in 1689. John, the 17th chief, was host to Dr Samuel Johnson and James Bowell on their tour of the Hebrides in 1773 – a plaque above the door at Lochbuie House commemorates their visit. Donald, the 20th chief, was born in 1816. He amassed a fortune as a merchant in Batavia in Java and used it to repurchase the Lochbuie estates which were, by then, being held by creditors for debts. Yet, even the 24th chief, Kenneth MacLaine's, efforts to keep the estates by launching himself as a singer came to nothing, and the Lochbuie estates were lost to an English bondholder.

Although the sett was first published by James Grant in 1886, the MacLaine of Lochbuie tartan is believed to date from the 18th century. The earliest example dates from 1810-20 and is from the Cockburn Collection. There is also a hunting version which first appeared in W. and A.K. Johnston's book of 1906.

Surnames with possible associations: MacCormick MacFadzean, MacGivra, MacIlvora, MacPhadden

# MacLaren

Earliest known date: 1831

Earliest source: Logan, 1831

Tartan type: Symmetrical

Sett: **B**48 Bk16 G16 R4 G16 Bk2 **Y**4

Clan crest: A lion's head erased Sable crowned with an antique crown of six (four visible) points Or, between tow branches of laurel issuing from a wreath at either side of the head both Proper

Clan motto and *slughorn* (slogan or warcry): *Creag an Tuirc* ("The boar's rock")

Badge: *Buaidh-chraobh na Labrhas* (Laurel)

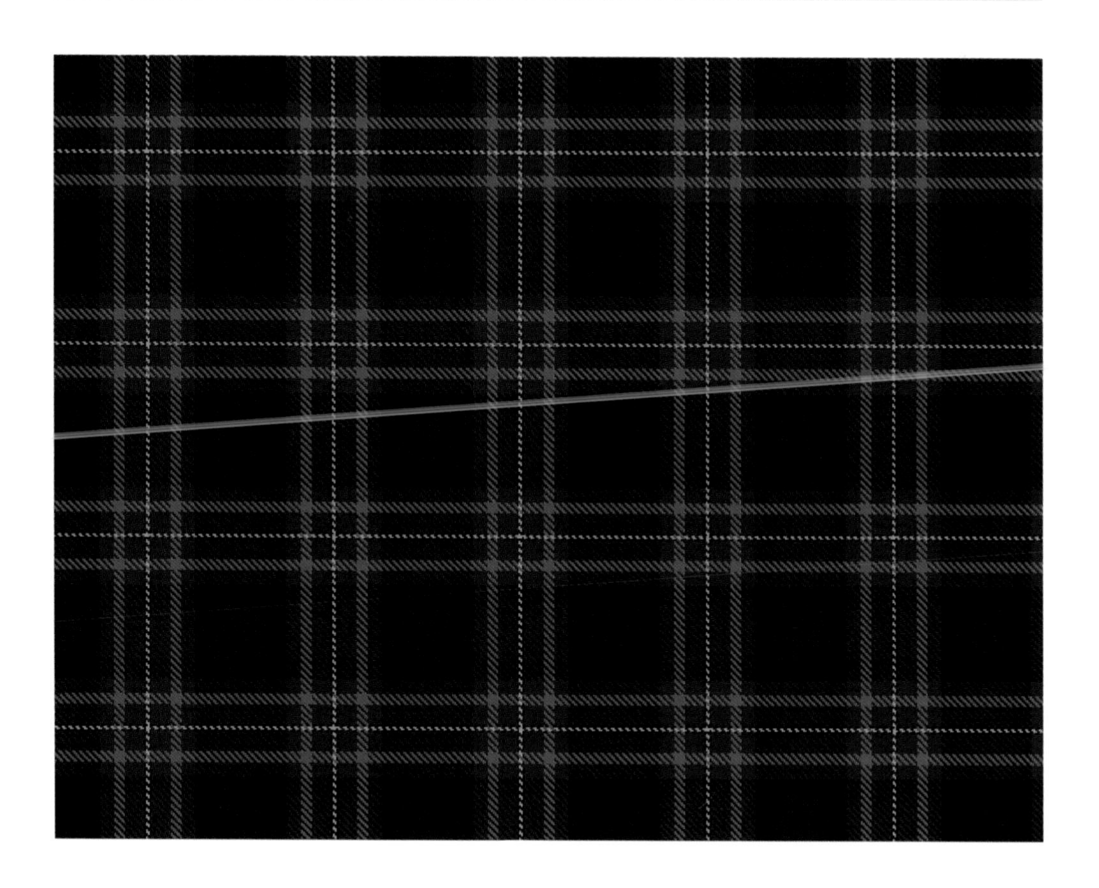

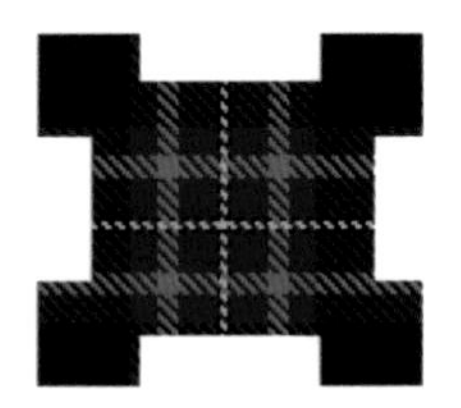

In Gaelic, the MacLarens are known as *Clann Mhic Labhrainn*, meaning the "sons of Laurence" (Laurence, Abbot of Achtow who was alive in the 13th century in Balquidder, the highland part of the princedom of Strathearn around Loch Voil and Loch Earn). The rallying point or "duthus" of the clan was *Creag an Tuirc* – "the Boar's Rock", near Achtow, which also provided the clan's *slughorn* (slogan or warcry). Three MacLaren nobles – Maurice of Tiree, Conan of Balquidder, and Laurin of Ardveche (Locherarnside) are recorded as signing the Ragman Rolls in 1296, in which they swore allegiance to the English king, Edward I, although later, in 1314, they probably supported Robert the Bruce at Bannockburn in his aims for an independent Scotland. In 1344, when the last Celtic earl of Strathearn was deprived of his holdings and title, the MacLarens came under pressure from new overlords: Balquidder passed into the hands of the Crown, which, in 1500, was granted to Janet Kennedy, the mistress of James IV.

In 1548, the MacLarens were invaded by the "Children of the Mist" – the dispossessed MacGregors, who were driven from their lands by the Campbells into Balquidder. In return for Campbell protection from the MacGregors, the MacLarens were forced to acknowledge the Campbells as their feudal superiors. Those who refused to submit sought their fortunes abroad. Some entered the service of Sweden: in 1647 "Johan Laurin" was made a nobleman with the name Lagergren, and in 1691 "Magnus Laurin" was ennobled with the name "Lagerstrom".

Royalist supporters, the MacLarens fought with Montrose in the cause of Charles I and when their Stewart king, James VII, called for help, the MacLarens followed him to fight in the battle of Killiecrankie (1689). The clan was also called out in 1715 and fought at Sheriffmuir and, in 1745, they rallied to the standard of the "Young Pretender", Charles Edward Stewart. At Culloden, the chief Donald MacLaren was captured, while Balquidder was attacked by Hanoverian forces. MacLaren managed to escape, however,and remained a fugitive until the amnesty in 1757. More recently, the chiefs recovered some of their clan lands including their rallying point, Creag an Tuirc, and, in 1957, the Lord Lyon decreed Donald MacLaren as MacLarane of MacLaren, Chief of the Clan, who was succeeded by his son, also Donald.

The MacLaren clan tartan was first described by Logan in 1831 and later published in a drawing by MacIan in 1847. Wilson & Sons, the Bannockburn weavers, had been producing the sett before 1820, but they called it "Regent". When George IV became king in 1820, the name Regent became outdated, but production of the sett continued. The MacLaren clan tartan differs only from the Fergusson (page 66) in having a yellow line in place of the white. A second MacLaren tartan was designed by I.G. Campbell MacLaren, approved by the chief and accepted by the Clan MacLaren Society in 1981 as the MacLaren Dress tartan.

*MacLaren Dress*

Surnames with possible associations: Lair, Lawrence, Lawrie, Lawson, Low, Lowson, MacFater, MacFeat, MacGrory, MacPatrick, MacPhater

# MacLean of Duart

Earliest known date: *c.*1810-20
Earliest source: Cockburn Collection,
Tartan type: Symmetrical
Sett: **Bk**2 R4 Az2 R24 G16 Bk2 W2 Bk2 Y2 Bk6 Az2 **B**8
Clan crest: A tower embattled Argent
Clan motto: "Virtue mine honor"
Badge: *Dearca fithich* (Crowberry)

The MacLeans of Duart, whose name in Gaelic is *MacGille Eoin,* meaning 'son of the servant of St John', are descended (like the MacLaines of Lochbuie) from Gillean na Tuaidh, 'Gillean the Battle-axe', who fought against the Norwegians at the battle of Largs in 1263.

In 1294, Gillemoir Mackilyn was a signatory of the Ragman Rolls, swearing fealty to the English king, Edward I. His son, Malise, however, was a supporter of Robert the Bruce, and his own son, Gillicullum, fought at Bannockburn. Gillicullum's son, Iain MacLean, settled in Mull. He had several sons, one of whom was Lachlan Lubanach, the progenitor of the MacLeans of Duart, and Eachann Reaganach, progenitor of the MacLaines of Lochbuie (see page 171). The brothers appear to have been supporters of the Lord of Lorn, but after some dispute, they became followers of the MacDonalds, Lords of the Isles. Luchlan Lubanach, who began building the Castle of Duart, overlooking the Sound of Mull, married Mary, daughter of the Lord of the Isles in 1367, and was made his lieutenant-general. Lachlan's son, Eachan Ruadh nan Cath, 'Red Hector of the Battles', fought and died for the Lord of the Isles at Harlow in 1411.

By the end of the century, the MacLeans held extensive lands in Mull, Tiree, Coll, Islay, Morvern and Lochaber. In 1496 the lands of Duart were erected into a barony by James IV. However, in 1501, James IV took to the field in person against Hector Odhar MacLean of Duart in an effort to remove the MacDonalds from the autonomous rule as Lords of Isles which was supported by the MacLeans. With the downfall of the last MacDonald lordship, the MacLeans began to struggle for power with the different branches of the Clan Donald trying to fill the void left by the fall of the Lordship of the Isles. The feud culminated at the battle of Traigh Ghruineard in Islay in 1598 when Sir Lachlan Mor MacLean was killed, it is said, by an elfin bolt from a black fairy whose services MacLean had spurned. Both clans were weakened – Sir Lachlan's death was avenged by his sons who massacred the Islay folk in a three-day blood-bath, and the Campbells, who had waited patiently on the sidelines, finally seized control of the island and its important trade route with Ireland.

In the 17th century, the MacLeans were staunch supporters of Charles I: in 1632 Lachlan MacLean of Morven was made a baronet. In 1651 Sir Hector, the 2nd Baronet called out the clan and lost his life at the battle of Inverkeithing. The estates were now heavily in debt, and once more the Campbells were on hand to take over the Duart lands. In 1689 Sir John, the 4th

Baronet, supported James VII. The direct Duart line was soon to be extinct: with the death of Sir Hector, the 5th Baronet, in 1750, the honors and chiefship were passed to Alan MacLean of Brolas. In 1911 Sir Fitzroy, the 10th Baronet (who had been at the Charge of the Light Brigade in the Crimean War and died aged 101), succeeded in reacquiring the ruins of Duart Castle, and the following year the clan gathered at their ancient home.

A sample of MacLean tartan dating from *c.*1810–20 is in the Cockburn Collection. Logan published a variation with a single azure stripe in 1831 which was rejected by the Smiths as an 'innovation', and the earlier version is now in general use today. D.C. Stewart also pointed out that the MacLean clan tartan is an 'inversion' of the Royal Stewart (page 241): the succession of colors is the same order and of the same proportions but the direction is reversed. The arrangement of black-white-black lines in the center of the Stewart is also in the MacLean, but moved to the red ground and here they are light blue-black-light blue.

Surnames with possible associations: Beath, Black, Clanachan, Garvie, Gillon, Lean, , MacBeath, Macbeth, MacCraken, MacIlduy, MacLergain, MacRankin, MacVeagh, MacVey, Paton

# MacLeod

Earliest known date: 1746
Earliest source: Logan, 1831
Tartan type: Symmetrical
Sett: **R**6 Bk4 G30 Bk20 B40 Bk4 **Y**4
Clan crest: A bull's head cabossed Sable, horned Or, between two flags Gules, staved of the first
Clan motto: 'Hold fast'
Badge: Juniper

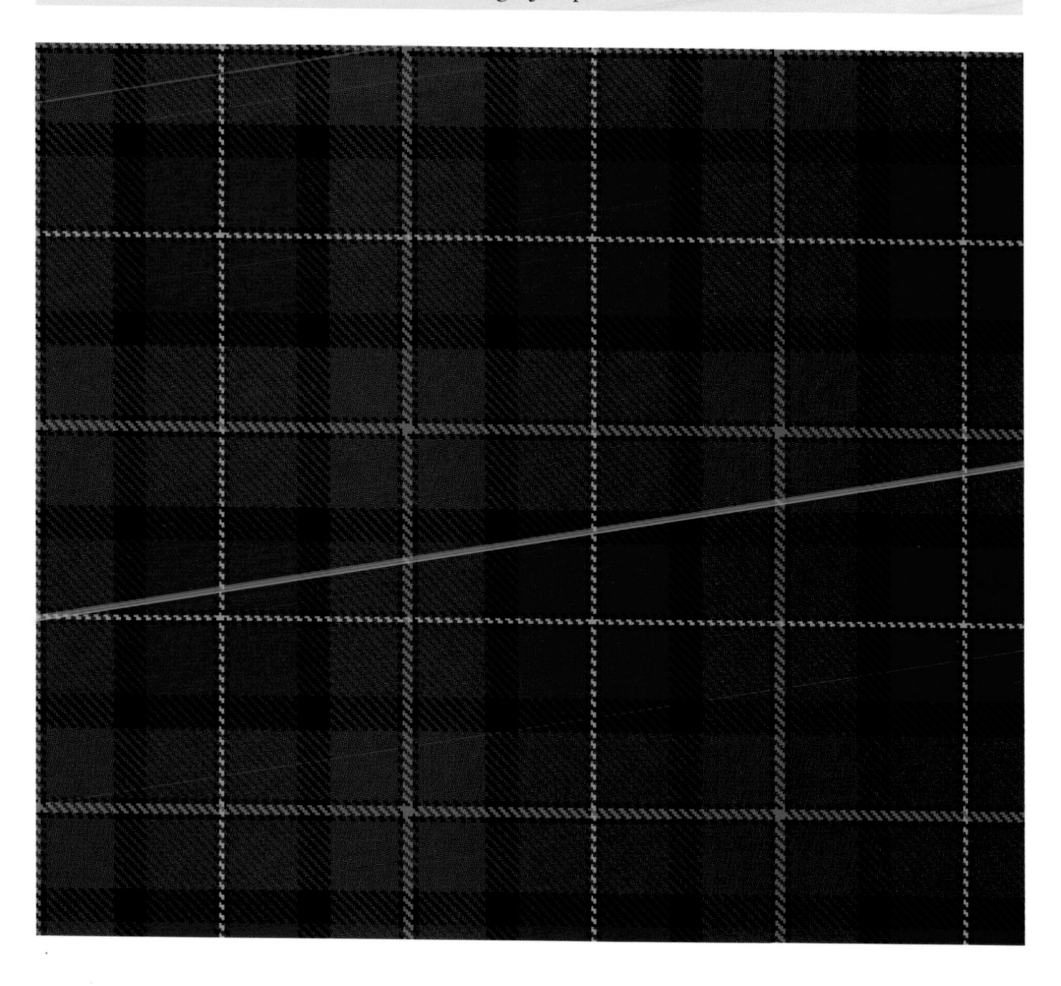

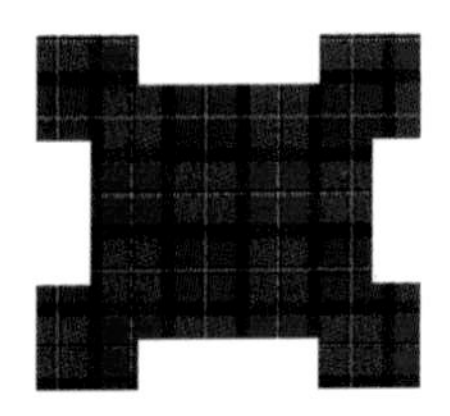

MacLeod means 'Son of Leod' and is apparently derived from the old Norse *Liotr* meaning 'ugly' – although in Anglo-Saxon, *leod* meant 'prince'. It is generally said that the ancestor of the MacLeods was Leod, son of Olaf the Black, King of the Isle of Man and the North Isles. Olaf died sometime around 1237 and was succeeded by his son Leod who inherited the islands of Lewis, Harris, and part of Skye. Leod also acquired Dunvegan on Skye (which remains the chief's seat even today) when he married the daughter of the Norwegian steward MacRailt.

Leod's two sons, Torquil and Tormod, became respectively the progenitors of the Siol Tormod, or MacLeods of Harris and Dunvegan, and the Siol Torquil, the MacLeods of Lewis (later 'of the Lewes'). Tormod is thought to have been the elder of the two and his chiefly descendants were subsequently styled MacLeod of MacLeod. Ian, the 4th chief, was alive in the 14th century and received the 'Fairy Flag' – supposedly a gift from a fairy he married, but more likely a fragment of a holy relic brought to Scotland from Constantinople by Harald Haardrade – and which is still preserved today at Duvegan.

The MacLeods followed the MacDonald Lords of the Isles to the battle of Haraw in 1411 but, when James IV set out to wrest power from the MacDonalds, the MacLeods withdrew their support. William, the 7th chief, was killed in a feud with the MacDonalds at the 'battle of the Bloody Bay' and was succeeded by Alastair Crotach 'the Hump-backed'. Despite his disability, Crotach successfully laid claim to Trotternish in 1542 (long held by the MacDonalds of Sleate), entertained James V at a mountainside feast in 1536, and built the famous 'Fairy Tower' at Dunvegan Castle. He also ordered the rebuilding of the church at Rodel in Harris: the church and splendid Crotach tomb are among the Hebrides' finest monuments. Crotach married Lochiel's tenth daughter – after the other nine had rejected him – and had three sons, the youngest of whom was Tormod, who became the 13th Chief.

Rory Mor, the 16th Chief, was knighted by James V in 1595. He settled the feud with the MacDonalds and was responsible for enlarging the Castle at Dunvegan. A great drinking horn named after him is kept at Dunvegan; it holds a bottle and a half of wine which must be drunk in a single draft, a ritual that forms part of the ceremonials of each new MacLeod chief. Norman, the 22nd Chief, entertained Boswell and Johnson at Dunvegan on their historic journey in the isles and had a magnificent portrait painted by Allan Ramsay in 1748 in which he wears the chiefly outfit of red MacLeod tartan.

The MacLeods of the Lewes refused to accept the superiority of their cousins at Dunvegan as chiefs until the head of their family, Torquil MacLeod of Lewes, was killed in 1597. The barony then passed to his son-in-law, Sir Rory MacKenzie of Cogeach, and representation of

*MacLeod - red*

the Siol Torquil passed to the senior cadets of the Lewes house, the MacLeods of Ramsay. In 1988, Torquil MacLeod of Ramsay was recognized by the Lord Lyon as MacLeod of the Lewes, Chief and Head of the baronial House under the MacLeod of MacLeod.

At a time when most people believed that the 'correct' tartan for the clan was the MacKenzie (see page 161), a tartan was recorded as The MacLeod Clan by Logan for MacIan's book in 1847 and, since then, this tartan has been used. It was officially approved by the 26th Chief, Norman Magnus, in 1910. A second MacLeod tartan, known as the MacLeod Red Clan tartan, was designed in 1982 by Ruairidh MacLeod and is based on the tartan worn by Norman, 22nd Chief, in the portrait by Allan Ramsay. The MacLeod of the Lewes (and Ramsay) tartan is the MacLeod of MacLeod yellow dress tartan which appeared in *The* Walter Scott in 1829.

Surnames with possible associations: Askey, Harold, MacCabe, MacCaig, Maccaskill, MacClure, MacCorkindale, MacCuaig, MacHarold, MacKaskill, MacLewis, MacLure, MacRaild

# MacMillan

Earliest known date:1847
Earliest source: MacIan
Tartan type: Asymmetrical
Sett: Bk 2Y12 Bk2 B8 Bk2 G12 B8 G12 Bk2 B8 Bk2 R16 W2 R16 Bk2 B8 Bk2Y12
Clan crest: A dexter and a sinister hand issuing from a wreath grasping and brandishing aloft a two-handed sword Proper
Clan motto: *Miseris succurrere disco* ('I learn to succor the unfortunate')
Badge: *Cuileann* (Holly)

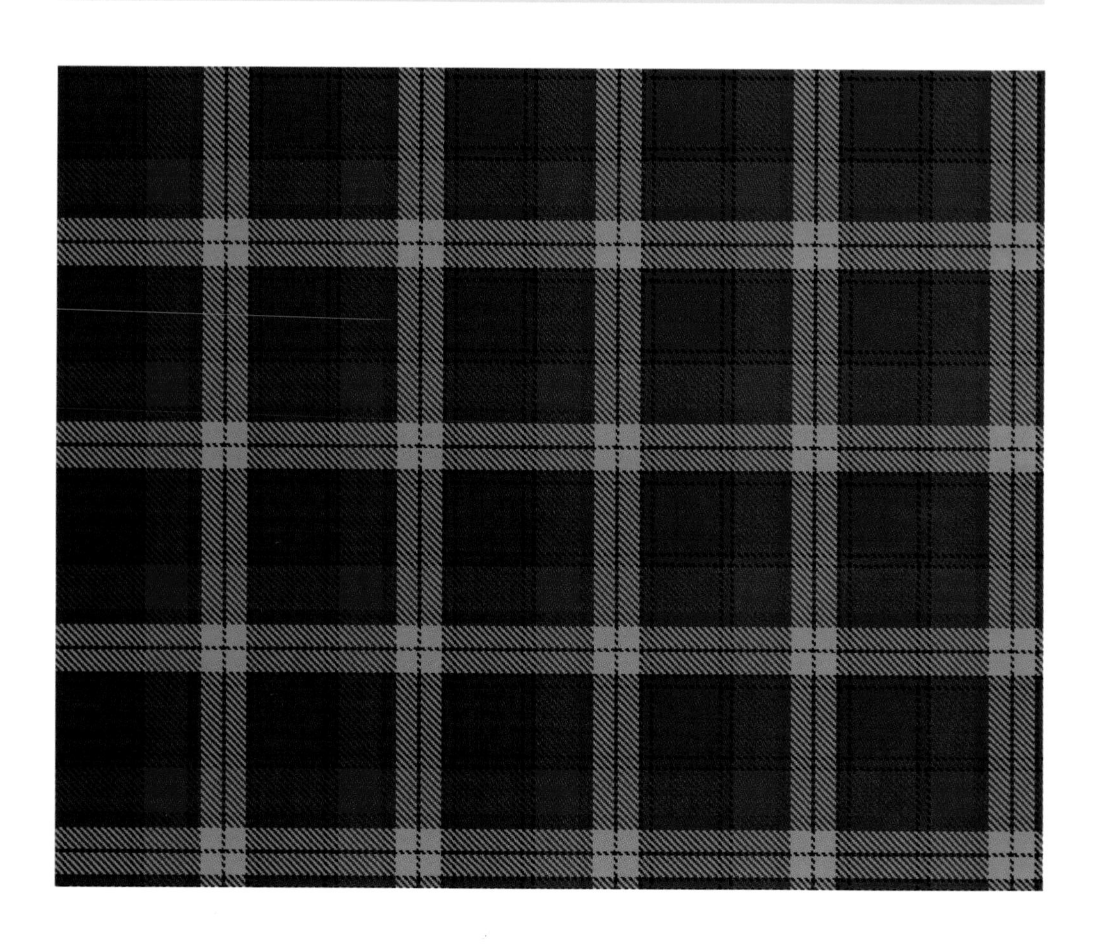

It is believed that the origins of the MacMillan clan lie in the ancient Celtic church: the name is derived from *Mac Mhaolain*, meaning 'Son of the Tonsured'. In pre-Reformation times, surnames in the Highlands were restricted to those of ancient birth, so the name implies descent from a monastic family, which was usually a branch of the local ruling house.

In the 12th century, Comac was appointed by Alexander I as Bishop of Dunkeld. Priests in the Celtic church were allowed to marry and one of Comac's sons, Gillie Chriosd, was the progenitor of the MacMillans. The name Mac Mhaolain also makes reference the type of shaven hairstyle worn by monks. This was not the Roman manner of a shaved ring at the crown of the head, but the more distinctive Celtic style of shaving the entire front of the head from ear to ear, leaving everything behind to grow long. The MacMillans seem to have remained keen on the barber's shop: in the Lord High Treasurer's accounts for 1473, there is an entry for payment to 'McMwlane the barbour [barber] for the leichcraft [leeching, or bleeding] done be him to the litl boys'.(Barbers doubled as surgeons at this time.)

A branch of the MacMillan clan was to be found on the shores of Loch Archaig in Lochaber during the reign of David I (1124–53). Tradition says that the MacMillans were moved from Loch Archaig by Malcolm IV (1153–65) and placed on Crown lands at Loch Tay in Perthshire, where they held the estate of Lawers. Robert the Bruce was was sheltered at Ben Lawers by the MacMillan chief, Maolmuire. The clan also fought for Bruce at Bannockburn in 1314. In the 14th century, the MacMillans were driven from Lawers and many moved south to Knapdale on the Argyllshire coast. In some parts of the county, the MacMillans are known as Na Belich 'The Bells'. In 1360, John, Lord of the Isles, granted them lands under a charter to last 'as long as the waves beat on the rock'. This tenure was commemorated in a carved inscription on a rock at Loch Suibhne. This is now gone – some say because of the Campbell's

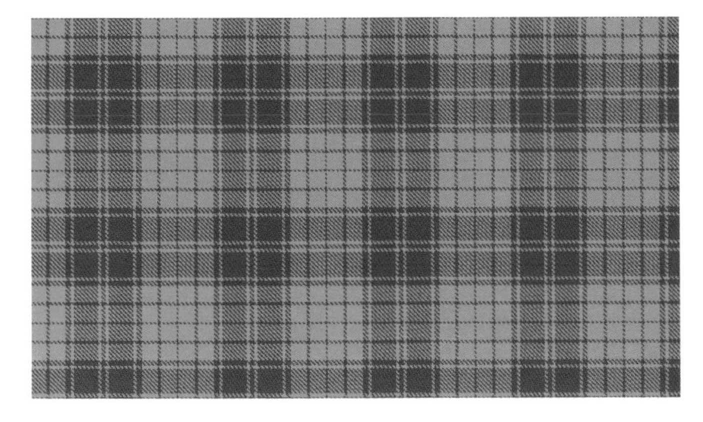

*Macmillan Dress*

*Macmillan Hunting*

chisels! The beautiful Celtic cross in the churchyard in Kilmory and the Round Tower near Castle Sween – both erected by Alexander, 5th Laird of Knapp and 12th Chief of Clan MacMillan – still bear testament to their occupation of the lands.

In time, however, the direct line of the MacMillans of Knap became extinct and, in 1742, the chiefship passed to Duncan MacMillan of Dunmore, an estate on the north side of Loch Tarbert. Duncan's son, Alexander MacMillan of MacMillan and Dunmore, settled the estates on his cousin, Duncan MacMillan of Laggalgarve. Although the MacMillans were staunch Jacobites, John MacMillan of Murlaggen of Lochaber refused to join the cause of Prince Charles Edward unless the Stewarts renounced their Catholic faith. His son, however, raised a company of men and fought at Culloden where he died. Donald MacMillan of Tulloch, who had surrendered to the Duke of Cumberland, was transported without trial, along with many of his men, to the English colonies in the West Indies. The old MacMillan lands were lost and the chiefship passed through a series of holders until 1951, when General Sir Gordon MacMillan of MacMillan was recognized at Chief of the Clan by decree of the Lord Lyon and established his seat at Finlaystone House in Renfrewshire.

The MacMillan clan tartan is referred to as an 'Ancient' tartan. This term is normally used to describe a lighter range of colors than in other tartans. The MacMillan Ancient resembles the Buchanan (page 34) and is derived from a drawing by MacIan in 1847 for the book *The Clans of the Scottish Highlands*. Logan, in the accompanying text to the illustration, stated that MacMillan Ancient was in fact identical to the Buchanan. There is also a MacMillan hunting tartan, and, a dress tartan in red and yellow, both of which were first recorded in *The Vestiarium Scoticum* in 1842.

Surnames with possible associations: Brown, MacBaxter

# MacNab

Earliest known date: c.1816

Earliest source: Logan, 1831

Tartan type: Symmetrical

Sett: **G**16 Cr2 G2 Cr2 G2 Cr12 R16 Cr2 R16 Cr12 G14 Cr2 **G**2

Clan crest: The head of a savage affrontee Proper

Clan motto: *Timor omnis abesto* ('Let fear be far from all')

Badge: Roebuckberry (Stone Bramble)

Like many other Highland clans, the MacNabs are of ecclesiastical descent. In Gaelic they are known as *Clann-an-Aba*, which means 'Children of the Abbott', and are descendants of the hereditary Celtic Abbots of Glendochart, who were themselves the *coarbs* or heirs of St Finian mac Fredach, a prince of the House of Lorn who founded the principal abbey in Glendochart and who died in around 703. It was the nephew of St Finian, and the younger son of Kenneth MacAlpin, the King of Scotland, called Abaruadh 'the Red Abbot', who was the progenitor of the MacNabs. For some 400 years, the MacNabs were also to be hereditary jewelers and armorers to the Campbells of Glenorchy. The MacNab lands on the side of Loch Tay stretched along the River Dochart to the head of the upper part of the Glendochart known as Strathfillan, with the chief's residence at Kinnell.

Angus MacNab was the brother-in-law of John Comyn (murdered by Robert the Bruce in 1306) and joined with the MacDougalls in opposition to Bruce. After the king's victory at Bannockburn, the MacNab charters were destroyed and their estates forfeited and given by Bruce to his loyal supporters. In 1336, Gilbert MacNab made peace with King David II and was granted a charter for the Barony of Bovain in Glendochart. Loyal to the Stewarts, the MacNabs, led by Iain Min, or 'Smooth John', fought with Montrose in 1645. Smooth John was captured after General Lesley besieged Montrose's castle at Kincardine and taken to Edinburgh where he was sentenced to death. On the eve of his execution, however, Smooth John escaped and later led 300 MacNab clansmen into battle at Worcester in 1651. Later chiefs did not support the Stewarts, however: in 1745, John MacNab, the 15th Chief, supported the Hanoverian succession. He was imprisoned by the Jacobites after the battle of Prestonpans in 1745 and confined in Doune Castle. He died in 1788 and was succeeded by Francis MacNab.

A famous producer (and drinker) of whisky, Francis was the subject of a splendid portrait by Sir Henry Raeburn (1756–1832) known as 'The MacNab'. On Francis's death in 1815, his nephew Archibald became chief. It now seemed as if an old prophesy was being fulfilled: it had been said that when a great storm blew a branch of a pine tree against the trunk of another, and grafted itself on to the trunk, the MacNabs would lose their lands. In 1828, the estates were in great debt and Archibald was obliged to sell. He emigrated to Canada and tried to establish a clan community there, but seriously overtaxed the resources of his clansmen in his efforts to repurchase the MacNab lands in Scotland. He died in France in 1860 and was succeeded by his daughter, Sophia, who was recognized as the 18th Chief. When Sophia died unmarried in Florence, Italy, in 1894, the chiefship became dormant. But, in 1955 the Lyon Court adjudged Archibald Corrie MacNab, the head of the House of MacNab of Arthurstone who had acquired the Kinnell estate in Perthshire from the Campbells, to be the 22nd Chief

*MacNab*

(his elder brother, James Alexander, had resigned his chiefship to him when the MacNab lands were regained). In 1970, James Charles MacNab of MacNab of Wester Kilmany in Fife, son of James Alexander, became the 23rd Chief of Clan MacNab, which also has a Clan Society with headquarters in Edinburgh.

The MacNab tartan has a structure identical to that of the Black Watch. The color changes – from black to crimson, blue to green, and green to scarlet – make it a most striking and attractive tartan. Logan was the first to record the pattern in 1831.

Surnames with possible associations: Abbot, Abbotson, Gilfillan

# MacNaughten

Earliest known date: 1831
Earliest source: Logan, 1831
Tartan type: Symmetrical
Sett: **Bk**2 Az2 R32 Az16 Bk24 G32 R32 Az2 **Bk**2
Clan crest: A tower embattled Gules
Clan motto:"I hoip in God"
Badge: *Lus Albanach* (Trailing Azalea)

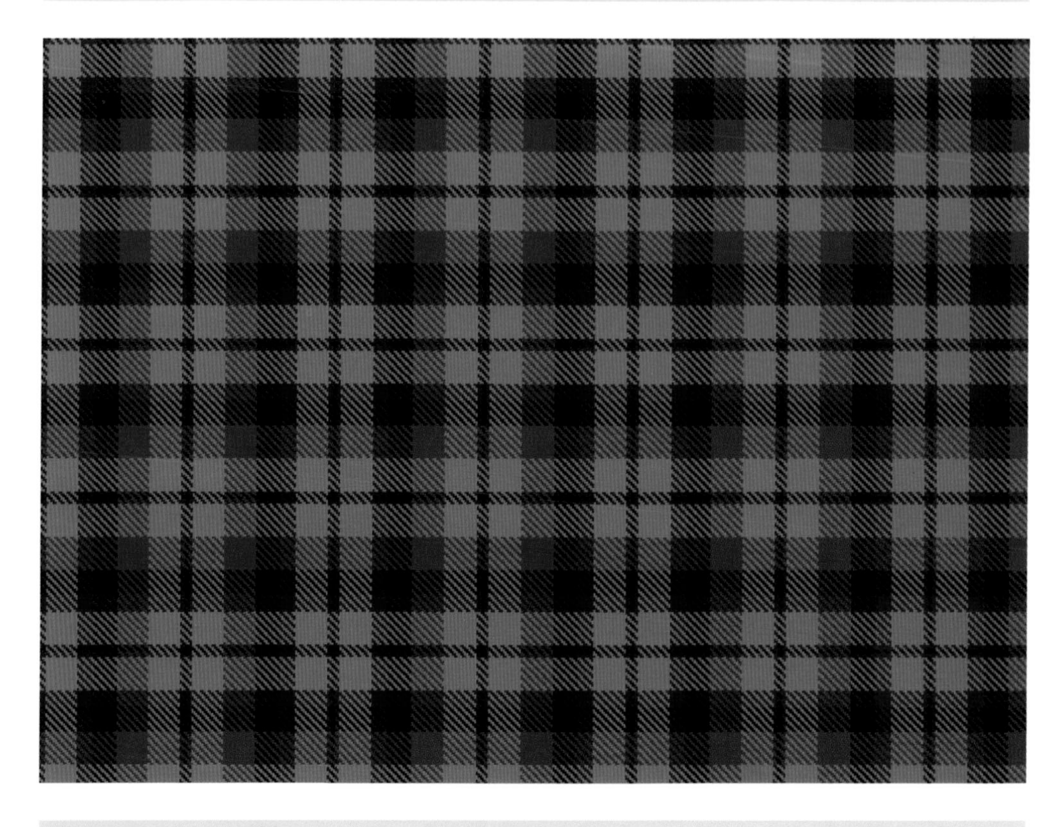

Surnames with possible associations: Hendrie, Hendry, Kendrick, MacEol, MacHendrie, MacHendry, MacKendrick, MacKenrick, MacKnight, MacNayer, MacNiven, MacNuyer, Porter

The name MacNaughten means "Son of Nectan", and the original Nectan was probably a chief who held power in Lorn in around 1200. Later in the century, the first chief was Malcolm MacNachtan, whose son, Gillechrist MacNachtan, was evidently a baron and who gave a church at the head of Loch Fyne to the Abbey of Inchaffray in around 1246. In 1292, Gilbert MacNachtan was one of the 12 great barons whose lands were formed by Act of Parliament into the new Sheriffdom of Argyllshire. In alliance with the MacDougalls, the MacNaughtens oposed Robert the Bruce's claims for the Crown of Scotland but they switched allegiance and fought for Bruce at Bannockburn in 1314. Duncan MacNaughten, whose father fought at Bannockburn, made his seat at Dundarave, and, in 1478, his grandson Alexander was knighted by James IV and fought at Flodden in 1513 – a battle in which MacNaughten was one of the few survivors.

Malcolm of Killearn, who became chief in 1603, was a Royalist and called out the clan in 1653 against Oliver Cromwell's occupation of Scotland. The rebellion was a shambles and made an enemy of the Argylls. MacNaughten was knighted after the Restoration of the monarchy but, thanks to Argyll's influence, was later denounced as an outlaw. Iain, or John, who was the next chief, fought for James VII under Viscount Dundee at Killiecrankie. Denounced as a Jacobite rebel, his estates were forfeited in 1690. His son, John MacNaughten of that Ilk and Dundarave, was the last of the direct line. Around 1700 he appaarently married a daughter of James Campbell of Ardinglass. Campbell appears to have deceived MacNaughten, however: drinking too much prior to his nuptials, MacNaughten found himself married to the elder daughter, rather than the younger! MacNaughten and the younger daughter fled to Ireland and Campbell received the 'gift' of the forfeited MacNaughten property in compensation.

The chiefship became dormant and was eventually settled on the descendants of the Irish branch of the family descended from John Dubh or 'Shane Dhu' who settled in Antrim around 1580 (his father was the second son of Sir Alexander MacNaughten, survivor of Flodden). In 1818, Edmund A. MacNaghten of Bushmill, West Antrim, was confirmed by the Lyon Court as Chief. In 1836, his brother and heir, Sir Francis MacNaughten of Dundarave was made a baronet. The present chief is Sir Patrick MacNaughten of MacNaughten.

The MacNaughten clan tartan was first recorded by Logan in 1831 and later, in 1850, by Smith. Other writers – and also the illustrator MacIan – omitted the black lines leaving a plain band of azure. This is now considered an error in copying and Logan's count, given above, is considered the correct one. The MacNaughten is also worn by the Vale of Atholl pipe band.

# MacNeil

Earliest known date: 1831
Earliest source: Logan, 1831
Tartan type: Symmetrical
Sett: **Y**6 Bk4 G24 Bk24 B28 **W**6
Clan crest: On a chapeau Gules furred Ermine, a rock Proper
Clan motto: *Buaidh no bas* ("Victory or death")
Badge: *Machall-monaidh* (Dryas, or mountain clover)

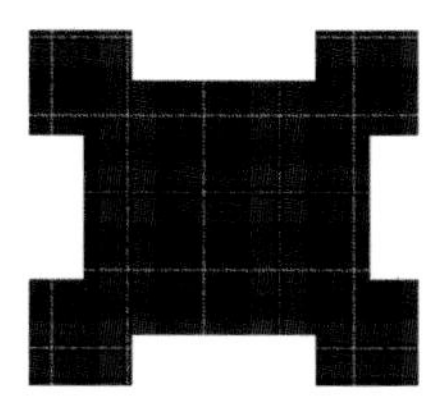

The Clan MacNeil take their name from Niall, a chief in the 13th or early 14th century who belonged to the dynastic family of Cowall and Knapdale, King of Ireland. The clan claims descent from Eoghan of Aileach, one of the sons of Niall of the Nine Hostages, King of Ireland in the 5th century. Tradition states that Eoghan's grandson, Aodh Niall, settled in Barra in around 1040, thereby founding the clan MacNeil in Scotland.

Neil MacNeil, 5th Chief of Barra, was described as a prince at the Council of the Isles held in 1252. His son, Neil Og, supported Robert the Bruce at Bannockburn in 1314 and was rewarded with lands in north Kintyre which were added to his barony of Barra. The MacNeils also held the island of Gigha off the coast to the south of Knapdale, and Taynish, on the mainland. In the reign of David II, the MacNeils held Barra under the Lords of the Isles, who granted a charter in 1427 to Gilleonan MacNeil, 9th Chief of Barra. After the forfeiture of the MacDonalds, Gilleonan MacRoderick MacNeil, 11th Chief of Barra, was given confirmation of Barra by the Crown in 1495. Furthermore, they were the hereditary keepers of Castle Swin in Knapdale in the 15th and 16th centuries. It was to this branch of the clan that the MacNeils of Colonsay belong.

In the 16th century, the MacNeils held state in their island fortress of Kismull. Independent-minded, the MacNeils had little respect for any authority – other than their own! Rory "the Turbulent", the 15th Chief, was arrested for piracy of an English ship near the end of the century, but managed to evade punishment by pleading with James VI that he thought it was a good idea to harass the English, whose Queen had been responsible for the death of James' own mother. By the 17th century, though, the MacNeils were, for the most part, accepting of the rule of central government. In 1688, Ruari Dubh, "Black Rory", 18th Chief of Barra, received a charter for Barra as a Crown Barony. Black Rory was a firm Jacobite and called out the clan to fight for James VII at Killiecrankie in 1689. He continued to remain loyal to the Stewart cause and rallied to the "Old Pretender" in 1715. Black Rory had three sons: the eldest, Gilleonan of Brevaig, was considered "weak" and was passed over in the succession; Roderick "the Dove of the West", who became the heir, and James of Ersary. Roderick and James went into exile in France but returned to Scotland on their father's death and supported the Rising of '45. Roderick was imprisoned, released in 1747, and died in 1763. Unlike other clans however, the MacNeil estates were not forfeited. His eldest son, Roderick "the Peaceful" had already died at Quebec in 1759, and the chiefship passed to "the Dove's" grandson, "Roderick the Gentle", who became the 20th Chief.

The direct line came to an end with his son General Roderick MacNeil of Barra, who also had to sell Barra in 1838. Consequently, the chiefship passed to the MacNeils of Ersary,

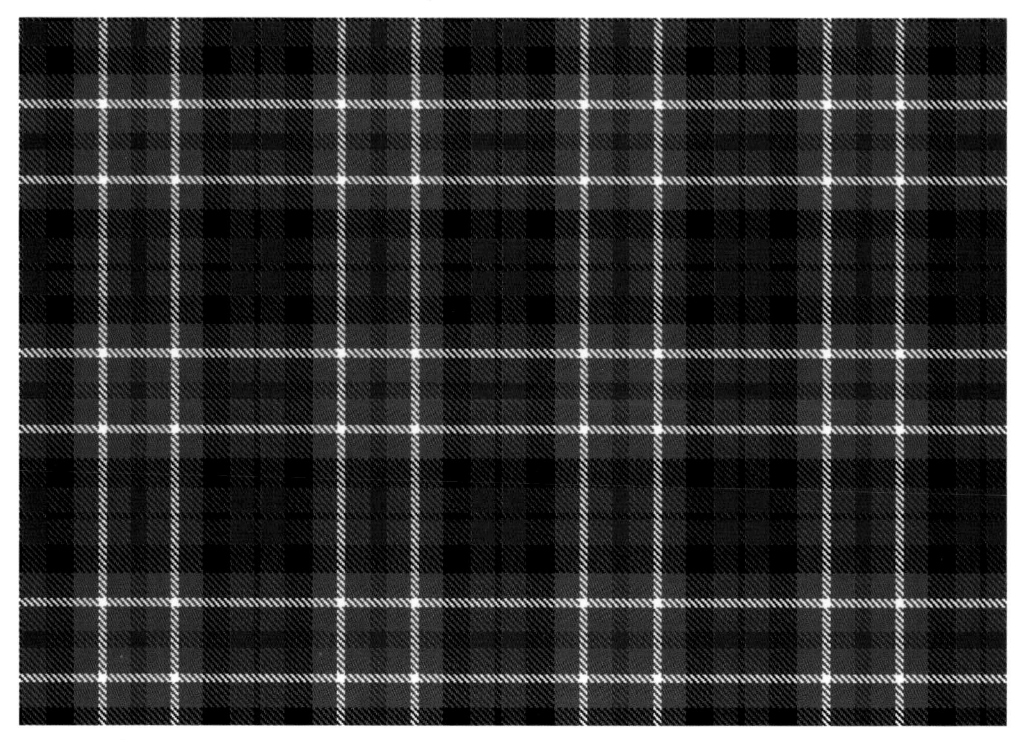

*MacNeil of Colonsay*

descendants of James, third son of "Black Rory". In 1937, American citizen, Robert Lister MacNeil became the 25th Chief of the name MacNeil. An architect by profession, MacNeil set about rebuilding and restoring Kismull Castle, the home of his forefathers. The present chief is Professor Ian Roderick MacNeil of Barra, who lives in Chicago, Illinois, USA.

The modern form of the MacNeil clan tartan differs slightly from the version first described by Logan in 1831, which had much broader dark lines enclosing the yellow stripe. *The Vestiarium Scoticum* in 1842 gave a version that was never generally adopted, while D.W. Stewart in 1898 gave another version with a thin white line with red guard lines which he claimed to be the oldest known version. A fifth tartan, the MacNeil of Colonsay clan tartan, belongs to a branch of the Clan MacNeil who are descended from a cousin, Torkill MacNeil.

Surnames with possible associations: MacGugan, MacNeilage, MacNeiledge, MacNeilly, Neal, Neil, Neilson, Nelson

# MacPherson

Earliest known date: 1819

Earliest source: Grant, 1886

Tartan type: Symmetrical

Sett: **R**2 Bk2 W2 R8 B8 Bk2 B4 Bk2 B8 Bk12 Y2 G16 R12 B2 **R**12

Clan crest: A cat sejant Proper

Clan motto: "Touch not the cat but a glove"

Badge: *Fraoch bhan* (White Heather)

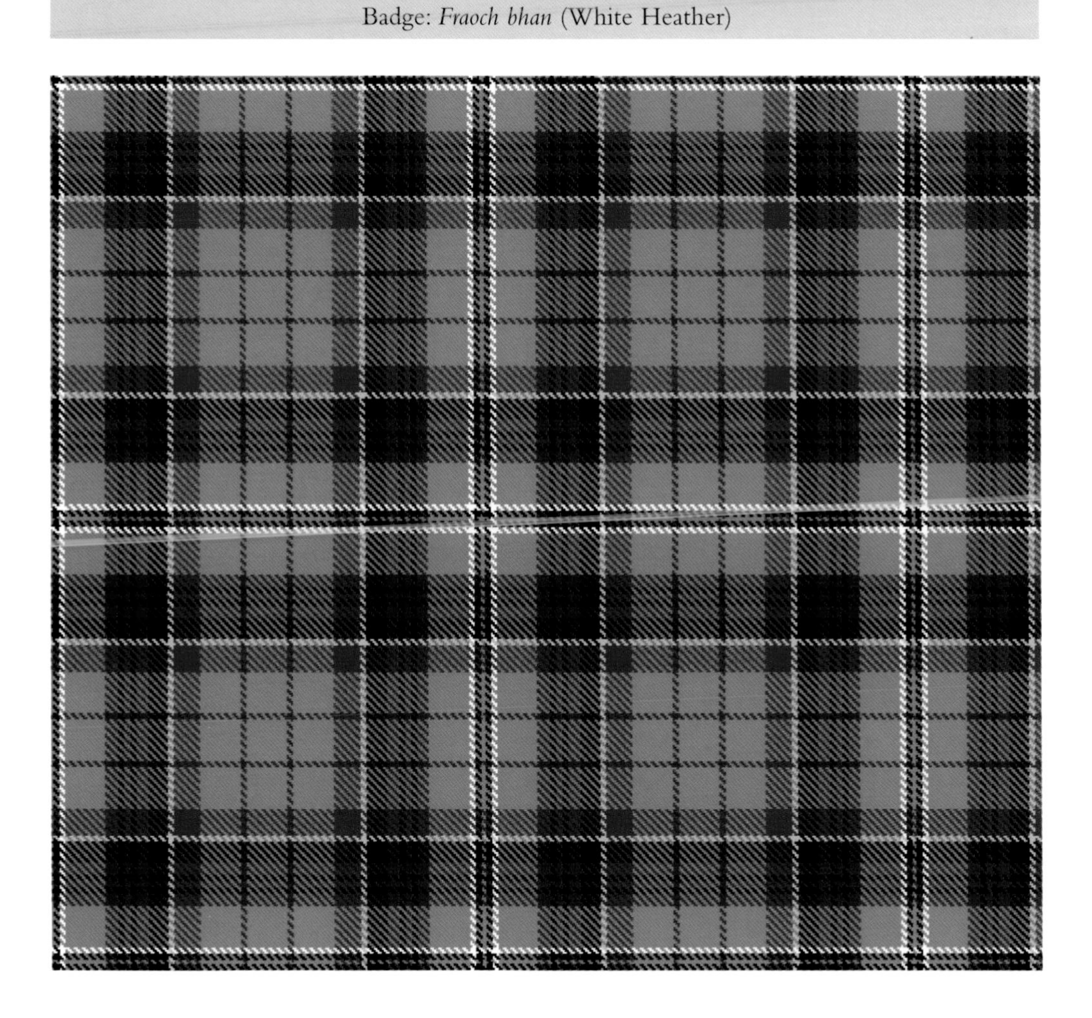

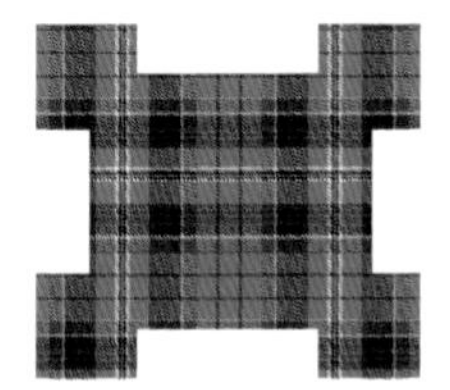

MacPherson is derived from *Mac a Phearsoin*, which means "Son of the Parson": the old Celtic church did not require their clergy to be celibate. The MacPhersons were part of the Clan Chattan Confederation. The progenitor of the clan is believed to have been Muireach, or Murdo, Cattenach, Chief of the Clan Chattan, who was also a Prior of Kingussie in Badenoch in 1173. Murdo married a daughter of the Thane of Cawdor and had two sons. The elder son, Gilli-Chattan Mhor, had a son, Dougal Doul, who became the 6th Chief of Clan Chattan, and from whom subsequent chiefs of the Clan Chattan descended.

Murdo's younger son was Ewan Ban. Clan tradition asserts that Robert the Bruce offered lands in Badenoch to him in 1309 on condition that the MacPhersons destroyed the Comyns. The MacPhersons style themselves as "the clan of the three brothers", and Ewan Ban also had three sons: Kenneth, ancestor of the MacPhersons of Cluny, Ian of Pitmean and Gillies of Invereshie. Kenneth of Cluny fought at Invernahaven in 1370 and left a son, Duncan, who was Parson of Laggan in 1438. His son Donald Mhor MacPherson – the first to bear MacPherson as a surname – was the ancestor of Andrew, probably the 8th chief, who acquired the great abbey-fortress of Grange in Strahisla in 1618. His son Ewan was a royalist who served under Montrose during the Civil War. His son Andrew MacPherson of Cluny died without an heir.

Duncan MacPherson of Cluny, the 10th Chief, lost his claim to lead the Clan Chattan in 1672 after the Lord Lyon ruled in favor of a Mackintosh chief. Duncan also had no sons, and he was succeeded as chief of Clan MacPherson by Lachlan MacPherson, 4th Laird of Nuid, in 1772. Lachlan's son, Ewan, was to become famous as a Highland leader during the Rising of 1745 when he defeated a superior force at Clifton Moor in Westmorland. After the defeat at Culloden, he evaded capture by the Hanoverian forces for nine years. Despite a reward of £1,000 for his capture, Ewan was hidden by his faithful clansmen in Badenoch until he escaped to France in 1755. In 1784, the forfeited Cluny estates were restored to Ewan's son, "Duncan of the Kiln" who got his name because his mother took refuge in a corn mill, where he was subsequently born. He accepted the defeat of the Jacobites and fought for the Crown during the American War of Independence. His son Ewan MacPherson of Cluny was recognized as Chief in 1873 but, by the end of the 19th century, the Cluny estates were bankrupt and were sold. Nevertheless, relics and regalia of the chiefs – including Sir Edwin Landseer's painting of "The Young Chief's First Ride" – as well as some of the old Cluny lands, were purchased by MacPherson clanspeople who formed the clan association and established the MacPherson Museum at Newtonmore in Badenoch.

The elaborate MacPherson clan tartan was being produced by Wilson's of Bannockburn at the start of the 19th century, although it was called "No.43, Kidd and Caledonian", and only

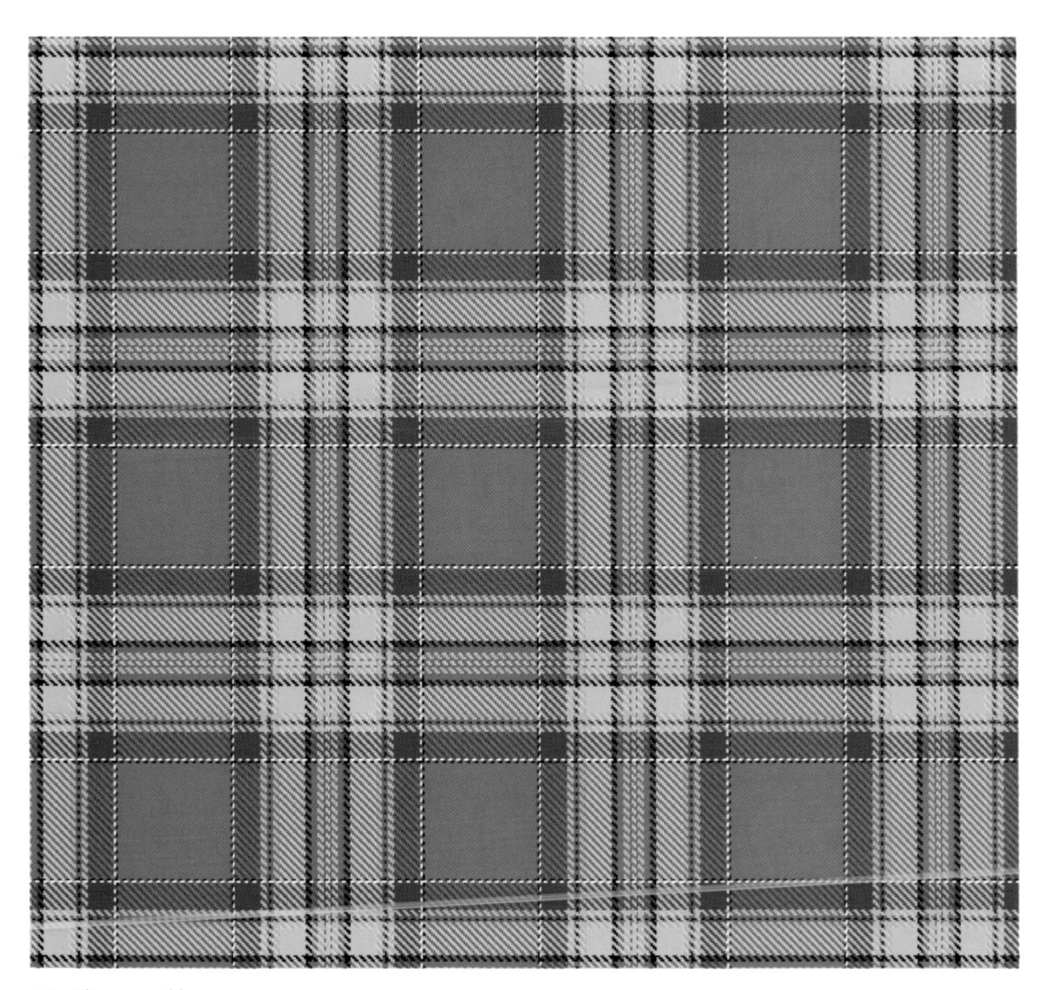

*MacPherson - older*

became "MacPherson" in 1822. The sett was recorded by Logan in 1831, but in his version there was significantly more red ground. The more 'compact' version worn today is closer to the count given by Grant in 1886, which he based on contemporary specimens of tartan.

Surnames with possible associations: Cattanach, Clark, Clarkson, Clerk, Cluny, Ferson, Gillespie, Gillies, Goudie, Gow, Lees, MacCunn, MacCurrach, MacFall, MacGoun, MacGown, MacLerie, MacLise, MacMurdo, MacMurdoch, Murdoch, Murdoson, Pearson, Smith

# MacQuarrie

Earliest known date (current sett): 1886
Earliest source: Grant, 1886
Tartan type: Symmetrical
Sett: **R**32 G2 R2 G2 R8 *G*24
Clan crest: A dexter arm in armour issuing from a coronet with five points and grasping a dagger
Clan motto and *slughorn* (slogan or warcry): *An Tarm Breac Dearg* ("The Army of the Checkered Red Tartan")
Badge: *Giuthas* (Pine Tree)

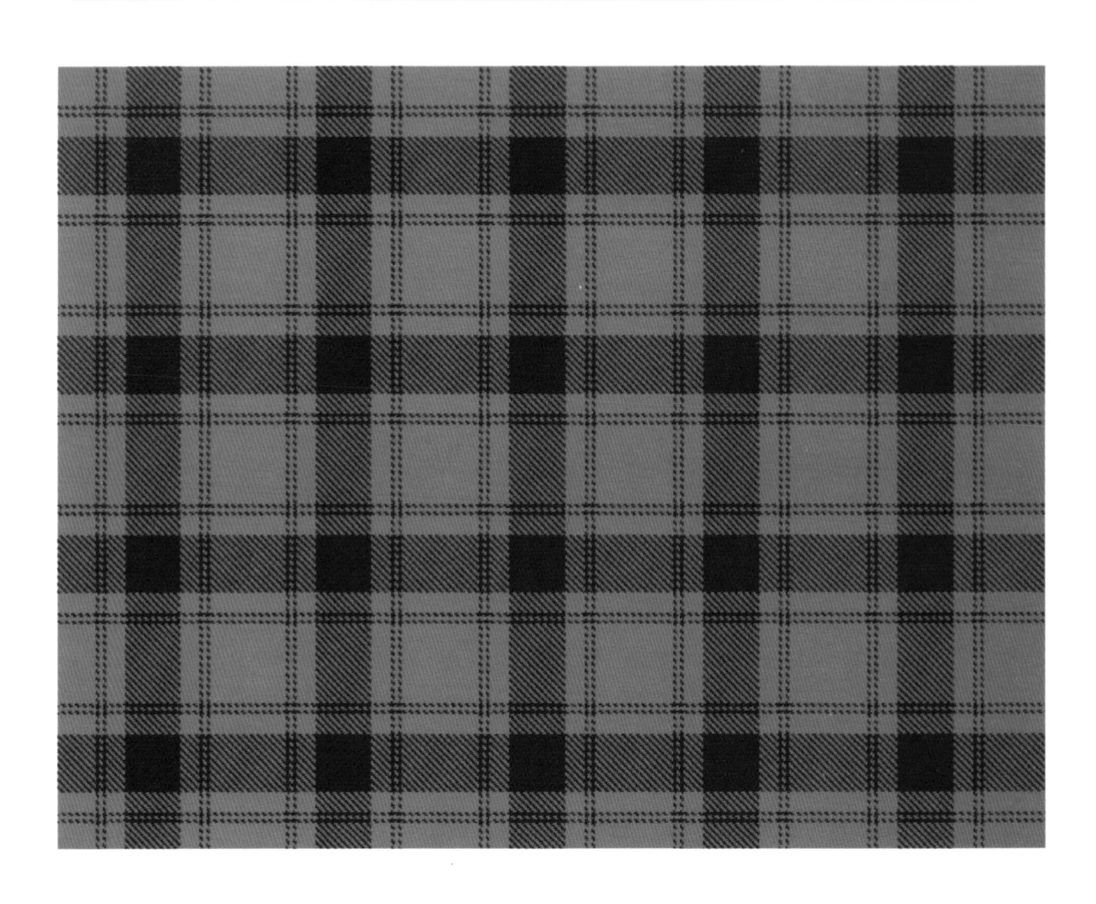

The name MacQuarrie comes from the Gaelic *Guaire*, which means "noble" or "proud". According to traditional genealogies, the clan's forefather, Guaire, was the brother of Fingon, ancestor of the MacKinnon chiefs. This seems likely since the MacKinnons at one time dominated the islands of Mull and Iona, which surround Ulva. The chiefs of the MacQuarries first appear in possession of Ulva, an island off Mull, as well as part of Mull itself. Iain, or John, MacQuarrie of Ulva is the first to be recorded: in 1463, it seems he was a member of the Council of the Isles as he witnessed a charter of MacDonald, Lord of the Isles and Earl of Ross.

Following the downfall of the MacDonald Lordship of the Isles, the MacQuarrie chiefs supported the MacLeans of Duart (see page 176) who were now the dominant power on Mull. John MacQuarrie appears to have died *c.*1473 and little else appears to have been recorded until 1609, when the Bishop of the Isles went to Iona as Commissioner for James VI. Among the chiefs of the isles who submitted fealty to the king was MacQuarrie of Ulva. In 1651, MacQuarrie of Ulva was slain – along with most of his clansmen – fighting alongside the MacLeans of Duart for Charles II against Cromwell's forces at the battle of Inverkeithing. Lachlan MacQuarrie, the 16th Chief, was the last "Lord of Ulva's Isle". He was obliged to sell Ulva in 1783.

His son, Major-General Lachlan MacQuarrie, the next chief, eventually managed to buy back the island and was eventually buried there in 1824. He had been Governor of New South Wales in Australia from 1809–21, being sent there to succeed Bligh – the famous captain of the mutinous ship *Bounty*, who had once more been deposed by officers commanding local troops! The MacQuarrie chief was, by all accounts, a better governor than Bligh: he helped transported convicts to become settlers once they were freed. His local popularity was reflected in the MacQuarrie River being named after him. The Major-General died without an heir and since then the chiefship has been vacant. The Clan MacQuarrie tartan in use today is the one illustrated by Grant in 1886, although an earlier specimen, with a greater proportion of red, had been collected in 1815 by the Cockburn Collection.

# MacRae

Earliest known date (for current sett): 1850

Earliest source: Smith, 1850

Tartan type: Symmetrical

Sett: **G**8 R2 G8 R8 B2 R2 B2 R2 B2 R8 B2 R2 B2 R2 B2 R8 W2 R2 B8 R2 B8 R2 W2 R8 G2 R2 G2 R8 G8 R2 **G**8

Clan crest: A cubit arm grasping a sword all Proper

Clan motto: *Fortitudine* ("With fortitude")

Badge: *Garbhag an t-sleibhe* (Fir Club Moss)

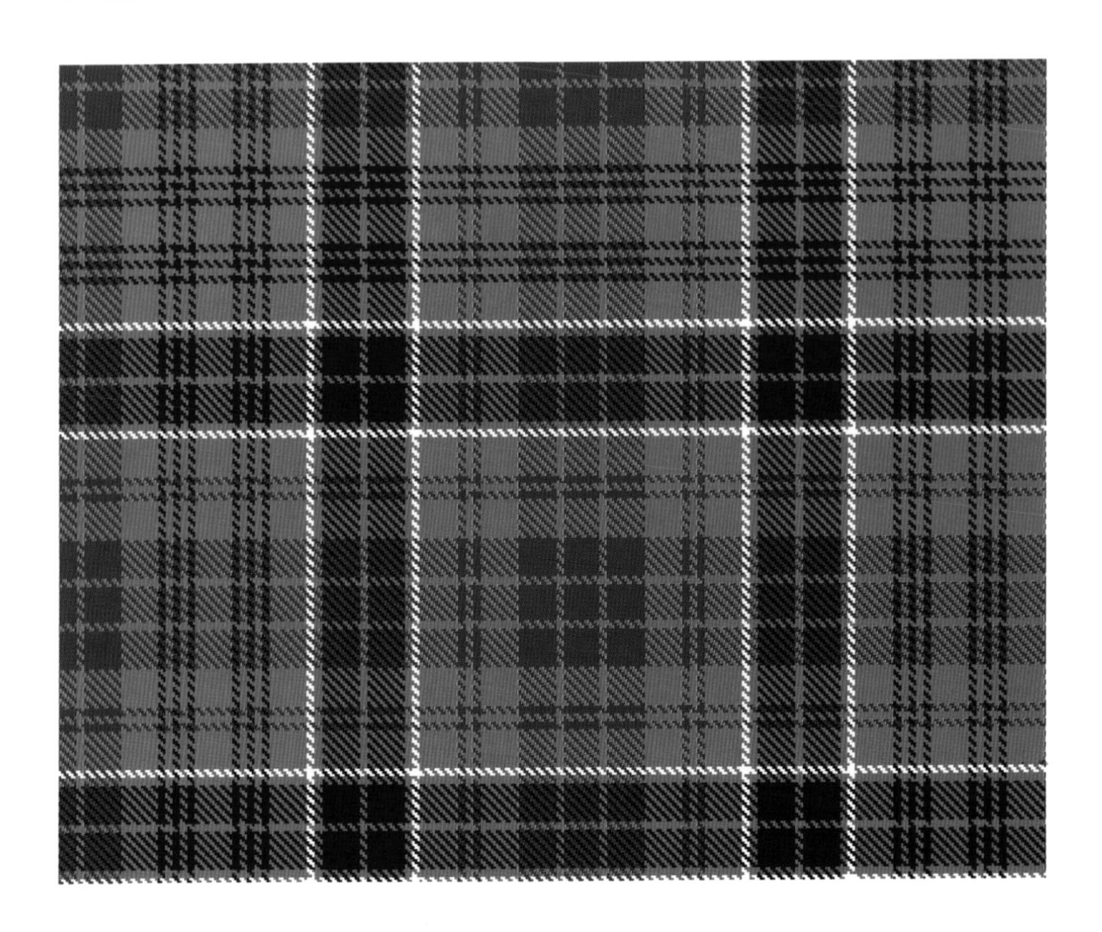

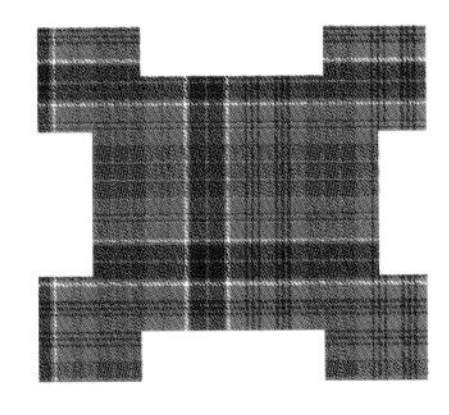

The name MacRae in Gaelic is *MacRath*, which means the "Son of Grace" and, like many other clan names, was probably of ecclesiastical origin. It was common as a first name in Scotland from the 5th to the 13th centuries, but was also used as a surname in Galloway, Ayrshire and in southern Perthshire in the 15th and 16th centuries. There are numerous spellings of the name: M'Crae, M'Crea and M'Creath are the most common (in Ireland it is most common as "Magrath"). The MacRae clan – sometimes known as "the Wild MacRaes" – seems to have been living in Lovat country in the 12th and 13th centuries before moving to Kintail, Ross-shire sometime in the 14th century.

The MacRaes were related to, and staunch allies of, the MacKenzie barons of Kintail: Duncan MacRae was constable of the MacKenzie stronghold of Eilandonan Castle. They were so loyal that they became known as "MacKenzie's shirt of mail". In 1539, when Donald Grumach MacDonald, 4th Chief of Sleate, besieged Eilandonan, he was killed by an arrow fired by a MacRae. As the fortunes of the MacKenzies prospered, so too did the MacRaes. Duncan MacCrae of Inverinate, was known as *Donnchaddh nam Pios*, or "Duncan of the Silver Cups" on account of his wealth and evidently splendid tableware! When the MacKenzies became the earls of Seaforth, the MacRaes became the hereditary keepers of Eilandonan, the Chamberlains of Kintail, and were also frequently vicars of the parish. The Reverend Farquhar MacRae (1598–1662) was Vicar of Kintail for 40 years, while his son, Reverend John MacRae of

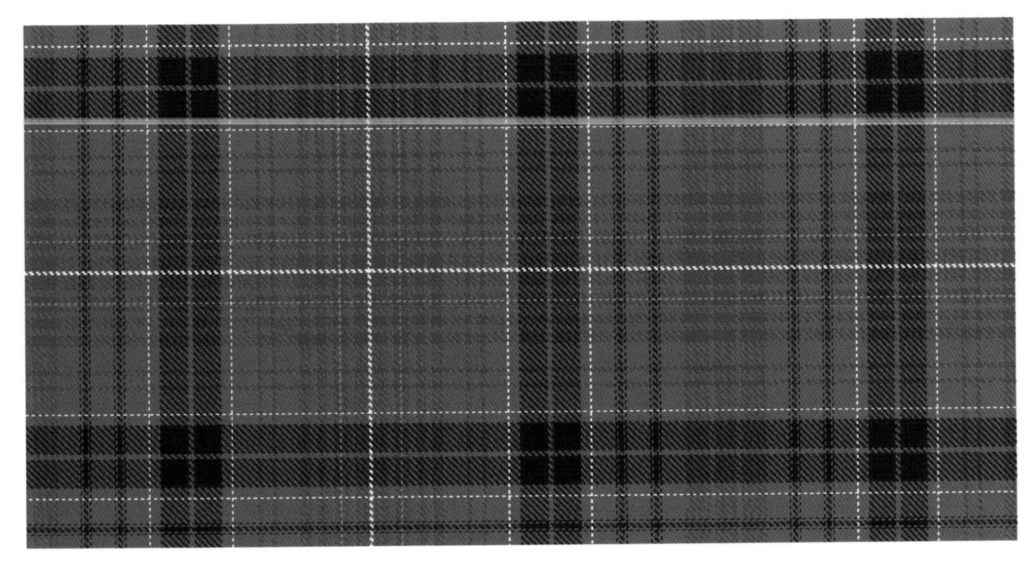

*MacRae - Princes Own*

*MacRae of Conchra*

Dingwall (1614–73) was the progenitor of the line of MacRaes of Conchra.

Jacobite supporters, the MacRaes fought at Sheriffmuir in 1715 but did not join the Rising in 1745 as a clan, although individuals did join the cause of the Young Pretender, Prince Charles Edward Stewart. Lieutenant Colonel John MacRae (b.1861) was Deputy Keeper at the Palace of Holyroodhouse and a member of the Royal Company of Archers which forms the bodyguard of the British monarch when in Scotland. In 1909, Sir Colin MacRae of Inverinate claimed chiefship of the Clan MacRae, but he was opposed by members of the house of Conchra descended from Reverend John MacRae of Dingwall. The chiefship has yet to be settled and the castle at Eilandonan, restored in the 1930s, still awaits the return of the chief.

The MacRae tartan was described by the Smith brothers in 1850 – albeit with an error in the thread count. A specimen of a different tartan, called "The Prince's Own" is in the collection of the Highland Society in London and dates from around 1816. A third tartan, described in 1893 by D.W. Stewart as a "Dress MacRae" of sapphire blue and white with a red line centered on the white and a yellow line centered on the blue, is said to have originated in a piece of knitting dating from the 18th century, itself as an indirect reconstruction of a tartan most probably used for the hose worn by the MacRaes of Conchra.

Surnames with possible associations: MacAra, MacCrae, MacCraw, MacCreath, MacGrath, Macra, MacRaith, MacRath, Raith

# Matheson

Earliest known date: 1850

Earliest source: Smith 1850

Tartan type: Symmetrical

Sett: **G**16 R8 G2 R2 G2 R48 B16 G8 R2 G2 R2 G8 R16 G2 R2 G2 R2 B16 G16 R4 **G**8

Clan crest: Issuing from a crown Or, a hand brandishing a scimitar fessways all Proper

Clan motto: *Fac et spera* ("Do and hope")

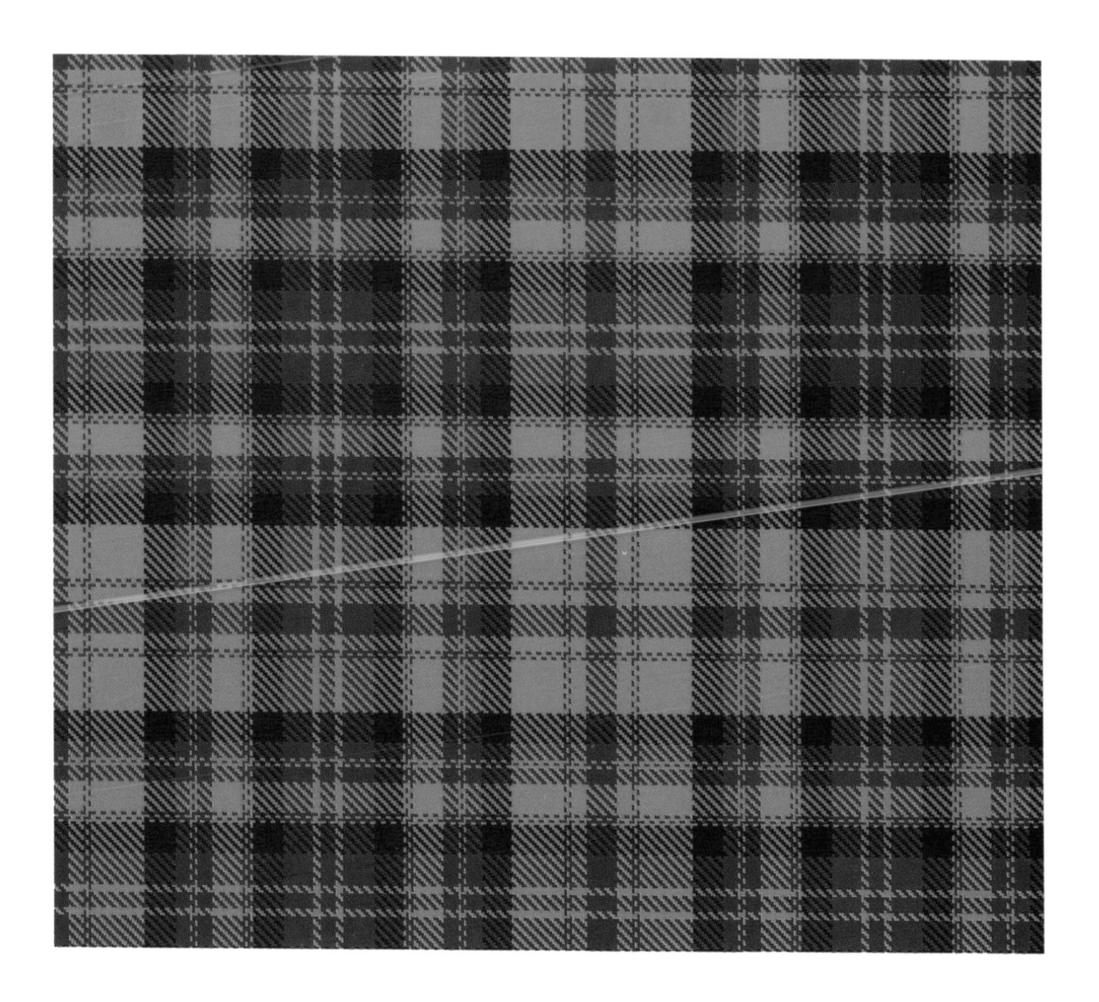

Some claim that the name Matheson is derived from *Mhic Mhathghamhuin,* meaning "Son of the Bear" since the supporters on the chief's coat of arms are two bears. Others, however, believe it may be derived from *MacMhathian* which means "Son of the Hero", an equally appropriate epithet. The Mathesons appear to have settled in the area around Lochalsh, Lochcarron and Kintail where they were granted lands by the Celtic earls of Ross. According to a manuscript from 1467, the first of the Matheson line was Mathan in 1263. He was the father of Murdoch, father of Duncan, father of Murdoch, father of Murdoch MakMakan of Bower, the chief in 1427.

From 1580 to 1602, chief of the clan Matheson appears to have been Murdoch Buidhe. He had two sons: Roderick of Fernaig, and Dougall of Balmacara who, in 1631, became Chamberlain of Lochalsh and a baillie to the earls of Sutherland. This line of the Matheson family settled on the north side of Loch Shin, hence Matheson of Shiness. Sir Donald Matheson of Shiness fought against the Jacobites during the Rising of 1715, while Alexander Matheson, along with his uncle Sir James Matheson, amassed a huge fortune trading in India and China. In 1827, they founded the trading house of Jardine Matheson, and, having bought the old family *duthus* of Lochalsh, Alexander was created a baronet in 1882.

Roderick of Fermaig, through whom the chiefly line descended, had one son, John, who became the father of John Mor of Fernaig, who made his money in cattle droving and became the owner of Bennetsfield in the Black Isle in 1688. His son, Alexander, was styled the 1st Chief of Bennetsfield, and his son John, fought at Culloden in 1745. He was succeeded by his son Colin who died in 1825. His son, Captain John of Bennetsfield. was the family historian and died childlessin 1843 leaving the Bennetsfield estate in a, debt-ridden state. The chiefship subsequently passed to his cousin, Heylin Fraser Matheson, the grandson of Colin of Bennetsfield's third son, Charles Mackenzie Matheson. Heylin's son, Colonel Betram Matheson of that Ilk, was confirmed in the chiefship by the Lord Lyon in 1963. The Colonel then nominated General Sir Torquil Matheson, 5th Baronet, as *tanastair* (successor). However, Major Sir Torquil succeeded his father as 6th Baronet in 1963 and Colonel Betram as Chief of the Clan Matheson in 1975, thereby uniting the baronetcy and the chiefship.

Although MacIan recorded two similar designs in *c.*1845, the tartan worn by the Mathesons is the design recorded by the Smith brothers in 1850. D.C. Stewart remarked that with its irregular character, it is likely that the design was a combination of elements of other tartans, in particular the MacDonald of Glengarry, which has a related structure.

Surnames with possible associations: MacMath, MacPhun, Massey, Mathie,

# Maxwell

Earliest known date: 1842
Earliest source: *The Vestiarium Scoticum*, 1842
Tartan type: Symmetrical
Sett: **R**6 G2 R56 Bk12 R8 G32 **R**6
Clan crest: A stag Proper attired Argent, couchant before a holly bush proper
Clan motto: *Reviresco* ("I grow strong again")

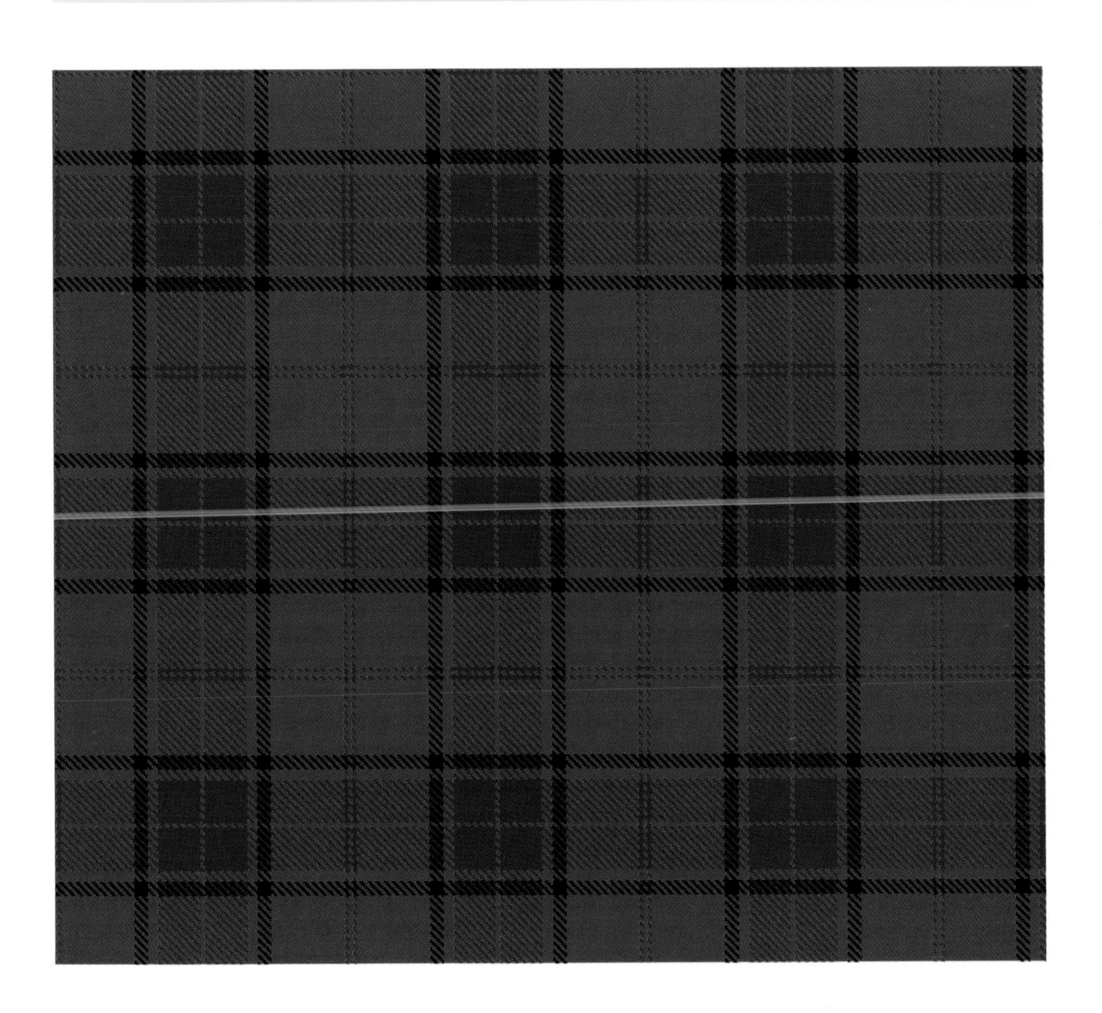

The origin of the Maxwell clan name is, according to tradition, Maccus Well, a pool in the River Tweed near to Kelso. Maccus is believed to have been a Norse chief during the reign of David I (1124–53), but it was members of the Maxwell family in the 13th century who were the ancestors of this Lowland family.

The first on record was Sir John Maxwell, Chamberlain of Scotland, who died in 1241without an heir. He was succeeded by his brother Sir Aymer who had two sons, Herbert and John – from the younger son are descended the Maxwell baronets of Cardoness, the Maxwells, Barons Farnham and Baronets of Calderwood, and the Maxwells, Baronets of Pollok, whose home, Pollok House was gifted to the city of Glasgow in 1967. In its grounds is the magnificent Burrell Collection of art. Sir Herbert, the elder son of Sir Aymer, signed the Rangman Roll in which he swore fealty to the English king Edward I in 1296. His son Eustace was the keeper of Caerlaverock Castle on behalf of his English overlords, but later, it seems, he became a supporter of Robert the Bruce in his struggle for an independent Scotland and fought with Bruce at Bannockburn in 1314.

Eustace's descendant – his great-grandson to the sixth degree – was created Lord Maxwell in 1440 and took his seat in the House of Lords. He had two sons: Robert, 2nd Lord Maxwell, and Sir Edward, from whom descend the Maxwells of Monreith, created baronets in 1681. Robert, 2nd Lord Maxwell, was succeeded by his son, John, 3rd Lord, who fought and fell at Flodden in 1513. His son, Robert, became the 4th Lord, and left two sons: Robert, 5th Lord, and Sir John, who became Lord Herries of Terregles. Robert, the 5th Lord, was created Warden of the Marshes by James V in 1542, but was captured at the battle of Solway later in the year. His son John, the 6th Lord, was awarded the earldom of Morton when the Regent was executed. He was later deprived of this title and died fighting the Johnstons. John, the 7th Lord, was linked to a number of intrigues and plots to restore the Catholic Mary, Queen of Scots to the throne: John remained a devout Catholic throughout the Protestant reformation. Following Mary's execution in 1587, and the Spanish Armada defeat in 1588, Lord Maxwell continued to communicate with King Philip of Spain in the hope of bringing about a Catholic revolution.

In 1608, in the continuing feud with the Johnstons, Lord Maxwell shot and killed Sir James Johnston – who at the time was attempting to reconcile the two families. Lord John Maxwell was executed in 1613 and was succeeded by his brother, Robert, 8th Lord Maxwell, who was later created Earl of Nithsdale. When his son Robert, 2nd Earl, died unmarried in 1667, succession to the earldom reverted to his cousin, John, 4th Lord Herries. His descendant, William, the 5th Earl, was a staunch Jacobite supporter who was captured at the battle of Preston in 1715. Taken to London as prisoner, he was tried and sentenced to death for treason.

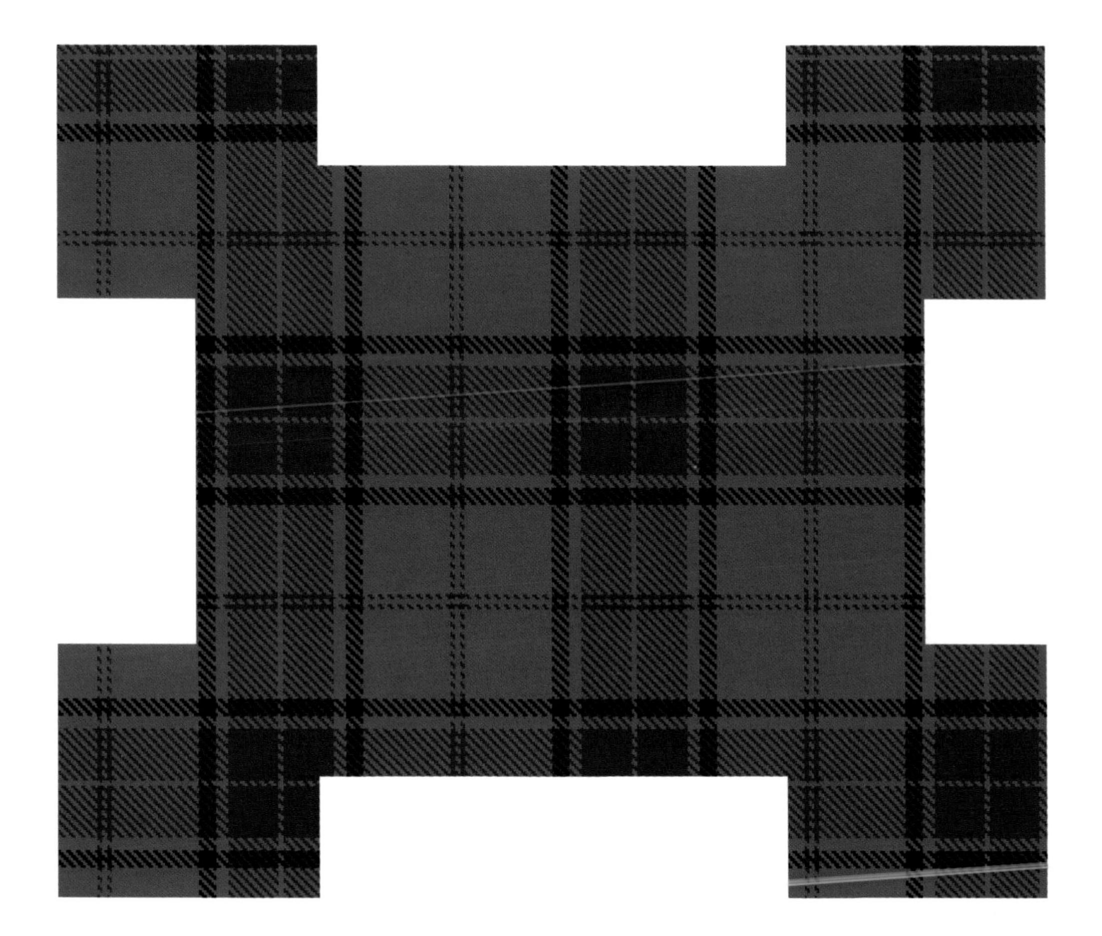

However, on the eve of his execution, aided by his wife, the earl escaped from the Tower of London disguised as a woman. The couple then fled to Rome, where the earl died in 1744. His great-grandson, William Constable-Maxwell, proved his claim to the Lordship of Herries in 1878, but the peerage was later to pass to the Duchess of Norfolk and, today, the chiefship of the clan is undetermined.

The Maxwell clan tartan first appeared in *The Vestiarium Scoticum* in 1842, where Lowland families like the Maxwells were first named. It is possible that the Maxwell tartan, like many others in the *Vestiarium*, was "invented" for publication by the Sobieski Stewart brothers. Nevertheless, many of those "invented" tartans are beautiful and, still in use today.

# Menzies

Earliest known date: 1893

Earliest source: D.W. Stewart, 1893

Tartan type: Symmetrical

Sett: **G**96 R8 G4 R8 G12 R4 G6 **R**18

Clan crest: A savage head erased Proper

Clan motto: *Vil God I Zal* ("Will God I Shall")

Badge: *Uinnseann* (Ash) and "Menzies' Heath"

The Scottish surname Menzies is the same as the English surname Manners (the ancestors of the Dukes of Rutland) both of which are likely to be derived from *Mesnieres*, in Normandy. It is important to remember that the letter "z" in Menzies is never pronounced like the "z" in zebra, because it is in fact, an old Scottish letter for a guttural "y" – a sound that is a cross between a "y" and a "g".

The first of the Menzies to appear on record were Robert de Meyneris, who signed a charter for grants of the lands of Culdares in Fortingall, Atholl to Sir Matthew de Moncrieff, and. David de Meyneris and Thomas de Meyneris, who witnessed the charter. Sir Robert was at the court of Alexander II around 1124 and quickly rose in royal favor: in 1249 he was made Chamberlain of Scotland and received a large tract of land in Rannoch, in the west of Atholl. This area had formed part of the abbey-lands of Dull, of which the king's ancestors had been hereditary abbots. Some historians now conclude that Sir Robert was also rewarded with a bride – possibly illegitimate – who was descended from the royal house, since two of Robert's sons were named Alexander and David, the names of the Scottish monarchs.

Alexander married Egidia, the daughter of James, the High Steward of Scotland,and was granted lands in Aberfeldy, Strathtay in 1296, as well as the lands of Weem (known as *Meinearach* in Gealic and which became the stronghold of the Clan Menzies), Fortingall in Atholl, Glendochart in Breadalbane, and Durisdeer in Nithsdale. His son, Sir Robert de Mengues, was a companion-in-arms of Robert the Bruce. In 1487, Sir Robert Menzies, 8th Chief, had his lands erected into the Barony of Menzies and, in 1488 built the castle of Weem, to replace Comrie Castle on the River Lyon until 1487 which had burnt down in 1487. In 1510, Sir Robert resigned the baronies of Ennoch and Weem to James IV, who regranted them as the free barony of Menzies, renaming the castle of Weem, the "Castle Menzies". This, too, was destroyed in a raid by the Stewarts of Garth, but by 1577, it had been rebuilt by James Menzies of that Ilk, who had sat as a baron in Mary, Queen of Scots' parliament.

In 1665, Sir Alexander Menzies of that Ilk was created Baronet of Nova Scotia and his brother, Colonel James Menzies of Culdares (from whom the present chiefly line descends) was a veteran of the Civil War in which he claimed he received no fewer than nine arrow(!) wounds in his legs doing battle with the marauding MacDonalds of Glencoe during the reign of Charles II (1660–85). Major Duncan Menzies of Fornock led his highlanders at the battle of Killiecrankie in 1689, while later, in 1715, Menzies of Culdares rallied to the cause of the "Old Pretender". Culdares was captured at Dunblane and spent many years in exile: when the "Young Pretender" landed in Scotland in 1745, Culdares was too advanced in years to serve in person. Instead he sent the prince his finest horse and the clan was led by Menzies of Shian

*Menzies Red and White*

who, along with his son, were killed in battle. The Menzies of Menzies baronetcy became extinct on the death of Sir Neil Menzies of Menzies, 8th Baronet, in 1910. The estates were sold in 1918 when Menzies' sister Egidia died, and soon Castle Menzies became run down and dilapidated. It was saved from complete ruin, however, when it was purchased in 1957 by the Menzies Clan Society which has since restored it as the clan heritage center.

The Menzies have several tartans: the oldest is perhaps the red and white dress tartan, which seems most appropriate as their *slughorn* (slogan or warcry) is *Gael 'us Dearg a suas* – "Up with the White and Red". A certified sample of this tartan dates from 1815 and is in the Collection of the Highland Society. The same sett, but in black and white, is used in mourning. The most popular tartan, and the one in general use is the Menzies hunting clan tartan woven in green and red. It was first recorded by D.W. Stewart in 1893.

Surnames with possible associations: MacIndeor, MacMenzies, MacMinn, MacMonies, Mein, Meine, Mennie, Meyners, Minn, Minnus, Murchie, Murchison,

# Montgomerie

Earliest known date: 1893
Earliest source: Stewart 1893
Tartan type: Symmetrical
Sett: **Bk**8 G10 Bk8 P56 Bk10 R10 **Bk**8
Clan crest: A lady dressed in ancient apparel Azure holding in her dexter hand an anchor and in her sinister the head of a savage couped suspended by the hair all Proper
Clan motto: *Garde bien* ("Watch well")

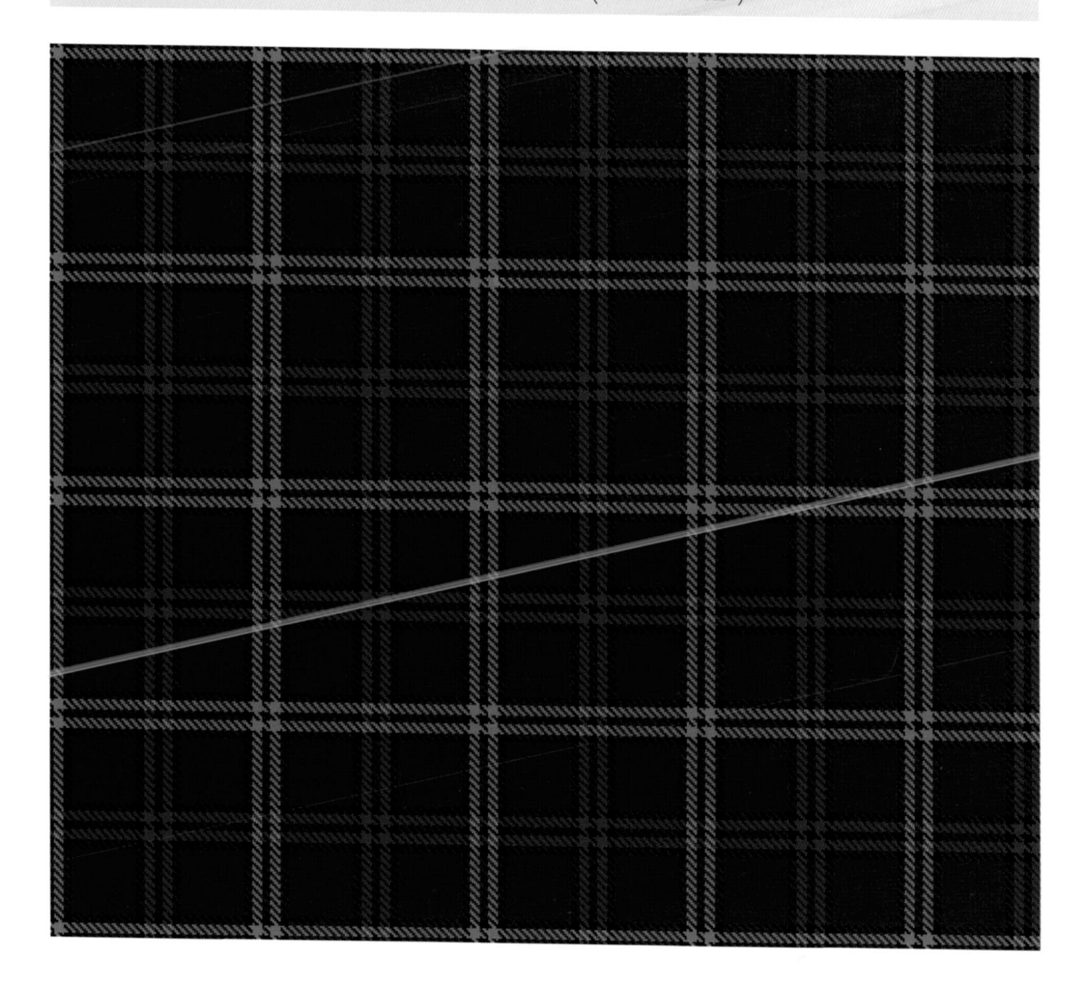

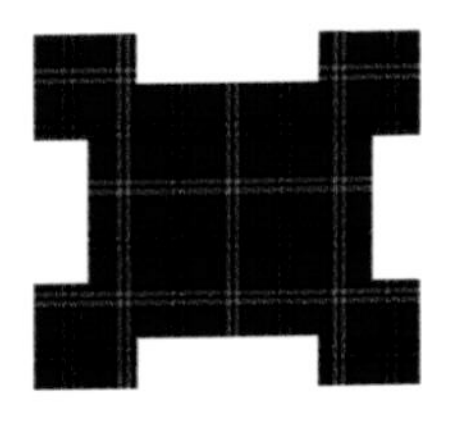

Montgomerie is an ancient Norman French name. Roger de Mundegumbrie, called "Roger the Great" held the castle of Saint Foy de Montgomery at Lisieux in France. His son, Roger de Montgomery, was joint governor of Normandy and accompanied his cousin, William the Conqueror, on the invasion of England. After the battle of Hastings in 1066, Roger was rewarded with the earldom of Arundel.

The first Montgomerie to appear in Scotland was Robert de Montgomerie, who probably arrived in 1147 in the retinue of Walter Fitzalan, the first High Steward of Scotland, and obtained lands in Renfrewshire. The first of his successors of note was John Montgomerie, 7th Earl of Eaglesham, who fought bravely at the battle of Otterburn in 1388, capturing Sir Henry Percy – the famous "Hotspur". The ransom paid by the Percys for Hotspur's release included building the castle of Polnoon for Montgomerie. Montgomerie then married Elizabeth, the daughter and heiress of Sir Hugh de Eglintoun, and so, through marriage, acquired the barony of Eglinton and Ardrossan.

Around 1445, Montgomerie's grandson, Sir Alexander, was created Lord Montgomerie. He had two sons: Alexander, and George, who was the ancestor of the Montgomeries of Skelmorlie. Alexander, who died before his father, left two sons: Hugh became 2nd Lord Montgomerie, and Robert, from whom descend the earls of Mount Alexander in Ireland. Hugh supported Prince James in his rebellion against his father James III, and fought at Sauchieburn in 1488. As reward, Montgomery was granted for life the isle of Arran and the keepership of Brodick Castle. In 1507, he was made the Earl of Eglinton and surviving the battle of Flodden in 1513, was part of the Parliament at Perth in October of that year which proclaimed the infant James V as king. He was succeeded by his grandson Hugh, 2nd Earl. When Hugh died in 1546, his son, Hugh 3rd Earl of Eglinton supported Mary, Queen of Scots and fought for her at Langside in 1568. Taken prisoner, the earl was declared guilty of treason. In 1571, he finally submitted and recognized James VI as king. Hugh, the 4th Earl, was shot in a feud with the Cunninghams, and his son, Hugh, the 5th Earl, died childless in 1612.

The earldom of Eglinton then passed to Sir Alexander Seton, the son of Margaret, the daughter of the 4th Earl, who had married Robert Seton, 1st Earl of Winton. Seton was a Protestant and, refusing to accept the religious policies of Charles I, fought with the Army of the Covenant during the Civil War. With the accession of Charles II, who agreed to Scotland's wishes regarding religious matters, Seton became a Royalist. Seton was captured at Dunbarton and was imprisoned in Berwick until the Restoration of the monarchy in 1660. Alexander, the 10th Earl, a distinguished politician, was unfortunately shot and killed by a poacher in 1769. His brother Archibald, the 11th Earl, raised the 78th Highlanders, while in 1839, Archibald,

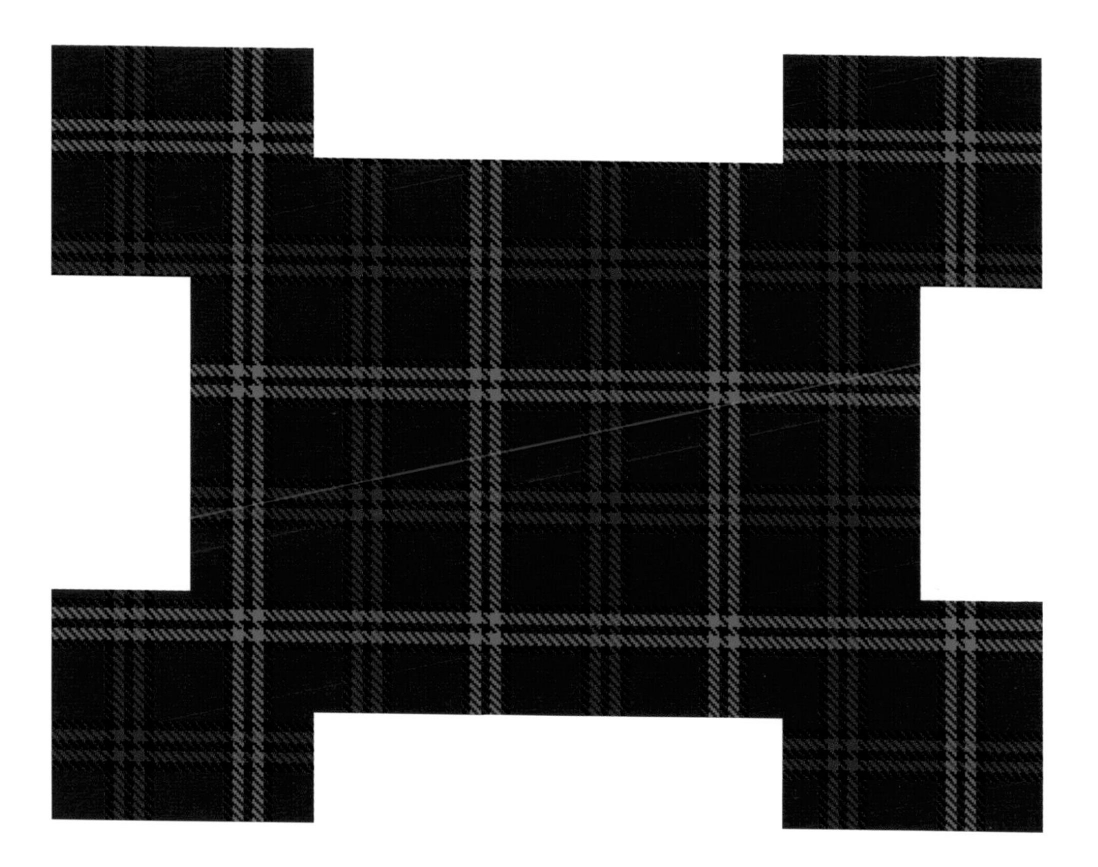

13th Earl organized the spectacular Eglinton Tournament, a display that recreated medieval jousting. As the male heir of the Seton line, he was made 1st Earl of Winton in 1859 and his son Archibald William, 14th Earl of Eglinton, was recognized by the Lyon Court at Chief of the Montgomeries in 1860.

According to the opinion of D.W. Stewart in 1893, the Montgmerie tartan could be traced back to the time of the Union in 1707, thereby making it one of the oldest Lowland tartans. He also noted that it had the rare feature of a plain purple background. The earlier publication, *The Vestiarium Scoticum of 1842*, contained a completely different pattern of three blue stripes on a green ground. D.C. Stewart noted in 1950 that such triple and quadruple stripes were frequent features of tartan designs in the *Vestiarium*.

# Morrison

Earliest known date: Not known

[Earliest source: Stewart, 1950. Clan Society founded 1906)

Tartan type: Symmetrical

Sett: **Bk**6 G28 Bk28 G4 B28 **R**6 (Morrison Clan Society Tartan)

Clan crest: Issuing from sea waves Azure crested Argent, a mount Vert, thereon a battlemented wall Azure masoned Argent, and issuing therefrom a cubit arm naked Proper, the hand grasping a dagger hilted Or

Clan motto: *Teaghlach Phabbay* ("Pabbay family")

Badge: *Sgod cladaich* (Driftwood)

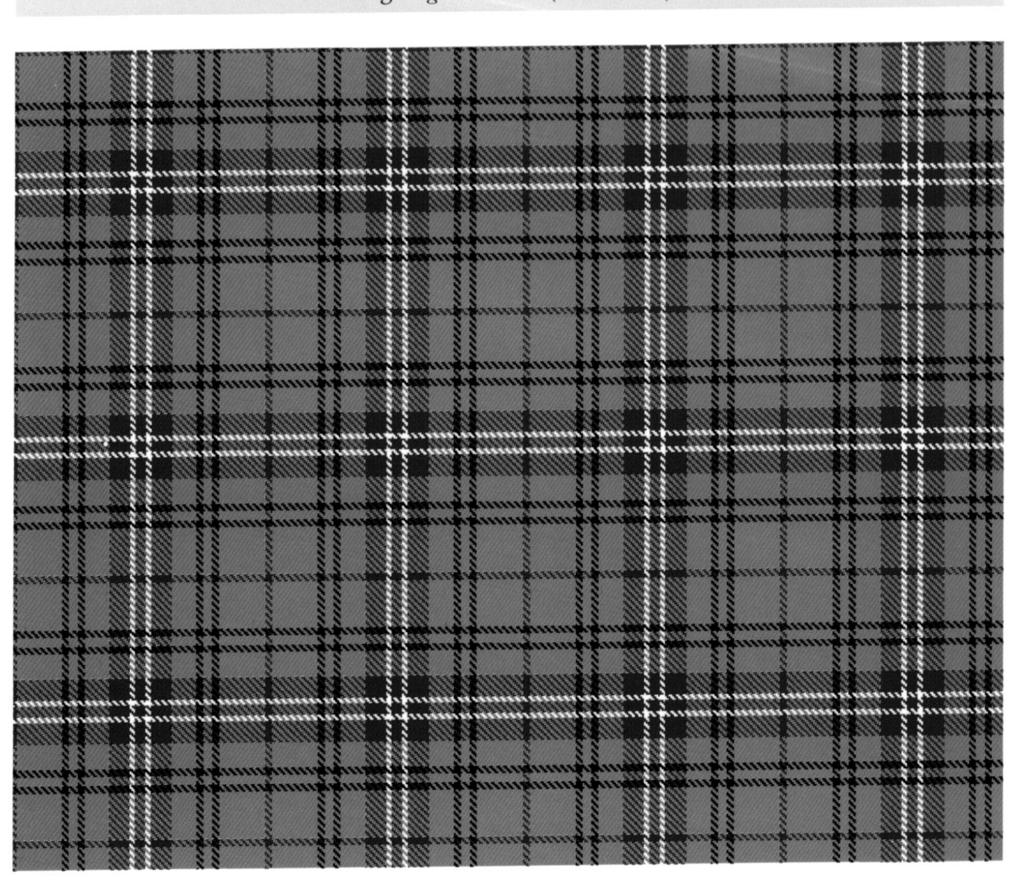

The Clan Morrison derives its name from an adaptation of the Gaelic *MacGillemhoire*. "Gillemhoire" means "follower, or devotee, of Saint Mary". The Morrisons of Perth and Lennox, whose name is adapted from the Gaelic *Moiris* or "Son of Maurice" (in Latin *mauricius* means "dark-skinned" or "swarthy") on the other hand, did not form a clan. From the "sons of Maurice" are descended the Morrison of Bognie, in Aberdeenshire.

The Highland clan of the Morrisons were the hereditary brieves (see below) of the island of Lewis in the Hebrides where they had their stronghold at Dun Eystein and their "big house" or Tigh Mor near Habost in Ness on the extreme north point of the "Long Island". A brieve, or brehon, (Gaelic, britheamh) was the local arbiter, or judge, who had the power to award compensation and settle disputes brought to him voluntarily by the parties involved. To each successive generation, the brieve handed down the customary laws known as the Brehon Laws. Acording to clan tradition, Gillemhoire was shipwrecked and was washed ashore on Lewis clinging to a piece of driftwood – hence the clan's plant badge. Gillemhoire has been claimed to be the son of King Olav of Norway, thereby making him the brother of Leod of Dunvegan, the progenitor of a second Lewis clan, the Macleods. Guillemhoire married the heiress of the Gows, or Clan Igaa, who held the Dun of Pabbay, a small isle in the Sound of Harris.

When, in 1493, the Crown finally broke the power of the MacDonald Lord of the Isles, years of unrest followed as the clans vied for power. The Morrisons were not a numerous clan and lived in harmony with their MacLeod kinsmen. The MacAulays, the third of the Lewis clans, however, killed Donald Ban, the brother of John Morrison, the brieve at Habost. The Morrison's sought revenge and raided Uig, but the MacAulays successfully appealed to the MacLeods for help. Consequently, the Morrisons were defeated at the Caws of Tarbert, and a joint force of MacAulays and MacLeods invaded their lands.

The feud was continued by the next Morrison chief, Uisdean, or Hucheon, who unsuccessfully invaded north Harris. On his deathbed in 1566, Hucheon confessed that he had cuckolded Ruari MacLeod of Lewis and openly admitted that he himself had fathered Lady Lewis's eldest son, Torquil. MacLeod disinherited Torquil, set his wife aside as an adulteress and took another wife. Torquil, now a half-brother to the Morrison chief, Iain Dubh Morrison, then allied himself to the MacKenzies of Kintail who now made claim to the island. In the bloody war that followed, Iain Dhub Morrison was slain (1601) by the MacLeods, who later captured and executed his eldest son and successor, Malcolm Mor Morrison. Eventually, in the early 17th century, the Macleods were overthrown, the MacKenzies secured power and their former allies, the Morrisons were driven from the island.

In the 20th century, a branch of the family, the Morrisons of Ruchdi in North Uist, who

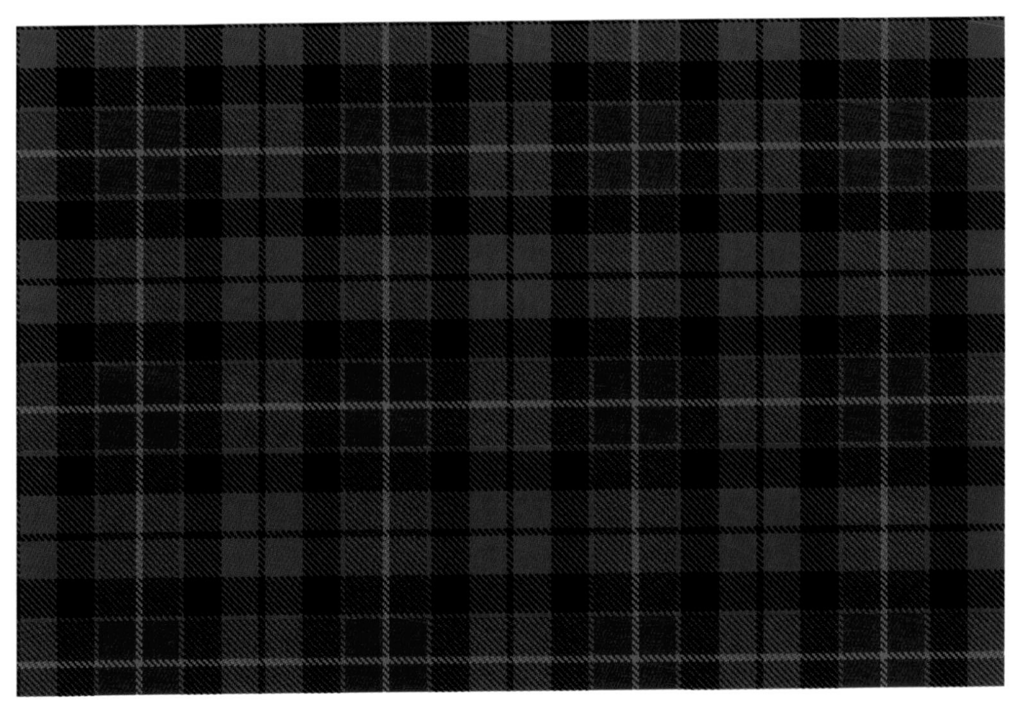

*Morrison Hunting*

claim descent from the Dun of Pabbay, were recognized by the Lord Lyon as the chiefly line, while John Morrison 1st Lord Margadale, who owned the island of Islay was created Regional Chief of the Morrisons of Islay.

The Morrisons have two tartans: the Morrison Clan Society tartan is the MacKay tartan to which a red line was added. D.C Stewart noted in 1950 that this MacKay tartan was a comparatively late tartan, although he did not give a date. Since the earliest sample of MacKay tartan dates from 1816 in the Cockburn Collection, we should assume a later date for the Morrison tartan. Furthermore, the Clan Society was founded in 1906, it is possible that this tartan dates from then. The second tartan, the Morrison Clan tartan has a red ground. It was approved and recorded by the Lyon Court in 1968, and is based on a sample which had been found between the pages of an old Morrison family bible dating from 1747. Although it is not necessarily of the same age, such an early relic is a rare example of an original tartan.

Surnames with possible associations: Brieve, MacBrieve,

# Munro

Earliest known date: 1850
Earliest source: Smith, 1850
Tartan type: Symmetrical
Sett: **G**4 Cr4 G4 R32 B2 Y2 R6 B12 R6 Y2 B2 R6 G32 R6 B2 Y2 **R**48
Clan crest: An eagle perching Proper
Clan motto: Dread God ("Fear God")
Badge: *Garbhag nan Gleann* (Common Club Moss)

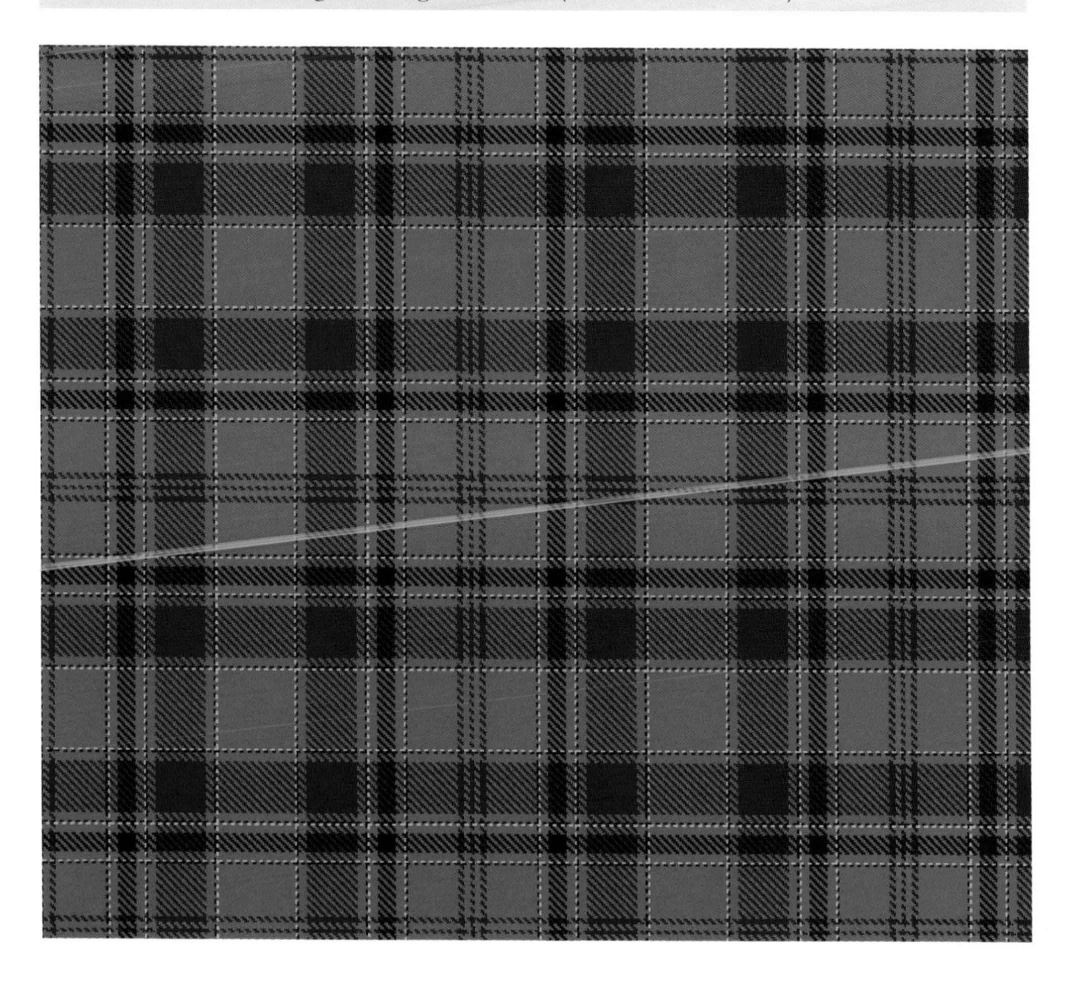

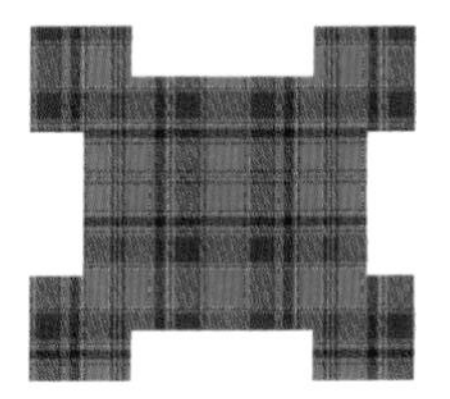

In Gaelic the Munros are known as *Clann Rothaich*, and the clan land was Ferindonald, meaning "Land of Donald", which is believed to have been the name of the first Munro chief. Donald received a charter for lands in Ross-shire as a reward for helping Malcolm II (1005–34) against Norse invaders. The lands were situated under Ben Wyvis, and extended from Loch Morie down the coastal plains of on the north side of the Firth of Cromarty. The title of their chief was Munro of Foulis and, in times of war, a fire was lit as a beacon on the highest tower of Castle Foulis, Evanton in Ross-shire, to call the clan together. The Munro *slughorn* (slogan or warcry) became *Caistel Folais'n a theine* – "Castle Foulis ablaze". (In fact the castle *was* fully ablaze when it burnt down accidentally in 1750, but was later rebuilt.)

According to Burke's Peerage, the 1st Munro of Foulis was Hugh, who died in 1126. Later, George Munro of Foulis is said to have received a charter from the Earl of Sutherland in the reign of Alexander II (1214–49) and Robert Munro in 1309, had a charter for lands in Strathspey and of Cupermakcultis. The first Munro chief on record, Robert de Munro (1341–69) appears to have married the niece of Queen Euphame Ross, the consort of king Robert II, who was also the half-sister of the Earl of Ross. Robert de Munro was killed fighting for William, Earl of Ross and Lord of Skye, who had confirmed Munro's possession of the lands of East Foulis and the Tower of Strath Skiach (the predecessor of Foulis Castle), in Ferindonald. Hugh of Munro, the next chief, was confirmed in the lands of West Foulis in 1394. When the MacDonald earls of Ross fell from power in 1476, the Munros acquired the Barony of Foulis in their own right directly from the Crown.

Robert Munro of Foulis was killed at the battle of Pinkie in 1547 fighting against the invading English. His son Robert had two sons, Robert and Hector, who were successively chiefs, and a third son George of Obsdale, from a second marriage. When Hector Munro of Foulis was chief, he was taken ill in 1589 and it is said that he used witchcraft (unsuccessfully) to offer up the life of his half-brother George as a substitute victim! Hector died in 1603 and was succeeded by his son Robert, known as the "Black Baron" who was made the 1st Baronet in 1634. He was also colonel of two Dutch regiments under King Gustavus Adolphus of Sweden during the Thirty Years War. The Black Baron was killed by a musket ball in 1638 and was buried at Ulm, Germany. At the time, the Swedish army contained no fewer than 27 field-officers and 11 captains of the surname Munro.

The Black Baron's son, the 2nd Baronet, also died abroad (in Holland in 1651) aged just 16. In an ironic twist of fate, the baronetcy – and the chiefship of the Clan Munro – along with the Foulis estates passed to Sir Robert Munro of Obsdale, the grandson of George, the "Substitute Victim", who became the 3rd Baronet of Foulis.

Presbyterians, the Munros followed their chief in support of William and Mary in the Revolution of 1688 and, in the next century, throughout the Jacobite unrest from 1689 to 1746, were loyal to the Government. Sir Robert, the 6th Baronet and a Hanoverian officer in the 37th Regiment, died at Falkirk. The events of the Jacobite Risings had left Foulis Castle in near-ruins and "the Scholar Chief" Sir Harry Munro, 7th Baronet, began rebuilding. The 9th Baronet, General Sir Charles Munro of Foulis led a division of Simon Bolivar's army which liberated much of South America. When his grandson, Sir Hector Munro, 11th Baronet, died in 1935, the baronetcy passed to a cousin, but Foulis Castle and the chiefship passed to his grandson, Patrick Munro of Foulis, who completed the restoration of the castle.

The Munro tartan in what is now considered its correct form with the spaces between the three green lines in crimson (not in scarlet, as described by Logan), was illustrated by the Smith brothers and by Smibert in 1850. In early versions of the tartan, such as the sample in the Cockburn Collection where it is called Locheil Cameron, the crimson stripes often appeared as bright pink.

Surnames with possible associations: Dingwall, Vass, Wass,

# Murray

Earliest known dates: Murray of Atholl, c.1810–20; Murray of Tullibardine, 1679

Earliest sources: Atholl, Cockburn Collection, 1810-1820; Tullibardine, Smith, 1850

Tartan Types: Symmetrical

Setts: Atholl: **B**24 Bk 4 B4 Bk4 B4 Bk24 G24 R6 G24 Bk24 B24 Bk2 **R6**

Tullibardine: **B**4 R2 B2 R4 B8 R4 B2 R2 Bk4 R2 B2 R48 B24 R4 G4 R16 G24 R8 B4 R4 **Bk**2

Clan crest: On a wreath Or and Sable, a demi-savage Proper wreathed about the temples and waist with laurel, his arms extended and holding in the dexter hand a dagger, in the sinister hand a key all Proper

Clan motto: Furth fortune and fill the fetters ("Find fortune and fill your boots")

Badge: *Aitionn* (Juniper)

The ancient Pictish kingdom of Moray (in Gaelic *Moireabh*) gives the Clan Murray its name. The kingdom was given to Freskin, who probably supported King David I's policy to pacify the northern provinces of Scotland and was granted a charter for part of Moray and the castle of Duffus. His grandson, William, became known as "de Moravia", which in Lowlands Scots became Murray. In addition to his heir Sir Walter, William de Moravia had several other sons: from one is descended the House of Murray of Tullibardine. The senior line of Murrays took the surname of Sutherland and became the earls of Sutherland in 1235. From then on, the chiefs of the Murrays were also the lords of Petty in Moray, and then, through marriage, also lords of Bothwell in Clydesdale in the 1250s.

Sir Walter Murray, 1st Lord Bothwell, was co-Regent of Scotland in 1255. Sir Andrew Murray, heir to the 3rd Lord Bothwell, supported the cause of an independent Scotland and with William Wallace, rose against the English king Edward I in 1297. Sir Andrew "the Patriot", fought and died at the battle of Stirling Bridge. Sir Andrew's heir, the 4th Lord, was Regent of Scotland. He died fighting the English at the battle of Halldon Hill in 1333. The last Murray lord, the 5th of Bothwell, married his cousin Joan, the daughter of Maurice Murray, Earl of Strathearn. When he died of the plague in 1360, Joan carried the Lordship of Bothwell to her second husband, the 3rd Earl of Douglas.

The chiefship of the Murrays then fell into uncertainty with several branches of the Name in Sutherland and Murray itself, and throughout Perthshire and Stirlingshire to the Borders. In 1542, however, the Murrays of Tullibardine in Strathearn became Chiefs of the Clan Murray. and by "Bands of Association" in 1586 and again in 1598, the various Murray lairds all across Scotland – Moray of Abercairny in Perthshire, Murray of Polmaise in Stirlingshire, Murray of Cockpool in Dunfriesshire, Murray of Cobairdy in Buchan, and the Murrays of Falahill and Blackbarony in the Borders – recognized the line of Sir John Murray, who was created 1st Earl of Tuillibardine in 1606. William, his son and heir, married Dorothy Stewart, the eldest daughter of John, 5th Earl of Atholl, whose inheritance was a vast estate of over 200,000 acres. The Stewart earldom of Atholl became a Murray earldom when their son John was confirmed in 1629 as the Earl of Atholl. In 1703, the Murrays reached the top of the peerage tree when they were created dukes of Atholl. The 1st Duke's younger son, was Lord George Murray, the Jacobite general and planner of the Rising of 1745. His elder brother, George, was a supporter of the Hanoverian succession, however and led a charge at Culloden, which broke the Hanoverian ranks but could not prevent the overall defeat of the Jacobites. He died in exile in the Netherlands in 1760.

Culloden was the last time the Highlanders of Atholl went to war, but the ceremonial

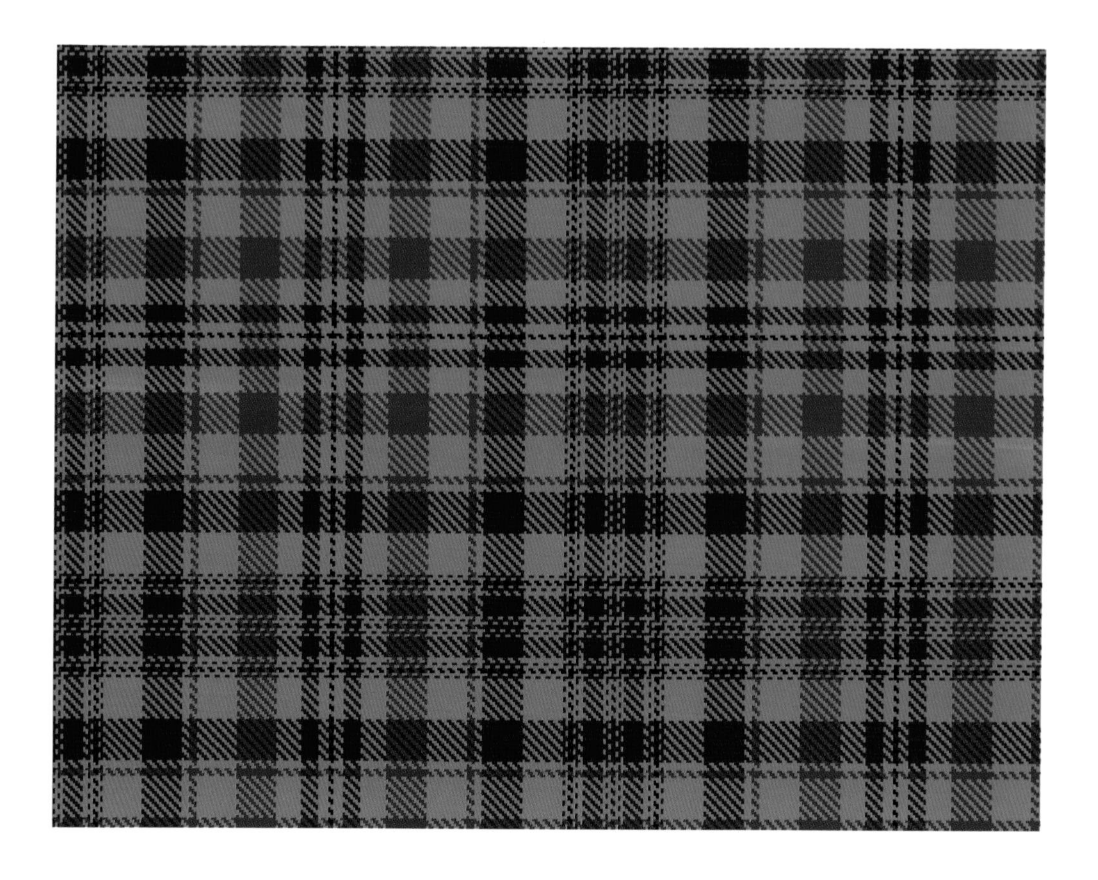

*Murray of Tullibardine*

bodyguard of the clan chiefs – the Atholl Highlanders – is unique in being the only private army in Britain. The Murray of Atholl tartan is also known as the Atholl district tartan and may have been in use by the Murrays of Polmaise around 1618 when Sir Robert Gordon wrote to the chief requesting that he remove the red and white lines from the plaids of his men so their dress would be in harmony with other septs. The Murray of Tullibardine clan tartan, was said by Grant in 1850 to have been adopted and worn by Charles, 1st Earl of Dunmore (the second son of the 1st Marquis of Tullibardine), in 1679, who was the Lieutenant-Colonel of the Royal Grey Dragoons, the "Scots Greys".

Surnames with possible associations: MacMurray, Moray, Piper, Small

# Nicolson MacNicol

Earliest known date: *c.*1845–7

Earliest source: McIan illustration, 1845–7

Tartan type: Symmetrical Sett: **R**12 G2 R12 Bk8 R2 Az2 R2 G16 R12 Bk2 R12 **G**2

Clan crest: Nicolson : A lion issuant Or armed and langued Gules

MacNicol: A hawk's erased erased Gules

Clan motto: Nicolson: *Generositate* ("By generosity")

Badge: Juniper

Clan motto: MacNicol: *Sgorr-a-bhreac* ("Scorrybreac" - the clan home on Skye)

Badge: Trailing Azalea

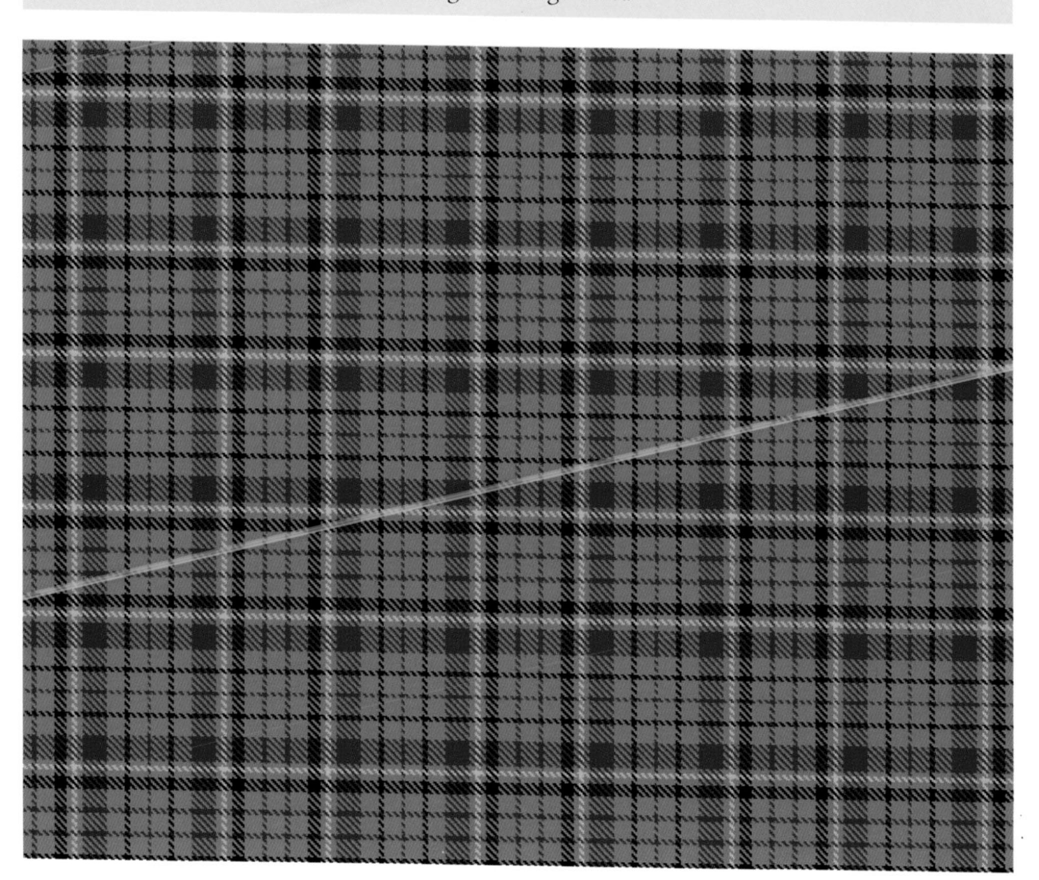

In 1985, the Lyon Court deliberated on the confusion between the Hebridean MacNicol clan and those on the mainland of Scotland whose name, over time, had become anglicized as Nicolson. The 4th Lord Carnock was recognized as Nicolson of that Ilk, chief of Clan Nicolson, while Iain Nicolson of Scorrybreac was recognized as MacNeacail of MacNeacail (MacNicol of MacNicol) and Scorrybreac, chief of the independent Clan MacNeacail, which had formerly been a cadet of the Nicolsons.

Both the Nicolsons and MacNicols are of Norse descent: Nicolsons perhaps deriving from the name "Olsen" or from Nicolassen. Tradition holds that Nicolassen eventually settled in Scotland after he was sent as an envoy from Norway in 1266 to conclude the Treaty of Perth which ceded the Hebrides to Scotland.

In the 16th century, a James Nicolson appeared as a lawyer in Edinburgh. Of his two sons, James became the bishop of Dunkeld in 1606, while John, the elder son, acquired the lands of Lasswade in 1592. His son, also called John, was created a baronet of Nova Scotia as Nicolson of that Ilk and Lasswade in 1629. In 1637, Thomas Nicolson became the 1st baronet of Carnock, near Stirling but the direct male line of the Nicolsons ended in 1808 and passed to Bishop James's grandson in Shetland, Major General Sir William Nicolson who served in America and India. He died in 1820 and was succeeded by his son, Admiral Sir Frederick Nicolson, and then by Arthur Nicolson, the ambassador to the Imperial Court at St Petersburg, Russia from 1906–10, who was created Baron Carnock of Carnock in 1916.

The MacNicols, whose name in modern Gaelic takes the form MacNeacail, held the lands of Scorrybreac, Skye and were part of the Council of the MacDonald Lord of the Isles. Following the collapse of the Lordship of the Isles, the MacNicols became followers of the MacDonalds of Sleate.. The clan was badly affected by the Highland Clearances in the 19th century, and the family was forced to abandon Scorrybreac and emigrate to New Zealand and Australia. In 1989, Iain Nicolson, chief of Clan MacNeacail unveiled a commemorative stone and set about developing a reacquired portion of Scorrybreac as a national park.

The Nicolson MacNicol clan tartan is a reconstructed sett by D.C. Stewart based on an illustration by McIan in around 1845 of a woman wearing a shawl, although Logan stated that they had not seen a tartan that was peculiar to the Nicolsons/MacNicols. Stewart noted that MacIan's drawing was open to various interpretations and his reconstruction should not be regarded as authentic: its status is simply listed as "Recorded" in the Scottish Tartans Society's *Register of All Publicly Known Tartans*.

# Ogilvie

Earliest known date: 1816
Earliest source: Stewart, 1893
Tartan type: Symmetrical
Sett: **W**2 Az8 Y2 Bk2 R12 W2 R8 W2 R12 Bk2 Y2 Az8 R2 **Az**8
Clan crest: A lady affrontee fro the middle upward Proper in Azure vestments holding a portcullis Gulles.
Clan motto: *A Fin* ("To the end")
Badge: *Sgitheach geal* (Hawthorn)

The Ogilvie lands are in Angus, a Pictish kingdom. When the Picts and Gales became united, the rulers of the former Kingdom of Angus became titled as "mormaer". By the 12th century, the mormaers had become styled in the English fashion as counts or earls. Gillebride, Earl of Angus gave the lands of Ogilvie (in old English, *Ocel-fa* meaning "high plain"), in Glamis, Forfarshire, sometime around 1172, to his third son, Gilbert who then also assumed the name of his property. Patrick de Ogilvie appears in the Raglan Rolls and from him descended the Ogilvies of that Ilk. When this line expired, the Ogilvies of Auchterhaus, founded by Sir Patrick Ogilvie of Wester Powrie became the stem-family and, in addition, they became the hereditary Sheriffs of Angus.

Sir Patrick commanded the Scottish forces in 1429 with Joan of Arc against the English in France. His younger son, Sir Walter Ogilvie was appointed Lord High Treasurer of Scotland in 1425 and, in 1430, was made an ambassador to England. His numerous sons included Alexander of Auchterhaus, the progenitor of the Ogilvies of Inchmartine, and Sir Walter of Lintratham, Treasurer of Scotland who was the ancestor of the Ogilvies of Airlie, the Earl of Deskford, Findlater, and of Seafield. Sir Walter's eldest son, Sir John Ogilvie of Lintratham, received a charter to the lands and castle of Airlie in 1459 and his son was elevated to the peerage as Lord Ogilvie of Airlie. In 1639, Charles I made James the 8th Lord the Earl of Airlie. Staunchly royalist, the Ogilvies supported Charles I, and, in the following century, several members of the family were attainted for the part they played in the 1715 and 1745 Jacobite risings. In 1778, however, Lord Ogilvie was pardoned, but it was not until an Act of Parliament in 1826 that the Airlie earldom was restored to David Ogilvie as 6th Earl.

The seats of the Airlie family are at the castle of Airlie and Cortachy Castle on the river South Esk. The Ogilvie tartan is one of the most complex: a version described by Logan in 1831 but, curiously, known until 1812 as Drummond of Strathallan – as the Ogilvies and Drummonds only became connected by marriage at this date – had over 90 color changes. If laid out on the usual 24-inch web, it would need to be woven at 64 threads per inch. The resulting fabric may have been finer than many used for kilts at that time and, therefore, it is possible that Logan's specimen was a silk plaid. According to D.W. Stewart, an earlier and less elaborate Ogilvie tartan was already in use prior to 1812, probably because of the difficulty of weaving the elaborate sett. The simplified version of the Ogilvie of Airlie tartan was certified by the chief in 1816.

Surnames with possible associations: Airlie, Findlater, MacGilchrist, Richardson, Storie

# Ramsay

Earliest known date: 1842

Earliest source: *The Vestiarium Scoticum*, 1842

Tartan type: Symmetrical

Sett: **R**6 Cr2 R60 Bk56 W4 **Bk**8

Clan crest: A unicorn's head couped Argent armed Or

Clan motto: *Ora et labora* ("Pray and work")

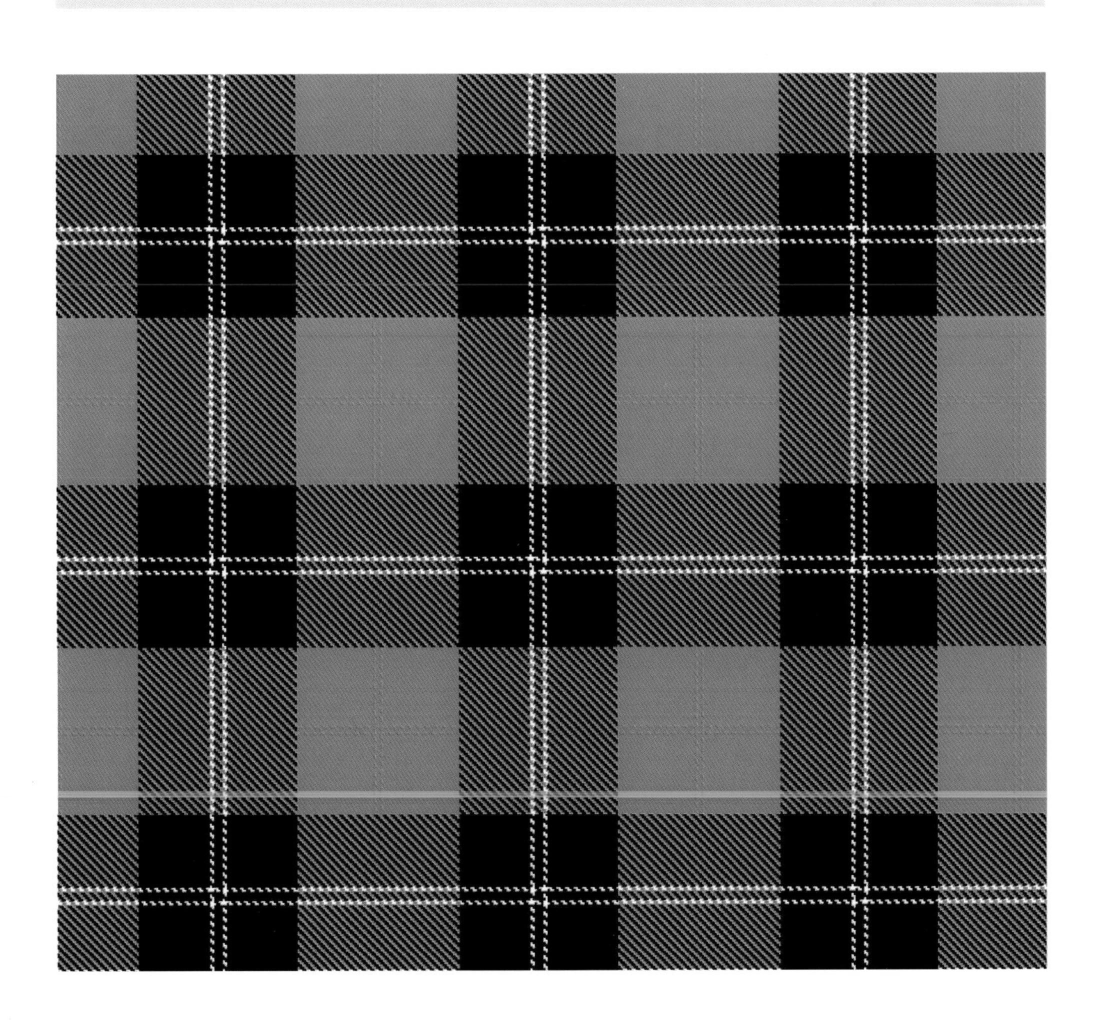

Sir Simon de Ramesie, a Norman-French knight, is believed to have been in the retinue of David I, and was living in Lothian in 1140 when he witnessed a charter to the monks of Holyrood. The de Ramesies flourished, so that by the 13th century there were five major branches of the house: Dalhousie, Auchterhouse, Banff, Forfar and Chatto.

William de Ramsay, most likely Sir Simon's descendant, swore fealty to Edward I and received lands of Dalwolsy, now Dalhousie, in 1296. Later, however, William supported King Robert the Bruce and, in 1338, his son Alexander defended Dunbar against the English forces. Alexander was made Sheriff of Teviotdale – an appointment that so infuriated William Douglas of Liddesdale that he captured Ramsay and imprisoned him in Hermitage Castle where he starved to death in 1342. In 1400, his descendant, Sir Alexander Ramsay, successfully held Dalhousie Castle (now a hotel) against a siege by Henry IV of England. His descendant, also called Alexander, was killed at Flodden in 1513 and Dalhousie passed to his son Nicholas.

One of Nicolas's great-grandsons, John Ramsay, killed the Earl of Gowrie and his brother Alexander Ruthven in 1600. They attempted to kidnap James VI in what is now known as the Gowrie Conspiracy. A grateful monarch made John Ramsay the Earl of Holderness and Viscount Haddington. In 1618, George Ramsay (John's eldest brother) was made Lord Ramsay of Melrose – a title he changed the following year to Lord Ramsay of Dalhousie. William, the 2nd Lord Ramsay was made Earl of Dalhousie in 1633, yet he opposed the religious policies of Charles I and raised a cavalry regiment for Parliament, to fight at Marston Moor in 1644.

The Ramsays continued in public service and contributed to the arts: Allan Ramsay, born in 1687, was a celebrated publisher and poet, author of "The Gentle Shepherd", while his son, also Allan, was one of the greatest portrait painters of the 18th century. The 9th Earl was governor-general of Canada from 1819 to 1832, while the 10th Earl, who was created Marquis of Dalhousie, was governor-general of India from 1847 to 1856. When he died in 1860 without a male heir, the marquisate became extinct, but the earldom continued and was passed to his cousin, William Maule, who was made Baron Panmure in 1831 and from whom the present chiefs descend. Their seat is now Brechin Castle in Angus.

The Ramsay tartan may have used an early MacGregor sett as its basis. This is because "Ramsay" was one of the names adopted by members of the Clan MacGregor when their own was proscribed under laws directed against the Clan from 1563 to 1775. It is possible, therefore, that the Ramsay tartan was in use long before it was first recorded in *The Vestiarium Scoticum*.

# Robertson (Clann Donnachaidh)

Earliest known date: 1831

Earliest source: Logan, 1831

Tartan type: Symmetrical

Sett: **R**2 G2 R18 B2 R2 G18 R2 B18 R2 G2 R18 G2 **R**2

Clan crest: A dexter hand holding up an imperial crown Proper

Clan motto: *Virtutis glorria merces* ("Glory is the reward of valor")

Badge: *An Raineach mhor* (Bracken)

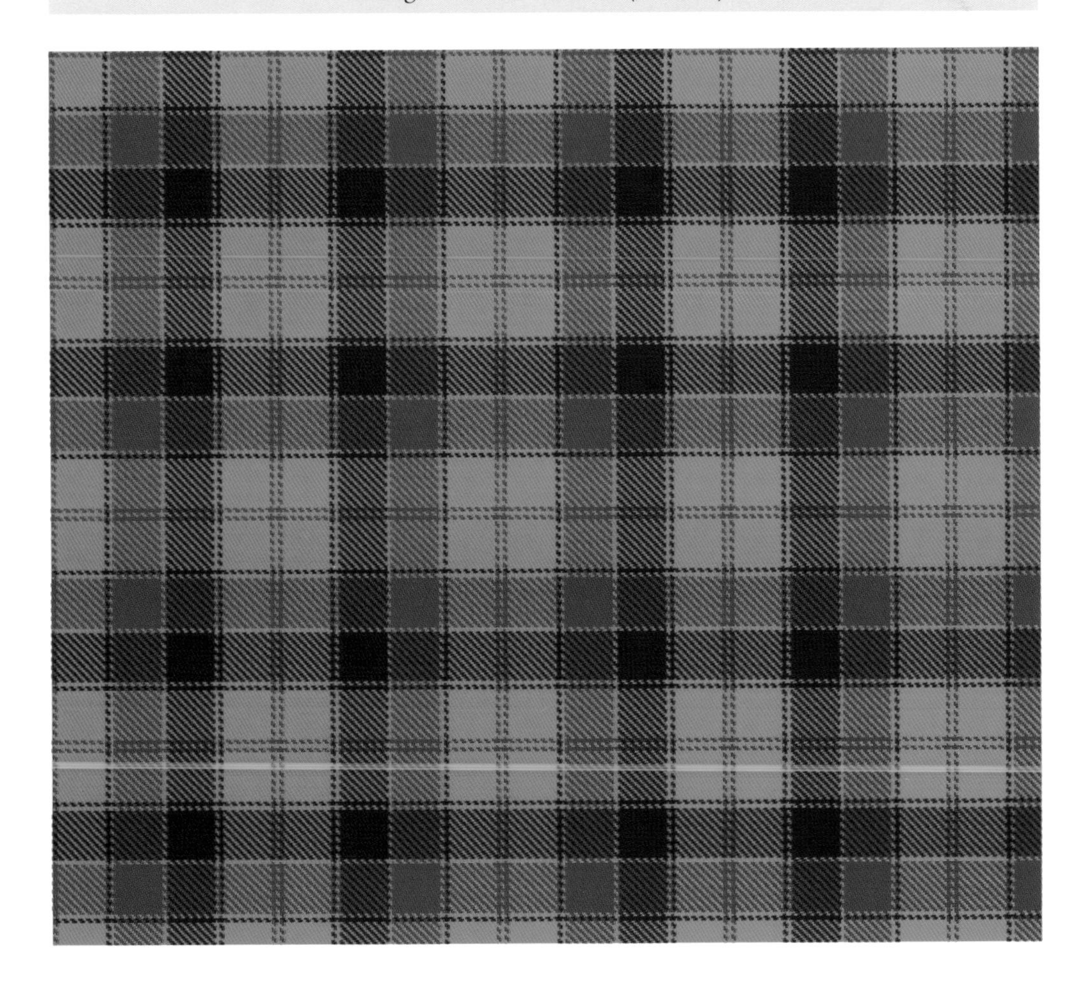

The chiefs of the Clan Robertson are descended from the Celtic "mormaers" or ruling princes of Atholl. The clan is more correctly called Clann Donnachaidh, which means "Children of Duncan", after their ancestor Robert Riabhach "Grizzled Robert" Duncanson, the 4th Chief of the Clan. His lands were elected into the Barony of Struan in 1451 by James II as a reward for the capture of Sir Robert Graham who had (under great provocation) murdered King James I in 1437 at Perth. Riabhach's son took the name Robertson, which thereafter became the clan and family name.

Like many clans, the Robertsons feuded with their neighbors, in this case the Stewarts of Atholl: the 6th chief, William Robertson, was killed by the Stewarts while trying to recover lands stolen from him, and the 8th chief was murdered. His brother inherited an estate so deeply in debt that a large portion of the lands had to be sold off. In early times, the chiefs had castles at Rannoch and at Invernack near Struan, and, until 1854, their principal residence was Dunalastair, or Mount Alexander, at the foot of Schiehallion in Rannoch. In 1606, John Robertson, a wealthy Edinburgh merchant with claims to kinship, transferred the title of the lands to Robertson of Struan.

In 1636, the chiefship was devolved to Donald, known as the "Tutor of Struan". Intensely loyal to the Stewart monarchy, Donald raised a regiment to fight for Charles I in the Civil War. Alexander, 17th Chief of Struan, was known as the "Poet Chief". He followed James VII into exile in France in 1690 and had his estates forfeited. He was pardoned in 1703, but would never swear fealty to the Hanoverian succession, calling the Clan Donnachaidh out in 1715 to support the "Old Pretender" and again in 1745 when they rallied to the side of the'Young Pretender", Prince Charles Edward Stewart. When the Poet Chief died, the chiefship passed to a kinsman, Duncan Robertson of Drumachuine. He was unable to take up the Robertson estates because he, too, had been forfeited for his participation in the 1745 Rising. In 1784, his son Alexander, the 15th chief, succeeded in having the Barony of Struan restored to him by the Crown. In 1854, George Robertson, the 18th Chief, sold off the Struan estates and, for many years, his successors lived in Kingston, Jamaica, although a Clann Donnachaidh Society was formed in Edinburgh in 1893.

Surnames with possible associations: Collier, Colyear, Dobbie, Dobson, Donachie, Duncanson, Dunnachie, Hobson, Inches, MacConachie, MacConnechy, MacConochie, MacDonachie, MacInroy, MacLagan, MacRobbie, MacRobert, MacRobie, Roberts, Robinson, Robison, Robson, Roy, Stark, Tonnochy

# Rose

Earliest known date: 1842
Earliest source: *The Vestiarium Scoticum*, 1842
Tartan type: Symmetrical
Sett: **G**8 R64 P18 Cr12 P4 Cr6 P4 Cr24 **W**6
Clan crest: On a chapeau Gules furred Ermine, a harp Azure
Clan motto: "Constant and true"
Badge: *Ros Mairi Fhiadhaich* (Wild Rosemary)

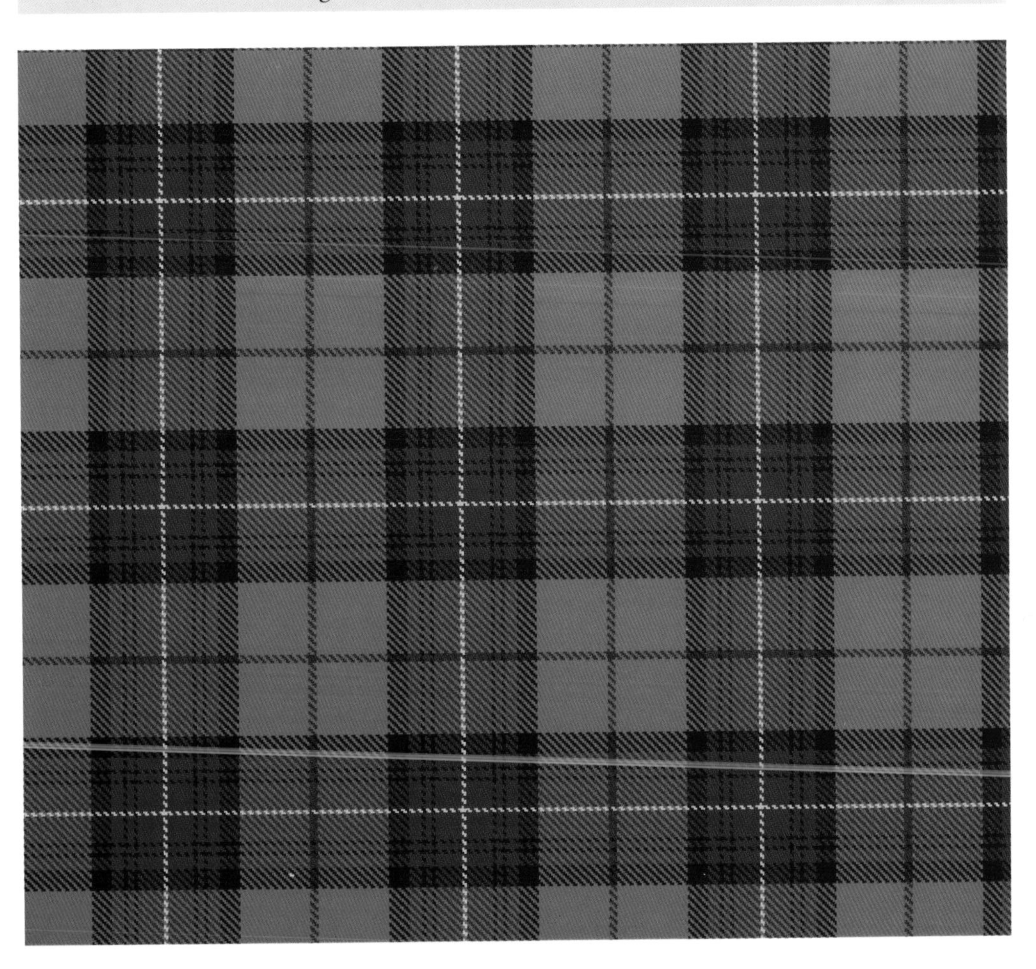

The family of the chief of the clan, Rose of Kilravock, originated in Ros, near Caen in Normandy, France. Along with two other families – the de Boscos and the de Bissets, with whom the Roses were related – the de Ros family settled first in Wiltshire and Dorset in England after the Norman Conquest in 1066. The de Ros first appear in Scotland in Nairn during the reign of David I, but they were first designated as "of Geddes", which is in Inverness-shire.

In 1219, Hugh de Ros appears as a witness to the foundation charter of Beauly Priory by Sir John de Bisset, whose family had by now settled in Lovat. Hugh's son and successor, also Hugh, acquired the Barony of Kilravock through his marriage to Mary, the daughter of Sir Andrew de Bosco and his wife Elizabeth (who was herself the daughter and heiress of Sir John de Bisset of Lovat!). Hugh was succeeded by his son William, who had two sons. Andrew, the younger son was the ancestor of Rose of Auchlossen in Mar, while Hugh (the eldest) married Janet, daughter of Sir Robert Chisholm, through whom he acquired large tracts of land in Strathnairn. Around 1460, the "Tower of Kilravock" a picturesque castle on the banks of the River Nairn was built by Hugh, 7th Baron, as a defense against the Rose's unruly neighbors. Mary, Queen of Scots stayed there, as did her son, James VI. The Rose family has occupied Kilravock Castle since it was built and it remains the family seat and chief's family home to this day. The Roses supported the Reformation and the 13th Baron opposed the religious policies of Charles I and led his clan against Montrose at the battle of Auldearn in 1645. Yet, when the king was handed over to Parliament by the Scots army, Rose was part of the Duke of Hamilton's expedition which planned to rescue him! At the outbreak of the 1715 Jacobite Rising, the Roses declared for the Government. In 1746, on the eve of the battle of Culloden, Hugh, the 16th Baron with Hanoverian sympathies, entertained Prince Charles Edward Stewart at Kilravock while the Duke of Cumberland occupied the Rose's house at Nairn!

The Rose Clan tartan appeared in *The Vestiarium Scoticum* in 1842 and was designated as "Dress" tartan. According to D.C. Stewart, in the colors were poorly reproduced in the accompanying plate – they appeared as mid-blue and scarlet. The *Vestiarium* text, however, specifies the colors as purple and crimson. Another Rose tartan, a hunting sett, was recorded by James Logan earlier in 1831.

Surnames with possible associations: Barron

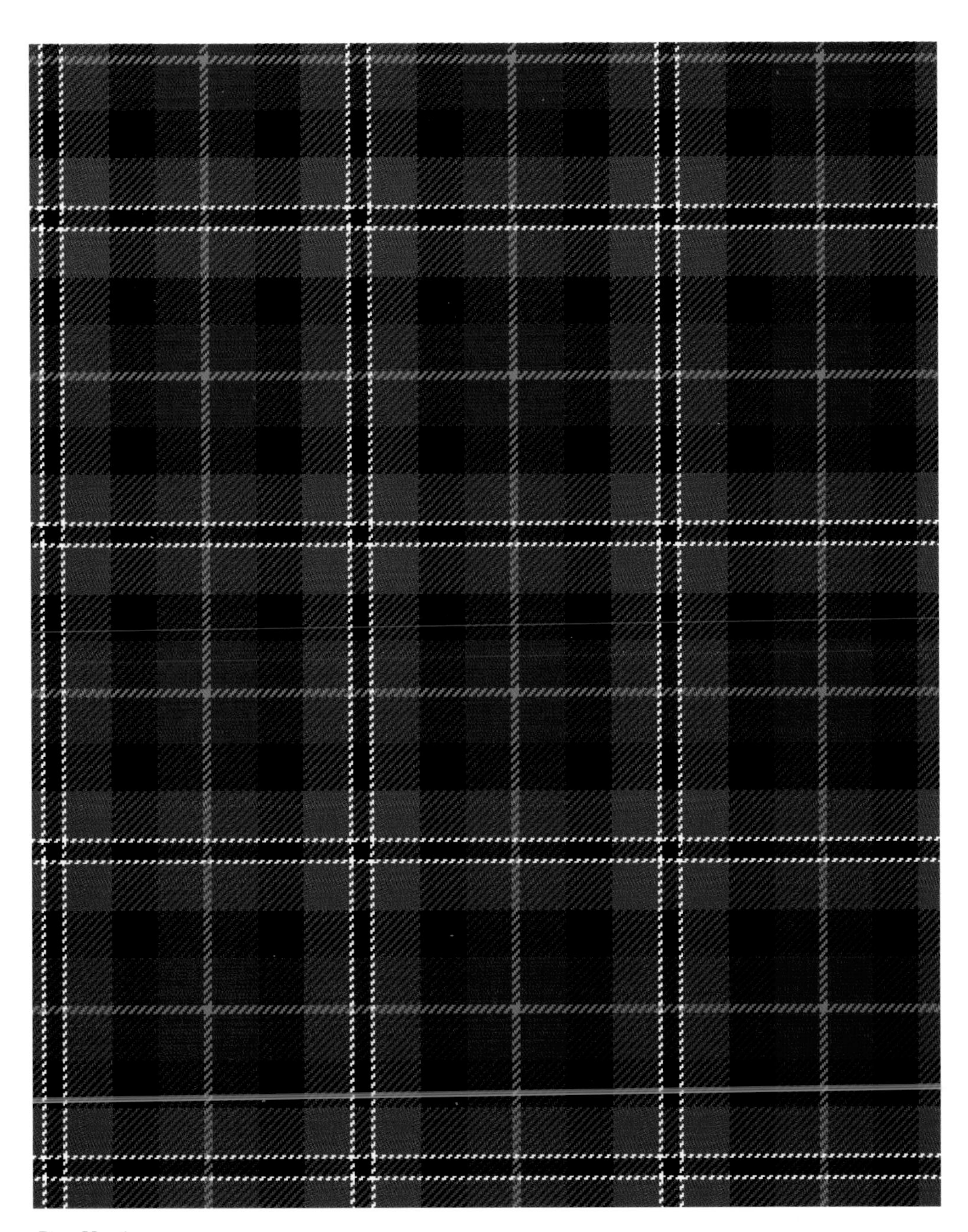

*Rose Hunting*

# Ross

Earliest known date: *c.*1810-1820

Earliest source: Cockburn Collection, 1810–20

Tartan type: Symmetrical Sett: **G**36 R4 G36 R36 G4 R8 G4 R36 B36 R4 B36 R36 B2 R2 B4 R2 B2 R36 B2 R2 B4 R2 B2 R36 G36 R4 **G**36

Clan crest: A hand holding a garland of juniper Proper

Motto: *Spem successus alit* ("Success nourishes hope")

Badge: *Aitionn* (Juniper

The Clan Ross is known to Highlanders as *Clann Aindreas* – the Sons of Andrew. Tradition maintains that the ancestors of the earls of Ross was the eldest son of Gilleoin na h-Airde or "Son of the follower of St Andrew". The first Earl of Ross, Malcolm, lived in the early 12th century. In 1214, Alexander II led his army to subdue the rebellion of the son of Donald Bane, a rival claimant to the Scottish throne. Alexander was assisted by the Ross chief, Fearchar Mac an t'sagirt (Son of the Priest), for which he was knighted. In 1234, Fearchar was formally recognized as the Earl of Ross.

Prominent throughout Scottish history, the Rosses fought in the struggle for independence from the Norse in the 13th century; at Bannockburn in 1314 and at Halidon Hill in 1333, where Hugh Ross, brother-in-law to Robert the Bruce, was killed in action. William, the 5th Earl of Ross, who died in 1372, left only a daughter who claimed the earldom as the Countess of Ross, and which was carried by her into the Clan Leslie. However, as the Leslies did not take the name of Ross, the chiefship passed to William's younger half-brother, Hugh of Rariches. He founded the House of Ross of Balnagowan.

Royalist supporters in the Civil War, some 1,000 clansmen were led by David, 12th Chief, against Oliver Cromwell's forces at the battle of Worcester in 1651. He was captured and imprisoned, while many of his clansmen were transported to the colonies in New England. He was succeeded as chief by his son, who died heirless. The chiefship then passed to a kinsman, Malcolm Ross of Pitcalnie. A claim was made by General George Ross, brother of Lord Ross of Hawkhead, and subsequently the Lyon Court recognized this claim to the chiefship. In 1903, however, the chiefship was restored to the "true" line when Miss Ross of Pitcalnie, near Tain, rematriculated the chiefly arms. In 1968, the chiefship passed to her heir, David Ross of Ross and Shandwick, who was a direct descendant through the male line of Fearchar Mac an t'sagairt.

The Clan Ross tartan in the Cockburn Collection is the tartan that is in use today. This is the oldest version dating from around 1810–20: Logan described a version in 1831, but he evidently gave an incorrect thread count. *The Vestiarium Scoticum* of 1842 also gives another erroneous version, although the Ross hunting tartan (*right*) is based on this scheme.

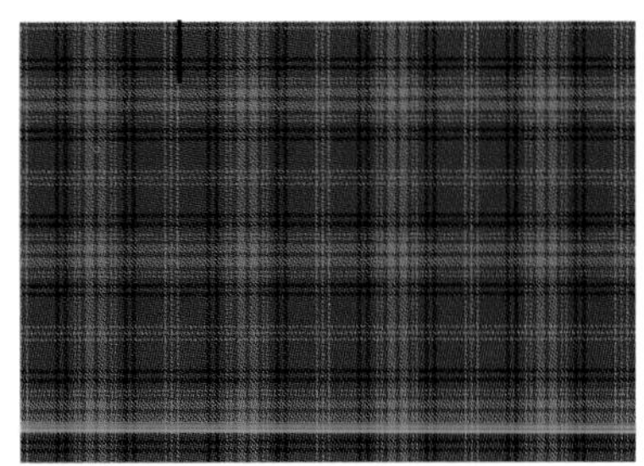

*Ross Hunting*

Surnames with possible associations: Corbet, Dingwall, Duthie, Fair, Gillanders, Haggart, MacTaggart, MacTier, MacTire, Taggart, Train

# Scott

Earliest known date: possibly 1829

Earliest source: Letter from Sir Thomas Dick Lauder to Sir Walter Scott, cited by Donald C. Stewart, 1950

Tartan type: Symmetrical

Sett: **G**8 R6 Bk2 R56 G28 R8 G8 W6 G8 **R**8

Clan crest: A stag trippant Proper, attired and unguled Or

Clan motto: *Amo* ("I love")

Badge: Blaeberry

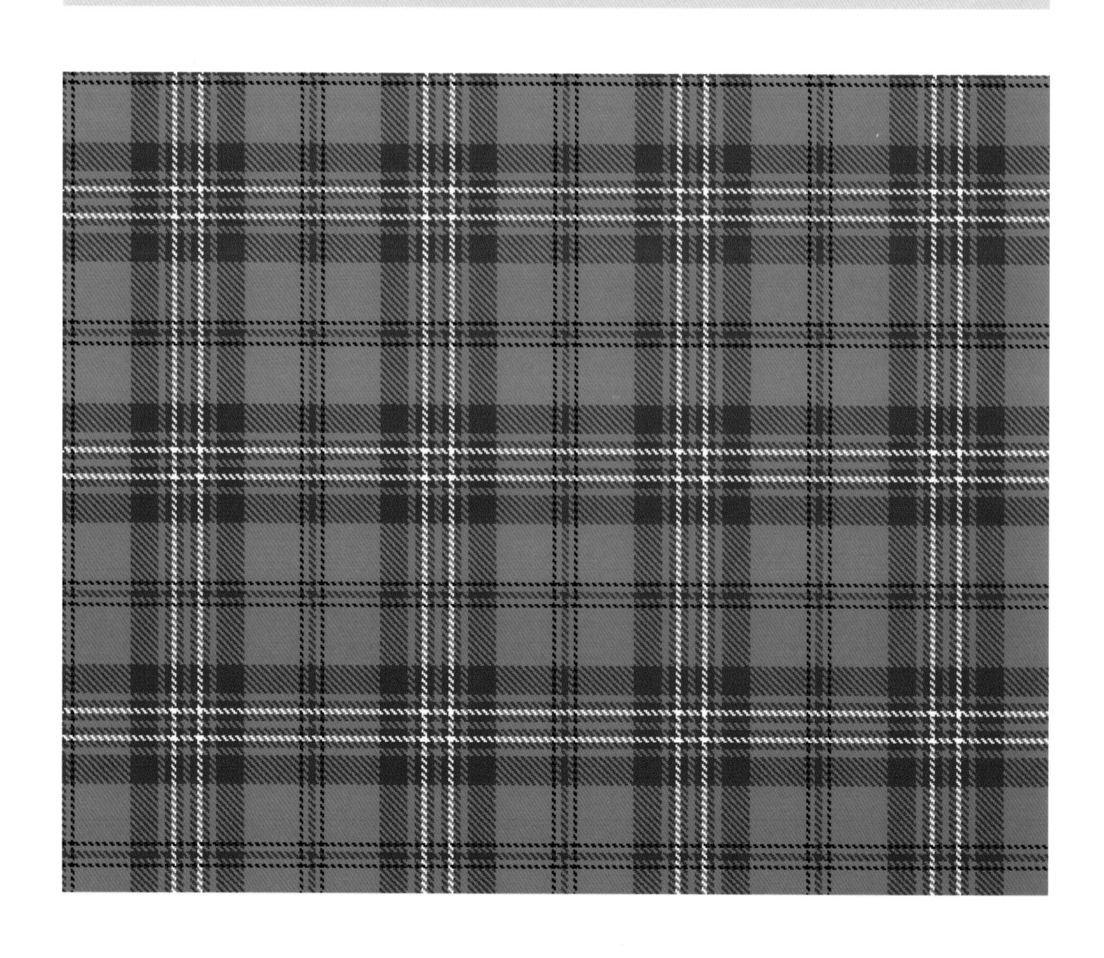

One Uchtredus filius Scoti was alive in 1130. He was the father of Richard, said to have had two sons: Richard, the ancestor of the Scotts of Buccleuch, and, Sir Michael, ancestor of the Scotts of Balweary. From Richard (the eldest son) descended Sir Richard, who through marriage acquired the Murthrockstone estates. He was appointed ranger of Ettrick Forest and built his home at Buccleuch. When Sir Richard died in 1320 he left a son, Sir Michael, who was a firm ally of Robert the Bruce and fought his cause at Halidon Hill in 1333, dying at the battle of Durham in 1346. Sir Michael left two sons: Robert, and Walter of Synton. Robert's descendant was Sir Walter, who was created Lord Scott of Buccleuch in 1600 and during the reign of James VI, fought in the Netherlands with the Prince of Orange.

Lord Scott died in 1611 and was succeeded by his son, also Walter, who was made Earl of Buccleuch in 1619. The second earl, Francis, supported the Covenant and opposed the religious policies of Charles I. He died aged 25, leaving two daughters who in turn became Countess of Buccleuch: Mary, who married Walter Scott of Highchester (of the Harden line of Scotts), became chief in her own right but when she died the peerage and chiefship passed to her sister, Anne, who married James, Duke of Monmouth, the illegitimate son of Charles II. On their wedding day in 1673, the couple were created Duke and Duchess of Buccleuch. The duke later rebelled against the Crown, his titles were forfeited and he was subsequently executed. But, as Anne had been specifically created duchess, her titles were not affected and she was succeeded by her grandson, Francis, who became the 2nd Duke of Buccleuch. Bellendean, near the head of Borthwick Water in Roxburghshire, in the heart of the clan chief's possessions, was the gathering place of the clan in times of war and "A Bellendaine" ("To Bellendean") remains the clan's *slughorn* (slogan or war-cry). The border seat of the dukes is the Castle of Branxholm, although the family also maintains three other great houses – and an internationally acclaimed art collection – of Drumlanrig, Bowhil and Boughton.

The earliest mention of the clan tartan known as "Red Scott" seems to have been in a letter from Sir Thomas Dick Lauder to Sir Walter Scott in 1829. The novelist Sir Walter Scott – who had stage-managed the important state visit of George IV to Edinburgh in 1822 and did a great deal to encourage the fashion for tartans in the 19th century – believed that Lowland Borders families in Scotland never had clan tartans, but instead used various patterns of black and white known as "Shepherd's Plaid". Smibert, in 1850, published such a design, which he said was prepared for Sir Walter Scott's "private" use in 1822.

Surnames with possible associations: Laidlaw

# Sinclair

Earliest known date: 1831

Earliest source: Logan, 1831

Tartan type: Symmetrical

Sett: **R**56 G32 Bk8 W2 Az12 **R**56

Clan crest: A cock Proper, armed and beaked Or

Clan motto: "Commit thy work to God"

Badges: *Conasg* (Gorse); White Clover

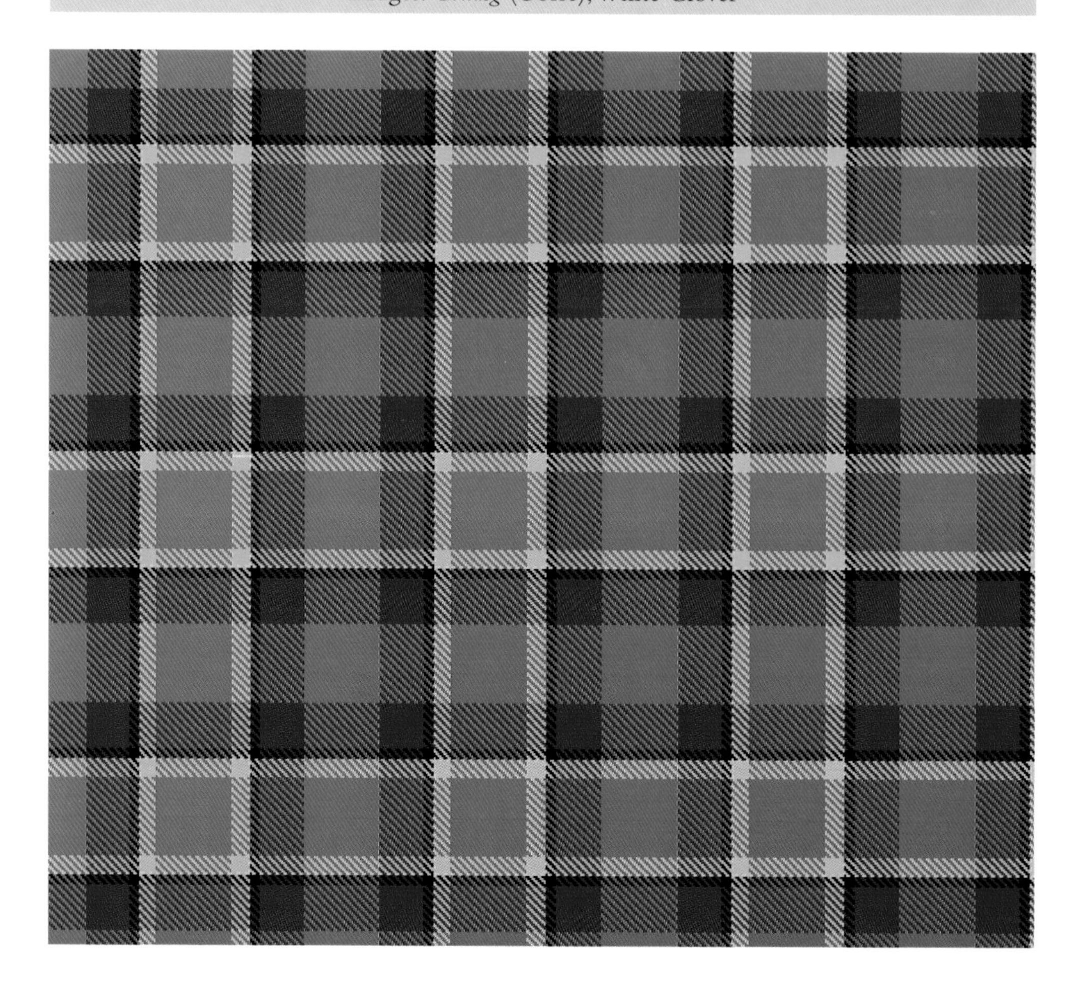

The name Sinclair, or St Clair, is derived from Saint-Clair-sur-Elle near St Lô in Normandy, France. The earliest record of the name dates from 1162 when Henry de St Clair received a charter of the lands of Herdmanston in Haddingstonshire from the Constable of Scotland. The St Clairs of Herdmanston were created peers in 1449, and the line of Lord Sinclair and the lands remain to this day.

The principal line of the Sinclairs, from which the clan chiefs descend, was founded by Sir William Sinclair, Sheriff of Edinburgh, Haddington, Linlithgow and Dumfries who was granted the Barony of Rosslyn in 1280. His son, Sir Henry Sinclair fought at Bannockburn and received a grant of lands in Pentland in 1317 as reward. His son, Sir William was "the kind and true St Clair" who died with Sir James Douglas in Spain *en route* to the Holy Land to bury the heart of Robert the Bruce. His grandson, Henry, Earl of Orkney and Lord High Admiral of Scotland, conquered the Faroe Islands in 1391, discovered Greenland and may also have voyaged to the New World, landing at Nova Scotia in Canada, and possibly even in Massachusetts, USA. His grandson, William, the last "Prince of Orkney", (he was compelled to resign Orkney by James III), was the founder of magnificent Rosslyn Chapel near Edinburgh. He was created Earl of Caithness in 1455 and bypassing his mentally ill eldest son, William "the Waster", the title passed to his second son, while the Rosslyn lands were settled on his third son from whom descended the lords Sinclair of Ravenscraig, chiefs of the blood of Sinclair until the line failed in 1784. In 1805, the earldom of Rosslyn passed to Sir James St Clair Erskine, Baronet, the ancestor of the Viscounts Thruso.

Of the Caithness line, the 2nd Earl died at Flodden; the 3rd Earl was killed during a rebellion in the Orkneys, while the 4th Earl was a supporter of Mary, Queen of Scots. He had several sons, the eldest of whom was John, Master of Caithness, who was starved to death by his father (for negotiating a peace treaty with the Murray clan without his permission) in the Castle of Girnigoe. Nevertheless, he did manage to become the ancestor of the 5th, 6th and 7th earls and of the Sinclairs of Murkill and Ratter! George, the 6th Earl, was so debt-ridden that, in 1672, he had to sell off much of the Sinclair lands. When he died without an heir in 1676, Sir John Campbell of Glenorchy, who now owned most of the mortgaged Sinclair estates, promptly married the widowed countess and claimed the earldom! The right to the titles was, however, disputed by George Sinclair of Keiss, a descendant of the 5th Earl, who seized the Sinclair estates by force. When he met the Campbells in battle on the banks of the Atimarlech, near Wick, the results were disastrous: so many Sinclairs were killed it was said the Campbells could cross the river without getting their feet wet.

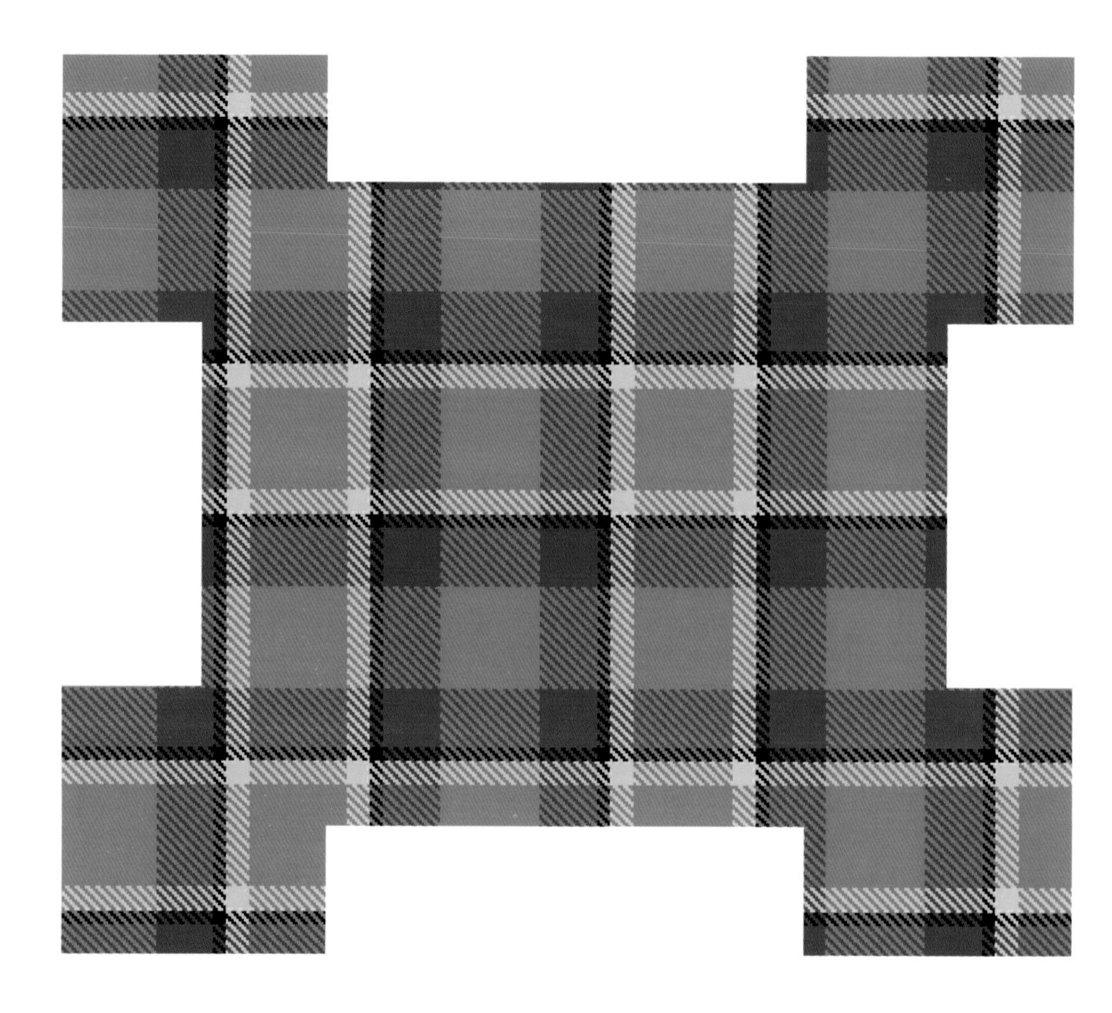

In 1681, the Sinclairs finally regained the earldom of Caithness through an Act of Parliament. Girnigoe Castle, on the rocky Caithness coast, near Wick, is the seat of the chief. A specimen of a Sinclair tartan also appears in a painting of Alexander, 13th Earl of Caithness (1790–1858). However, the usual tartan is that given by Logan in 1831. In 1951, the Lord Lyon recoded the Sinclair tartan in its smallest proportions, but the sett can be multiplied at the discretion of the weaver.

Surnames with possible associations: Clyne, Linklater, Lyall, Mason

# Skene

Earliest known date: 1850
Earliest source: Smith, 1850
Tartan type: Symmetrical
Sett: **B**2 R6 G18 R6 B2 R6 **B**18
Clan crest: A dexter arm issuing from the shoulder out of a cloud, holding forth a triumphal crown Proper
Clan motto: *Virtutis regia merces* ("A palace the reward of bravery")

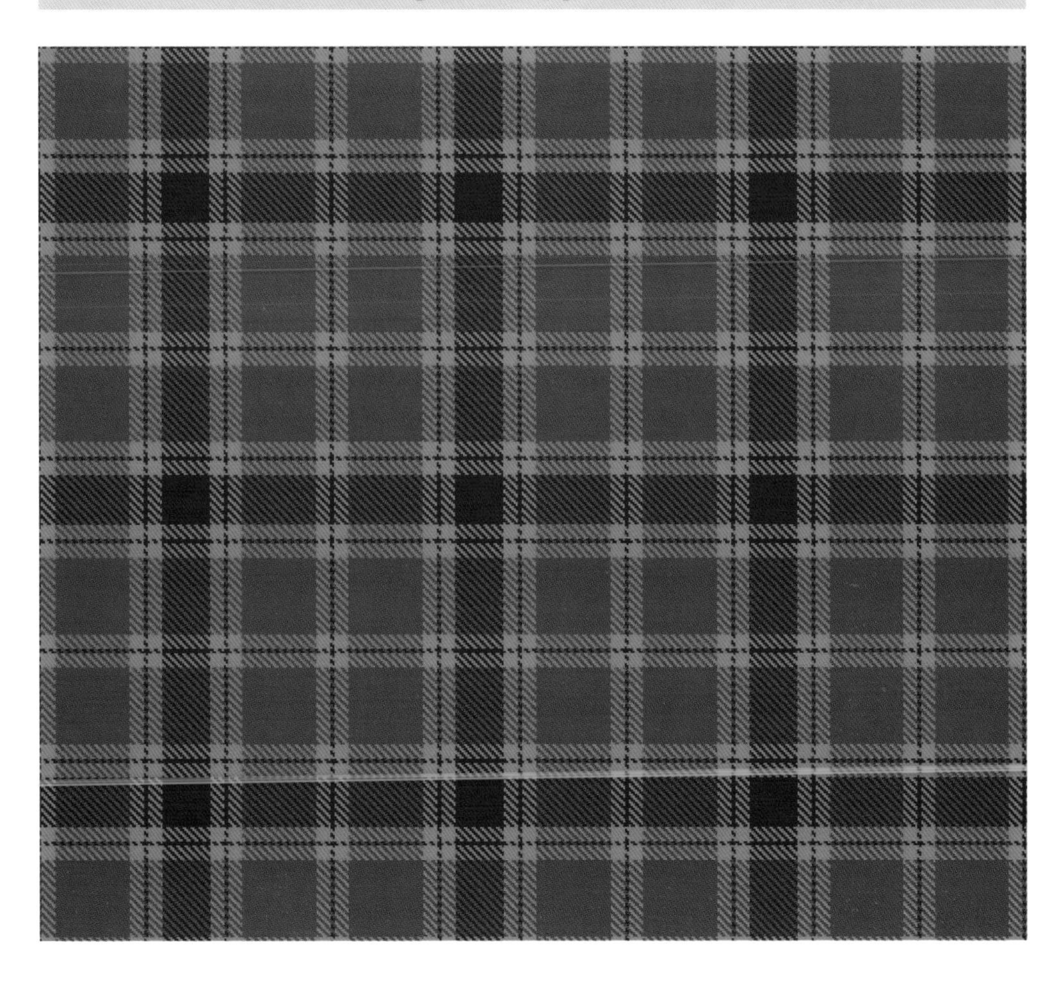

In Gaelic, Clan Skene is known as *Siol Sgeine* or *Clann Donnachaidh Mhar.* Legend tells that the founder of the Clan Skene was the younger son of Robertson of Struan who is said to have saved the life of the king by killing a ferocious wolf using only his small dagger or *sgian*. The reward for his courage was a grant of lands in Aberdeenshire, which he promptly named after his trusty blade. At Skene House, a carving of the arms of the chief has one of the earliest representations of Highland dress.

The first to bear the name was John de Skene who lived in the 11th century during the reign of Malcolm III. After the king's death, John became a supporter of Donald Bane, a rival to king Edgar for the throne of Scotland. John's lands were forfeited and were only restored when the Skenes joined Alexander's army in 1118. In the next century, John and his son Patrick de Skene appear in the Ragman Rolls of 1296 as swearing fealty to Edward I, but the Skenes were staunch supporters of Robert the Bruce, and, after his victory, the Skene lands were erected into a barony. In later times, the Skenes were forced into exile for their support of Charles I – the chief becoming part of the Swedish army of King Gustavus Adolphus. The family of Skene of Skene became extinct in the direct line in 1827, when the estates were devolved on James, 4th Earl of Fife, nephew of the last Skene of Skene. Other prominent branches of the family flourished, however: representation of the Skenes passed to the Skenes of Halyard, who were descended from Andrew of Auchorie, a second son of James, the 12th Chief, who died in 1605. The Halyards would later found Skeneborough on the shores of Lake Champlain in Canada. James Skene descended from the Skenes of Rubislaw, said to be Sir Walter Scott's inspiration for Ivanhoe, as did William Forbes Skene (1809–93) the celebrated historian of Scotland.

This tartan appeared in Wilson of Bannockburn's pattern book of 1819 where, in common with most early collections (including Logan's *The Scottish Gael* of 1831) it was called "Logan". It first became called Skene in the Smith's work in 1850, but here the fine lines were given as green and not blue. Grant's version of 1886, which used samples of tartan that were in use at the time, is the closest version to Wilson's pattern, and is the one in current use today. It is similar to the Robertson tartan – in keeping with the tradition that as the Skenes descended from the Robertsons of Struan.

Surnames with possible associations: Cariston, Dis, Dyce, Halyard, Halyard

# Stewart

Earliest known dates:
Royal Stewart Royal Family: *c.*1800 Source: Logan, 1831
Stewart of Appin:1820 Source: D.C. Stewart, 1950
Stewart of Atholl: pre-1842 Source: *The Vestiarium Scoticum*,1842
Tartan types: Symmetrical
Setts: Royal: **R**72 Az8 Bk12 Y2 Bk2 W2 Bk2 G16 R8 Bk2 R4 **W**2
Appin: **G**4 R4 Az2 B4 R48 G4 R4 B16 R4 G4 R8 G48 R4 Az2 B4 **R**6
Atholl: **R**12 Bk2 R40 Bk16 G6 Bk2 G4 Bk2 **G**44
Clan crest: A pelican Argent, winged Or, in her nest feeding her young Proper
Clan motto: *Virescit vulnere virtus* ("Courage grows strong at a wound")
Badges: *Darag* (Oak); *Cluaran* (Thistle)

In addition to the royal house of Stewart, who became the monarchs of Scotland, there were three main branches of Stewarts in the Highlands during the 14th and 15th centuries: the Stewarts of Appin, of Atholl, and of Balquidder. The clan takes its name from the hereditary office of Steward of Scotland, granted to their ancestor, Walter fitzalan by King David (1124–53), along with extensive lands in Renfrewshire and East Lothian. This office was the most important in the kingdom, and after the Stewarts became monarchs themselves, the office was settled on the heir-apparent. Today, Prince Charles is the Great Steward of Scotland.

Walter married Robert the Bruce's daughter and when Bruce's son David II died childless, he was succeeded by Bruce's grandson, Robert Stewart, who reigned as Robert II. The male line of royal Stewarts continued until the reign of Mary, Queen of Scots, and, as a family, the Stewarts held the throne of Scotland and later, England, until Queen Anne's death in 1714.

The Royal Stewart tartan is probably the best known of all the Scottish tartans. The personal tartan of the present Queen, it was worn by George IV during his state visit to Edinburgh in 1822 and was later adopted by George V for the House of Windsor (the present royal family) to mark their links with the royal house of Stewart from which they are descended through George I of Hanover (crowned 1714), the great-grandson of James VI and I, the Stewart king of Scotland and England (1603). When George V stated that this tartan could be worn by all members of his family, his words were taken to mean all the people of the British Empire. Consequently, since clansmen wear the tartan of their chief, all subjects of the British monarch can properly wear the Royal Stewart tartan!

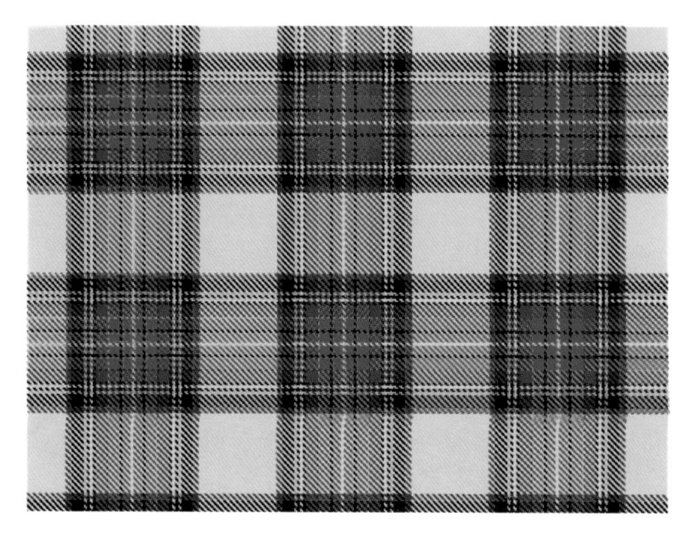

*Stewart Dress*

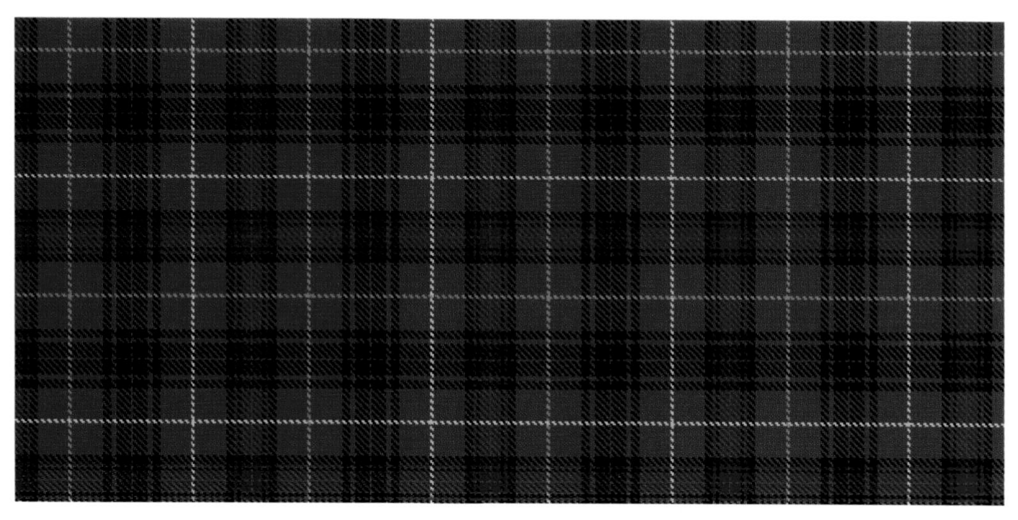

*Stewart Hunting*

In addition to this, the clan also have a Stewart dress tartan (another popular symbol of Scotland), an asymmetrical Hunting Stewart general clan tartan, the Old Stewart clan tartan, (known as "Stewart of Bute" and sometimes regarded as the clan tartan as distinct from Royal Stewart), and, the Prince Charles Edward tartan, (also known as the "Earl of Moray"). This tartan, said to have been worn by Bonnie Prince Charlie when he was at Holyrood in 1745–6, is an earlier version of the Royal Stewart with the red ground very much reduced.

Of the other main branches of the clan, the Stewarts of Appin are descended from Sir John Stewart of Bonkyl (d.1298), the younger son of Alexander, the 4th Steward of Scotland. Duncan, 2nd of Appin was Chamberlain of the Isles to James IV, while Allan the 3rd of Appin established the great *gilfine* (branch-clan of subsidiary families) by dividing his lands between his five sons: Duncan (4th of Appin); John, the ancestor of the Stewarts of Strathgarry; Dugald of Achnacone; James of Fasnacloich, and, Alexander of Invernahyle. The Stewart of Appin Clan tartan, unlike other Stewart tartans, has a pattern that is closer to the group that includes some MacDonald and Clan Chattan designs.

The Stewarts of Atholl descend from the "Wolf of Badenoch", Alexander Stewart, Earl of Buchan, the brother of Robert III. In 1437, Joanna, the widowed queen of James I married the "Black Knight of Lorne" a descendant also of Alexander, the 4th Steward of Scotland. Her son by this marriage, Sir John Stewart of Balveny was grated the earldom of Atholl by his half-brother, James II. The clan tartan design is apparently a relic worn by a Stewart of Atholl during the 1745 Jabobite Rising when the Stewarts rallied to support Bonnie Prince Charlie.

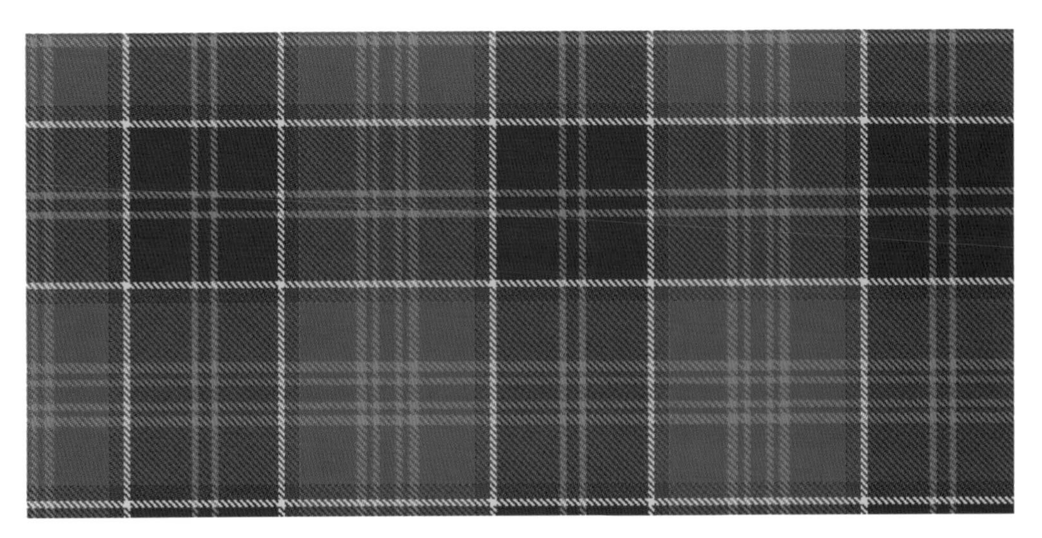

*Stewart of Appin Hunting*

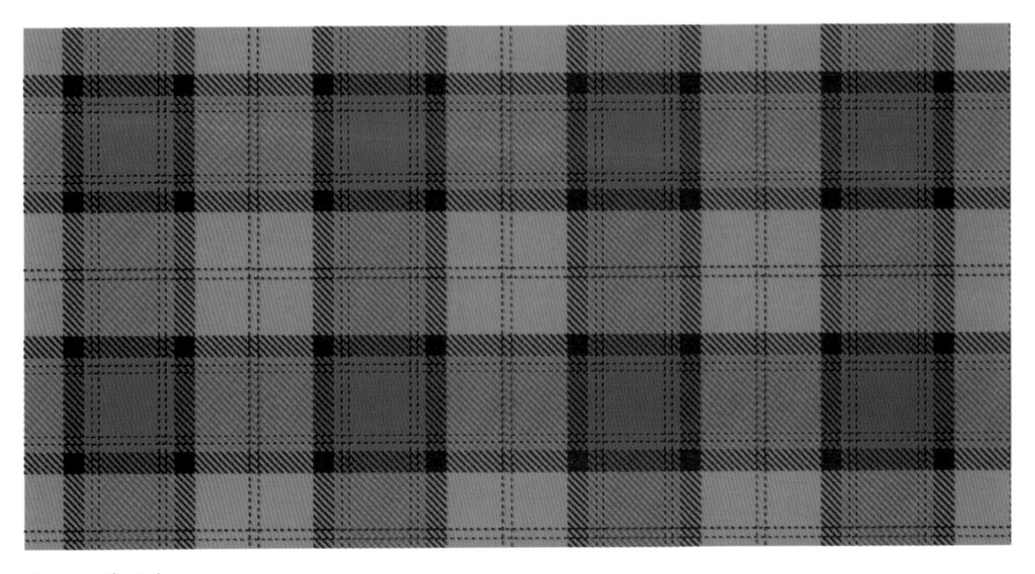

*Stewart of Attol*

Surnames with possible associations: Cook, Crookshanks, Cruickshanks, Duilach, France, Francis, Garrow, Jameson, Jamieson, Lombard, MacCamie, MacCloy, MacGlasham, MacMunn, MacMurtie, Moodie, Munn, Sharp, Stewart

Stewart of Appin: MacCombich, MacLae, MacLea, MacLeay, MacMichael

# Sutherland

Earliest known date: 1618

Earliest source: *The Vestiarium Scoticum*,1842

Tartan type: Symmetrical

Sett: **G**12 W4 G48 Bk24 B6 Bk4 B4 Bk4 B24 R2 B2 **R**6

Clan crest: A cat-a-mountain sejant rapant Proper

Clan motto: *Sans peur* ("Without fear")

Badge: *Canach* (Cotton Sedge)

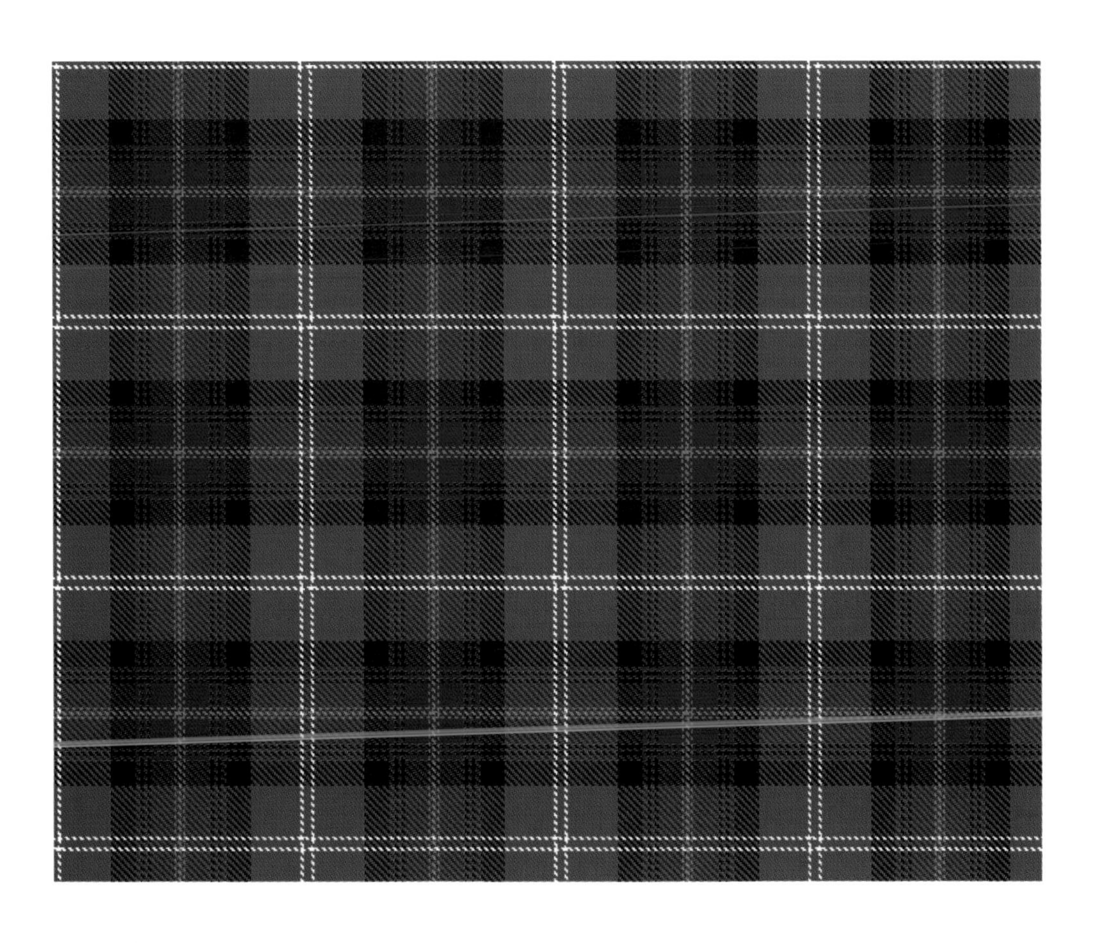

The Sutherland clan take their name from the land in the far north of Scotland that was called *sudrland* (southland) by the Norse because it was south of their settlements in the Orkneys and Caithness, and was originally the southern part of this ancient earldom. The chiefs of the clan Sutherland are descended from Freskin, a Flemish nobleman who owned lands in Scotland and in the Welsh borders.

Around the turn of the 12th century, King David awarded Sutherland to Freskin's grandson, Hugh of Moray, who was then called Lord of Sutherland. His son, William, was created Earl of Sutherland in around 1235. Hugh's brother (also William), meanwhile, was in Moray and took the surname Murray, becoming the ancestor of the dukes of Atholl. Kenneth, the 4th Earl of Sutherland, died fighting the English at Halidon Hill in 1333, while the 5th Earl's first marriage was to Princess Margaret, daughter of Robert the Bruce. Their son was heir to the Scottish throne but died of plague in 1361, while the later earls descended from his second wife. Robert, the 6th Earl, married the daughter of the "Wolf of Badenoch" – Robert III's ferocious brother. The earl also built Dunrobin – which simply means "Robin's castle" – and this has remained the main seat and stronghold of the Sutherland earls ever since. When John, 8th Earl, went mad in 1494, his son-in-law, Adam Gordon, seized Dunrobin and the earldom for himself and claimed that the rightful heir – Alexander Sutherland – was both mad and illegitimate. Gordon's wife, Elizabeth, became Countess in her own right when her husband died. She was succeeded by her grandson, John Gordon, 11th Earl, known as "Good Earl John", who was poisoned in 1567.

John, the 16th Earl, returned to using the surname Sutherland in place of Gordon. In 1715, as Lord Lieutenant, he raised his men for King George and garrisoned Inverness against the Jacobites. The 17th Earl died leaving only a daughter and heiress, Elizabeth. In 1771 she was confirmed by the House of Lords as Countess of Sutherland in her own right. Her husband, the Marquis of Stafford, was created 1st Duke of Sutherland in 1833. The 2nd Duke transformed the somewhat grim and forbidding Dunrobin between 1835 and 1850 into a more appealing building, enlisting the help of Sir Charles Barry, the architect of the Houses of Parliament. On the death in 1962 of the 5th Duke of Sutherland, the earldom and the dukedom of Sutherland were separated: chiefship of the clan and the earldom passed to his niece, Elizabeth, 22nd Countess of Sutherland, while the dukedom was inherited by the Earl of Ellesmere, a descendant of a younger son of the first duke.

Two Sutherland tartans are recognized. It may have been this Sutherland clan tartan that was mentioned in 1618 in a letter from Sir Robert Gordon instructing Murray of Pulrossie to remove the red and white lines so that their dress would be in harmony with the other septs.

*Black Watch*

The "Old Sutherland" with its red and white lines may, pre-date this letter. The "New Sutherland" is identical to the Black Watch – although it is sometimes woven in lighter colors. Furthermore, the Black Watch is kilted (folded) to show the blue, but when worn by the Argyll and Sutherland Highlanders, the material is kilted to show the green.

Surnames with possible associations: Duffus, Federith, Norman, O'May

# Urquhart

Earliest known date: *c.*1810–20

Earliest source: Cockburn Collection, 1810–20

Tartan type: Symmetrical

Sett: **Bk**4 G18 Bk12 B2 Bk2 B2 Bk2 B12 **R**6

Clan crest: Issuant from a crest coronet Or, a naked woman from the waist upwards Proper, brandishing in her dexter hand a sword Azure, hilted and pommelled Gules, in her sinister hand, a palm sapling Vert.

Clan motto: "Meane well speak well and doe well"

Badge: *Lus-leth-an-t-Samhraidh* (wallflower)

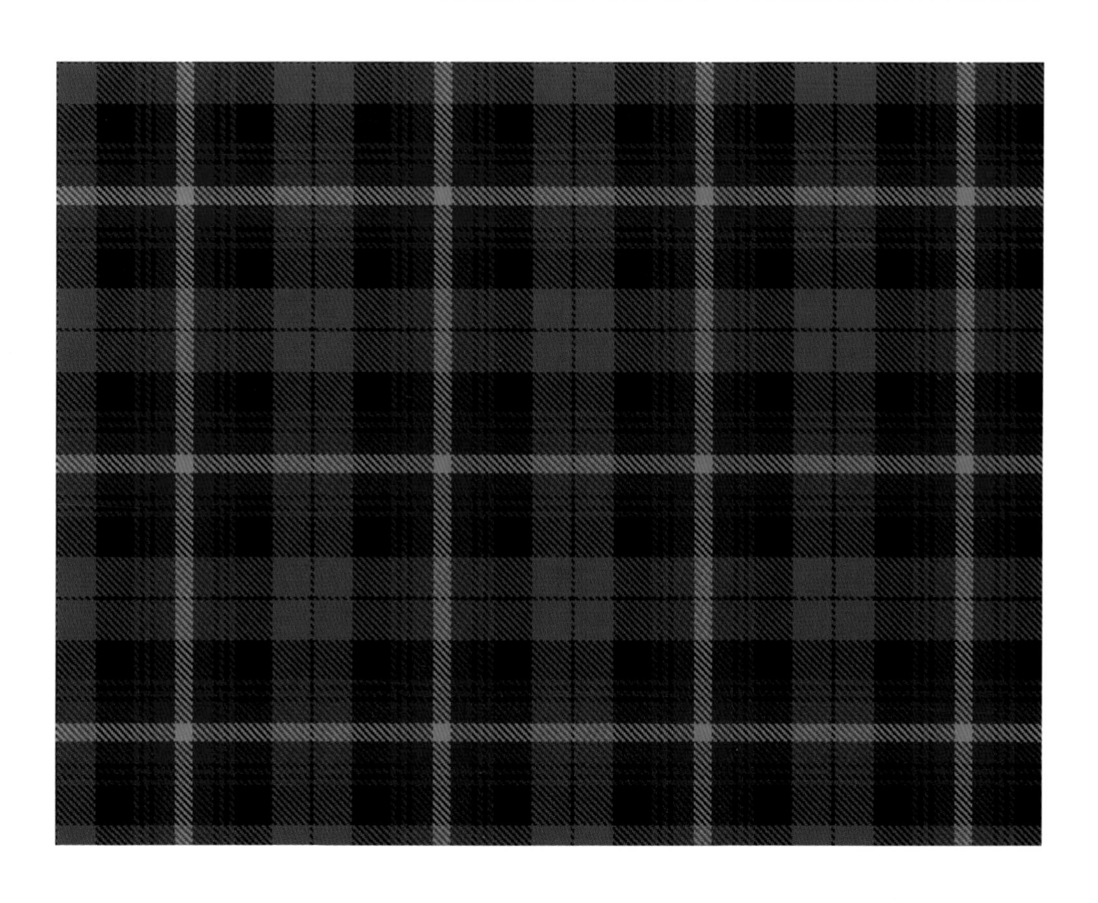

The Urquharts are the descendants of a sea-faring tribe, which settled at Cromarty. The chiefs acquired land along the south side of the Cromarty Firth stretching to Airchart (Urquhart), from where they derive their name. The meaning of the name itself is controversial: some say Urquhart means "on a rowan wood", others "on a rapid torrent", while many settle on it meaning "the fort on the knoll" because of Castle Urquhart's position overlooking Loch Ness.

The first recorded Urquhart ancestor was William de Urchard, who is said to have defended the Motte of Cromarty against the English during the time of William Wallace. Around 1358, his son, Adam de Urchard became the Sheriff of Cromarty, a position which became hereditary. Alexander, the 7th Sheriff had two sons: the younger son, John, founded the House of Craigfintry, while Walter, the eldest, was the grandfather of Thomas Urquhart who was knighted by James VI. Sir Thomas's son, also called Thomas, was a scholar and writer who translated the works of the French author Rabelais and wrote a number of curious works including the modestly titled *The True Pedigree and Lineal Descent of the Most Ancient and Honourable Family of Urquhart Since the Creation*. He was also a soldier, joining the army of Charles I and fighting at the battle of Worcester in 1651 where he was taken prisoner. When he was freed, Sir Thomas returned to the Continent, where it is said he died of laughter in 1660 celebrating the Restoration of the English monarchy! Thomas left no heir and on his death the chiefship passed to the line of Urquhart of Craigfintry, represented by John Urquhart of Cranston whose fortress of Castle Craig on the Cromarty Firth is still the seat of the Urquhart chief. The direct line of this house expired in 1741 on the death of Colonel James Urquhart and the chiefship passed to the nearest male relative, William Urquhart of Meldrum, a descendent of John, the Tutor of Cromarty (the guardian of Sir Thomas "the scholar"). The last member of this family line was Major Beauchamp Urquhart who died of his wounds in the Sudan in 1898. The arms and chiefship of the Urquharts was dormant until 1959, when a male heir was "found" in the USA: Wilkins F. Urquhart of Louisiana, chief of Clan Urquhart, was a descendant of 18th century Urquharts of Braelangswell who had emigrated to America.

The Urquhart tartan was registered in 1981 by the clan chief Kenneth Tryst Urquhart. This is a slight variation on the sample in the Cockburn Collection, which has a slightly broader red stripe (known as Urquhart Broad Red). The Smith brothers, writing in 1850, say that their sample of Urquhart tartan dated from shortly before 1822. Another registered tartan is the Urquhart White Line, which is used as the Dress tartan.

# Wallace

Earliest known date: 1842

Earliest source: *The Vestiarium Scoticum*, 1842

Tartan type: Symmetrical

Sett: **Bk**2 R16 BK16 **Y**2

Clan crest: Issuant from a crest coronet of strawberry leaves Or, a dexter arm vambraced, the hand brandishing a sword all Proper.

Clan motto: *Pro libertate* ("For liberty")

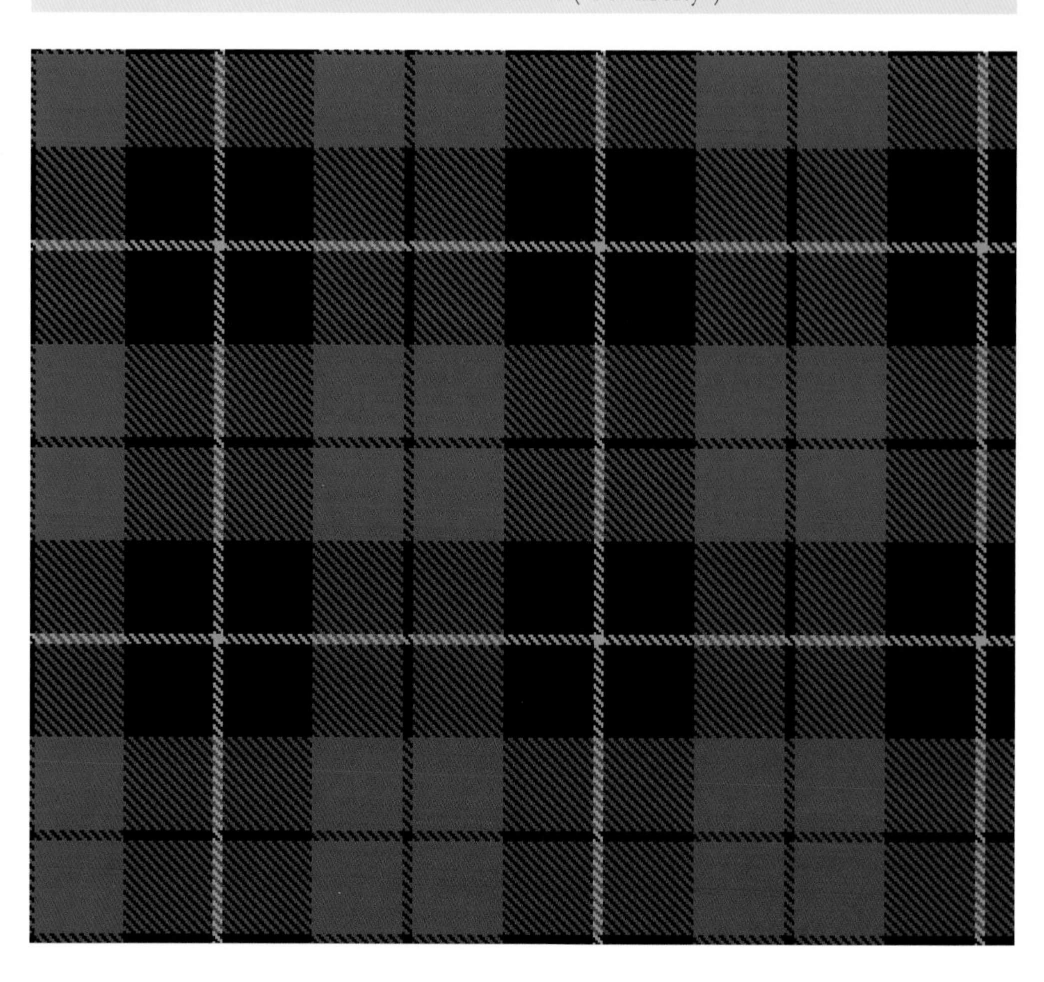

Some say that the name Wallace comes from *Waleis*, meaning "Welshman" – which was a common name in England in the 12th century – while others maintain it is derived from *Walensis*, which in Scotland meant a Briton from the Strathclyde region. Whatever its exact origins, the name Wallace was in use in the 12th century in Ayrshire and Renfrewshire.

Richard Wallace of Riccarton (Richardston), the founder of the Wallaces, was a vassal of the High Steward of Scotland and a landholder near Kilmarnock from around 1165. His grandson, Adam Walays, 3rd Chief of Riccarton, had two sons: Adam, the eldest who inherited the family estates in Ayrshire, and, Malcolm, who received lands in Elderslie and Auchinbothie, Renfrewshire. Malcolm was the father of Scotland's greatest hero, Sir William Wallace of Elderslie, born *c.* 1274. Malcolm Wallace refused to submit to Edward I of England in 1296. He and his eldest son Andrew were executed, but his wife fled to Dundee with their youngest son, William. By 1297, William Wallace had rallied sufficient men to undertake a guerrilla war against the English and had his greatest victory – against overwhelming odds – at Stirling Bridge. In 1298, however, Wallace was defeated at Falkirk. He escaped the English but in 1305 was betrayed. Taken to London, Wallace was tried for treason and hanged at Smithfield on 23 August 1305.

From Adam Wallace, 4th Chief of Riccarton, are descended the Wallaces of Craigie, Ayrshire. In 1669 Hugh Wallace of Craigie was made a baronet of Nova Scotia, but the representation of the line was to pass eventually to the Wallaces of Cairnhill who, through marriage, inherited estates at Busbie and Cloncaid in Ayrshire.

The Wallace tartan's first recorded appearance was in The Vestiarium Scoticum in 1842. D.C. Stewart writing in 1950 claimed that the Wallace tartan was known from samples in early collections – although he does not say which collections! He also wrote that his father D.W. Stewart, stated that the Wallaces were known to have also worn the MacLean of Duart tartan (page 177) but again, does not give reasons for this.

Surnames with possible associations: Wallis

# Wemyss

Earliest known date: 1842

Earliest source: *The Vestiarium Scoticum*, 1842

Tartan type: Symmetrical

Sett: **R**8 G2 R48 Bk8 R8 Bk24 W2 Bk24 **R**8

Clan crest: A swan Proper

Clan motto: *Je pense* ("I think")

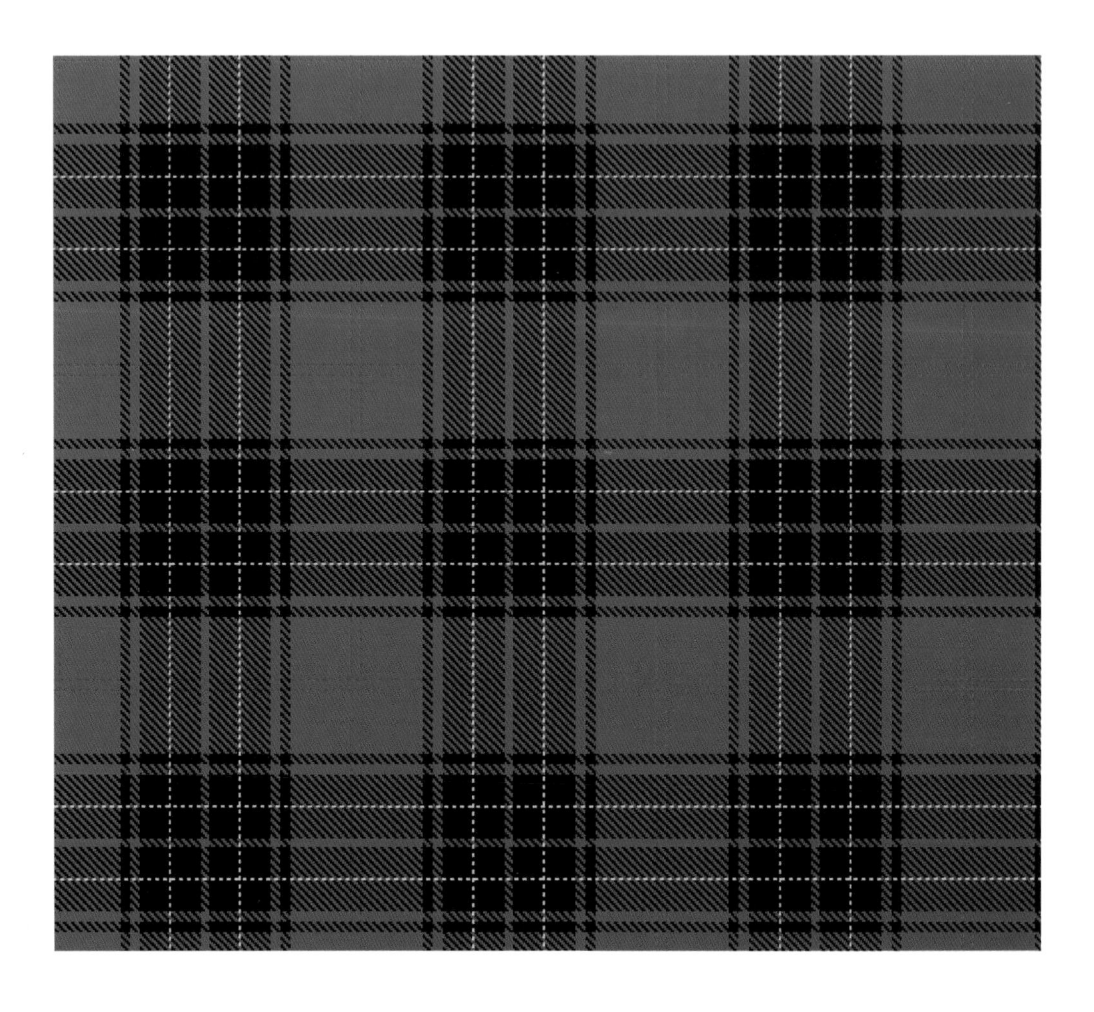

The name Wemyss is derived from the Gaelic *uaimh* which means "cave" and is believed to refer to the two caves with their ancient Pictish markings on the rockfaces below the "MacDuff Castle" at East Wemyss near Kirkcaldy in Fife. The Wemyss are descended from a younger son of the MacDuffs, Gillemichael MacDuff, Earl of Fife who obtained the lands from his father in around 1160.

In 1296, Sir Michael swore fealty to the English king Edward I, but then changed his allegiance to support Robert the Bruce which resulted in the "old" Wemyss Castle (at East Wemyss, and known locally as MacDuff's Castle) being sacked by English troops. A new and enlarged castle was built at West Wemyss by Sir John Wemyss in 1564–65 and here Mary, Queen of Scots first met her future husband, Henry, Lord Darnley. Sir John's descendant, John Wemyss born in 1586, was knighted in 1618 and created a baronet of Nova Scotia in 1625, with a charter to the barony of New Wemyss in the province. He was created a baron in 1628 and later Earl of Wemyss by Charles I. In 1745 the Wemyss supported the Jacobite cause. The earl's eldest son, David, Lord Elcho, was colonel of a troop of royal horse guards. Following the defeat at the battle of Culloden, Elcho fled to France. In his absence he was convicted of treason and his estates forfeited to the Crown. When he died in Paris in 1787, he was succeeded by his brother, Francis, who changed his name to Charteris. From him, the present earls of Wemyss and March are descended. His maternal grandfather was the notorious Colonel Francis Charteris, known as the "Rapemaster General of Great Britain"! He had amassed a huge fortune through gambling but was drummed out of the British Army for cheating at cards and out of the Dutch Army for theft! Such was his disgrace that when he died it is said that "mourners" at his funeral threw dead dogs and offal on his grave!

The chiefship of the name of Wemyss, as well as the estates in Fife, were, devolved onto a second brother, James Wemyss of Wemyss and Chief of the Name. He was the Member of Parliament for Sutherland, and in 1757 married Lady Elizabeth Sutherland. In 1800 the famous Sutherland Highlanders were raised by General William Wemyss of Wemyss. A corridor of Wemyss Castle is still carpeted with the Sutherland, rather than the Wemyss, tartan which was first recorded in 1842 in *The Vestiarium Scoticum*.

# Index

# Useful Addresses

## Collections:

The Carmichael Collection at the West Highland Museum, Fort William, Argyll, Scotland
The Cockburn Collection at the Mitchell Library, North Street, Glasgow, Scotland
The Highland Society of London Collection at the National Museum of Scotland, Queen Street, Edinburgh, Scotland

## Tartans on the Web:

www.tartans.scotland.net

Tartans of Scotland: The Official Register of all Publicly Known Tartans. This web site produced in association with the Scottish Tartans Society contains information on over 2,500 registered tartans, the different types of tartans and how they are made, as well as how to read a tartan, tartan 'facts' and Highland dress. There is a Tartan Index with color illustrations of tartans.

### www.scottishtartans.co.uk

Peter MacDonald Tartan Design and Consultancy

As well as a brief history of tartan and a 'Tartan of the Month', which focuses on one of the rarer tartans, this site also gives information of the design of tartan for clan societies, corporations and multi-national companies. Individuals, too, can commission their own individual tartan design!

# Bibliography

Cheape, Hugh, *Tartan: The Highland Habit,* National Museums of Scotland, 1991
Dunbar, J. Telfer, *History of Highland Dress,* B.T Batsford, 1978
Hesketh, Christian, *Tartans,* Weidenfeld and Nicholson, 1961
Innes, Sir Thomas, *The Tartans of the Clans and Families of Scotland,* Johnston & Bacon, 1971
Way, George and Squire, Romilly, *Clans and Tartans,* Harper Collins, 2000
Grange, R.M.D, *A Short History of the Scottish Dress,* Burkes Peerage, 1966
Sir Ian Moncrieffe of that Ilk and Hicks, David, *The Highland Clans,* Barrie and Rockliff, 1967
Stewart, Donald C., *The Setts of the Scottish Tartans,* Oliver and Boyd, 1950
Urquhart, Blair, *Tartans,* Apple Press, 1994
MacDonald, P., *The 1819 Key Pattern Book – One Hundred Original Tartans,* 1996 available from P MacDonald.

# Credits